McGraw-Hill's
GED
Social Studies

**The Most Comprehensive and Reliable
Study Program for the GED Social Studies Test**

Kenneth Tamarkin
Jeri W. Bayer

Reviewers

Marsha Davis, Instructional Facilitator, New York City Board of Education,
Office of Adult and Continuing Education

Marianne Dryden, Foreign Language Education,
University of Texas at Austin

Sara Gabbard, Education Resource Consultant,
Adult Learning Resource Center, Des Plaines, Illinois

Lamar Gailey, Director, Adult Literacy,
Lanier Technical College, Oakwood, Georgia

Thomas Hollamby, Teacher,
Adult Education, Oxnard, California

J. L. "Jan" Morris, CFCS, ABE/GED Instructor,
South Florida Community College, Avon Park, Florida

McGraw-Hill

New York Chicago San Francisco Lisbon London Madrid Mexico City
Milan New Delhi San Juan Seoul Singapore Sydney Toronto

1 2 3 4 5 6 7 8 9 0   QPD/QPD   1 0 9 8 7 6 5 4 3 2

ISBN 0-07-140702-2

McGraw-Hill books are available at special quantity discounts to use as premiums and sales promotions, or for use in corporate training programs. For more information, please write to the Director of Special Sales, Professional Publishing, McGraw-Hill, Two Penn Plaza, New York, NY 10121-2298. Or contact your local bookstore.

This book is printed on acid-free paper.

Table of Contents

PART I: CRITICAL THINKING SKILLS IN SOCIAL STUDIES

Acknowledgments

Photo on page 3 from the Library of Congress.

Excerpt on page 13 from *Margaret Mead: Some Personal Views* by Margaret Mead. Reprinted with permission of Walker & Company, 435 Hudson Street, New York, NY, 10014.

Excerpt on page 15 reprinted with permission from the January 1991 issue of *Public Management* (PM) magazine published by the International City/County Management Association, Washington, D.C.

Photo on page 20 by Peter Menzel Photography/Material World.

Excerpt on page 20 from Hine and Faragher, *The American West,* Yale University Press, 2000. Reprinted by permission.

Excerpt on page 69 from *Let Nobody Turn Us Around: Voices of Resistance, Reform, and Renewal* by Manning Marable and Leith Mullings. Reprinted by permission of Rowman & Littlefield Publishers.

Poster on page 71 from the Library of Congress.

Cartoon on page 72 from the Library of Congress.

Photo on page 73 from the Library of Congress.

Excerpt on page 83 from *Let Nobody Turn Us Around: Voices of Resistance, Reform, and Renewal* by Manning Marable and Leith Mullings. Reprinted by permission of Rowman & Littlefield Publishers.

Excerpt on page 87 from "The Ballot or the Bullet" speech by Malcolm X. Copyright © 1965, 1989 by Betty Shabazz and Pathfinder Press. Reprinted by permission.

Excerpt on page 87 from *Let Nobody Turn Us Around: Voices of Resistance, Reform, and Renewal* by Manning Marable and Leith Mullings. Reprinted by permission of Rowman & Littlefield Publishers.

Excerpt on page 87 reprinted with permission of the Anti-Defamation League.

Excerpt on page 88 from "I Have a Dream" by Martin Luther King Jr. Reprinted by arrangement with The Heirs to the Estate of Martin Luther King, Jr., c/o Writers House Inc, as agent for the proprietor. Copyright 1963 by Martin Luther King, Jr. Copyright renewed 1991 by Coretta Scott King.

Excerpts on pages 88 and 89 from *Illustrated History of Europe* by Frederic Delouche. Originally published by Cassell & Co. Reprinted by permission.

Excerpts on pages 90 and 91 from Hine and Faragher, *The American West,* Yale University Press, 2000. Reprinted by permission.

Excerpt on page 94 from pages 5–6 of Prologue from *Freedom in the Western World* (Volume II of *A History of Freedom*) by Herbert J. Muller. Copyright © 1963 by Herbert J. Muller. Reprinted by permission of HarperCollins Publishers, Inc.

Photo on page 112 from Culver Pictures, Inc.

Photo on page 112 courtesy of the Massachusetts Historical Society.

Excerpts on pages 123 and 125 © Microsoft Corporation. All rights reserved. Reprinted with permission from Microsoft Corporation as made available through Microsoft® Encarta® Encyclopedia 99.

Excerpt on pages 126–127 from "Political System", Encyclopedia Britannica On-line, accessed February, 2001. Reprinted by permission.

Drawing on page 140 from the Library of Congress.

Photo on page 140 by AP/Wide World Photos.

Photo on page 140 from the Library of Congress.

Photo on page 141 © Bernard Hoffman/Time Pix.

Drawing on page 141 by James Eights (1798–1882), Pearl Street from Maiden Lane. Watercolor on paper, c. 1850, Albany Institute of History & Art. Bequest of Ledyard Cogswell, Jr.

Poster on page 142 from the Library of Congress.

Excerpt on page 150 from *Let Nobody Turn Us Around: Voices of Resistance, Reform, and Renewal* by Manning Marable and Leith Mullings. Reprinted by permission of Rowman & Littlefield Publishers.

Photo on page 151 from Ellis Island Research.

Poster on page 151 from the Library of Congress.

Excerpt on page 155 from *A Future Perfect* by John Micklethwait and Adrian Woolridge, copyright © 2000 by John Micklethwait and Adrian Woolridge. Used by permission of Times Books, a division of Random House, Inc.

Excerpt on page 156 from "Taino Restoration" by Rick Kearns, as appeared in *Native People's Magazine.* Reprinted by permission of Rick Kearns, freelance writer/poet.

Photo on page 157 by NASA/Photo Researchers, Inc.

Map on page 160 from *World Geography* by John Hodgdon Bradley, Silver Burdett Ginn, 1954. Reprinted by permission.

Map on page 163 from *The Nine Nations of North America.* Copyright © 1981 by Joel Garreau. Reprinted by permission of Houghton Mifflin Company. All rights reserved.

Photos on page 165 from UCLA Geography, Air Photo Archives.

Drawing on page 166 from *The State of the Environment,* United Nations Environmental Programme, 1984. Reprinted by permission.

Excerpt on page 173 from "Urban Development" by Dora Crouch, in *Cities: The Forces That Shape Them,* Cooper-Hewitt Museum, 1982. Reprinted by permission of Rizzoli International Publications.

Photo on page 173 by Nikos Desyllas/Superstock, Inc.

Photo on page 254 by SEF/Art Resource, NY.

Photo on page 254 by Mark Antman/Phototake, Inc.

Excerpt on page 262 from "Motion Picture," from Microsoft® Encarta® Encyclopedia 2001. © 1993–2000 Microsoft Corporation. Portions reprinted with permission from Microsoft Corporation as made available through Microsoft® Encarta® Encyclopedia 2001. All rights reserved.

Cartoon on page 265 by Jean-Loup Charmet/SPL/Photo Researchers, Inc.

Excerpt on page 266 from "A Reservoir of Suffering Humanity" by Richard Rhodes, from *Visions of Technology*, edited by Richard Rhodes. Copyright © 1999 by Richard Rhodes. Excerpted with the permission of Simon & Schuster.

Photo on page 268 © Reuters NewMedia Inc./CORBIS.

Excerpt on page 268 from *Ingenious Pursuits: Building the Scientific Revolution* by Lisa Jardine, 1999. Reprinted by permission of Doubleday, a division of Random House.

Excerpt on page 276 from "Man & Machines," *Technology and Culture*, Melvin Kranzberg and William H. Davenport, eds.

Excerpt on pages 278 and 279 reprinted with the permission of Simon & Schuster from *The Greatest Inventions of the Past 2,000 Years* by John Brockman. Copyright © 2000 by John Brockman.

Photo on page 280 by Tom McHugh/Photo Researchers, Inc.

Excerpt on page 280 from "The Act of Invention: Causes, Contexts, Continuities, and Consequences," by Lynn White, Jr. in *Technology and Culture*, Melvin Kranzberg and William H. Davenport, eds.

Excerpt on page 283 from "A great man before a great audience," *Harvard Magazine*, 101, November/December 1998. Reprinted by permission.

Photo of Parthenon on page 284 by Steve Vidler/Superstock, Inc.

Photos of Forbidden City and Colosseum on page 284 by Milt and Joan Mann. Cameramann International.

Photo of Amida Byodoin Temple on page 284 from Scala/Art Resource, NY.

Photo of Gandan Monastery on page 284 by Dean Conger/CORBIS.

Photo of Mayan Ruins in Guatemala on page 284 © Barnabas Bosshart/CORBIS.

Excerpt on page 285 from "Cities" in Encyclopedia Britannica.

Excerpts on pages 286–287, 289,291, and 299 from *Illustrated History of Europe* by Frederic Delouche. Originally published by Cassell & Co. Reprinted by permission.

Painting on page 300 courtesy of The Saint Louis Art Museum. Private Collection.

Cartoon on page 302 from the Library of Congress.

Cartoon on page 303 from *Illustrated History of Europe* by Frederic Delouche. Originally published by Cassell & Co. Reprinted by permission.

Excerpt on page 376 from *The Future Once Happened Here: New York, D.C., L.A., and the Fate of America's Big Cities* by Fred Siegel. Copyright © 1997 by Fred Siegel. Reprinted with permission of The Free Press, a Division of Simon & Schuster, Inc.

Photo on page 378 © Ron Watts/CORBIS.

Excerpt on page 381 from "An Unforeseen Revolution: Computers and Expectations, 1935–1985," by Paul Ceruzzi, in *Imagining Tomorrow: History, Technology, and the American Future,* Joseph Corn, ed., MIT Press, 1986. Reprinted by permission.

Excerpt on page 382 from "Faces and Activism of the Asian Pacific-American Community," by Alice H. Yang. Adapted, with permission from the publisher, from *Perspectives: Readings on Contemporary American Government,* © 1997. Close Up Foundation, Alexandria, Virginia.

Excerpt on pages 382–383 from Sandra Day O'Connor, Madison Lecture, "Portia's Progress," by Sandra Day O'Connor. 66 N.Y.U. L. Rev. 1546, 1552–53, 1557, 1558, 991. Reprinted by permission of New York University Law Review.

Excerpt on page 385 from "Cleaning up the Land: Tribal colleges train a new generation of Environmentalists," *Mind and Spirit,* 1, October/November 1998. Reprinted by permission of The American Indian College Fund.

Excerpt on page 386 from *Love Canal: My Story,* by Lois Marie Gibbs. Reprinted by permission.

Painting on page 389 by Jean-Louis David (French, 1748–1825), "Napoleon Crossing the Alps," Canvas (1800), Musée de Versailles. Giraudon/Art Resource, NY.

The editor has made every effort to trace ownership of all copyrighted material and to secure the necessary permission. Should there be a question regarding the use of any material, regret is hereby expressed for such error. Upon notification of any such oversight, proper acknowledgment will be made in future editions.

To the Student

If you're studying to pass the GED Tests, you're in good company. In 1999, the most recent year for which figures are available, the American Council on Education GED Testing Service reported that over 750,700 adults took the GED Test battery worldwide. Of this number, more than 526,400 (70 percent) actually received their certificates. About 14 percent of those with high school credentials, or about one in seven, have a GED diploma. One in twenty (5 percent) of those students in their first year of college study is a GED graduate.

The average age of GED test-takers in the United States was over 24 in 1999, but nearly three quarters (70 percent) of GED test-takers were 19 years of age or older. Two out of three GED test-takers report having completed the tenth grade or higher, and more than a third report having completed the eleventh grade before leaving high school.

Why do so many people choose to take the GED Tests? Some do so to get a job, to advance to a better job, to attend college, or to qualify for military service. More than two out of every three GED graduates work toward college degrees or attend trade, technical, or business schools. Still others pursue their GED diplomas to feel better about themselves or to set good examples for their children.

More than 14 million adults earned the GED diploma between 1942 and 1999. Some well-known graduates include country music singers Waylon Jennings and John Michael Montgomery, comedian Bill Cosby, Olympic gold medalist Mary Lou Retton, Delaware Lieutenant Governor Ruth Ann Minner, Colorado's U.S. Senator Ben Nighthorse Campbell, Wendy's founder Dave Thomas, Famous Amos Cookies creator Wally Amos, and Triple Crown winning jockey Ron Turcotte.

This book has been designed to help you, too, succeed on the GED Test. It will provide you with instruction in the skills you need to pass and plenty of practice with the kinds of test items you will find on the real test.

What Does GED Stand For?

GED stands for the Tests of **General Educational Development.** The GED Test Battery is a national examination developed by the GED Testing Service of the American Council on Education. The certificate earned for passing the test is widely recognized by colleges, training schools, and employers as equivalent to a high school diploma. The American Council reports that almost all (more than 95 percent) of employers in the nation employ GED graduates and offer them the same salaries and opportunities for advancement as high school graduates.

The GED Test reflects the major and lasting outcomes normally acquired in a high school program. Since the passing rate for the GED is based on the performance of graduating high school seniors, you can be sure your skills are comparable. In fact, those who pass the GED Test actually do better than one-third of those graduating seniors. Your skills in communication, information processing, critical thinking, and problem solving are keys to success. The test also places special emphasis on questions that prepare you for entering the workplace or higher education. Much that you have learned informally or through other types of training can help you pass the test.

Special editions of the GED Test will include the Spanish language, Braille, large print, and audiocasette formats. If you need special accommodations because of a learning or physical disability, your adult education program and testing center can assist you.

What Should You Know to Pass the Test?

The GED Test consists of five examinations called Language Arts, Writing; Social Studies; Science; Language Arts, Reading; and Mathematics. On all five tests, you are expected to demonstrate the ability to think about many issues. You are tested on knowledge and skills you have acquired from life experiences, television, radio, books and newspapers, consumer products, and advertising. Your work or business experiences may be helpful during the test. You can expect the subjects to be interrelated. This is called *interdisciplinary* material. For example, a mathematics problem may include a scientific diagram. Or a social studies question may require some mathematical skills.

Keep these facts in mind about specific tests:

1. The **Language Arts, Writing Test** requires you in Part I to recognize or correct errors, revise sentences or passages, and shift constructions in the four areas of organization, sentence structure, usage, and mechanics (capitalization and punctuation). Letters, memos, and business-related documents are likely to be included.

In Part II you will write an essay of 200 to 250 words presenting an opinion or an explanation on a topic familiar to most adults. You should plan and organize your ideas before you write, and revise and edit your essay before you are finished.

2. Three of the five tests—**Social Studies, Science,** and **Mathematics**—require you to answer questions based on reading passages or interpreting graphs, charts, maps, cartoons, diagrams, or photographs. Developing strong reading and critical thinking skills is the key to succeeding on these tests. Being able to interpret information from graphic sources, such as a map or cartoon, is essential.

3. The **Language Arts, Reading Test** asks you to read literary text and show that you can comprehend, apply, analyze, synthesize, and evaluate concepts. You will also read nonfiction and show that you can understand the main points of what you are reading.

4. The **Mathematics Test** consists mainly of word problems to be solved. Therefore, you must be able to combine your ability to perform computations with problem-solving skills.

Part I of the Mathematics Test will permit the use of the Casio *fx*-260 calculator, which will be provided at the test site. The calculator will eliminate the tediousness of making complex calculations. Part II will not permit the use of the calculator. Both parts of the test will include problems without multiple-choice answers. These problems will require you to mark your answers on bubble-in number grids or on coordinate plane graphs.

Who May Take the Tests?

About 3,500 GED Testing Centers are available in the fifty United States, the District of Columbia, eleven Canadian provinces and territories, U.S. and overseas military bases, correctional institutions, Veterans Administration hospitals, and certain learning centers. People who have not graduated from high school and who meet specific eligibility requirements (age, residency, etc.) may take the tests. Since eligibility requirements vary, you should contact your local GED testing center or the director of adult education in your state, province, or territory for specific information.

What Is a Passing Score on the GED Test?

A passing score varies from area to area. To find out what you need to pass the test, contact your local GED testing center. However, you should keep two scores in mind. One score represents the minimum score you must get on each test. The other is the minimum average score on all five tests. Both of these scores will be set by your state, province, or territory and must be met in order to pass the GED Test.

Can You Retake the Test?

You are allowed to retake some or all of the tests. The regulations governing the number of times that you may retake the tests and the time you must wait before retaking them are set by your state, province, or territory. Some states require you to take a review class or to study on your own for a certain amount of time before retaking the test.

THE GED TESTS

Tests	Minutes	Questions	Content/Percentages
Language Arts, Writing			
Part I: Editing (multiple choice)	75	50	Organization 15% Sentence Structure 30% Usage 30% Mechanics 25%
Part II: the Essay	45	1 topic: approx. 250 words	
Social Studies	70	50	World History 15% U.S. History 25% Civics and Government 25% Economics 20% Geography 15%
Science	80	50	Earth and Space Science 20% Life Science 45% Physical Science 35% (Physics and Chemistry)

Language Arts, Reading	65	40	Literary Text 75%
			    Poetry 15%
			    Drama 15%
			    Fiction 45%
			Nonfiction 25%
			    Informational Text
			    Literary Nonfiction
			    Reviews of Fine and Performing Arts
			    Business Documents

Mathematics			
Part I: Calculator	45	25	Number Operations and Number Sense 20–30% Measurement and Geometry 20–30%
Part II: No Calculator	45	25	Data Analysis, Statistics, and Probability 20–30% Algebra, Functions, and Patterns 20–30%
	Total: 7¼ hours	Total: 240 questions and 1 essay	

How Can You Best Prepare for the Test?

Many community colleges, public schools, adult education centers, libraries, churches, community-based organizations, and other institutions offer GED preparation classes. While your state may not require you to take part in a preparation program, it's a good idea if you've been out of school for some time, if you had academic difficulty when you were in school, or if you left before completing the eleventh grade. Some television stations broadcast classes to prepare people for the test. If you cannot find a GED preparation class locally, contact the director of adult education in your state, province, or territory.

What Are Some Test-Taking Tips?

1. **Prepare physically.** Get plenty of rest and eat a well-balanced meal before the test so that you will have energy and will be able to think clearly. Intense studying at the last minute probably will not help as much as having a relaxed and rested mind.

2. **Arrive early.** Be at the testing center at least 15 to 20 minutes before the starting time. Make sure you have time to find the room and to get situated. Keep in mind that many testing centers refuse to admit latecomers. Some testing centers operate on a first come, first served basis; so you want to be sure that there is an available seat for you on the day that you're ready to test.

3. **Think positively.** Tell yourself you will do well. If you have studied and prepared for the test, you should succeed.

4. **Relax during the test.** Take half a minute several times during the test to stretch and breathe deeply, especially if you are feeling anxious or confused.

5. **Read the test directions carefully.** Be sure you understand how to answer the questions. If you have any questions about the test or about filling in the answer form, ask before the test begins.

6. **Know the time limit for each test.** The Social Studies Test has a time limit of 70 minutes (1 hour 10 minutes). Work at a steady pace; if you have extra time, go back and check your answers.

7. **Have a strategy for answering questions**. You should read through the reading passages or look over the materials once and then answer the questions that follow. Read each question two or three times to make sure you understand it. It is best to refer back to the passage or graphic in order to confirm your answer choice. Don't try to depend on your memory of what you have just read or seen. Some people like to guide their reading by skimming the questions before reading a passage.

Use the method that works best for you.

8. Don't spend a lot of time on difficult questions. If you're not sure of an answer, go on to the next question. Answer easier questions first and then go back to the harder questions. However, when you skip a question, be sure that you have skipped the same number on your answer sheet. Although skipping difficult questions is a good strategy for making the most of your time, it is very easy to get confused and throw off your whole answer key.

Lightly mark the margin of your answer sheet next to the numbers of the questions you did not answer so that you know what to go back to. To prevent confusion when your test is graded, be sure to erase these marks completely after you answer the questions.

9. Answer every question on the test. If you're not sure of an answer, take an educated guess. When you leave a question unanswered, you will always lose points, but you can possibly gain points if you make a correct guess.

If you must guess, try to eliminate one or more answers that you are sure are not correct. Then choose from the remaining answers. Remember that you greatly increase your chances if you can eliminate one or two answers before guessing. Of course, guessing should be used only when all else has failed.

10. Clearly fill in the circle for each answer choice. If you erase something, erase it completely. Be sure that you give only one answer per question; otherwise, no answer will count.

11. Practice test-taking. Use the exercises, reviews, and especially the Posttest and Practice Test in this book to better understand your test-taking habits and weaknesses. Use them to practice different strategies such as skimming questions first or skipping hard questions until the end. Knowing your own personal test-taking style is important to your success on the GED Test.

How to Use This Book

This book will guide you through the types of questions you can expect to find on the GED Social Studies Test. To answer the questions successfully, you will need to focus on getting the meaning from what you have read. You will be reading selections about U.S. history, world history, economics, civics and government, and geography. In addition, you will be using information from graphs, maps, cartoons, photographs, and other visual materials.

Before beginning this book, you should take the Pretest. This will give you a preview of what the Social Studies Test includes, but, more important, it will help you identify which areas you need to concentrate on most. Use the chart at the end of the Pretest to pinpoint the types of questions you have answered incorrectly and to determine which skills you need the most work in. You may decide to concentrate on specific areas or to work through the entire book. We strongly suggest you do work through the whole book to best prepare yourself for the GED Test.

This book has a number of features designed to help make the task of test preparation easier and more effective.

- The first four chapters isolate the four critical thinking skills covered on the Social Studies Test—comprehension, application, analysis, and evaluation. *Comprehension* refers to the ability to understand and draw conclusions about a passage. *Application* is the ability to take information or knowledge gained from one situation and use it to answer questions about another, similar situation. *Analysis* consists of breaking a passage into logical parts and thinking about how the parts fit together. *Evaluation* involves examining information to determine its accuracy and importance. The first four chapters isolate these skills and give plenty of practice exercises to help you understand and develop your abilities.

- Chapters 5 through 10 cover themes in social studies as defined by the National Council for Social Studies. Each chapter introduces a theme, such as *Time, Continuity, and Change* and *Global Connections.* The theme is then developed and explained with a broad range of readings and graphics from U.S. history, world history, economics, civics, and geography. Exercises accompany the readings to check understanding and to give you practice answering questions similar to those you will find on the GED Social Studies Test.

- A variety of passages and graphics are used in each chapter, including traditional selections as well as more modern materials that offer different points of view. Passages are often presented with graphics in interdisciplinary studies. Readings are sometimes paired to offer revealing comparisons between periods or events in history.

- The Answer Key explains the correct answers for the exercises. If you make a mistake, you can learn from it by reading the explanation that follows the answer and then reviewing the question to analyze the error.

- The following icons have been used throughout the chapters to indicate which subject area of social studies is being presented.

 U.S. History

 World History

 Civics & Government

 Geography

 Economics

After you have worked through the ten chapters in this book, you should take the Posttest. The Posttest is a simulated GED Test that presents questions in the format, at the level of difficulty, and in the percentages found on the actual GED Test. The Posttest will help you determine whether you are ready for the GED Social Studies Test. The evaluation chart at the end of the test will help you locate the areas of the book you need to review.

After you have reviewed, the Practice Test can be used as a final indicator of your readiness for the GED Test. This test also has the same format, level of difficulty, and percentages as the Posttest and the GED Social Studies Test.

Social Studies

Directions: Before beginning to work with this book, take this Pretest. The purpose of this test is to help you determine which skills you need to develop in order to pass the GED Social Studies Test.

The Social Studies Pretest consists of 50 multiple-choice questions. The questions are based on maps, charts, graphs, cartoons, photographs, and reading passages.

Answer each question as carefully as possible, choosing the best of five answer choices and blackening in the answer grid. If a question seems

to be too difficult, do not spend too much time on it. Work ahead and come back to it later when you can think it through carefully.

When you have completed the test, check your work with the answers and explanations at the end of the section.

Use the evaluation chart on page 24 to determine which areas you need to review most. For the best possible preparation for the GED Social Studies Test, however, we advise you to work through this entire book.

Pretest Answer Grid

1	① ② ③ ④ ⑤		18	① ② ③ ④ ⑤		35	① ② ③ ④ ⑤
2	① ② ③ ④ ⑤		19	① ② ③ ④ ⑤		36	① ② ③ ④ ⑤
3	① ② ③ ④ ⑤		20	① ② ③ ④ ⑤		37	① ② ③ ④ ⑤
4	① ② ③ ④ ⑤		21	① ② ③ ④ ⑤		38	① ② ③ ④ ⑤
5	① ② ③ ④ ⑤		22	① ② ③ ④ ⑤		39	① ② ③ ④ ⑤
6	① ② ③ ④ ⑤		23	① ② ③ ④ ⑤		40	① ② ③ ④ ⑤
7	① ② ③ ④ ⑤		24	① ② ③ ④ ⑤		41	① ② ③ ④ ⑤
8	① ② ③ ④ ⑤		25	① ② ③ ④ ⑤		42	① ② ③ ④ ⑤
9	① ② ③ ④ ⑤		26	① ② ③ ④ ⑤		43	① ② ③ ④ ⑤
10	① ② ③ ④ ⑤		27	① ② ③ ④ ⑤		44	① ② ③ ④ ⑤
11	① ② ③ ④ ⑤		28	① ② ③ ④ ⑤		45	① ② ③ ④ ⑤
12	① ② ③ ④ ⑤		29	① ② ③ ④ ⑤		46	① ② ③ ④ ⑤
13	① ② ③ ④ ⑤		30	① ② ③ ④ ⑤		47	① ② ③ ④ ⑤
14	① ② ③ ④ ⑤		31	① ② ③ ④ ⑤		48	① ② ③ ④ ⑤
15	① ② ③ ④ ⑤		32	① ② ③ ④ ⑤		49	① ② ③ ④ ⑤
16	① ② ③ ④ ⑤		33	① ② ③ ④ ⑤		50	① ② ③ ④ ⑤
17	① ② ③ ④ ⑤		34	① ② ③ ④ ⑤			

PRETEST

1. During the Civil War, Delaware, Maryland, Kentucky, and Missouri were "border states" that remained with the Union in spite of the fact that they were slave states. Which of President Lincoln's positions at the beginning of the Civil War was most probably influenced by the status of these four states?

   (1) his request that Robert E. Lee become chief strategist for the North
   (2) his reluctance to issue an order for the emancipation of all slaves
   (3) his call for Union volunteers to fight the Confederate rebels
   (4) his reluctance to mandate a draft of young men into military service
   (5) his agreement with Congress to raise taxes to pay for the war effort

Questions 2 and 3 refer to the following quote.

> "Justice of this kind is obviously no less shocking than the crime itself, and the new 'official' murder, far from offering redress for the offense committed against society, adds instead a second defilement to the first."
>
> —U.S. Supreme Court Justice Brennan in a 1975 dissenting opinion on a controversial issue

2. In the preceding quote, what does "official murder" refer to?

   (1) suicide
   (2) mercy killing
   (3) assassination
   (4) the death penalty
   (5) manslaughter

3. Based on the quote, what can we infer about Justice Brennan?

   (1) He supports pardoning those on death row.
   (2) He is in favor of life imprisonment for murder.
   (3) He is against capital punishment in all situations.
   (4) He believes in severe sentences for convicted killers.
   (5) He supports capital punishment as a deterrent.

PRETEST

Questions 4 and 5 refer to the following picture and paragraph.

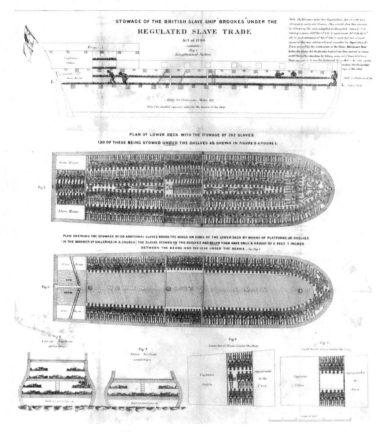

Slave ships like the notorious *Brookes* became floating coffins for many of the Africans kidnapped and sold for transport into slavery in North America and the West Indies. This deck plan of the vessel was issued under the auspices of British antislavery advocate Thomas Clarkson; it protested the leniency of the Act passed in 1788 to regulate the British slave trade. Under the Act, ships were permitted to sail with their human cargo packed in claustrophobic density. Carrying 454 slaves, the *Brookes* allowed 6' x 1'4" for each adult male; 5'10" x 11" for each woman; and 5' x 1'2" for each boy. Horrifying in its straightforward, almost clinical presentation of Middle Passage conditions, this became one of the most widely circulated items in the graphic arsenal of American abolitionists.

4. Which of the following reasons best explains why the diagram of the slave ship *Brookes*, was so widely distributed?

    (1) to warn black Africans to be careful of kidnapping by white slave traders
    (2) to elicit sympathy in the United States and Great Britain for victims of the slave trade
    (3) to be used by shipbuilders to determine dimensions for new slave ships
    (4) to encourage people to enter the blacksmith trade to produce more chains
    (5) to drum up more business for the company that designed the ship

5. Why did Clarkson believe that the Regulated Slave Act of 1788 was too lenient?

    (1) It allowed slave traders to get away with transporting slaves under inhumane conditions.
    (2) It limited the number of slaves that could be captured and imported by British slave traders.
    (3) It didn't allow slave traders to treat their cargo like objects of disdain and ridicule.
    (4) It gave slaves too much of an opportunity to escape before they reached the United States.
    (5) It didn't support the costs required to bring slaves back to health and prepare them for auction.

Questions 6–8 refer to the following passage.

In 1890, the journalist Jacob Riis published a book titled *How the Other Half Lives*, which contained photographs and detailed descriptions of the deplorable life in New York's tenement district. About this problem Riis wrote: "The remedy that shall be an effective answer to the coming appeal for justice must proceed from the public conscience. Neither legislation nor charity can cover the ground. The greed of capital that wrought the evil must undo it, as far as it can now be undone."

6. According to Riis, how could New York's tenements in 1890 best be improved?

   (1) by enacting new legislation
   (2) by appealing to charity
   (3) by changing capitalistic greed
   (4) by demanding justice
   (5) by asking more questions

7. With which of the following positions on today's poverty and discrimination would Riis likely agree?

   (1) Each individual should pull himself up by his own bootstraps.
   (2) Government's funding for social programs should be cut.
   (3) The states themselves must pass legislation to correct the problem.
   (4) A booming, growing economy will automatically solve the problem.
   (5) Private industry is morally responsible for helping to correct social problems.

8. Based on the values expressed in the quote, to which of the groups below would Riis likely have given support?

   (1) New York's "Four Hundred," the self-appointed social elite
   (2) machine politicians who had the power to give jobs
   (3) private citizens who established the cities' settlement houses
   (4) a group lobbying to pass antipoverty legislation
   (5) businessmen who believed in the theory of social Darwinism

9. Which of the following is an example of American imperialist policy?

   (1) sending food and medical assistance to drought-stricken Ethiopia
   (2) the purchase of Alaska from the czar of Russia in 1867
   (3) blockading Cuba to prevent Soviet ships from entering the western hemisphere
   (4) controlling most of the Panama Canal Zone until 1979
   (5) the bombing of Libya in retaliation for terrorist acts

10. President Grover Cleveland refused to annex Hawaii to the United States after learning that a majority of the natives preferred being ruled by their queen, Liliuokalani. In making this decision, he was abiding by the principle of rule by "consent of the governed" put forth by which of the following documents?

   (1) the Declaration of Independence
   (2) the Monroe Doctrine
   (3) the Constitution
   (4) the Emancipation Proclamation
   (5) the idea of Manifest Destiny

Questions 11–13 are based on the following passage.

"The SS had given the order to destroy us and burn the camp. April 11, 1945: We were to be shot at 3 P.M.; the British arrived at 11 A.M."

The writer of these words, Fania Fenelon, was a survivor of the German concentration camp at Auschwitz-Birkenau. She was one of the lucky European Jews of World War II. Six million others were slaughtered by the Nazis for no other reason than that they were Jewish and thus considered to be racially inferior to Germans. The dimensions of this holocaust were not fully understood until after the invasion of Germany by the Allied forces. The shock waves caused by such a revelation of man's inhumanity to man are still being felt today.

11. The above passage describes which belief of some Germans taken to the extreme?

(1) isolationism
(2) imperialism
(3) progressivism
(4) jingoism
(5) racism

12. Which of the following does the author of this piece exhibit?

(1) racism
(2) humanitarianism
(3) nationalism
(4) sectionalism
(5) materialism

13. According to the passage, why was Fania Fenelon's life spared?

Because of
(1) sudden S.S. intervention
(2) the fact that she was not German
(3) the timely arrival of the British
(4) a Nazi officer's sympathy toward her
(5) shock about former Holocaust murders

Question 14 is based on the following passage.

As telecommunications increasingly entwines itself with educational, social, financial, and employment opportunities, those communities lacking access will find themselves falling further behind the rest of society. The Internet has the potential to empower its users with new skills, new perspectives, new freedoms, even new voices; those groups who remain sequestered from the technology will be further segregated into the periphery of public life.

14. What is the purpose of this paragraph?

(1) to glorify the advances made by telecommunications technology
(2) to specify the skills and perspectives made possible by the Internet
(3) to give communities ideas for accessing more technology
(4) to express concern about those who don't have access to the Internet
(5) to predict that everyone will have equal opportunities due to the Internet

Questions 15 and 16 are based on the following cartoon.

Entitlements are government-funded programs such as Medicare and Social Security that provide financial assistance to individual Americans.

—Michael Ramirez, Copley News Service

15. Which of the following best expresses the main idea of the cartoon?

The government has
(1) decided to cut funds for entitlement programs
(2) decided to increase funds for entitlement programs
(3) decided to create new entitlement programs
(4) decided not to touch entitlement programs
(5) no authority over funding for entitlement programs

16. Which of the following best expresses the cartoonist's opinion?

(1) The government has too much money.
(2) Entitlement programs are over-funded.
(3) Entitlement programs are under-funded.
(4) Entitlement programs are essential to America.
(5) Entitlement programs deserve support.

Questions 17–19 are based on the following list of U.S. government actions.

***Brown v. Board of Education of Topeka* decision (1954)**—separate educational facilities for blacks and whites declared inherently unequal by the Supreme Court

Central High School, Little Rock, Arkansas (1957)—federal troops sent by the president to escort black students into a previously all-white school

U.S. Commission on Civil Rights (1957)—by authority of the president's office, allowed the U.S attorney general to enforce voting rights in the states

Civil Rights Act (1964)—outlawed racial discrimination in public accommodations and by employers, unions, and voting registrars

Voting Rights Acts (1965, 1970)—stopped the use of literacy tests for voter qualification and gave greater power to the federal government to protect citizens' voting rights

PRETEST

17. Which of the following federal actions was primarily the work of the judicial branch?

    (1) the *Brown* v. *Board of Education of Topeka* decision

    (2) the dispatch of federal troops to Central High School in Little Rock

    (3) the enforcement of voting rights in all the states

    (4) the outlawing of racial discrimination in public facilities

    (5) the prohibition of literacy tests to qualify people to vote

18. Which of the following federal actions most directly affected the voiding of a New York State law requiring voters to be able to write in English?

    (1) the *Brown* v. *Board of Education of Topeka* decision

    (2) the dispatch of federal troops to Little Rock, Arkansas

    (3) the passage of the Civil Rights Act

    (4) the founding of the U.S. Commission on Civil Rights

    (5) the passage of the Voting Rights Acts

19. Which of the following federal actions led to greater opportunity in the workplace and at the ballot box?

    (1) the *Brown* v. *Board of Education of Topeka* decision

    (2) the dispatch of federal troops to Little Rock, Arkansas

    (3) the founding of the U.S. Commission on Civil Rights

    (4) the passage of the Civil Rights Act

    (5) the passage of the Voting Rights Acts

Question 20 is based on the following map.

POPULATION DISTRIBUTION IN IOWA

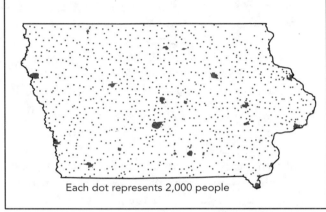

Each dot represents 2,000 people

U.S. Bureau of the Census

20. Iowa is one of the flattest states in the United States. Based on the information on the map, which of the following inferences can be made about population distribution in Iowa?

    (1) Farming is still a major industry and influence in the state of Iowa.

    (2) Flatlands allow for an even distribution of population.

    (3) Iowa is being drained of its population by the Sunbelt.

    (4) Iowa is one of the most heavily populated states.

    (5) There are few big cities on the plains of the United States.

21. Eastern European, Asian, and Hispanic immigrants to the United States often make their first home in large groups in low-rent city neighborhoods. The neighborhoods, or "urban villages," are often known by ethnically oriented nicknames such as Little Italy and Germantown. Which of the following best explains why newly arrived immigrants are drawn to the urban villages?

    (1) Immigrants don't speak English well enough to survive in neighborhoods where English is spoken.
    (2) Immigrants want to separate themselves from all contacts from and memories of what they left behind.
    (3) Urban villages help immigrants to blend in quickly and easily with mainstream America.
    (4) Urban villages provide the cushion of a familiar cultural background within a larger, unfamiliar city.
    (5) Urban villages provide excellent business opportunities and chances to climb out of poverty quickly.

22. The focus of the U.S. workforce has changed over the last 150 years. According to the Department of Commerce, 68.6 percent of the labor force was engaged in farming in 1840. The number had fallen to 31 percent by 1910. Farm occupations were held by 1.6 percent of the working population in 1990.

    Which of the following conclusions does this data support?

    (1) Farming is not profitable.
    (2) Farming is no longer necessary.
    (3) Most farming is done by large corporations.
    (4) Farming is becoming increasingly popular.
    (5) Farming is no longer a major occupation.

Questions 23–25 are based on the following information.

Federal, state, and local governments levy taxes to raise money for their operations. Most people in the United States pay at least one of the following taxes.

Income tax—a percentage of wages, profits, and other income paid to federal, state, and local governments

Social Security tax—percentage of wages paid into a public insurance fund that can be drawn on upon retirement

Capital gains tax—money paid to the federal government out of profits from the sale of land, buildings, stocks, and other capital assets

Property tax—money paid (usually to a local government) by the owner of real estate

Sales tax—money paid to federal, state, or local governments on the purchase of goods or services

23. When Amy and Mark Hill bought a new couch for their apartment, they had to pay an additional percentage of the price as a tax. What kind of tax did they pay?

    (1) income tax
    (2) Social Security tax
    (3) capital gains tax
    (4) property tax
    (5) sales tax

24. The Smith family recently sold some stock that they had bought several years earlier. The stock was worth twice as much as when they had bought it. What kind of tax did they have to pay on the profit they made from the stocks?

    (1) income tax
    (2) Social Security tax
    (3) capital gains tax
    (4) property tax
    (5) sales tax

25. The Fernandez family owns a house in Los Angeles. In July they got a bill from the state showing the amount of taxes they owed on their house. What kind of tax did they owe?

    (1) income tax
    (2) Social Security tax
    (3) capital gains tax
    (4) property tax
    (5) sales tax

Questions 26–29 are based on the following passage.

The Great Wall of China is reputed to be the only human-made feature visible from space. Although it was once thought to have been built entirely during the Ch'in Dynasty between 221 and 208 B.C.E., it is now believed to have been started earlier.

The 15-foot-high, 25-foot-wide, 1,500-mile-long structure was undoubtedly erected to keep out invading barbarians. To the common people of the empire, who had been forced to build the wall, it was not worth it, however. The wall, and other public works accomplished by the Ch'in Dynasty, had taken a great toll on the wealth and human life of the country. As a result, an indignant population rose up in rebellion against the Ch'in Dynasty, and in 207 B.C.E the Han Dynasty began.

Because of its rich history and magnificent appearance, the Great Wall attracts tourists, scientists, and historians to this day and will continue to do so for generations.

26. According to the author of this passage, why was the Han Dynasty able to come into power?

 (1) Barbarians were not effectively prevented from invading the empire under the Ch'in Dynasty.
 (2) It had started the work on the wall, controlled it all along, and took credit for its creation.
 (3) The common people rebelled against the empire that had forced them to work on the Great Wall.
 (4) The Ch'in emperor lost all his personal wealth in the creation of the Great Wall.
 (5) The Great Wall had become famous and attracted tourists who supported the Hans.

27. What is the main idea of this passage?

 (1) The emperor of the Ch'in Dynasty was a slave driver.
 (2) Invading barbarians were a problem in ancient China.
 (3) The common people of ancient China were very poor.
 (4) People today overestimate the importance of the Great Wall.
 (5) The human achievement of the Great Wall is widely appreciated.

28. With which of the following opinions would this author most likely agree?

 (1) The building of the pyramids of Egypt was not worth the human sacrifice it involved.
 (2) The pyramids of Egypt are also intriguing to people today because of the human effort they represent.
 (3) The pyramids of Egypt would probably be visible to a human standing on the moon.
 (4) The human significance of the pyramids of Egypt is greater than that of the Great Wall.
 (5) The human significance of the pyramids of Egypt is not as great as that of the Great Wall.

29. The writer has not directly stated, but would support, which of the following statements?

    (1) Astronauts have taken a personal interest in the history of the Great Wall of China.
    (2) The common people of the Ch'in Dynasty were the ones who provided the labor in constructing the Great Wall.
    (3) Work on the Great Wall was started before the Ch'in Dynasty came into existence.
    (4) The Great Wall is a stunning human achievement and was probably worth the effort it took.
    (5) The common people of today's China still resent the use of forced labor to build the Great Wall.

Questions 30 and 31 are based on the following cartoon.

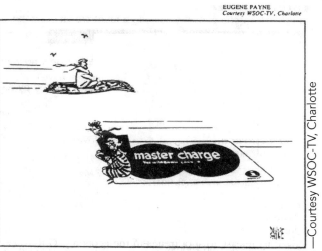

America's magic carpet

—Courtesy WSOC-TV, Charlotte

30. Based on the information in the cartoon, the artist would likely agree with which of the following statements?

    (1) Americans' spending is greater than it has ever been.
    (2) Americans' spending has fallen off because of inflation.
    (3) Americans' spending is supported more and more by credit.
    (4) Americans' spending far exceeds the spending of foreign consumers.
    (5) Americans' spending habits are going to drive the economy into a tailspin.

31. By comparing a credit card to a flying carpet, what is the artist suggesting about Americans?

    (1) They are riding high on consumer debt.
    (2) They expect a free ride.
    (3) They put trust in their financial future.
    (4) They are as rich as Arabian sheiks.
    (5) They use credit cards to purchase carpets.

Questions 32 and 33 are based on the following map.

TIME ZONES ACROSS NORTH AMERICA

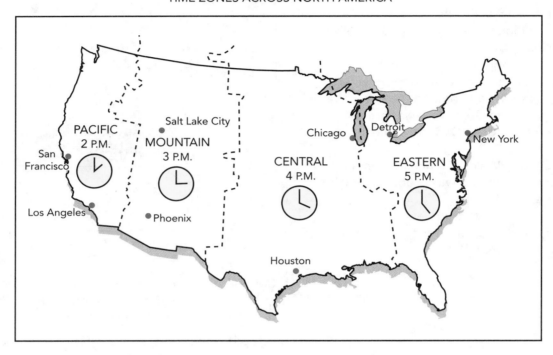

32. According to the time zones map, what time is it in San Francisco when it is midnight in Chicago?

(1) 9:00 A.M.
(2) 10:00 P.M.
(3) 11:00 P.M.
(4) 1:00 A.M.
(5) 2:00 A.M.

33. What time is it in New York when it is midnight in Salt Lake City?

(1) 5:00 A.M.
(2) 10:00 P.M.
(3) 2:00 A.M.
(4) 1:00 A.M.
(5) 9:00 P.M.

PRETEST

Questions 34 and 35 are based on the following passage.

The male form of a female liberationist is a male liberationist—a man who realizes the unfairness of having to work all his life to support a wife and children so that someday his widow may live in comfort; a man who points out that commuting to a job he doesn't like is just as oppressive as his wife's imprisonment in a suburb; a man who rejects his exclusion, by society and most women, from participation in childbirth and the engrossing, delightful care of young children—a man, in fact, who wants to relate himself to people and the world around him as a person.

—Margaret Mead, "Some Personal Views"

34. What is the writer's opinion about gender roles in American society?

(1) Males and females should remain in those roles that are best suited to their gender.
(2) Women should work outside the home and men should stay at home with the kids.
(3) Women should make fewer demands on men so that men will be more relaxed.
(4) Males can take on all of the roles of females in this world of modern technology.
(5) Men and women should both be able to perform roles not traditionally assigned to them.

35. What is the source of much frustration for modern men, according to the writer?

(1) demands that they reverse roles with women and stay at home
(2) pressure to assume only traditional male roles and responsibilities
(3) employers who do not pay them enough to allow their wives to stay at home
(4) their own inability to relate as someone other than just a breadwinner
(5) the lack of excitement and thrill in their lives once they marry

Questions 36 and 37 are based on the following passage.

The Noble and Holy Order of the Knights of Labor was organized in 1869 for all workers, regardless of race, sex, nationality, craft, or skill level. They believed that organized labor could meet the force of big business.

The Knights were opposed to strikes, except as a last resort, and child and convict labor. They favored a federal bureau for labor statistics, equal pay for both sexes, and an eight-hour workday.

The organization peaked at over 700,000 members but quickly lost its strength after the Haymarket Square riot in Chicago in 1886. The riot started during a meeting to protest police brutality against striking Knights. Violence erupted when a bomb was thrown into a police-controlled crowd. Seven policemen and ten workers were killed, and 117 people were injured. There was no proof that the Knights caused the violence, but public opinion turned against them.

36. What was the cause of the downfall of the Noble and Holy Order of the Knights of Labor?

   (1) spontaneous, unprovoked revolts by its members
   (2) suspicions about the cause of the Haymarket Square riot
   (3) continual police brutality and harassment toward its strikers
   (4) the amount of work time lost by its members on strike
   (5) the ineffectiveness of its leaders in reaching the group's goals

37. Which of the following is supported by the information given in the passage?

   (1) The Knights of Labor succeeded in keeping peace among black and white workers.
   (2) The events of 1886 proved that the Knights of Labor were dishonest and untrustworthy.
   (3) The Knights of Labor kept the growth of monopolies and other big businesses to a minimum.
   (4) The Knights of Labor's importance was in articulating the demands of laborers to big business.
   (5) The federal government established child labor laws as a result of the Knights of Labor's influence.

Questions 38 and 39 refer to the following passage.

Economists and business leaders are increasingly blaming the lack of affordable housing for the slowdown in major regional economies across the United States. In New England, the mid-Atlantic States, the Southeast, California, and portions of the Pacific Northwest, high housing costs have been shown to be causing or contributing to labor shortages. Housing costs contribute to labor shortages by encouraging out-migration from high-cost areas and discouraging migration to these areas; diminished productivity due to lateness and absenteeism caused by long commutes as workers seek housing affordability far from developed worksites; and unacceptable recruitment, retention, and wage rate distortions.

—Excerpted from *America's Cities: Opposing Viewpoints* by Richard C. Lerlauto, Daniel N. Hoffman, and David C. Schwartz

38. What inference can you make based on the passage?

(1) Construction workers don't earn as much as they should.
(2) New Yorkers and Virginians have cheap housing.
(3) There is probably a full labor force in Massachusetts.
(4) Arizona probably doesn't have a labor shortage.
(5) The population has been decreasing in New Mexico.

39. Which of the following would have the *least* impact on the issue described?

(1) increased wages for workers in high housing cost areas
(2) political lobbying for rent control legislation in California
(3) wage decreases for workers who arrive late
(4) the development of cheaper construction materials
(5) housing subsidies for employees of companies in New Jersey

Questions 40 and 41 refer to the following map.

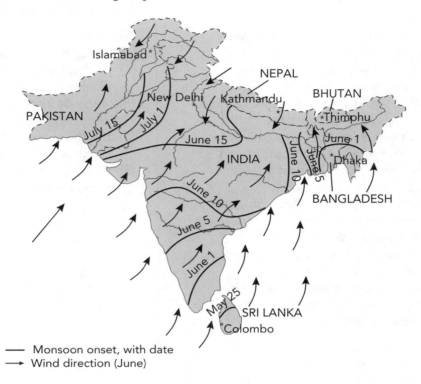

— Monsoon onset, with date
→ Wind direction (June)

40. This weather map of India features the onset of the monsoon. The monsoon is the summer rainy season that blows in from the Indian Ocean. From this map, what can you tell about the weather in India in mid-June?

(1) Southern India is still very hot and dry.
(2) Half of the country is being soaked with rain.
(3) Sri Lanka has recovered from the monsoon.
(4) Pakistani crops are well-watered and flourishing.
(5) Southeast winds are pushing the rains northward.

41. Which of the following can be seen on this map?

(1) the border between India and Pakistan
(2) that Istanbul is the capital city of Turkey
(3) that there are numerous cities in Southern India
(4) that the monsoon season affects all of India
(5) where the Himalayan Mountains are in Nepal

PRETEST

Questions 42 and 43 refer to the following graph.

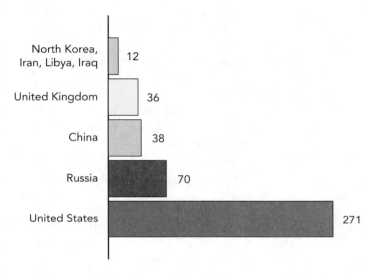

MILITARY BUDGETS, IN BILLIONS ($ 1998)

North Korea, Iran, Libya, Iraq — 12
United Kingdom — 36
China — 38
Russia — 70
United States — 271

42. Which of the following can be concluded from the information in the graph?

(1) The United States is concerned about the military capabilities of Iraq and Libya.
(2) The United States spends nearly four times more on the military than Russia.
(3) Russia has recently begun to pour more money into its military arsenal.
(4) The United Kingdom is a military concern to the United States.
(5) Russia used to compete fiercely with the United States in a race for military superiority.

43. Who might use the information in this graph to support their position?

(1) U.S. government officials who want to make a case for increasing defense spending
(2) Libyan officials who want to reassure their citizens that they have nothing to fear from the United States
(3) U.S. citizens who would like to see more tax money spent on education than on the military
(4) British politicians who want a larger defense budget so that the U.K. can compete with China
(5) U.S. generals who want raises in their salaries and improved working conditions

44. Before Prohibition, Carry Nation lectured across the United States, speaking against alcohol use. She also was arrested for breaking up saloons with a hatchet. Eventually, Nation became a symbol for the temperance movement. To which of the following women is Carry Nation's fame most similar?

(1) Susan B. Anthony, a militant advocate of women's rights, arrested for voting
(2) Betsy Ross, the woman who is said to have made the first American flag
(3) Eleanor Roosevelt, a president's wife and outspoken civil rights advocate
(4) Charlotte Parkhurst, a woman who disguised herself as a man and went to work as a stagecoach driver
(5) Geraldine Ferraro, the first woman nominated for vice president by a major party

Questions 45 and 46 refer to the graph below.

WHAT IS NOT RECYCLED?

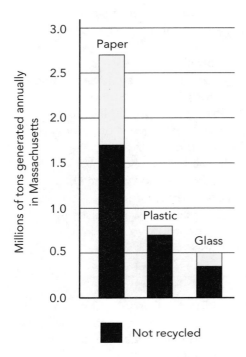

Not recycled

45. Using the information in the graph, which of the following statements cannot be proven?

    (1) Paper makes up the largest portion of the trash in Massachusetts.

    (2) A greater percent of glass than plastic is recycled in Massachusetts.

    (3) More than half of what could be recycled in Massachusetts wasn't.

    (4) More paper is being recycled than glass and plastic combined.

    (5) The recycling efforts have been steadily increasing in Massachusetts.

46. Which of the following is an *unlikely* explanation of the information presented by the graph?

    (1) It feels more convenient to just throw something away. Recycling requires a special effort.

    (2) Many businesses still don't recycle or encourage their employees to recycle at home.

    (3) Almost everything we buy is wrapped in layers of wasteful and excessive packaging.

    (4) No one in Massachusetts is interested in recycling and the state may become a garbage capital.

    (5) Recycling efforts have never been fully funded or supported by state and local officials.

47. When you are hired for a job in the United States you are required to complete an I-9 form to state your identity and legal residence status. In addition to completing the form you must submit one or two documents as proof of what you have claimed. On the following page is a list of the acceptable documents. Under what circumstances would your documentation *not* be sufficient?

    (1) if you present an unexpired refugee travel document

    (2) if you present a voter registration card and an original birth certificate

    (3) if you present a driver's license with your photograph

    (4) if you present a school record and a Native American tribal document

    (5) if you present of Certificate of Naturalization

PRETEST

LISTS OF ACCEPTABLE DOCUMENTS

List A		List B		List C
Documents that Establish Both Identity and Employment Eligibility	OR	**Documents that Establish Identity**	AND	**Documents that Establish Employment Eligibility**

List A — Documents that Establish Both Identity and Employment Eligibility

1. U.S. Passport (unexpired or expired)

2. Certificate of U.S. Citizenship (*INS Form N-560 or N-561*)

3. Certificate of Naturalization (*INS Form N-550 or N-570*)

4. Unexpired foreign passport, with *I-551 stamp or* attached *INS Form I-94* indicating unexpired employment authorization

5. Alien Registration Receipt Card with photograph (*INS Form I-151 or I-551*)

6. Unexpired Temporary Resident Card (*INS Form I-688*)

7. Unexpired Employment Authorization Card (*INS Form I-688A*)

8. Unexpired Reentry Permit (*INS Form I-327*)

9. Unexpired Refugee Travel Document (*INS Form I-571*)

10. Unexpired Employment Authorization Document issued by the INS which contains a photograph (*INS Form I-688B*)

OR

List B — Documents that Establish Identity

1. Driver's license or ID card issued by a state or outlying possession of the United States provided it contains a photograph or information such as name, date of birth, sex, height, eye color, and address

2. ID card issued by federal, state, or local government agencies or entities provided it contains a photograph or information such as name, date of birth, sex, height, eye color, and address

3. School ID card with a photograph

4. Voter's registration card

5. U.S. Military card or draft record

6. Military dependent's ID card

7. U.S. Coast Guard Merchant Mariner Card

8. Native American tribal document

9. Driver's license issued by a Canadian government authority

For persons under age 18 who are unable to present a document listed above:

10. School record or report card

11. Clinic, doctor, or hospital record

12. Day-care or nursery school record

AND

List C — Documents that Establish Employment Eligibility

1. U.S. social security card issued by the Social Security Administration (*other than a card stating it is not valid for employment*)

2. Certification of Birth Abroad issued by the Department of State (*Form FS-545 or Form DS-1350*)

3. Original or certified copy of a birth certificate issued by a state, county, municipal authority or outlying possession of the United States bearing an official seal

4. Native American tribal document

5. U.S. Citizen ID Card (*INS Form I-197*)

6. ID Card for use of Resident Citizen in the United States (*INS Form I-179*)

7. Unexpired employment authorization document issued by the INS (*other than those listed under List A*)

Source: Form I–9

Question 48 refers to the photograph below. It shows a family from the Eastern European country of Albania sitting with all of their material possessions.

48. Which of the following statements can you infer from this photograph?

   (1) This family is wealthy by Albanian standards.
   (2) Albanians lead a very isolated life.
   (3) A donkey is the only form of transportation available.
   (4) The father and mother play traditional roles in the family.
   (5) T.V. gives this family a view of life in many other places.

Questions 49 and 50 refer to the passage below.

"The West has been the great word of our history. The Westerner has been the type and master of our American life." When the future president Woodrow Wilson wrote these words in 1895 he was neither the first nor the last to so grandly interpret the American West. That "great word" was never pure fact but was always tinged deeply with myth, and though interpretations of the facts change, the myth survives. The history of the West has been consistently revised in accord with the dream.

Centuries before they first sailed to the Americas, Europeans were dreaming of unknown lands to the west, places inhabited perhaps by "the fabulous races of mankind," men and women unlike any seen in the known world. The people might be frightening, but their world would surely be a paradise, a golden land somewhere beyond the setting sun.

—Excerpted from *The American West* by Robert V. Hine and John Faracher

49. According to this passage, which of the following is true?

   (1) People who moved westward were inspired by a myth.
   (2) People who moved westward were ultimately disappointed.
   (3) The West has always been a known entity.
   (4) Woodrow Wilson didn't visit the West until 1895.
   (5) All Americans have positive feelings about the West.

50. Which historical idea best summarizes the American attitude toward the West as it is described here?

   (1) Manifest Destiny
   (2) Separate but Equal
   (3) Uncle Sam Wants You
   (4) Live Free or Die
   (5) Iron Curtain

Answer Key

1. **Analysis (2)** Lincoln did not issue an order for emancipation for the entire country out of loyalty to the four border states that remained with the Union.

2. **Comprehension (4)** Of all the choices given, only the death penalty, or capital punishment, could mean the same as "official murder."

3. **Analysis (3)** Justice Brennan says the "official murder, . . . adds instead a second defilement to the first." This shows his opposition to capital punishment.

4. **Analysis (2)** The passage tells us that Clarkson was an antislavery advocate and that this picture was part of the arsenal of American abolitionists. Both of these clues indicate that the picture was being used to object to slavery and create sympathy for its victims.

5. **Evaluation (1)** The leniency of the Slave Act was in the room it gave slave traders to treat slaves so badly. The fact that conditions like those depicted in the etching of the ship were allowed to persist supported Clarkson's claim that the Act was too permissive.

6. **Comprehension (3)** In his statement Riis says, "The greed of capital that wrought the evil must undo it."

7. **Analysis (5)** In his statement Riis points out, "The greed of capital that wrought the evil must undo it." By capital, he means private industry. Riis would likely agree with the position that private industry is morally responsible for helping to correct social problems.

8. **Evaluation (3)** Riis believed that justice should come from the public conscience, as represented by private citizens who established settlement houses. Choice (1) is incorrect because the "Four Hundred" do not represent the public conscience. Choices (2) and (5) are incorrect because machine politicians and businessmen who believed in social Darwinism are the very ones Riis attacked for creating the conditions. Choice (4) is incorrect because Riis says legislation cannot undo the evil.

9. **Application (4)** An example of American imperialist policy was the U.S. control of most of the Panama Canal Zone, because it was a case of the United States controlling a foreign territory.

10. **Evaluation (1)** In making his decision, President Grover Cleveland was abiding by the principles of rule by "consent of the governed" put forth by the Declaration of Independence.

11. **Application (5)** The passage says, "Six million others were slaughtered by the Nazis for no other reason than that they were Jewish and thus considered to be racially inferior to Germans."

12. **Analysis (2)** The writer shows concern for the concentration camp inmates and is upset by "man's inhumanity to man."

13. **Comprehension (3)** Only choice (3) is mentioned as a reason for why the author's life was not taken.

14. **Comprehension (4)** The last sentence of the paragraph expresses the author's concern for those who don't have access to the Internet.

15. **Comprehension (1)** The figure on the left represents the government. The knife it holds represents the cuts it intends to make on the figure on the right. The "food," or money, will come from entitlements.

16. **Analysis (2)** The entitlement figure is drawn as a hog and represents overfeeding, or over-funding. By representing the U.S. government as Uncle Sam holding a knife, the cartoonist is expressing the opinion that entitlements have grown too much.

17. **Application (1)** Of the choices, only (1) was the result of action of the judicial branch. The other choices were the result of actions of either the legislative branch or the executive branch.

18. **Application (5)** According to the passage, the Voting Rights Acts outlawed restrictions on voting. Choices (1), (2), (3), and (4) did not involve the issue of literacy tests for voters.

19. **Application (4)** The Civil Rights Act is the only one that mentions employers as well as voting rights.

20. **Analysis (2)** Since there is an even distribution of population in Iowa, as shown on the map, it can be inferred that lowlands allow for an even distribution of population. None of the other conclusions is supported by the map.

21. **Analysis (4)** Immigrants would be attracted to areas in U.S. cities that provide them with something familiar. Many immigrants speak English, so the language problem would not be a deciding factor. Urban villages would help immigrants adapt to the new culture but not necessarily help them blend in quickly or offer any particular business opportunities outside of the urban village.

22. **Comprehension (5)** Because of the decline in the percentage of the labor force involved in farming, farming is no longer a major U.S. occupation. The figures do not refer to profits, the need for farming, or who does the farming.

23. **Application (5)** When people purchase products, they usually pay a sales tax. The other choices do not involve the retail sale of ordinary goods.

24. **Application (3)** Because the Smith family made a profit on the sale of stocks, the money paid out was a capital gains tax. The other choices do not involve the sale of land, buildings, stocks, or other assets.

25. **Application (4)** Because the Fernandez family owns property, they owed a property tax. The other taxes are not paid on property currently owned.

26. **Comprehension (3)** The passage states that the Ch'in Dynasty lost all its power when the people who were forced to work on the Great Wall finally rebelled.

27. **Comprehension (5)** Choice (5) is the main idea of the passage. Choices (1), (2), and (3) are details and facts from the passage. Choice (4) is the opposite of what is stated in the last paragraph of the passage.

28. **Analysis (2)** The author is enthusiastic about the Great Wall despite the suffering it caused. Therefore, he would probably feel the same about the pyramids of Egypt.

29. **Analysis (4)** Even though the author states that the people who built the Wall did not feel it was worth the effort, he also states that the Wall holds great fascination for people today.

30. **Evaluation (3)** In the cartoon the flying carpet is a credit card. This suggests that Americans' spending habits have not been curtailed by inflation but have been supported more and more by credit.

31. **Evaluation (1)** The mythical magic carpet rides high. By comparing a credit card to a magic carpet, the artist is suggesting that American consumers think they are "riding high," or experiencing financial success because of the ability to finance purchases with credit.

32. **Application (2)** Since San Francisco lies in the Pacific time zone, which is two hours behind Chicago, which lies in the central time zone, it would be 10:00 P.M.

33. **Application (3)** Since Salt Lake City, Utah, lies in the mountain time zone, which is two hours behind New York, which lies in the eastern time zone, it would be 2:00 A.M.

34. **Evaluation (5)** Men staying at home to care for young children is a reverse of their usual role, just as women working outside the home is a role reversal for them. The writer makes it clear that she thinks that both reversals should be acceptable choices.

35. **Analysis (2)** The writer implies that men are frustrated because of society's confining rules regarding appropriate behavior.

36. **Analysis (2)** The paragraph states that public opinion turned against the Knights after the Haymarket Square riot.

PRETEST

37. Evaluation (4) The Knights served an important purpose in stating clearly the goals of organized labor. The passage does not provide enough information for us to conclude anything else.

38. Analysis (4) Because Arizona is in the Southwest, which is not mentioned as one of the regions impacted by high housing costs, there is not likely to be a labor shortage there since housing costs there are affordable. The other choices are contradicted by the information given.

39. Analysis (3) Decreasing wages of late workers would not help to address the issue of labor shortages due to high housing costs. The other choices could conceivably help address the issue because they are consistent with the information in the passage.

40. Comprehension (2) The lines only indicate the onset, or start, of the monsoon. We cannot assume from the map that the monsoon quickly passes. Also, the arrows indicate that the wind direction is primarily from the southwest or northeast, not from the southeast. Pakistan is the last area to remain dry.

41. Comprehension (1) The map shows the borders between countries, but does not identify any but capital cities, or indicate mountain ranges. While the monsoon season does eventually impact most of the country of India (as well as other countries, e.g., Pakistan, Nepal, Bhutan, and Bangladesh), it does not affect the northernmost part of the country.

42. Comprehension (2) Choices (1) and (4), regarding military concerns, are not reflected in the graph, nor is history (5) or new policies (3). The only information that is clearly evident from the graph is how much more the United States spends than Russia.

43. Application (3) It would be difficult to make a case for increased military spending given how much more the United States invests over any other country. Libya could hardly be reassuring to its citizens on the basis of the information here, nor could much of a case be made by the

British since the U.K. is almost on a par with China. The only legitimate use that could be made of the graph would be by citizens in the United States who would like to see their money spent on something else, especially since the United States military budget is so much bigger than that of other nations.

44. Application (1) Like Nation, Anthony advocated an initially unpopular cause. Both were arrested for supporting their causes. Both were seen as symbols of women's movements. Ross and Parkhurst had no real political impact. Roosevelt and Ferraro were neither arrested for their convictions nor representatives of specific movements.

45. Analysis (5) The graph does not show the results of recycling over time, so it is impossible to say that they have been either increasing or decreasing.

46. Evaluation (4) If (4) were true, then the bars on the graph would all be dark blue.

47. Comprehension (3) A driver's license only establishes identity and thus needs to be combined with another document that establishes employment eligibility.

48. Evaluation (5) We can use our knowledge about the television to infer (5). There is no evidence in the picture that supports the other statements.

49. Comprehension (1) Choices (2)–(5) are contradicted by the passage. However, it is clear from what is said that the mythological appeal of the West has always been a major factor in attracting people to it.

50. Analysis (1) Manifest Destiny refers to the idea that it is America's fate to expand westward and to claim the lands there as its own.

Evaluation Chart

Use the preceding answer key to check your answers to the Pretest. Then find the item number of each question you missed and circle it on the chart below to determine the skills in which you need the most work. For each question that you missed, review the skill pages indicated.

Skill Area/ Content Area	Comprehension (pages 27–42)	Application (pages 43–58)	Analysis (pages 59–98)	Evaluation (pages 99–115)
U.S. History	6, 13, 14, 15, 42	9, 17, 18, 19, 43	1, 4, 16, 35, 36	5, 8, 10, 34, 37
World History	26, 27	11	12, 28, 29	
Civics & Government	2		3, 7, 45	46
Geography	40, 41, 49	32, 33	20, 21, 50	48
Economics	22, 47	23, 24, 25	38, 39	30, 31

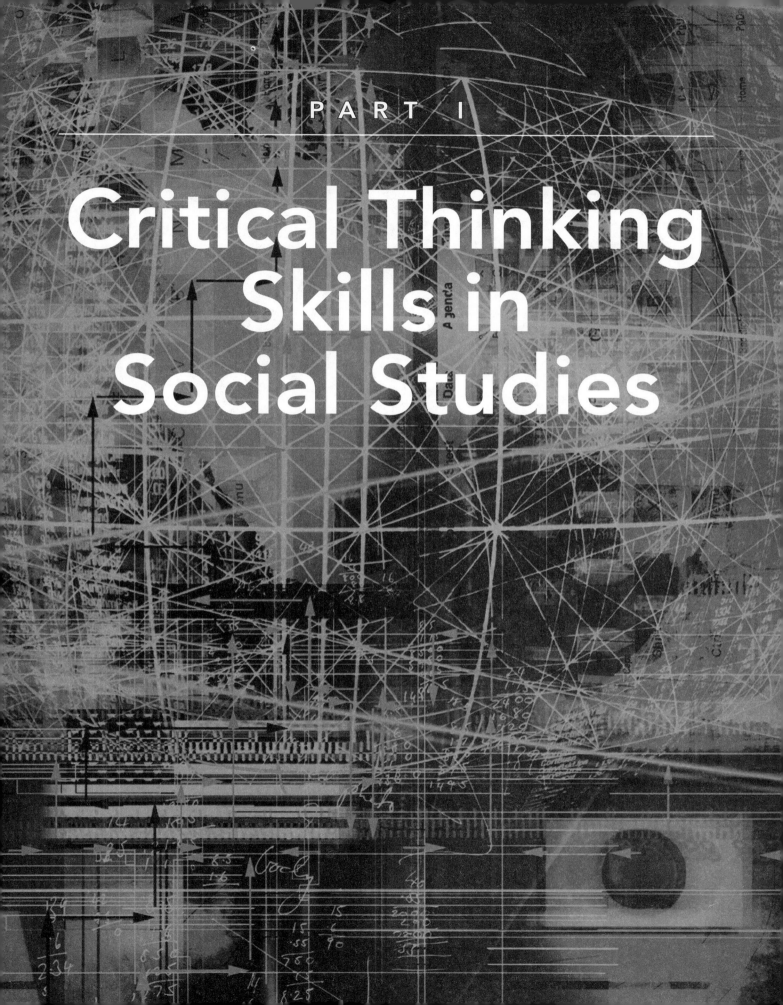

Critical Thinking Skills in Social Studies

Chapter 1

Comprehending Social Studies Materials

When you **comprehend** something, you understand what it means. For example, if you comprehend football, you are familiar with its objectives and rules, you recognize the role of each of the players, and you can appreciate the value of each play. Furthermore, if you are attending a game with someone who has never seen football before, you are able to explain the game so that the person can follow it.

The GED Social Studies Test will assess your ability to comprehend passages, forms, quotes, graphs, charts, maps, and cartoons. To demonstrate your comprehension of these materials, you will need to

- summarize the main idea
- restate information
- identify implications

Summarizing the Main Idea

Summarizing the main idea in social studies materials means finding the key thought. When someone simplifies a lengthy article into a few short sentences, that person is providing a summary of the information in the article. News reporters, for example, must frequently explain a long speech or a detailed event in just a few sentences. When they do this, they are summarizing the main idea.

The main idea of a speech, article, or report is often stated near its beginning or its end, since the speaker or writer wants to give the idea the primary emphasis. Sometimes the main idea is not stated directly. The author gives the details, but the reader must **infer,** or "read between the lines," to determine the key thought. In some cases, a title may be a clue to identifying the main idea.

Read the passage below, and in the question that follows circle the choice that best indicates the main idea.

On January 31, 1948, nearly a million people waited in the hot sun of India to mourn the assassination of Mohandas K. Gandhi, a thin brown man of seventy-eight who had died as he had lived—a poor private citizen without official title, position, or academic honors. Yet heads of state from all over the world were there to show respect for this friend of the oppressed and the United Nations lowered its flag and interrupted its sessions in tribute. Gandhi had demonstrated to the world the effective strategy of nonviolent civil disobedience toward unjust laws. Humanity had lost an international symbol of nonviolence and mourned for itself as much as for the man.

What is the main idea in this passage?

(1) the irony of life in general and one man's life in particular
(2) humankind's loss of a unique activist
(3) that Gandhi never held an official public title or position
(4) that Gandhi died a poor man
(5) a plea for more international understanding and love

In answering this question, it would help to go back to the last sentence of the passage: "Humanity had lost an international symbol of nonviolence and mourned for itself as much as for the man." This concluding sentence summarizes the main idea of the passage, so choice (2) would be the correct answer. All of the other sentences in the paragraph give details about how unusual and well respected Gandhi was.

GED PRACTICE

EXERCISE 1

Questions 1 and 2 refer to the following passage.

"For a thousand days I would serve as counsel to the president. I soon learned that to make my way upward, into a position of confidence and influence, I had to travel downward through factional power plays, corruption, and finally outright crimes." These are the words of John Dean, who served in President Richard Nixon's administration during the Watergate crisis. His testimony against his employer led to calls for Nixon's impeachment.

President Nixon made his resignation speech on August 8, 1974, after three articles of impeachment had been voted against him by the House of Representatives. Only one other president in history, Andrew Johnson, had ever faced the prospect of impeachment proceedings. No president had ever resigned from office before. Though Richard Nixon was never convicted of a crime or even brought to trial for one, to many people he remains a symbol of abuse of power.

1. What is the writer's main purpose in this passage?

   (1) to make a case for the elimination of the impeachment process as ineffective and outdated
   (2) to compare the corruption of Andrew Johnson's presidency with Richard Nixon's
   (3) to persuade the reader that former President Nixon was unjustly accused of abusing power and deserves our sympathy
   (4) to remind us of the abuse of power in Nixon's administration during his term as president
   (5) to point out that John Dean's testimony against Richard Nixon is what led to the former president's resignation

2. What does *impeachment* mean, as used in the passage?

   (1) finding a public official innocent
   (2) convicting a public official of serious crimes
   (3) bringing formal charges against a public official
   (4) the imprisonment of a public official
   (5) the resignation of a public official

Answers are on page 395.

Summarizing the Main Idea in Illustrations

You will work with several major types of visual materials throughout this text, including graphs, charts, tables, maps, and political cartoons. Each of these types of illustrations serves a particular purpose.

Graphs make comparisons of numbers or amounts by using lines, bars, circles, or pictures. They show patterns. There are several types of graphs.

- Line, bar, and area graphs show trends at a glance.

- Circle graphs or pie charts show how parts of a thing relate to the whole.

- Picture graphs, or pictographs, use symbols representing the subject being studied.

Charts and **Tables** are concise reference tools. They list information in orderly rows and columns with easily readable headings and captions.

Maps give information about specific geographic areas, highlighting such data as weather, population, and routes for traveling.

Political cartoons express opinions about political events in a humorous and pointed way.

When you read a graph, chart, table, cartoon, or map, you will need to grasp the main idea of the picture quickly before you can use the information. To do this, you will need to translate the picture into words. Look at the following example.

This is a circle graph. It looks like a pie that has been cut into pieces. The title of the graph is "U.S. Immigrants by Country of Birth: 1997."

U.S. IMMIGRANTS BY COUNTRY OF BIRTH: 1997

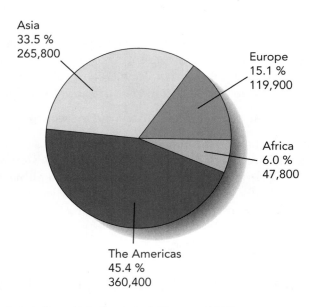

Asia
33.5 %
265,800

Europe
15.1 %
119,900

Africa
6.0 %
47,800

The Americas
45.4 %
360,400

Graph from U.S. Statistical Abstract 1999

Looking quickly at this graph, you can see that the main idea is that immigrants to this country come from many diverse places in the world. The largest number (45.4% of the total) come from other countries in the Americas, followed by Asia, which contributes 33.5%. People also immigrate from Europe and Africa.

GED PRACTICE

EXERCISE 2

Questions 1 and 2 refer to the following circle graph.

WORLD POPULATION GROWTH, 1995–2000

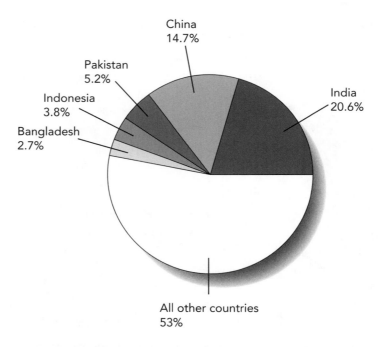

China
14.7%

Pakistan
5.2%

Indonesia
3.8%

Bangladesh
2.7%

India
20.6%

All other countries
53%

1. What is the main idea of this graph?

   (1) There are more people in the rest of the world than there are in these five Asian countries.
   (2) Bangladesh, Indonesia, and Pakistan do not have large populations.
   (3) The lack of birth control options accounts for the increased population growth in Asian countries.
   (4) Starvation and disease curb the growth of population in some countries.
   (5) Five countries in Asia contributed nearly half of the world's population growth between 1995 and 2000.

2. Which of the following is *not* a conclusion that may be drawn from the graph?

   (1) In several Asian countries there are probably conditions which lead to population growth that do not exist in the rest of the world.
   (2) More than one-third of the world's increased population from 1995 to 2000 lives in just two countries.
   (3) New government limits on family size and a disease epidemic may limit the population growth in Asia.
   (4) If you don't consider Asia when discussing population growth, you will miss a big piece of the picture.
   (5) The five countries specified on this graph probably need to take measures to limit population growth.

Questions 3 and 4 refer to the following line graph.

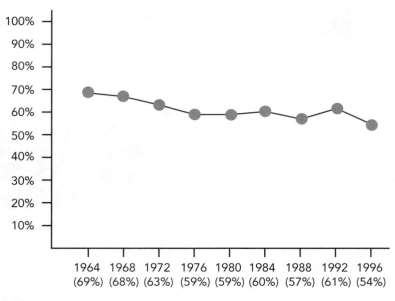

VOTER TURNOUT, 1964-1996 (By Percent)

— U.S. Census Bureau

3. What is the main idea of this graph?

(1) Voter turnout has been dropping steadily since 1964.
(2) Many people who are eligible to vote do not vote.
(3) There were more registered voters in 1992 than in 1988.
(4) The percentage of Americans who vote has declined over the past 30 years.
(5) People are more likely to vote in difficult economic times.

4. Which of the following conclusions *cannot* be drawn from the graph?

(1) The number of Americans of voting age declined between 1964 and 1972.
(2) Interest in voting among Americans has declined since the Vietnam War.
(3) The biggest change in the percentage of people who voted was between 1992 and 1996.
(4) Voter turnout is not dependent on which political party holds the office of president.
(5) The percentage of Americans who voted in 1960 was probably higher than the percentage that voted in 2000.

Answers are on page 395.

You will get more practice using these and other kinds of graphs, charts, tables, maps, and cartoons as you work through the other exercises in this book.

Restating Information

Restating information is "putting it into your own words," or paraphrasing. By paraphrasing the speaker's words, you are showing that you understand what has been said.

One situation in which restating information is useful is in client-centered therapy. Certain psychologists believe that a good way to help troubled patients work through their problems is to restate information that the patient offers. Through this method, the psychologist gives the patient a chance to understand his or her situation better. A typical dialogue between a doctor and a patient in which information is restated might go like this:

Doctor: What is troubling you today? You look worried.

Patient: I haven't been sleeping well lately.

Doctor: You have had trouble with insomnia.

Patient: Well, yes. I'm afraid I'm going to lose my job.

Doctor: So you are fearful of being unemployed. Do you have a reason to be afraid?

Patient: Yeah, sorta. I got really mad the other day and told off a couple of people at work. One of them was my boss.

Doctor: Oh, you were angry with your supervisor. Can you tell me more about that?

Patient: My boss is so hard on me. I don't think he likes me, really, so he picks at everything I do, and I just got fed up.

What do you think this doctor would say next?

Doctor: _____

_____

Because the psychologist has been consistently restating the patient's words, you probably wrote something like "So you feel your boss is too critical of you." When you restate information, your words and phrasing may be different from the original words, but the meaning is the same.

Read the passage below and choose the correct restatements that follow.

The Virginia Split

It is interesting how the geography of an area can influence its culture and politics. The South Atlantic region of the United States provides a good example. There are three topographical features that were important to the development of the region—the Tidewater, with low-lying land and large rivers; the Piedmont, with gently rolling hills above the falls of the rivers; and the Appalachian Mountains.

The Tidewater and the Piedmont were settled primarily as plantations, but the mountains presented a barrier that was insurmountable for the Virginia gentleman farmers. The mountains and the valleys west of them were settled instead by a people different from the farmers—in culture, religion, nationality, and economy. So different were they, in fact, that when Virginia seceded from the Union in 1861, western Virginia seceded from Virginia and fought on the side of the small farmers and non-slaveholding people of the North.

Directions: Based on what you have read, place a check mark before the correct restatements of the ideas from the above passage. As you check off each restatement, underline the words and phrases in the passage that say the same thing as those in the passage.

_____ (a) The people who settled what is now West Virginia were from a different social and economic group from those who settled Virginia.

_____ (b) The Tidewater is a land of gently rolling hills above the fall of the rivers.

_____ (c) West Virginia is largely mountainous, whereas Virginia is an area of gently rolling hills and low-lying river basins.

_____ (d) Virginia joined the Confederacy in 1861.

_____ (e) West Virginia seceded from the Union when the Civil War broke out in 1861.

You should have checked off (a), (c), and (d). The words from the passage that are restated are as follows:

(a) "The mountains and the valleys west of them were settled instead by a people different from the farmers—in culture, religion, nationality, and economy."

(c) "the Tidewater, with low-lying land and large rivers; the Piedmont, with gently rolling hills above the falls of the rivers . . . "

(d) "when Virginia seceded from the Union in 1861 . . . "

EXERCISE 3

Questions 1–3 refer to the following passage.

The terrorist tactic of hostage taking is becoming all too common around the world, and a primary target is the American citizen. The U.S. Army considers this to be enough of a threat to its servicemen overseas that it has informally set policies to guide soldiers through such an experience. Some of the suggestions that might help ensure a hostage's freedom from captivity and preserve the country's and the victim's own personal dignity are:

• Remain calm, courteous, and cooperative.

• Do not provide any pertinent information to the terrorists or appear capable of giving information that could be used to their advantage.

• Do discuss unimportant personal information with the captors—family, favorite sports, etc.

• Do listen to the terrorists talk about their cause, their beliefs, and their reasons for taking hostages, but do not praise or debate them.

• Form a chain of command among military and civilians present and sustain communication among hostages as much as possible.

1. Which of the statements below best describes a common practice of terrorists who seize hostages?

(1) Terrorists are usually calm and courteous in such circumstances.
(2) U.S. military servicemen are always harmed in such situations.
(3) Terrorists promise the release of obedient hostages.
(4) Terrorists often try to take Americans as hostages.
(5) Terrorists never release their hostages.

2. Which of the following is recommended as proper behavior for hostages taken by terrorists?

(1) Do not let the terrorists talk about their ideology to you.
(2) Make sure to communicate as often as possible with other hostages.
(3) Do not provide any personal background about yourself to the terrorists.
(4) Give the terrorists any information that will help their cause.
(5) Do not cooperate with the terrorists in any way.

3. Which of the following is *not* recommended by the article?

    (1) Appear to be cooperative in unimportant ways.
    (2) Tell the terrorists that you know something that could help their cause.
    (3) Listen to the terrorists, but don't comment on their views.
    (4) Make sure that you continue to communicate with your fellow hostages.
    (5) Discuss family and personal issues with the terrorists.

Answers are on page 395.

Restating Information from Illustrations

On the GED Social Studies Test, you will also be asked to restate information that is presented in graphs, charts, tables, maps, and cartoons. Giving directions is a form of restating information that you have probably already used in your daily life. As a passenger in a car, you may help the driver find the correct route by putting into words what you see on a map. Look at the map shown in the example below.

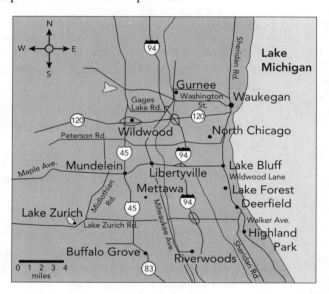

In giving directions to someone driving from downtown Libertyville to the corner of Washington Street and Sheridan Road in downtown Waukegan, you might say,

> "Take Maple Avenue in Libertyville east to Sheridan Road. You will pass Interstate 94. Turn left on Sheridan Road. Follow Sheridan Road north until you reach Washington Street in Waukegan."

In order to guide someone this way, you would have to know the directions north, south, east, and west.

Which direction is Waukegan from North Chicago? _____

Which direction is Lake Bluff from Libertyville? _____

Which direction is Buffalo Grove from Mundelein? _____

You should have said that Waukegan is north from North Chicago, Lake Bluff is east from Libertyville, and Buffalo Grove is south from Mundelein.

On road maps, some streets are usually heavier and darker than others. On many maps that heavier, darker color indicates a U.S. interstate or state highway. On this map the interstate is indicated with a symbol, 🛡94. The number of the interstate is 94.

A scale of miles is usually provided in the legend of a road map. A legend explains any symbols that are used in a map. A scale of miles may be shown in inches (one inch = 50 miles, for example) or by marks spaced equally along a line.

According to the scale on the map on the previous page, about how many miles is it

from Lake Bluff to North Chicago? _____

from Riverwoods to Mettawa? _____

The distance in the first question is three miles, and in the second it is about eight miles.

When you put into words the meaning of numbers in a chart, you are also restating information. For example, the chart below presents the percentage of women represented in four categories of occupations.

WOMEN AS A PERCENTAGE OF ALL EMPLOYEES IN SELECTED OCCUPATIONS IN 1997

Registered nurses	92%
Teachers, except college and university	74%
Secretaries, stenographers, typists	98%
Personal-service occupations	73%

Source: *The Ultimate Field Guide to the U.S. Economy,* The New Press, 2000

Here is one restatement of the information in this chart: "In 1997 almost no men were secretaries, stenographers, and typists." What is another restatement you could make?

_____

_____

_____

You could have written that nearly three-quarters of the teachers in 1997 (except those who worked in colleges and universities) were women. Another possible restatement is that in 1997 there were at least four occupations dominated by women.

EXERCISE 4

1. **Directions:** Look at the map on page 36 and write instructions for the most direct way to get from Lake Zurich to Wildwood.

   _____

   _____

   _____

   _____

   _____

2. Study the chart below. Restate two pieces of information presented in the chart.

THE COSTS OF MILITARY AND SOCIAL PROGAMS

Military program	Cost	Social Program
1 attack submarine	$2.3 billion	Head Start for 500,000 kids
1 F-22 bomber	$161 million	Pell grants for 100,000 students
1 Army division in Europe	$2.0 billion	Funding for 50,000 new teachers

Source: _The Ultimate Field Guide to the U.S. Economy,_
The New Press, 2000

   _____

   _____

   _____

   _____

   _____

   _____

Answers are on page 395.

Identifying Implications

So far, you have practiced two ways of showing your comprehension of passages and illustrations: by summarizing the main idea and by restating information. A third way to show that you understand information is by being able to identify implications. Implications are ideas that are suggested, or implied, but not stated directly. A writer implies ideas; a reader infers meaning from ideas.

Advertisements in newspapers and magazines and commercials on television make suggestions all the time. For example, at election time you may have seen many commercials for political candidates. These commercials often show a candidate in a pleasant setting; for example, at home with his or her family. The commercial does not have to state that the candidate is a stable, happy, family person. It implies this fact by showing a smiling family.

Read the following paragraph to identify its implications.

> Equality and fairness in the U.S. military are twentieth-century concepts. In fact, it was not until after World Wars I and II were fought and won that technical expertise and a cooperative spirit in leadership were rewarded by promotions through the ranks in the military.

What implication is made in this paragraph about the promotion system in the U.S. military before the twentieth century?

_____

_____

The author has implied that prior to the twentieth century, promotions in the U.S. military were based on criteria other than technical expertise and a cooperative spirit; therefore, promotions were unequal and unfair. The writer states in the first sentence that equality and fairness are new to the military. The writer then describes the "new" promotion system as an example of fairness and equality. You can infer that the author believes the previous system was unfair.

EXERCISE 5

Questions 1–3 are based on the following passage.

Needs are defined as food, shelter, and clothing. Wants are defined as extras in life—vacations, television sets, jewelry, etc. Wants and needs can mean different things to different people, but generally social scientists agree that economic groups can be fairly well classified by the amount of money they spend on needs versus wants.

The very poorest people in the world live at a bare subsistence level. At best, they have just enough food and shelter to stay alive. On a rung above this level on the economic ladder are the working poor, those who spend $9 out of every $10 on things they need and only $1 out of every $10 on what they want out of life. The middle-income group spends about $8 out of $10 on needs and the remaining $2 on wants, and the upper-income group spends only $4 out of $10 on needs.

1. What is the implication of the figures listed?

   (1) The wealthier a person is, the fewer needs he or she has.
   (2) Wealthy people want more than those at the lower end of the economic ladder.
   (3) The lower one's income, the more material things one needs to get by.
   (4) The middle income group is the best at balancing wants and needs.
   (5) As one's income goes up, one has more money to spend on wants.

2. What has the author implied about the poorest people in the world?

   (1) They cannot even provide for all their own needs.
   (2) They are not concerned about their wants.
   (3) They should be given monetary assistance by the government.
   (4) They are uneducated and unable to deal with money.
   (5) They are not considered to be in any economic group.

3. Philosopher Henry David Thoreau said, "Superfluous wealth can buy only superfluities." If *superfluous* means "excess" or "unnecessary," of which group of people was Thoreau speaking?

   (1) the poorest people in the world
   (2) the working poor
   (3) the middle-income group
   (4) the upper-income group
   (5) shopowners and lawyers

Answers are on pages 395–396.

Identifying Implications in Illustrations

You can draw implications from illustrations as well as from written materials. Line graphs are particularly effective in showing trends from which we may draw implications. A quick look at a line graph can reveal increases, decreases, uneven movements, or leveling off of numbers. Look at the following graph of unemployment rates.

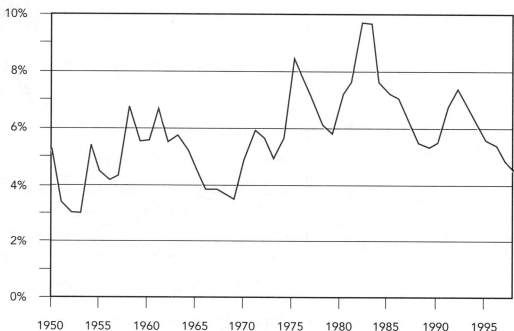

Notice that the graph has a title, "Unemployment Rate, 1950–98." It has figures going up the vertical axis that represent the percentage of unemployed workers in the United States and dates along the horizontal axis that show the period of time that the graph represents. Between 1950 and 1998 the line on the graph fluctuates between 3% and almost 10%. The implication is that over a given period of time the rate of unemployment in the United States can vary greatly. In more recent years, however, the trend appears to be toward decreasing rates.

EXERCISE 6

Questions 1 and 2 are based on the following graph.

TAX RECEIPTS, BY SOURCE, 1960–98

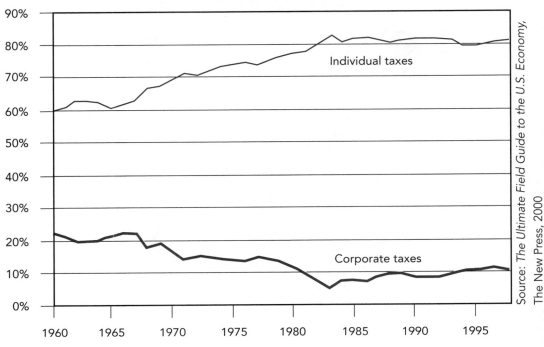

Source: *The Ultimate Field Guide to the U.S. Economy,* The New Press, 2000

1. What trend do the lines in the above graph imply?

    (1) Over time, individuals are paying more taxes while corporations are paying less.
    (2) Corporations were paying about the same amount of taxes in 1998 as they were in 1960.
    (3) Individuals should not have to pay as much in taxes as corporations.
    (4) If corporations were to pay more taxes, individuals would also have to pay more.
    (5) Individuals will never again have to pay as much in taxes as they did in 1983.

2. Which of the following conclusions does the graph support?

    (1) Corporations don't need to pay as much tax as individuals because there are more people than companies in the United States.
    (2) Individuals were making more money than corporations in the 1980s and thus paid more in taxes.
    (3) Since 1960 the gap between how much of the tax burden is carried by individuals versus corporations has been widening.
    (4) The gap between the tax burdens of individuals and corporations will probably continue to be wide over the next 10 years.
    (5) Corporations pay less in taxes because the government wants to help them out.

Answers are on page 396.

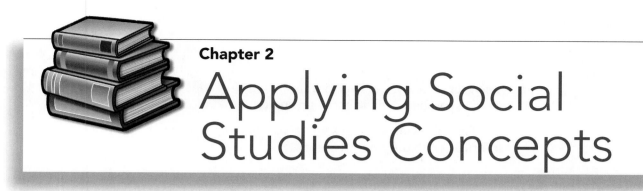

Chapter 2

Applying Social Studies Concepts

Have you ever taken a first-aid course and had to use your knowledge to help an injured child, friend, or co-worker? Have you ever taken a driver's education class and then had to apply that knowledge behind the wheel in real traffic? If so, you were applying your knowledge to real situations.

One of the most important goals of learning is developing the ability to apply facts, concepts, and theories in new situations. On the GED Social Studies Test you will have to demonstrate this ability by

- applying given theories, ideas, or facts in a different situation
- applying remembered ideas in a different situation

Applying Given Ideas

The community you live in might have a recycling program. You might see a brochure from your community with the following information:

New Neighborhood Recycling Program

These items will be picked up on the curbside weekly:

Newspaper, junk mail, cardboard, paperboard, steel cans, and glass

Bring these items to the Middle School parking lot the second Saturday of every month:

Aluminum cans, plastic bottles

Based on the brochure, indicate what you should do with each item if you are interested in participating in the recycling program. Write **C** for curbside, **M** for Middle School, and **U** for undetermined.

_____ **1.** the flyer from the local supermarket advertising weekly specials

_____ **2.** an empty tomato sauce can

_____ **3.** an empty Clorox Bleach bottle

_____ **4.** an empty Cheerios box

To answer these questions correctly, you need to apply the information given in the recycling brochure and your knowledge of the items described. You should know that flyers are always made from paper, so the correct response for 1 is C. Some cans on the grocery shelf are steel, and some are aluminum. It is not stated whether the empty tomato sauce can is steel or aluminum, so the correct response for 2 is U. Clorox bleach is always packaged in a plastic bottle since a glass bottle would be too dangerous.

Therefore, the correct response for 3 is M. Cheerios boxes are always made from paperboard, so the correct response for 4 is C.

The following exercises will give you more practice in applying information to different situations.

EXERCISE 1

Directions: Read the passage below. Indicate a correct application of the Supreme Court ruling by writing *yes* on the line before the statement and an incorrect application by writing *no*.

In 1954, the Supreme Court of the United States reversed an earlier controversial ruling. In 1896, the Supreme Court had ruled in the case of *Plessy* v. *Ferguson* that separate but equal facilities for blacks and whites were correct and legal. But the decision of 1954, called *Brown* v. *the Board of Education of Topeka*, ruled that blacks had equal rights to the same public schools as whites because separate educational facilities were deemed inherently unequal. Public schools were ordered to desegregate "with all deliberate speed."

Which of the following would be a correct application of the 1954 ruling?

_____ **1.** busing children from black inner-city schools to white or racially mixed schools in the same district

_____ **2.** setting up African American history courses in high schools and colleges

_____ **3.** establishing the United Negro College Fund to send poor, college-bound blacks to black colleges

_____ **4.** using diversity criteria in admissions policies at public universities and colleges

_____ **5.** establishing "magnet" schools that attract students of all races

Answers are on page 396.

EXERCISE 2

Directions: Read the Fourth Amendment to the U.S. Constitution below and complete the exercise that follows.

The right of the people to be secure in their persons, houses, papers, and effects, against unreasonable searches and seizures, shall not be violated, and no warrants shall issue, but upon probable cause, supported by oath or affirmation, and particularly describing the place to be searched, and the persons or things to be seized.

For each of the examples below, write *yes* if the Fourth Amendment would allow the action. Write *no* if the Fourth Amendment would not allow the action. Write *N/A (not applicable)* if the Fourth Amendment does not apply to the situation.

_____ 1. Acting on an anonymous tip that Joan Jones is selling stolen stereos from her apartment, detectives enter her home and search for the stolen items.

_____ 2. When Jean was out sick, her co-worker, Lillian, searched her desk for some paper clips that she needed.

_____ 3. After observing Sam Smith repeatedly selling illegal drugs at a street corner, undercover detectives get a warrant to search Smith's house for illegal drugs.

_____ 4. In a campaign against drunk driving, officers pulled over one car every 15 minutes, tested the driver for sobriety, and searched the car for alcohol.

Answers are on page 396.

EXERCISE 3

Questions 1 and 2 refer to the following passage.

When people hear the word *monopoly*, probably the first thing they think about is the popular board game. In business terminology, however, a monopoly is the exclusive control over a money-making activity.

In 1890, the U.S. government passed a law called the Sherman Anti-Trust Act that outlawed price-fixing (an agreement between companies to set their prices), underproduction of goods, market sharing, and any other form of monopolizing among producers of a similar product. However, public utilities such as gas, electric power, and water companies are exempted from these restraints. These government-sanctioned monopolies are permitted to exist so that essential services are not duplicated and natural resources are not wasted.

1. According to the Sherman Anti-Trust Act, which of the following is an example of an illegal monopoly?

   (1) the existence of only one power company in a city, giving consumers no choice of whom to obtain service from
   (2) a computer company whose growth is well beyond that of any of its competitors
   (3) a hamburger chain's restaurants, all of which belong to the same system of franchises
   (4) the oil refineries in a state agreeing on a minimum price to set for gasoline
   (5) a public university system in a state setting minimum and maximum tuition rates for the schools in its system

2. Which of the following is an example of a legal monopoly?

   (1) a cable television company given the exclusive license to service a particular community
   (2) a supermarket chain that sells items at a loss until its prices force its competitors out of business
   (3) a long-distance telephone company that agrees with its competitors to lower prices five percent
   (4) a health-care network that takes over all the hospitals and clinics in a region
   (5) a drug company that limits the availability of its new vaccine so that it can keep the price high

Questions 3 and 4 refer to the following passage.

Many Americans today complain that we are quickly becoming a bilingual country—the primary and secondary languages being English and Spanish. They resent the concessions made to the non-English-speaking minority. Yet the first European settlers in the New World were Spanish. Christopher Columbus himself was sailing under the flag of Spain when he "discovered" the North American continent in 1492. Saint Augustine, Florida, was founded in 1566 by the Spanish and was the first European settlement in the United States or Canada. As early as 1630, Spanish padres of the Roman Catholic faith established missions in territories now known as the states of California, Texas, Arizona, and New Mexico. Perhaps if more Americans were reminded of this Spanish influence on our country's history, they would be more tolerant of our non-English-speaking minority.

3. With which of the following groups would the author of this article be likely to agree?

Those who
(1) are trying to get a law passed in the United States to make English the official language of the U.S.
(2) want to ban the use of Spanish in bilingual classes in public elementary and secondary schools
(3) support the use of two languages—French and English—in Canada, where the French played a large role in founding the country
(4) maintain that the Native Americans should be given free land and other special rights as original inhabitants of this part of the world
(5) send teachers of English as a second language all over the world to help those who have the desire to learn our language

4. Which of the following facts would best support the writer's opinion?

(1) In the past, the children of immigrants to the United States learned and used English.
(2) One hundred years ago, schools for Indians forbade the use of native languages.
(3) English is quickly becoming the world language for business, science, and technology.
(4) In the former French colonies of West Africa, French is used by government officials.
(5) Throughout Europe, fluency in more than one language is the norm, not the exception.

Question 5 refers to the following passage.

Death Valley did not come by its name by whim or chance. Death Valley is an arid desert in southeastern California that was named in 1849 by one of 18 survivors of an original party of 30 who had attempted to cross it in search of a shortcut to the California goldfields. The Rocky Mountains, too, are well deserving of their name, as are Crater Lake in Oregon and Great Salt Lake in Utah.

In other parts of the world as well, cities, bodies of water, and landforms have been named for their physical characteristics. The Diamond Coast in southwestern Africa, for instance, gets its name from its valuable resource, and Buenos Aires in Argentina for its "fair winds."

5. Which of the following would this author probably agree was named for its physical attributes as described in the article above?

   (1) Cape Horn in Chile, after its first successful navigator's birthplace in the Netherlands
   (2) San Juan, capital city of Puerto Rico, named for Saint John by its Spanish founders
   (3) the Hwang Ho (Yellow River) of China, for the color it develops as it picks up silt along its course
   (4) the city of Philadelphia (City of Brotherly Love) in Pennsylvania, so called by its Quaker founders to reflect their highest hopes for the community
   (5) New Delhi, the capital city of India, which was built on a site three miles from the original city of Delhi

Answers are on page 396.

Special Item Types

Another way the GED Social Studies Test will test your ability to apply given ideas in a different situation is by using an item type similar to the one on page 49. In this type of item, certain categories are defined and then specific situations are given. You will need to read the categories carefully to understand the differences between them. Then read the situations to match them up with the information given. If you have trouble with these questions, you might use a process of elimination. In other words, go through the categories and decide which ones do not fit. In this way, you may be able to narrow your choices. Try using this method as you read the following information.

EXERCISE 4

Questions 1–4 refer to the following information.

Propaganda is a method by which information is provided in such a way as to influence or slant the opinion or feelings of the audience that receives the message. Listed below are five techniques used by propagandists.

Name calling—attaching an unfavorable name to an idea, person, or group of people in order to influence the attitude of the audience against the idea or people

Glittering generalities—speaking in high-sounding but general and vague terms to influence positively the feelings of the audience toward a subject

Bandwagoning—advising people to do something because "everyone" does it, because it is popular, or because it is the "in" thing to do

Transferring—associating the respect, prestige, or power of one person or object with another person so that the audience is influenced favorably

Card stacking—choosing only specific, favorable points that support a cause and ignoring the unfavorable points

1. A manufacturer of laundry detergent introduces a "revolutionary new" product that dissolves grease "like magic." Which propaganda technique is being used?

   (1) name calling
   (2) glittering generalities
   (3 transferring
   (4) bandwagoning
   (5) card stacking

2. A radio commercial suggests that all residents of Rapid Falls, Idaho should subscribe to the *Rapid Falls Gazette* since 85 percent of the households there subscribe to the paper. The announcer adds that "40,000 households can't be wrong." Which propaganda technique is being used?

   (1) name calling
   (2) glittering generalities
   (3) transferring
   (4) bandwagoning
   (5) card stacking

3. While campaigning through the South, a candidate for the presidency of the United States appeared in a church on the same platform with a leader of the fundamentalist Christian movement. Which propaganda technique is being used?

    (1) name calling
    (2) glittering generalities
    (3) transferring
    (4 bandwagoning
    (5) card stacking

4. During a debate, the Republican candidate for office calls his Democratic opponent a "tax-and-spend liberal" despite the Democrat's record of shown fiscal restraint. Which propaganda technique is being used?

    (1) name calling
    (2) glittering generalities
    (3) transferring
    (4) bandwagoning
    (5) card stacking

Answers are on pages 396–397.

Applying Given Ideas in Graphics

In addition to applying ideas from reading passages, the GED Social Studies Test will also ask you to apply given ideas or facts from graphics such as political cartoons, maps, tables, charts, and graphs.

Look at the line graph below. See if you can use the information in the graph to answer the questions that follow it.

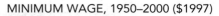

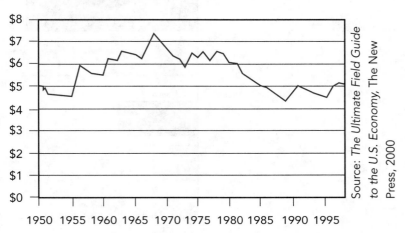

MINIMUM WAGE, 1950–2000 ($1997)

Source: *The Ultimate Field Guide to the U.S. Economy*, The New Press, 2000

According to this chart, over the 40-year period from 1960–2000, has the minimum wage gone up, gone down, or stayed about the same?

Based on the information given in the graph, would you recommend that the minimum wage be increased, decreased, or kept the same?

What is your reason for your choice?

_____

_____

After being adjusted for inflation, the minimum wage was higher in the 1960s and 1970s than it was in 2000. Therefore, you should have answered that the minimum wage has gone down.

Based on the information in the graph, you could recommend an increase in the minimum wage to get it closer to what it used to be in the 1960s and 1970s.

The following exercise will give you more practice in applying information from a graph.

EXERCISE 5

Questions 1 and 2 refer to the following graph.

SHARE OF TOTAL FINANCIAL WEALTH
(BY GROUPS OF HOUSEHOLDS)

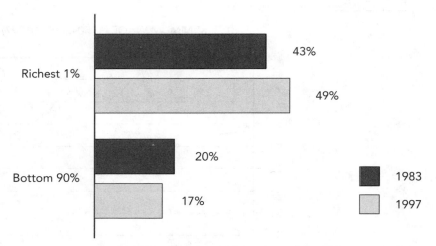

Source: *The Ultimate Field Guide to the U.S. Economy,* The New Press, 2000

1. Given the information in the bar graph, what action would an advisor be most likely to recommend to improve the equality of wealth distribution in the United States?

   (1) abolish the death tax, so that the children of the wealthiest Americans do not have to pay a tax on money they inherit
   (2) give school vouchers to all parents, so that parents who send their children to private schools can save money
   (3) lower the tax rates of all taxpayers, so that every taxpayer has a 5% reduction in income taxes
   (4) provide universal health-care coverage for all Americans who have assets less than 10 million dollars
   (5) create a national sales tax on all goods and services in order to raise more revenue for the government

2. Who would be most likely to use this bar graph?

   (1) the CEO (Chief Executive Officer) of a major corporation while arguing for more compensation and stock options
   (2) union negotiators for a major industry while arguing for a large three-year salary increase for the workers
   (3) politicians trying to replace the graduated income tax, which has higher rates for higher incomes, with a flat-rate tax
   (4) conservative analysts who argue that the free market creates more wealth and benefits for everyone
   (5) a congressman running for reelection who wants to show how most people in his district are better off

Answers are on page 397.

Applying Remembered Ideas

You have practiced applying ideas and facts from reading passages and graphics to different situations. Now you will learn to apply knowledge you have gained from prior learning or experience rather than from written passages.

For example, if you saw a movie about a Vietnam veteran going back to the site of his worst wartime experiences, you could understand his emotions much better if you had prior knowledge of the horrors of the Vietnam conflict. You could apply that prior knowledge to decide for yourself whether his performance was convincing. If you also had prior knowledge of other American wars and the reactions of veterans to their experiences, you would be better able to understand the actions of the Vietnam veteran.

On the GED Tests and in the exercises in this book, you will be expected to apply prior knowledge of events, people, and ideas to new situations.

In some cases, you may not be familiar with the person, place, or thing being discussed. This does not mean that you cannot pass the GED Social Studies Test. Keep in mind that the following sections of this book will give you a lot of information about social studies issues. Reading newspapers and magazines and listening to the news while you are preparing for the test will also give you valuable information about social studies and keep you aware of current events. When you are taking the test, if you cannot recall what is being discussed in a test item, do not panic. Simply make the most reasonable choice and move on to the next item.

In your daily life, you already know how to apply prior knowledge to new situations. For example, when you read the newspaper or listen to a newscast, it is often assumed that you are familiar with some information.

Suppose in the fall of 2000 you saw the following headline:

News Analysis: Falling Short of Peace After Camp David

This headline assumes that the reader will know that Camp David refers to a meeting of Israelis and Palestinians hosted by the United States. You can expect that the article to follow will be about the Israeli-Palestinian conflict.

The following exercise will give you practice in applying remembered ideas to reading passages.

EXERCISE 6

Directions: In order to answer the following questions, you must apply some prior knowledge. Circle the number of the correct choice.

1. For Americans, one of the most difficult periods of the twentieth century was the Great Depression of the 1930s. Which of the following situations is most like the Great Depression of the 1930s?

    (1) the violent era of apartheid in South Africa, in which the white and black populations were strictly segregated
    (2) the collapse of the Russian economy and resulting widespread poverty following the fall of Communism
    (3) the decline of the United Kingdom as a great power after the devastation of World War II
    (4) the dictatorship of "Papa Doc" Duvalier in Haiti, in which basic human rights were abused
    (5) the conflict between India and Pakistan over control of the disputed province of Kashmir

Questions 2 and 3 are based on the following passage.

Once upon a time, gray wolves roamed freely throughout North America, filling an important niche in an abundantly diverse chain of wildlife. Today, that chain is broken, largely because of the demise of predators like wolves, whose numbers plummeted a century ago as a result of bounty hunters working to protect livestock.

The good news is that in recent years, the wolf has made a comeback. The comeback is so good, says the U.S. Fish and Wildlife Service, that the wolf no longer needs to be classified as an endangered species.

2. What information does the article assume the reader knows?

    (1) that wolves are dangerous animals who should not live near people
    (2) that a large predator like a wolf can help keep an ecosystem healthy
    (3) that it is no longer necessary to worry about protecting livestock
    (4) that a species classified as endangered will soon become extinct
    (5) that environmental extremists want to protect dangerous animals

3. Which of the following did people interested in protecting livestock know a century ago?

    (1) how to effectively kill all the dangerous large animals that might hurt people

    (2) that disrupting the ecosystem could have unexpected consequences

    (3) that wolves are an essential part of the environment

    (4) that killing large predators could have a negative impact

    (5) that every living thing in an ecosystem could have an important function

Answers are on page 397.

Applying Remembered Ideas and Facts in Graphics

On the GED Social Studies Test, you will be required to apply your knowledge of social studies concepts, events, places, and people to questions based on graphic materials. For example, political cartoons often depend on your outside knowledge in order to provide humor and to make their point.

Look at the political cartoon below.

—Bob Gorrell. Courtesy Creators Syndicate.

At the time of these presidential debates, one of the most popular programs on television was a game show called "Who Wants to Be a Millionaire?" On the show, contestants are asked questions, and if they are not sure of the answer, they can poll the audience or phone a friend.

Candidate Al Gore had a reputation for changing his positions according to public opinion. Candidate George W. Bush had a reputation for not knowing policy details. Which of the two candidates in the cartoon is probably Al Gore? Which is probably George W. Bush?

_____

_____

What do you think is the cartoonist's opinion of the two candidates?

_____

_____

_____

_____

Al Gore is the candidate saying "I'd like to poll the audience." George W. Bush is the candidate saying "Could I please phone a friend?"

The cartoonist appears to be dissatisfied with both candidates.

 Now look at the following bar graph.

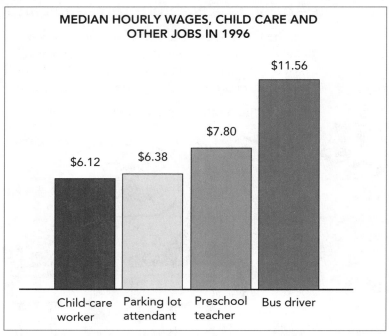

MEDIAN HOURLY WAGES, CHILD CARE AND OTHER JOBS IN 1996

- Child-care worker: $6.12
- Parking lot attendant: $6.38
- Preschool teacher: $7.80
- Bus driver: $11.56

Source: *The Ultimate Field Guide to the U.S. Economy,* The New Press, 2000

Which of the jobs in the graph are filled mostly by men? Which of the jobs are filled mostly by women? What else is an important difference between these jobs?

_____

_____

_____

_____

_____

What do you think are the main points of the graph?

_____

_____

_____

Parking lot attendants and bus drivers are mostly men. Child-care workers and preschool workers are mostly women.

Another important difference between these jobs is that the parking lot attendants and bus drivers work with machines, while the child-care workers and preschool workers work with children.

The main points of the graph are that men's jobs are generally higher paid than women's jobs, and that working with machines seems to be more highly valued in our society than taking care of our children.

The following exercise will give you more practice in applying prior knowledge to visual graphics.

GED PRACTICE

EXERCISE 7

Questions 1 and 2 are based on the following cartoon.

1. In this cartoon, with which of the following does the cartoonist assume the reader is familiar?

   (1) current women's fashions
   (2) the story of Cinderella
   (3) angels with magic powers
   (4) the women's movement
   (5) women's traditional role

2. What does the cartoonist imply that women today dream about?

    (1) a life of leisure and pleasure
    (2) marrying a rich, handsome man
    (3) help with housecleaning
    (4) helping others meet their goals
    (5) being successful in business

 Questions 3 and 4 are based on the following bar graph.

WORLD SALES OF SELECTED MULTINATIONALS AND GROSS NATIONAL PRODUCT OF SELECTED COUNTRIES IN 1996 (IN BILLIONS OF $1996)

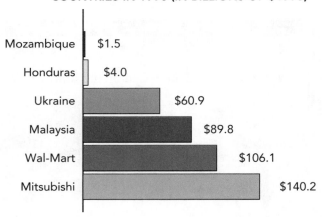

Source: *The Ultimate Field Guide to the U.S. Economy*, The New Press, 2000

3. Which of the bars on the graph represents a company rather than a country?

    (1) Mozambique
    (2) Honduras
    (3) Ukraine
    (4) Malaysia
    (5) Mitsubishi

4. What would be a reasonable conclusion that could be drawn from the information on the graph?

    (1) Countries with a small gross national product have a great potential for growth.
    (2) Small countries are at a disadvantage when dealing with large multinational corporations.
    (3) The sales of the largest companies are larger than the gross national product of any country.
    (4) Large companies have gotten too large and powerful and need to be broken up into smaller units.
    (5) In order to have more control over their own economies, smaller nations should merge.

Answers are on page 397.

Chapter 3

Analyzing Social Studies Materials

When you analyze something, you break it down into its basic parts, or elements, to better understand how it works.

For example, suppose you are an investigator for your local fire department, and have to figure out the cause of a fire. You might want to interview an eyewitness, who might be able to tell you where she first saw smoke. You might want to examine the damage inside to look for physical clues. In order to arrive at the correct cause, you need to look at all the evidence carefully.

When you read social studies materials, you must also analyze. You look at specific ideas and pieces of information to better understand the point being made by a writer, graphic artist, or cartoonist. You can analyze written information in a number of ways. On the GED Social Studies Test, you will be tested on your ability to analyze material in these ways:

- distinguishing facts from opinions and hypotheses
- distinguishing conclusions from supporting statements
- recognizing information that is designed to persuade an audience
- recognizing unstated assumptions
- identifying cause-and-effect relationships
- recognizing the point of view of a writer in a historical account
- recognizing the historical context of a text
- identifying comparisons and contrasts
- determining the implications, effects, and value of presenting visual data in different ways

Distinguishing Facts from Opinions and Hypotheses

When we read, we often see facts, opinions, and hypotheses. It is important to be able to distinguish one from the other. **Facts** are statements that can be proved to be true. **Opinions** are statements about the writer's feelings or ideas about a topic and are influenced heavily by one's background, values, and outlook on life. Often, an opinion cannot be proved or disproved. **Hypotheses** are conjectures that are made for the purpose of explaining an event. Hypotheses may be proved or disproved with the passage of time or the acquisition of more information about why or how events occur.

The different types of written material in a newspaper illustrate the differences between facts, opinions, and hypotheses. News articles are based largely on facts. Editorials and featured columns can present a writer's opinions along with the facts. In a news article a reporter can also report on a hypothesis being made by a newsmaker. In an editorial or a featured column, the writer can create a hypothesis in an attempt to explain events or predict future events.

The examples below show how facts, opinions, and hypotheses differ.

- It is a fact that California experienced the greatest population growth of any state in the United States in the second half of the 20th century. Census figures from the states can be examined to prove that this is true.

- It is an opinion, however, that California is the best part of the country in which to live because that is a statement based on a person's values, background, and outlook on life.

- It is a hypothesis that if Southern California cleans up its air pollution and reduces traffic congestion, people will continue to move to the area.

Read the passage below. Then place an **H** on the line next to every hypothesis that might explain why the event occurred.

> Over the period of one year, the motor vehicle death rate from accidents in nineteen states decreased significantly over the previous year's figures. Research has shown that the two most important factors that determine the survival of a victim in a serious traffic accident are (1) whether the victim is restrained in the car and (2) whether medical attention is immediately available.

Based on the information in the above passage, which of the hypotheses listed might explain why traffic fatalities were reduced?

_____ (1) The states instituted tough drunk-driving laws.
_____ (2) The states hired more highway patrol officers to catch speeders.
_____ (3) The states increased the number of trauma centers and paramedics to handle victims of traffic accidents.
_____ (4) The states adopted laws requiring passengers to wear seat belts.
_____ (5) The states required more frequent driver examinations for senior citizens and teenagers.

Only (3) and (4) are reasonable explanations of the reduction in motor vehicle fatality rates. Both of them address the two criteria that affect the survival of victims of traffic accidents. None of the other choices has a direct relationship to the immediate access to medical care and the restraint of passengers in the vehicle. Choices (3) and (4) may be proved or disproved by comparing the number of motor vehicle fatalities both before and after the number of trauma centers and paramedics were increased and before and after the seat belts were required.

EXERCISE 1

 Questions 1–4 refer to the following passage.

Some jobs are more stressful than others, and air traffic controllers are considered to have one of the most stressful. This belief has been backed up by the fact that controllers have a high incidence of stress-related disorders like chronic anxiety and alcoholism. Many people believe, too, that the reason for the high level of stress is the responsibility that controllers have for the safety of passengers. However, such reasoning does not explain the low rate of stress disorders among airline pilots, who have much more direct responsibility for people's safety.

Recent studies have attempted to explain this discrepancy by naming poor labor-management relations as the main source of the controllers' stress.

Controllers who were interviewed complained that their recommendations for providing safety backups and other measures were not being considered by their employers or the Federal Aviation Administration. Interestingly, too, the studies concluded that the most conscientious of the workers were the ones most prone to experience stress—because of their high level of concern for safety.

1. Which of the following is a hypothesis that may be drawn based on the information in the passage?

    (1) Shortening the working hours of air traffic controllers would result in a reduction of their stress-related disorders.
    (2) Providing proof that management is implementing the controllers' recommendations would reduce stress.
    (3) Providing ongoing counseling services for the victims of stress would reduce their stress levels.
    (4) Ensuring that all planes are no more than 20 years old would lower stress levels among air traffic controllers.
    (5) Reducing the number of daily scheduled flights would reduce stress levels among air traffic controllers.

2. Which of the following is a fact about air traffic controllers that the author could support with data?

    (1) There is a relatively high rate of alcoholism among air traffic controllers.
    (2) There is a low incidence of stress disorders among the controllers.
    (3) Pilots suffer from significantly more anxiety than controllers do.
    (4) The only source of air traffic controllers' stress is poor labor-management relations.
    (5) The controllers are not taken seriously by the Federal Aviation Administration.

3. According to the passage, air traffic controllers have which of the following opinions?

   (1) Some jobs are more stressful than others because they have more impact on people's lives.
   (2) An air traffic controller's job is more stressful than a pilot's because it is more important.
   (3) No one in authority is paying attention to controllers' safety recommendations.
   (4) The more conscientious airline workers experienced the most stress.
   (5) Airline executives have no concern for safety, only for maximizing profits.

4. Which of the following has been shown in recent studies?

   (1) The main reason for air traffic controllers' high level of stress is their concern for passengers' comfort and safety.
   (2) Air traffic controllers should be more conscientious about passengers' safety and less concerned about their work benefits.
   (3) Chronic anxiety causes most air traffic controllers to become alcoholics requiring extensive treatment programs.
   (4) The negative attitudes of air traffic controllers lead to poor labor-management relations and low worker morale.
   (5) A correlation exists between how conscientious air traffic controllers are and the amount of stress they experience on the job.

Answers are on page 397.

Facts, Opinions, and Hypotheses in Illustrations

Facts, opinions, and hypotheses can also be found in illustrations such as political cartoons and drawings. As you look at the following graphics, think about whether the information being presented is based on facts, opinions, or hypotheses.

The real purpose of a political cartoon is to express the opinion of the cartoonist—a view of a political or social issue as the artist sees it. What is the artist's opinion in the following cartoon?

—Steve Kelley, *The Union Tribune*, Copley News Service

Notice that there are four people in the cartoon, each representing a different group as shown by their label. Three of these people (labeled "parents," "teachers," and "courts") are arguing over a book labeled "prayer issue." The boy, labeled "students," is alone at the blackboard, being ignored by the other three, while he is incorrectly doing a basic math problem. This picture illustrates the opinion that:

Students' education is being _____ while the prayer issue is being debated by the people who should be helping them to _____

You should have completed the first blank with *ignored* or *neglected*, since none of the adults is paying any attention to the student. The second blank should be completed with *learn*, since that should be the concern of parents, teachers, and the courts.

GED PRACTICE

EXERCISE 2

Questions 1 and 2 refer to the cartoon below.

TOM FLANNERY
Courtesy Baltimore Sun

The American Dream House

—Used with permission of Angela R. Flannery.

1. **What is the opinion of this cartoonist about the American dream to own a home?**

   It is
   (1) worth the struggle and sacrifice that it demands
   (2) threatened by increasingly high costs
   (3) becoming less desirable than apartment living
   (4) as attractive and as popular as ever
   (5) a realistic goal for most people

2. Which of the following facts is supported by the cartoon?

(1) The cost of new homes has decreased in the past decade.
(2) Only two-parent families can afford to buy new homes.
(3) The cost of new homes has gone up 100 percent in the past decade.
(4) People are buying smaller homes because they are more affordable.
(5) Owning their own home is only a dream for most Americans.

Answers are on page 397.

GED PRACTICE

EXERCISE 3

Look at the pictograph below on U.S. Exports to the major warring nations in World War I and circle the answer that represents the most plausible hypothesis that may be made.

U.S. EXPORTS TO THE MAJOR WARRING NATIONS

$ = $100 million   c = $10 million

Nations	1914	1915	1916
Major Allied Powers			
United Kingdom	$$$$$$	$$$$$$$$$cc	$$$$$$$$$$$$$$$$cc
France	$$	$$$$	$$$$$$ccc
Russia	cccc	ccccc	$$$c
Major Central Powers			
Germany	$$$cccc	ccc	c
Austria-Hungary	cc	c	'
Turkey	c	'	–

1. In April 1917 the United States entered the war against the Central Powers. Based on the graph, what hypothesis can be made about why the United States entered the war?

(1) Economically, the United States had already aligned itself with the Allied Powers.
(2) The Central Powers were depressed economically and would, therefore, be easy to defeat.
(3) The United Kingdom was receiving almost five times as much aid as Czarist Russia.
(4) The Central Powers did not need help financially, while the Allied Powers did.
(5) The cause of the Allied Powers was more just than the cause of the Central Powers.

Answers are on page 397.

Distinguishing Conclusions from Supporting Statements

Distinguishing a conclusion from supporting statements is a crucial part of understanding what you read. Writers will often present a conclusion as if it is just one more fact. As a reader, you must be able to determine which statements a writer makes are provable facts and which statements are conclusions that the writer is trying to draw from those facts.

Look at this accident report:

> I was heading north on Broadway. At Central Street I began to make a left turn. A '98 Chevy was coming south on Broadway. As I turned, the '98 Chevy struck the side of my car. According to the police, who quickly came to the scene, the Chevy's tire skid marks showed that it was going 50 mph when the driver hit the brakes. There was a 30-mph speed limit on Broadway. The driver of the Chevy was driving recklessly and was responsible for the accident.

Which part of this accident report is a conclusion being drawn by the writer?

_____

_____

What facts does the writer give to support that conclusion?

_____

_____

_____

The writer's conclusion is that the driver of the Chevy was driving recklessly and was responsible for the accident.

The facts that support this conclusion are that the Chevy struck the side of the writer's car, and the tire skid marks show that the Chevy was going 50 mph and that the speed limit was 30 mph.

EXERCISE 4

Directions: Read the paragraphs below. Circle the letter of the choice that best indicates the conclusion that may be drawn from the information given.

1. Prior to the 1980s, the U.S. home finance system was stable, easy to understand, and acceptable to lenders and home buyers alike. The basic home loan, or mortgage, was steady for a 30-year period, during which the rate of interest for the mortgage was fixed and unchangeable. Beginning in the 1980s, the system started to become more complex. By 1992, lenders were offering home loans for 15-, 20-, or 30-year periods at a maximum 8 percent interest rate. Home buyers were also offered ARMs (adjustable-rate mortgages) that started at a 4.5 percent interest rate for the first year but could change every year during the life of the loan.

Which of the following statements expresses the conclusion of the paragraph?

(1) In the 1990s adjustable-rate mortgages started at 4.5 interest.
(2) Beginning in the 1980s, the mortgage system started to become much more complex.
(3) Beginning in the 1980s, home buyers had to settle for a 15-year mortgage at a fixed rate.
(4) Prior to the 1980s, home buyers could get a 30-year mortgage at a fixed rate of 8 percent.
(5) Adjustable-rate mortgages did not exist before the 1980s.

2. Adults have obligations to the children they bring into this world. Infants are incapable of caring for themselves and will not develop normally without proper love and discipline. Society sets up laws, therefore, to ensure the normal growth of its young. Parental neglect is generally considered to involve the disregard of the physical, emotional, and moral needs of children under the age of 18 and is punishable in most states by imprisonment, fines, or removal of children from the home.

Based on the passage, which of the following does the writer believe?

(1) Punishments for adults guilty of parental neglect are too severe.
(2) Parents have responsibility for the proper development of their children.
(3) Parental neglect can be caused by strict enforcement of existing laws.
(4) Society needs to do more to protect the welfare of its children.
(5) Parents can have only a very limited influence on their children.

Answers are on page 397.

EXERCISE 5

Questions 1 and 2 refer to the following passage.

In possibly the first action of its kind, a coalition of union, community, and religious groups negotiated an agreement with the city of Vacaville, California, requiring certain employers to give a year's notice of plant closings or major cuts in operations. The agreement was limited to those companies attracted to the city by the offer of tax-supported financial aid.

1. Which of the following conclusions can be drawn from this paragraph?

   (1) When union, community, and religious groups unite, they can demand anything they want from a city.
   (2) The city of Vacaville, California, has limited the number of private companies that may move there.
   (3) Cooperation among certain groups in Vacaville, California, has given some employees there a chance to plan their futures.
   (4) Labor agreements between city and community groups must be limited to companies benefiting from tax breaks.
   (5) Unions, communities, and religious groups often cooperate with each other to accomplish a common goal.

2. Which of the following employers would be subject to this agreement?

   (1) a Vacaville company that loses a big government contract, goes bankrupt, and closes all its operations
   (2) a Vacaville company that sells shares of stock to employees who eventually become the owners
   (3) a tax-supported Vacaville company that is shut down overnight because of safety and health violations
   (4) a company given tax incentives that merges with a larger company and moves its operations 50 miles away
   (5) a fast-food restaurant in Vacaville that lays off its part-time workers because of a decrease in sales

Questions 3 and 4 refer to the following passage.

Economic researchers at the Federal Reserve and the Internal Revenue Service reported that during the 1980s America's super-rich became even richer. The richest 1 percent of American households (all of them at least millionaires) accounted for 37 percent of private net worth in 1989, up from 31 percent in 1983. In fact, by 1989 the top 1 percent of American households had a greater net worth than the bottom 90 percent of American households. This surge in wealth among the super-rich was the first significant rise in wealth concentration since the Roaring Twenties.

3. What conclusion can be drawn from this passage?

(1) The Roaring Twenties were boom years for the super-rich.
(2) During the 1980s, most Americans became wealthier.
(3) More households were among the super-wealthy during the 1980s.
(4) Money given to the wealthy will "trickle down" to the poor.
(5) The same families have been among the super-wealthy since the 1920s.

4. Which of the following inferences about the late 1980s can be drawn from the passage?

(1) The gap between the super-rich and the rest of the American people grew even wider.
(2) The bottom 90 percent of the American people became poorer than they had been before.
(3) The tax structure was adjusted to treat rich and poor the same and improve fairness.
(4) More than half of the American people grew richer as the nation grew wealthier.
(5) Most Americans experienced the same surge in wealth as Americans did in the 1920s.

Question 5 refers to the following passage.

Only five generations ago, it was forbidden by law to teach slaves to read and write. Today some of the greatest novelists, playwrights, and poets produced in the United States are African American. Less than 60 years ago, black people were barred from professional athletics; today they dominate them. Black popular music, relegated to obscurity as "race music" in the early twentieth century, now largely defines U.S. popular culture. As late as 1960, the majority of African Americans had never been permitted to vote in a presidential election, and were largely excluded from the political system in the South. Today, there are over 10,000 black elected officials, and black voters comprise the essential core group for a liberal and progressive political coalition in national elections. African Americans have done more than make "contributions": they have instead largely reshaped and redefined what U.S. life and society are about. All these gains were the results of the struggles of ordinary people. Our struggle continues.

—Excerpted from *Let Nobody Turn Us Around: Voices of Resistance, Reform, and Renewal*, ed. by Manning Marable and Leith Mullings

5. What is the main conclusion drawn in this passage?

(1) Today some of the greatest writers produced in the United States are African American.

(2) African American athletes now dominate many professional sports that used to bar them.

(3) Black popular music was dismissed as "race music" in the early twentieth century.

(4) Black voters comprise the essential core group for a liberal coalition in national elections.

(5) African Americans have largely reshaped and redefined what U.S. life and society are about.

Answers are on pages 397–398.

EXERCISE 6

Look at the bar graph below. Notice that it has a title, "Number of Immigrants to the United States," a horizontal label (across the bottom axis of the graph) of "Years," and a vertical label (up the left axis) of "In Millions." Bars of various heights represent variations in numbers of immigrants throughout the years.

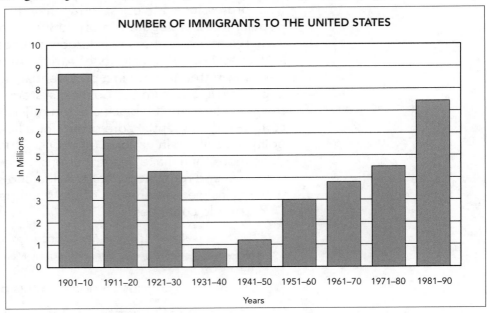

Place an **F** next to a fact that is directly given in the bar graph. Place a **C** next to the conclusions that may be drawn from the graph. Place an **X** next to statements that are neither facts directly stated in the graph nor conclusions that may be drawn.

_____ (a) During the 1970s the nationalities of the predominant immigrant groups changed from European to Indo-Chinese.

_____ (b) In the decade starting in 1921, slightly more than 4 million immigrants came to the United States.

_____ (c) The decades from 1931 to 1950 mark the period when immigration to the United States was at its lowest.

_____ (d) Between 1901 and 1910 nearly 9 million people immigrated to the United States.

_____ (e) A 1953 law called the Refugee Relief Act stopped the decreasing trend of immigration to the United States.

_____ (f) No significant changes in immigration patterns are foreseen for the coming decades.

_____ (g) Immigration to the United States was at its highest during the early twentieth century.

_____ (h) In the 1980s, the number of immigrants to the United States was the greatest since the beginning of the twentieth century.

Answers are on page 398.

Recognizing Information That Is Designed to Persuade an Audience

Look at this campaign poster from 1944 for Franklin Delano Roosevelt, who was President of the United States during the Depression and World War II.

What features in the poster were designed to persuade people to vote for Roosevelt?

_____

_____

   You might have noticed the caption "Our Friend," or you might have noticed the hands of working people of different races, or the child who symbolizes the future, or the image of Roosevelt himself looking very presidential.

   Political posters and cartoons are often designed to persuade an audience.

EXERCISE 7

Questions 1 and 2 are based on the following political cartoon.

1. **What image is Robert Pryor trying to make you think of when you look at this cartoon?**

   (1) a filmmaker editing a film
   (2) a person lost in a fun house
   (3) an insect caught in a spider's web
   (4) a scientist trying to solve a problem
   (5) a tourist lost in a foreign place

2. **What is the point the cartoonist is trying to make?**

   (1) President Nixon was caught in a lie by tapes of his conversations.
   (2) President Nixon was the victim of persecution by his enemies.
   (3) Nixon's poor appearance on television cost him the presidency.
   (4) President Nixon was overwhelmed by the details of being president.
   (5) The Nixon Library had difficulty finding films of his presidency.

Political posters and cartoons are not the only graphics that are designed to persuade an audience. Question 3 is based on the following photograph.

3. This photograph was taken in Richmond, Virginia, in April 1865 at the end of the Civil War. What might have been the message the photographer was trying to convey?

(1) It is important to preserve our architectural heritage.
(2) The rewards of war are worth the sacrifice.
(3) Poor construction can be very dangerous.
(4) The nation needs to heal the wounds of war.
(5) War brings terrible and total devastation.

Answers are on page 398.

Recognizing Unstated Assumptions

When someone makes an assumption about something, that person takes a fact or an idea for granted. In newspaper or television editorials, the writers or speakers often take for granted certain ideas that may or may not be true. By doing this, they attempt to influence your opinion.

For example, in a commercial, an individual with dandruff is shown as a social outcast until he uses a particular shampoo to get rid of the problem. The unstated assumption is that dandruff-free people are popular, while those with dandruff are not. A further assumption is that the use of a certain product will increase your popularity. It is important to be able to know when this kind of subtle persuasion is being used. If you can clearly understand unstated assumptions in what you read or hear, you will be better able to make informed decisions.

Read the statement below carefully to discover the underlying, unstated assumption made by the writer.

All people caught and convicted of DUI (driving under the influence) should be sent to mandatory Alcoholics Anonymous meetings.

What is the unstated assumption about people who have been convicted of a DUI?

_____

Your answer should include the word *alcoholics*. For the writer to state that all DUI drivers should be sent to AA meetings assumes that they are all alcoholics. In fact, while they may be drunk at the time they are caught, they may not be alcoholics.

EXERCISE 8

Read the statements below. In the space provided, write the underlying unstated assumption behind each one.

1. The United States should use its power to prevent small developing countries from turning from capitalism to socialism.

What does the writer assume about socialism?

_____

2. Finally the people of mainland China can enjoy the benefits of Westernized society and escape, at least partially, the dreariness of their past existence.

What does the writer assume about China before Westernization?

_____

3. The dress was punk, the music was 50,000 watts, the style was slamdance, but there would be no trouble at this rock concert. This concert was a Christian rock festival.

What does the writer assume about rock concerts?

_____

4. The leaders of Las Vegas, Nevada did such a great job of governing in the last decade of the twentieth century, that their metropolitan area was the most rapidly growing one in the United States.

To what does the writer attribute the growth of Las Vegas?

_____

5. By greatly increasing military spending, the Reagan Administration brought about the collapse and breakup of the Soviet Union.

What does the writer assume about the breakup of the Soviet Union?

_____

_____

Answers are on page 398.

GED PRACTICE

EXERCISE 9

Questions 1–4 are based on the following passage.

The Corrections Corporation of America was formed in the early 1980s. It is an investor-owned corporation established to make a profit by running prisons as businesses. Excesses are eliminated, bureaucracy is avoided, employees are trained and paid adequately, and costs are constantly monitored. Though the corporation does not set policy, it runs everything else and manages the facilities toward the goal of turning a profit.

This ever-present concern for the bottom line bothers some of the critics of this bold new idea. Mark Cunniff, executive director of the National Association of Criminal Justice Planners, said pointedly, "The private sector is more concerned with doing well than doing good." For this reason, CCA was expected to be a short-lived company despite the fact that people like former Tennessee governor Lamar Alexander called the idea of a privately run prison "bold" and "impressive." He pointed out that private contractors have been running hospitals for years and have shown they can do it without cost overruns. "If private management is good enough for our sick mothers, it's good enough for our murderers and rapists," he concluded.

1. What unstated assumption is made by former governor Alexander?

(1) Private companies are more concerned about sick people than they are about prisoners.
(2) Private corporations are quite capable of setting as well as carrying out government policy.
(3) Though private contractors have done a good job of running hospitals, they may not do so well with prisons.
(4) Running private prisons would require management skills similar to those needed for running private hospitals.
(5) Cost overruns are unavoidable in large institutions such as hospitals and prisons.

2. Mark Cunniff, executive director of the National Association of Criminal Justice Planners, is quoted in the passage. He says, "The private sector is more concerned with doing well than doing good."

   From the quote, which of the following can you infer that Mr. Cuniff believes?

   (1) Private companies are concerned with effectively and efficiently performing social service.
   (2) Private companies are more concerned with producing a profit than performing good deeds.
   (3) Private citizens are more concerned with their own health needs than that of other people.
   (4) Private citizens are more concerned with having good hospitals than good, well-run prisons.
   (5) Private organizations currently provide most of the country's well-run social services.

3. On the basis of former governor Alexander's statement about Tennessee's prisons, what does his chief concern seem to be?

   (1) untrained employees
   (2) unfair policies
   (3) managing prisons effectively
   (4) overcrowding
   (5) too much red tape

4. According to the passage, how does the Corrections Corporation of America run prisons as businesses?

   (1) It sets and implements fair and reasonable policies.
   (2) It examines excesses and efficiencies in its operations.
   (3) It asks employees to work for less, but offers other incentives.
   (4) It improves the way bureaucracy is handled without cost overruns.
   (5) It operates facilities in such a way that they can make a profit.

Answers are on page 398.

Unstated Assumptions in Illustrations

The information that goes into tables, charts, graphs, and other illustrations is sometimes obtained on the basis of underlying, unstated assumptions. It is a good practice to question how valid or true some data is.

A table or chart is an organization of many facts into a small space. Tables and charts can be useful in many situations.

The chart below reports the results of a survey. The title, "Paying What the Job's Worth," gives us an idea of what the survey was about. Notice that occupations are listed along the left side of the chart, and the headings "paid too little," "paid about right," and "paid too much" are listed across the top. Percentages across from each listed occupation tell us how many of the people surveyed viewed the pay scale for that job as too little, too much, or about right according to the contribution the job makes to society. What assumptions did the interviewer make about the people responding to this survey?

PAYING WHAT THE JOB'S WORTH			
843 respondents were asked how they feel "about the amount of income that different kinds of people receive for the contribution they make to society."			
OCCUPATION	PAID TOO LITTLE	PAID ABOUT RIGHT	PAID TOO MUCH
Movie stars/ top entertainers	0.5%	18.8%	80.7%
Professional athletes	2.9%	18.2%	78.8%
Top executives	1.3%	24.3%	74.4%
Physicians	2.4%	27.5%	70.1%
Government officials	4.7%	25.1%	70.2%
Landlords	5.1%	41.8%	53.1%
Skilled blue-collar workers	8.7%	48.3%	43.1%
Union factory workers	14.4%	55.8%	29.9%
Scientists	22.7%	55.8%	21.4%
Middle-level managers	21.1%	69.2%	9.6%
Owners of small business	43.5%	52.5%	4.0%

One assumption the interviewer must have made is that the people responding to the survey knew how much money each job pays. Another assumption the interviewer must have made is that the respondents had some idea of what contributions each job makes to society.

Look at the following cartoons. Think about what assumptions are being made by the cartoonist.

EXERCISE 10

Questions 1–3 are based on the following cartoons.

—Reprinted with special permission from King Features Syndicate.

—Reprinted with special permission from King Features Syndicate.

1. What assumption is the cartoonist making about his readers?

   (1) They will agree with his views.
   (2) They will be offended by the cartoons.
   (3) They have no interest in politics.
   (4) They are concerned with math and correct pronunciation.
   (5) They are familiar with the cartoon characters.

2. The subject of the first cartoon is the tax policy of Republican President George W. Bush. Which of the following unstated assumptions does the cartoonist make?

    (1) The dignity of the President must be respected.
    (2) The public needs to get behind the President.
    (3) The President's tax policy makes no sense.
    (4) Good economic times are ahead.
    (5) The President needs to worry more about math.

3. The subject of the second cartoon is the Senate confirmation hearings for former Senator John Ashcroft, who had been nominated to become Attorney General. What assumption is the cartoonist making about Senator Ashcroft?

    (1) He can be trusted to keep his word to uphold all the laws.
    (2) He will be no match for his more clever opponents.
    (3) He has a speech impediment, which undermines his credibility.
    (4) He cannot be trusted to protect those he formerly opposed.
    (5) He will have no difficulty being confirmed by the Senate.

Answers are on page 398.

Identifying Cause-and-Effect Relationships

When we analyze social studies material for causes and effects, we connect important events with the conditions that made them happen. Without thinking about it, you connect causes with effects every day. For example, in recent winters, the United States experienced such extremes in temperatures that the frost line reached Florida, damaging the state's orange crop. Many oranges were lost. On the television news, it was predicted that consumers would soon be forced to pay higher prices for orange products at stores.

A number of results stemmed from this single cause: sudden cold temperatures. A couple of them are listed below.

Cause	Effect
freezing temperatures	damaged orange crop
damaged orange crop	fewer oranges harvested

What effect might come from the cause shown below? Write one.

Cause   **Effect**

fewer oranges harvested   _____

You may have written *higher prices for orange products*, since a short supply of a commodity leads to higher prices. You can probably think of other causes and effects stemming from this event. For example, higher prices for orange products (cause) might mean that fewer orange products would be bought (effect). Also, a damaged Florida orange crop (cause) might mean the sale of more California oranges (effect).

Effects normally follow causes in time. However, sometimes an effect appears in a sentence before the cause, even though the effect follows the cause in time. The statement below is an example of this inverted written order.

Effect

America finally turned its attention to the exploration of space largely because of

Cause

the Soviet Union's launching of *Sputnik* in the late 1950s.

GED PRACTICE

EXERCISE 11

Questions 1–3 are based on the following passage.

The working-class residents of this industrial complex 35 miles from the city of São Paulo have had the sorry distinction of living in a "chemical laboratory" where they serve as test animals for what has turned out to be an experiment to determine both the long- and short-term effects of air and water pollutants on humans. According to measurements taken in 1980 by a government agency, every day the factories of Cubatão were discharging ten thousand tons of toxic gases and particulate matter into the atmosphere. In one slum neighborhood the level of air contamination was twice what the World Health Organization considered capable of producing excess mortality. In 1977 a device installed there by the state government to measure pollutants in the air broke down after 18 months because it was strained beyond its capacity. Moreover, the levels of acid rain in Cubatão exceeded those to be found anywhere on the planet.

The 1980 investigation found that on a daily basis industrial plants were dumping 2600 tons of poisonous wastes into adjacent rivers, which were all certifiably lifeless. Detergent foam, clouds of steam, and green sludge were the signature elements of Cubatão's waterways, which ceaselessly disgorged deformed, dead fish and assorted foul stenches.

The effects of this ecological violence on the nearly one hundred thousand citizens of Cubatão were predictably disastrous. The incidences of birth defects were said to exceed those to be found elsewhere in the country, and unconfirmed reports of gruesomely deformed infants—babies born without brains, and kittens born without limbs—added to Cubatão's disrepute. The city had Brazil's highest infant mortality rate. As many as half of the city's inhabitants were believed to be suffering from some form of lung disease.

The story of the ruin of Cubatão involves elephantine miscalculation, which may be attributed to a number of uniquely Brazilian tendencies. Indifference to risk, especially as it might affect people on the lower end of the social scale, obviously was a factor. This same attitude has made Brazil a leading importer of dangerous pesticides. The primary victims of these agrochemicals are the farmworkers who are constantly exposed to them; the primary beneficiaries are the multinational companies that dump in Brazil products banned in "First World" countries, or that sell chemicals in Brazil under circumstances in which proper warnings are not given to those who will use them.

—Excerpted from *The Brazilians* by Joseph A. Page

1. Which of the following is *not* an effect of Cubatão's factories discharging tons of toxic gases and particulate matter?

   (1) high levels of air contamination in poor neighborhoods
   (2) having the highest infant mortality rate in Brazil
   (3) inhabitants suffering from high levels of lung disease
   (4) farmworkers being exposed to dangerous pesticides
   (5) Cubatao being called "the most polluted place on Earth"

2. If pollution in Cubatão was reduced, which of the following would likely be an effect?

   (1) more industrial development
   (2) more toxic gases released
   (3) longer life expectancy
   (4) increased birth defects in babies
   (5) greater food production

3. Given the information in this passage, what would Brazil be most likely to do?

   (1) take immediate action to protect the Amazon rain forest
   (2) support miners who have illegally moved onto Indian land
   (3) develop effective programs to prevent the extinction of species
   (4) promote organic farming as an alternative to the use of pesticides
   (5) encourage family planning and improved prenatal care

Answers are on page 399.

Not all events that happen are connected by a cause-and-effect relationship. Sometimes there may be no cause-and-effect relationship even though one is claimed. Politicians do this all the time. For example, they are quick to take credit for a booming economy and equally quick to distance themselves from a struggling one.

Part of the ongoing political debate in the United States is over cause and effect. Conservatives tend to distrust government and want to decrease its role. They think that private citizens, companies, and organizations should take the lead in handling many of the challenges of our society. Liberals see a much greater role for government as a regulator of the private sector and a provider of services.

For each of the following cause-effect scenarios, place a **C** if you would expect a conservative to believe the scenario, and place an **L** if you would expect a liberal to believe the scenario.

_____ 1. If the welfare system were drastically cut back, people would take more responsibility for their lives, and be better off. Private charities would take care of those few who could not help themselves.

_____ 2. If government environmental regulations were cut back, companies would take advantage of the situation, resulting in greater pollution.

_____ 3. The federal government should work towards establishing national educational standards and provide additional funding to public schools to help them reach those standards.

_____ 4. If taxes were cut for individuals and companies, the money would be invested in the economy, leading to greater economic growth and prosperity.

A conservative would most likely believe 1 and 4, since both scenarios trust more in the private sector than in government. A liberal would most likely believe 2 and 3, since liberals believe that government is needed to regulate business and has a role to play in providing services such as education.

EXERCISE 12

Questions 1 and 2 are based on the following passage.

Conservative behaviorists discuss black culture as if acknowledging one's obvious victimization by white-supremacist practices (compounded by sexism and class condition) is taboo. They tell black people to see themselves as agents, not victims. And on the surface, this is comforting advice, a nice cliché for downtrodden people. But inspirational slogans cannot substitute for substantive historical and social analysis. Although black people have never been simply victims, wallowing in self-pity and begging for white giveaways, they have been—and are—*victimized*. Therefore, to call on black people to be agents makes sense only if we also examine the dynamics of this victimization against which their agency will, in part, be exercised. What is particularly naïve and peculiarly vicious about the conservative behavioral outlook is that it tends to deny the lingering effect of black history—a history inseparable from though not reducible to victimization. In this way, crucial and indispensable themes of self-help and personal responsibility are wrenched out of historical context and contemporary circumstances—as if it is all a matter of personal will.

This ahistorical perspective contributes to the nihilistic threat within black America in that it can be used to justify right-wing cutbacks for poor people struggling for decent housing, child-care, health care, and education. And . . . although liberals are deficient in important ways, they are right on target in their critique of conservative government cutbacks for services to the poor. These ghastly cutbacks are one cause of the nihilistic threat to black America.

—Excerpted from *Let Nobody Turn Us Around: Voices of Resistance, Reform, and Renewal*, ed. by Manning Marable and Leith Mullings

1. From this passage, what would you expect to be an effect of cutting back support for decent housing, child-care, health care, and education?

    (1) Cutbacks will stimulate personal responsibility in poor people and lead them to rely on self-help.
    (2) Poor people will wallow in self-pity and beg for renewed privileges and giveaways.
    (3) Government action will have no lasting impact on the daily lives of most poor people.
    (4) Poor people will suffer as a result of these cutbacks, and their ability to cope will be hurt.
    (5) Poor people will reevaluate their dependence on government handouts and support conservatives.

2. When the author refers to victimization in black history, he is probably referring to all except which of the following periods?

   (1) the period of slavery, in which many black people were owned by others and denied all basic human rights
   (2) the Civil Rights era, during which blacks were attacked for peacefully demonstrating for their rights
   (3) the era of segregation, when under the guise of "separate but equal," blacks were denied equal rights and living conditions
   (4) the racism and violence of the Ku Klux Klan, who intimidated and attacked blacks who threatened the status quo
   (5 racial profiling, in which police officers are more likely to assume that blacks are to be suspected of crimes

Answers are on page 399.

Recognizing the Point of View of a Writer in a Historical Account

Historical accounts are attempts to tell a story. By necessity, all stories are told from a point of view. Usually, we see American history from the point of view of the Northern Europeans who have been the dominant group for most of our history, wielding the most political and economic power.

Howard Zinn, in his *A People's History of the United States,* has a deep understanding of the importance of point of view in understanding history. In the book he states, "Thus, in that inevitable taking of sides which comes from selection and emphasis in history, I prefer to try to tell the story of the discovery of America from the viewpoint of the Arawaks, of the Constitution from the standpoint of the slaves, of Andrew Jackson as seen by the Cherokees, of the Civil War as seen by the New York Irish, of the Mexican war as seen by the deserting soldiers of Scott's army, of the rise of industrialism as seen by the young women in the Lowell textile mills, of the Spanish-American war as seen by the Cubans . . . the postwar American empire as seen by peons in Latin America. And so on, to the limited extent that any one person, however he or she strains, can see history from the standpoint of others."

The 2000 presidential election was one of the closest in our nation's history. George W. Bush was the Republican candidate, and Al Gore was the Democratic candidate. Below are three political cartoons drawn before the winner of the election was known. What do you think was the point of view of each cartoonist?

—DANZIGER, TRIBUNE MEDIA SERVICE, www.danzigercartoons.com. Reprinted by permission.

—Scott Stantis, Copley News Service.

ANOTHER PUNCH HOLE PROBLEM

—Reprinted with special permission from King Features Syndicate.

The first cartoonist shows the Bush family in a very negative light. It is reasonable to assume that this cartoonist is taking the Democratic point of view about the election.

The second cartoonist is satirizing the hand recount that Al Gore and the Democrats were advocating. (Remember that the donkey is often used as the symbol of the Democratic Party.) It is reasonable to assume that this cartoonist is taking the Republican point of view about the election.

The third cartoonist is criticizing both sides. It appears that he is taking the point of view of a concerned citizen who is worried more about the Constitution than he is about who wins the election.

EXERCISE 13

Questions 1–4 are based on the following information.

Since black Africans were forcibly brought to America as slaves, their situation and future have been major issues. Following are five different points of view towards the condition and treatment of blacks in the United States. In the quotes that follow, decide which of the five points of view is being represented.

Black integration—work for a society in which color is insignificant and where individual achievement and hard work largely determine the life chances of most black people

Black nationalism—work for blacks to place their energies in building economic and social institutions that would provide goods and services to other black people

Transformation—work to dismantle all forms of class hierarchy and social privilege

White liberalism—express sympathy toward blacks

White supremacy—justify the oppression of blacks by claiming that white dominance must be preserved

1. "A segregated district or community is a community in which people live, but outsiders control the politics and the economy of that community. They never refer to the white section as a segregated community. It's the all-Negro section that's a segregated community. Why? The white man controls his own school, his own bank, his own economy, his own politics, his own everything, his own community— but he also controls yours. When you're under someone else's control, you're segregated. They'll always give you the lowest or the worst that there is to offer, but it doesn't mean you're segregated just because you have your own. You've got to *control* your own. Just like the white man has control of his, you need to control yours."

   —Excerpted from "The Ballot or the Bullet" by Malcolm X, 1964

   (1) black integration
   (2) black nationalism
   (3) transformation
   (4) white liberalism
   (5) white supremacy

2. "I am a Communist because I am convinced that the reason we have been forcefully compelled to eke out an existence at the lowest level of American society has to do with the nature of capitalism . . . I am a Communist because I believe that black people, with whose labor and blood this country was built, have a right to a great deal of the wealth that has been hoarded in the hands of the Hughes, the Rockefellers, the Kennedys, the DuPonts, all the superpowerful white capitalists of America." (Angela Davis, 1970)

   —Excerpted from *Let Nobody Turn Us Around: Voices of Resistance, Reform, and Renewal*, ed. by Manning Marable and Leith Mullings

   (1) black integration
   (2) black nationalism
   (3) transformation
   (4) white liberalism
   (5) white supremacy

3. The National Alliance "will do whatever is necessary to achieve this White living space and to keep it White. We will not be deterred by the difficulty or temporary unpleasantness involved, because we realize that it is absolutely necessary for our racial survival."

   —Excerpted from the Anti-Defamation League investigative summary report, 1998

   (1) black integration
   (2) black nationalism
   (3) transformation
   (4) white liberalism
   (5) white supremacy

4. "I have a dream that one day on the red hills of Georgia the sons of former slaves and the sons of former slaveowners will be able to sit down together at the table of brotherhood.

   "I have a dream that one day even the state of Mississippi, a desert state sweltering with the heat of injustice and oppression, will be transformed into an oasis of freedom and justice.

   "I have a dream that my four little children will one day live in a nation where they will be judged not by the color of their skin but by the content of their character."

   —Martin Luther King, 1963

   (1) black integration
   (2) black nationalism
   (3) transformation
   (4) white liberalism
   (5) white supremacy

Answers are on page 399.

Recognizing the Historical Context of a Text

The world has changed greatly over the years. It is important when reading a historical text to recognize the conditions of the time when it was written and to evaluate the writing in that context.

Look at these three accounts of Germany. One was written during the period of the Roman Empire, almost two thousand years ago. One was written in 1775, during the period of the Enlightenment in Europe. The third was written in 1928. Beneath each account, write which time period you believe it is from, and the evidence you used to make your decision.

Germany today is as France was at the time of Francis I. The taste for literature is beginning to spread; we must wait for Nature to cause true geniuses to be born, as under the governments of Richelieu and Mazarin. The soil that produced one Leibniz can produce others.

—Excerpted from *Illustrated History of Europe*, ed. by Frederic Delouche

In the first place, our people must be freed from the hopeless chaos of internationalism and deliberately, systematically trained to be fanatically nationalist. . . . In the second place, we shall tear our people away from the absurdity of parliamentarianism by teaching it to fight the folly of democracy and recognize the need for authority and command. Thirdly, we shall free the people from pathetic faith in external aid, faith in the reconciliation of peoples, in world peace, in the League of Nations and in international solidarity; and thereby we shall destroy those ideas. There is only one right in this world and that is might. . . .

—Excerpted from *Illustrated History of Europe*, ed. by Frederic Delouche

---

They do nothing, public or servant, without bearing arms. But custom decrees that no one shall do so until the city has judged him capable. So, in the Assembly itself, one of the leaders, or the father, or his relations decorate the young man with a buckler and a javelin, which are the equivalent of a toga, the first honours of youth. Before that, they are regarded as belonging to a house; thereafter, they belong to the State. Outstanding nobility or great merit on the part of their fathers may win the favour of a leader for very young men: they attach themselves to others who are stronger or more experienced, and there is no shame in being of their number.

—Excerpted from *Illustrated History of Europe*, ed. by Frederic Delouche

---

The first selection is a letter written in 1775 from Frederick II, King of Prussia, to Voltaire. All the people mentioned in the passage lived in Europe in the period after the Renaissance. In addition, the optimistic tone and interest in literature and intellectual achievement are characteristic of the 17th and 18th centuries in Europe.

The second selection is from a speech of Adolf Hitler's in 1928. In the speech he clearly lays out his Nazi philosophy, which he carried out when he came to power in the 1930s. The violent philosophy that directly led to World War II should be recognizable. He also refers directly to the League of Nations, which was created after World War I.

The third selection is from *Germania*, written by the Roman historian Tacitus in about 98 C.E. He describes a primitive, warlike society. He also mentions such items as a buckler, javelin, and toga, which would help place this writing in Roman times.

EXERCISE 14

Question 1 is based on the following passage.

Though European explorers believed they had discovered "Mundos Novus"—a New World—for thousands of years the Western Hemisphere had been home to peoples with histories and dreams of their own. Native Americans lived in more than two thousand distinct cultures, spoke hundreds of different languages, and made their livings in scores of dissimilar environments. Columbus called the people of the Caribbean *los Indios*, mistakenly thinking he had arrived in the East Indies. Within a half-century "Indian" had passed into English, used to refer to all Native Americans, ridiculously lumping together Aztec militarists, Hopi communalists, and Pequot horticulturists. Just as the term *European* includes dozens of nationalities, so the term *Indian* encompasses an enormous diversity among the native peoples of the Americas.

—Excerpted from *The American West* by Robert Hine and John Faragher

1. What point made in this passage could be considered "present-mindedness" or judging the past using current information and perspectives?

    (1) European explorers believed they had discovered a New World.
    (2) Native Americans lived in more than two thousand distinct cultures.
    (3) Columbus was the first to call the people of the Caribbean Indians.
    (4) It was ridiculous to lump together very different peoples with one name.
    (5) The term European includes dozens of very different nationalities.

Questions 2 and 3 are based on the following passage.

In our time the frontier myth has become an anachronism, no more than a refuge for extreme conservatism, but it need not be so. The frontier story must be reformulated and refit to the realities of our history, providing us with a national myth not only to "match our mountains," but to match the needs and aspirations of a new century. The Indians offer heroic examples of resistance, survival, and adaptation. No story in our history is more inspiring than their tale of persistence and resurgence. Although today we may approach the pioneer story with ambivalence, that intellectual experience can be illuminating. The settlers stood alone against authority but also welcomed the assistance of an active government. They went their own way, but they also believed in community. They were not only male, but female, not only white and Anglo, but German, African, Mexican, and Asian. The frontier is our common past, and it binds us all together, like a continental warming blanket. The frontier is also our common future. The struggle to build a humane and equitable society out of the legacies of colonialism continues, and we must continue struggling to resolve the dilemmas of development. The frontier remains, as Willa Cather expressed it, our "road of destiny." It will not cease to color our next century.

—Excerpted from *The American West* by Robert Hine and John Faragher

2. When was this passage most likely written?

   (1) at the end of the twentieth century
   (2) in the middle of the twentieth century
   (3) at the end of the nineteenth century
   (4) at the beginning of the nineteenth century
   (5) at the end of the eighteenth century

3. According to the author, what part of the frontier myth has stood the test of time?

   (1) the heroic resistance, survival, and adaptation of Native Americans
   (2) the courage of the settlers who stood alone against authority
   (3) the settlers' willingness to accept the assistance of the government
   (4) the importance of Germans, Africans, Mexicans, and Asians
   (5) the crucial role that women played in settling the frontier

Answers are on page 399.

Identifying Comparisons and Contrasts

When you **compare** two things, you look for ways in which they are similar. **Contrasting** things is looking for ways in which they are different. Comparison and contrast are often used to analyze topics in Social Studies. Cartoonists will often use comparison and contrast in order to make their point. For example, look at the cartoon below.

HECK OF A WAY TO RUN A RAILROAD

The people and objects in the cartoon are labeled according to what they symbolize. The engineers who are running the "Social Security" train are labeled "Senate" and "House" to symbolize the U.S. Congress. To the dismay of the elderly couple on the "Social Security" train, this "railroad's" workers are tearing apart the same train that they are trying to keep running.

In drawing such a comparison, the cartoonist is implying that the Social Security system is being _____ by the Congress of the United States and probably will not _____ much longer. Looking at the expression on the faces of the elderly couple, you can infer that what is happening to the Social Security system is _____ to our senior citizens. If you did not know it already, you could also infer that the elderly _____ on Social Security to support themselves.

Your exact words may vary, but they should have been similar to the following:

" . . . the Social Security system is being *destroyed* (or *dismantled*) by the Congress of the United States and probably will not *last* much longer." In the faces of the older man and woman you can see fright and disbelief, or puzzlement, so you can infer that the situation is *frightening* to them, probably because of how important Social Security is to them financially. You can infer that the elderly *depend* on Social Security for financial support just as train passengers depend on the train to get them where they need to go.

EXERCISE 15

Questions 1–3 are based on the following cartoon.

CRAIG MACINTOSH
—Reprinted with permission from *Star Tribune*, Minneapolis.

1. According to the cartoon, what does the cartoonist think about nuclear waste disposal?

   It is
   (1) no longer considered a serious problem
   (2) being handled carefully by trained technicians
   (3) of concern only in out-of-the-way places
   (4) getting much too close for comfort
   (5) the responsibility of all citizens

2. From the way the characters are dressed, what can you infer about nuclear waste disposal?

   It is
   (1) safe enough to be handled in an average person's garage
   (2) handled more easily in cooler weather than warmer weather
   (3) so dangerous that protective suits must be worn when handling it
   (4) no more serious than handling yard waste in a backyard
   (5) being handled safely and competently by ordinary citizens

3. On what are the humor and impact of this cartoon based?

    (1) the contrast between the dismayed ordinary homeowner and the cheerful people handling the waste
    (2) comparing the old-fashioned homeowner with the modern waste disposal workers
    (3) contrasting the space-age suits of the waste disposal workers with the crumpled clothes of the homeowner
    (4) contrasting the complexity of nuclear waste disposal with the simple solution of dumping it in someone's garage
    (5) comparing finding a nuclear waste disposal site with checking on the elderly during a period of hot weather

Question 4 is based on the following passage.

Liberal Moslems now stress a basic democratic principle shared immediately with the other monotheistic religions, Judaism and Christianity—the principle of spiritual equality and brotherhood. It is perhaps more emphatic in the gospel according to Mohammed, if only because all men alike were dwarfed by the transcendent mightiness of Allah; Maude Royden went so far as to say that Islam "proclaimed the first real democracy ever conceived in the mind of man." In keeping with this principle, which entered Moslem law as a theory of political and civil equality, Mohammed shared the concern of Jesus and the prophets of Israel over the habitual oppression of the poor; he attacked the extreme economic inequalities that limited the real freedom of the many. More explicitly, according to tradition, he insisted on racial equality: "The white man is not above the black nor the black above the yellow; all men are equal before the Maker." His religion would accordingly have an advantage over Christianity in the conversion of Africans and Asiatics. He was also most explicit in his concern to free simple worshipers from the priesthood, with its stock in ritual or sacrament, that everywhere stood between them and God, and that might live off them when not exploiting them. A Moslem needed no priest, not even a church, in performing his daily worship; or in a mosque he might still pray alone, in true spiritual equality with all other Moslems bowed down before Allah. The caliph of Islam was never a pope, nor did its clerics have the possibly awful power of sacraments essential to salvation.

—Excerpted from *Freedom in the Western World* by Herbert J. Muller

4. According to the passage, which of the following is *not* a common element of Islam, Judaism, and Christianity?

    (1) spiritual support for democratic principles
    (2) promoting spiritual equality and brotherhood
    (3) explicit insistence on racial equality
    (4) concern for the plight of the poor
    (5) belief in monotheism, or one God

Determining the Implications, Effects, and Value of Presenting Visual Data in Different Ways

Presenting visual data in different ways can have an effect on its impact. For example, look at this line graph of the median weekly earnings of full-time workers from 1970–2000. What are some conclusions you can draw from this graph?

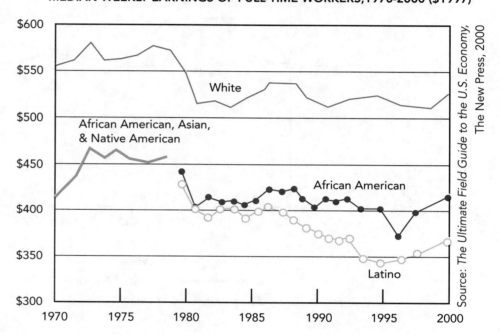

MEDIAN WEEKLY EARNINGS OF FULL-TIME WORKERS, 1970-2000 ($1997)

Source: *The Ultimate Field Guide to the U.S. Economy*, The New Press, 2000

You might conclude from the graph that until recently, real wages had been relatively steady for the past 20 years. You might also conclude that real wages in 2000 were lower than they were 30 years earlier. You could also clearly see that Whites earn significantly more than African Americans or Latinos.

The same data could be presented this way:

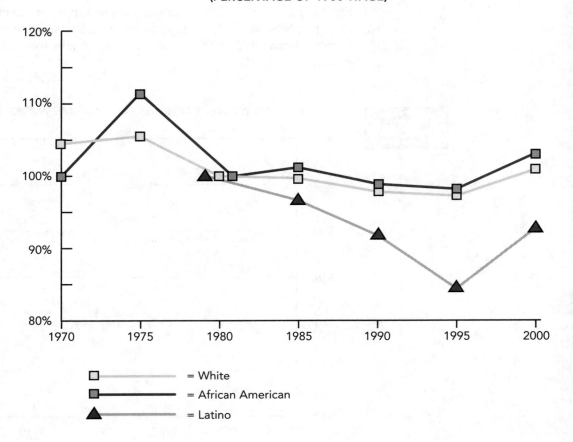

**MEDIAN WEEKLY EARNINGS OF FULL-TIME WORKERS, 1970–2000
(PERCENTAGE OF 1980 WAGE)**

What is one conclusion that you could make from the first graph that you cannot make from the second one?

_____

_____

From the second graph, you cannot conclude that whites earn significantly more than African Americans.

EXERCISE 16

Question 1 is based on the following cartoon.

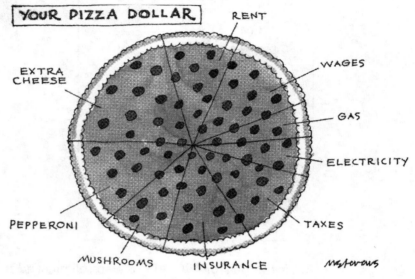

—©The New Yorker Collection, 1992, Mick Stevens.
From cartoonbank.com. All Rights Reserved.

1. What is the main conclusion that you can draw from this cartoon?

    (1) Each slice of a pizza pays for something else.
    (2) Taxes are the main reason pizza prices are so high.
    (3) More than half the price of a pizza pays for overhead.
    (4) Cutting back on cheese would reduce pizza prices.
    (5) Pizza workers should be getting a larger piece of the pie.

Question 2 is based on the following graph.

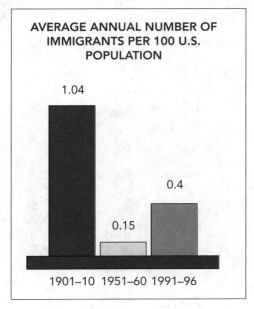

AVERAGE ANNUAL NUMBER OF
IMMIGRANTS PER 100 U.S.
POPULATION

1.04

0.15

0.4

1901–10   1951–60   1991–96

2. If the bar for 1901–1910 were eliminated from this graph, what conclusion would be lost?

(1) Most people living in the United States are either immigrants or the descendants of immigrants.
(2) The number of immigrants entering the United States was much higher at the beginning of the century than at the end of the century.
(3) Annual immigration as a percentage of total population dramatically increased toward the end of the century.
(4) Annual immigration as a percentage of total population was at its highest at the beginning of the century.
(5) Contrary to the opinions of some conservatives, immigration has helped the United States economy.

Answers are on page 399.

Chapter 4

Evaluating Social Studies Materials

When you must make a major purchase—like a car—you often *evaluate* your financial situation and your transportation needs before you shop. Once you are out in the marketplace, you continue to evaluate. You judge the vehicles you see as to how well you can afford them and how well they are made.

In studying social studies, you also need to evaluate information. You must be able to judge the value or logic of an idea. You also have to be able to understand how and why people make the decisions that they do. Most important, you need to be able to determine when a decision has been based on sound logic. In this section you will learn how to evaluate material in social studies in five ways:

- judging the extent to which information satisfies criteria
- recognizing the role that values play in beliefs and decision making
- judging the adequacy of facts
- comparing and contrasting different viewpoints
- recognizing logical fallacies and identifying faulty reasoning

Judging Information

In order to judge the worth or value of something, you must have standards or reference points to go by. A secretary's typing ability is judged by the **criteria** of speed and accuracy. The value of a movie is measured by its entertainment level, its cinematography, its acting and direction. A newspaper article is evaluated by its adequacy of facts, its style of writing, and its objectivity (the writer's abstention from opinion or bias).

If you know and understand the criteria by which something is judged, you are better prepared to evaluate it. For example, if you know the legal requirements for a good and binding contract, then you are better prepared to enter into one. Some of the criteria for a legally binding contract on the sale of goods include:

1. a clear written offer by the buyer or buyer's representative

2. a clear written acceptance of the offer by the seller or seller's representative

3. a settlement of the deal that is agreeable and clear to both buyer and seller

4. a clear exchange of something valuable between the buyer and seller

5. no illegal activity involved in the deal by either the buyer or the seller

Judge whether the situation described below constitutes a legally binding contract according to the criteria listed above. If it does, write *yes* in the space next to it. If the situation does not, write *no* in the space, and write the number of the criterion that the case does not satisfy.

_____ A husband and wife both shake hands with a neighbor in an agreement to purchase a used car for $5,000 from him, and the neighbor, in turn, agrees to hand over the title to the automobile upon receipt of the money.

You should have written *No, 1 and 2*. Though an offer to purchase the car is made, and the seller accepts the offer, neither the offer nor the acceptance is in writing. Therefore, no legally binding contract exists.

EXERCISE 1

Directions: In the following cases, judge whether the situation described constitutes a legally binding contract according to the criteria. If it does, write *yes* on the line. If the situation does not, write *no* on the line. For each *no* answer, write the number of the criterion that the case does not satisfy.

_____ **1.** A private pilot agrees to pick up 100 pounds of marijuana in Mexico and deliver it to a buyer in Texas.

_____ **2.** The lawyer of a woman who owns an apartment approves the lease application for two friends who want to rent the apartment for one year. The lawyer accepts the friends' deposit on the first month's rent with a typed agreement that both the friends and the owner will sign.

_____ **3.** After much discussion and haggling over price, an owner of a small bookkeeping business tells a computer salesman that he will seriously consider buying a computer only if he can get it for $300 less than the salesman's "final" offer.

_____ **4.** A poor but diligent farmer signs a note promising to feed and house a laborer in his home in compensation for the work the laborer has agreed, in writing, to do on his land.

Answers are on page 400.

EXERCISE 2

Directions: Read the passage below. Be prepared to judge the theory described in the passage.

In 1964, anthropologist Ashley Montagu edited a startling book entitled *The Concept of Race*. In the book, Montagu and nine other writers stated that the concept of race is a myth that leads to the perpetuation of errors.

According to Montagu, skin color and physical features are not necessarily accurate indicators of a person's ancestry. He believes that the term *ethnic group* might be a better term than *race*.

For each of the facts below, write *(1)* in the blank if the fact would help support Montagu's theory, *(2)* if the fact would dispute Montagu's theory, and *(3)* if the fact would have no bearing on Montagu's theory.

_____ **1.** Ashley Montagu is a white man.

_____ **2.** Montagu has supported this theory since at least 1941.

_____ **3.** The use of the term *race* has had a long history and, in fact, is prevalent even today among many people.

_____ **4.** There are obvious differences among groups of people in the world that seem fairly easy to define and categorize by "race."

_____ **5.** Ashley Montagu is one of America's most distinguished anthropologists, having taught at numerous universities.

_____ **6.** The book *The Concept of Race* contains contributions from nine other distinguished scientists besides Montagu who all support the theory.

Answers are on page 400.

Recognizing Values

What beliefs do you hold nearest and dearest to your heart? What would you die for? If you could be doing anything you wanted to right now, what would it be? These questions all focus on your personal values.

Your beliefs and values influence the big decisions that you must make in life. In understanding social studies material, you must be able to recognize how an individual's values affect the decision he or she makes.

For example, Martin Luther King, Jr. is known to have put great value on civil disobedience as a nonviolent means of resolving conflict. Because of his beliefs, he advised his followers to avoid using violence at all cost during the struggle for civil rights in the 1950s and 1960s. Thus, even though opponents to the Civil Rights movement at times used excessive physical force to intimidate protesters, there were almost no incidents of violent retaliation, and the success of the movement reflects King's value of nonviolence.

Fill in the words that best summarize the values of the person described in the case below.

A senator does not believe that she could ever have an abortion because it is morally repugnant to her. She personally feels that abortion should not be legalized. A survey shows, however, that her constituency is overwhelmingly in favor of a law permitting abortion. The senator votes "yes" on the bill to legalize abortion.

The senator apparently values _____

over _____

You should have written something similar to *her responsibility to her constituency* over *her personal beliefs*. In other words, the feelings of those who elected her override her own personal feelings.

EXERCISE 3

Directions: For each of the following statements, supply the most accurate words that reflect the values of the person described in each case.

1. A young man wants very much to settle down and save enough money to get married and to buy a home and a good-running car. However, he has been instilled with a strong belief in the responsibility of every American citizen to serve his country. His decision to join the U.S. Army was affected primarily by his sense of

_____

2. A scientist is asked to work on a prestigious project to develop a neutron bomb, a weapon he despises because it is designed to destroy on impact living things, not buildings. When the scientist refuses the project, it shows that he values his

_____

over his _____

Answers are on page 400.

GED PRACTICE

EXERCISE 4

Questions 1–4 refer to the following passage.

The derogatory term "Yankee imperialist" has not always been applied to Americans. Prior to the Spanish-American War in 1898, the United States was strongly isolationist and did not concern itself with issues involving other parts of the world.

The Spanish-American War grew out of the American public's growing desire to expand American territory and interests and out of a general "war fever."

Several of the larger American newspapers began to capitalize on the Cuban struggle for independence from Spain, sensationalizing abuses Spanish military forces were committing against the Cubans.

Public outrage reached its peak with the sinking of the battleship *Maine*, which was sent to the Havana harbor to protect U.S. citizens and property in Cuba. Though the cause of the explosion was never discovered, President McKinley approved a congressional resolution demanding immediate Spanish withdrawal from Cuba. A few days later Spain declared war.

The congressional resolution stated that the United States was not acting to secure an empire. However, the terms of the Treaty of Paris that officially ended the war required that Spain cede the Philippines, Puerto Rico, and Guam to the United States. For good or ill, the United States had expanded. It had become a world power, admired by some who felt the United States now had an altruistic concern for smaller nations. Others detested the United States for what they believed to be imperialistic bullying of countries in its way.

1. According to this writer, what values of Americans most directly triggered the U.S. decision to enter the war against Spain in 1898?

    (1) a desire to help and protect the less economically fortunate in this world
    (2) a belief that democracy is the only fair form of government and that military rule is unjust
    (3) an overriding desire to maintain peace and harmony in the Western Hemisphere
    (4) an abhorrence of social injustice and a belief in their responsibility to the oppressed
    (5) a sense of outrage about danger to American lives and property abroad

2. What change in American values resulted from the Spanish-American War?

    (1) The public became more wary of electing indecisive candidates for high public office.
    (2) Nationalism increased as Americans found ways to strengthen their internal society and economy.
    (3) Standing apart from the rest of the world lost its importance and the United States saw itself as a player in international conflict.
    (4) The U.S. adopted a materialistic policy of acquiring property and increasing capitalistic ventures inside and outside the United States.
    (5) The public developed a cautious, wait-and-see attitude toward getting involved in further conflicts with other world powers.

3. Those who use the term "Yankee imperialist" against the United States would most likely also agree with which of the following?

    (1) The Peace Corps was established to help Third World countries develop their own economic bases.
    (2) Puerto Rico should be made a permanent colony of the United States.
    (3) The United States had no right to invade the small Caribbean island of Grenada in 1983.
    (4) The Philippines can blame its economic woes on the U.S. decision to grant it independence in 1946.
    (5) The United States entered the Vietnam conflict because of its concern for the well-being of Southeast Asia.

4. From the information presented in the passage, which was not a contributing factor to the start of the Spanish-American War?

    (1) American newspapers' sensationalizing reports
    (2) the sinking of the battleship *Maine*
    (3) the American public's "war fever"
    (4) the United States' policy of isolationism
    (5) the demand for Spanish withdrawal from Cuba

Answers are on page 400.

Judging the Adequacy of Facts

Have you ever told one of your favorite jokes to a friend, only to have him or her appear bewildered after you delivered the punch line? If you considered why the joke failed, you may have learned that you omitted an important detail. When facts are lacking in a story, confusion or misinterpretation of the story is likely to result.

When important facts are omitted, you cannot make an informed decision. Suppose, for example, that you overheard a debate about the purchase of a new fleet of buses for your city's transit system. One group supports the buying of American-made buses. These buses cost more than the foreign-made buses that another group wants. To be able to judge how you feel about the issue, you need to know all the facts. You need to know

- the cost of each fleet of buses

- the city's financial situation

- the level of quality of the bus each company manufactures

- the impact the purchase of a foreign product over an American product is likely to have on American jobs

All of these considerations may have some influence on what your final position will be. Similarly, when you read social studies materials, you must be able to determine whether the facts are adequate to support the writer's conclusion or point of view.

Certain information is missing in each case below. On the line provided, indicate what facts are needed to answer each question.

Case 1

Intelligence (IQ) tests were improved dramatically by French psychologist Alfred Binet when he found a way to measure judgment, comprehension, and reasoning skills. In what ways could Binet have made his test bias-free, also?

_____

You should have written *How are the tests biased?* In order to answer the question, you need to know in what ways the IQ test is biased.

Case 2

The number of registered voters in favor of gun control in a county increased by 50 percent before the last election. However, the defeated candidate for the U.S. Congress, who supported gun control, did not benefit directly from this increase in the number of registered voters. In fact, he lost the election by the same margin of votes as he did the last time he ran. Why didn't the candidate get more votes if the number of registered voters supporting his cause increased by 50%?

_____

You should have written the question *How many of the registered voters in the county who support gun control actually voted in the election?* or

What were some of the other important issues in the election besides gun control? The fact that the information tells you that the number of registered voters increased by 50 percent does not mean they voted. Also, there is the possibility that even if they voted they might have chosen a different candidate on the basis of issues other than gun control.

EXERCISE 5

Questions 1 and 2 are based on the following passage.

"Equality of right under the law shall not be denied or abridged by the United States or by any state on account of sex." So read the Equal Rights Amendment proposed in 1972. Opponents of the amendment insisted, however, that it meant that anti-family, pro-abortion, pro-homosexual, and anti-privacy laws would be passed.

As a result, the amendment was defeated in 1982. Ten years had passed since the first of 35 states ratified it. Thirty of these states had approved the amendment within the first year of its proposal. By law, three-fourths of the state legislatures, or 38 states, had to approve it to make it a part of the U.S. Constitution.

If there had been more time, the amendment probably would have been ratified. In two major opinion polls just a few weeks before the ERA's defeat, it was reported that the majority of American citizens supported the amendment.

1. Which of the statements in the article is *not* adequately supported by facts?

   (1) A majority of Americans supported the ERA at the time of its defeat.
   (2) Thirty-eight states needed to ratify the amendment to make it law.
   (3) The ERA might have passed if there had been more time.
   (4) Its opponents were fearful of the ramifications of the ERA.
   (5) A clear majority of the states approved of the ERA.

2. Which of the following statements is supported by the information provided in the passage?

   (1) Organizations working for the ERA had more popular support than governmental support.
   (2) As a result of the defeat of the ERA, men are given more consideration in parental custody cases than they were before.
   (3) Since the 1982 defeat of the ERA, single-parent, female-headed families have become more numerous and more poverty-stricken.
   (4) Gay rights and welfare mothers' groups supported the ERA and worked for its ratification.
   (5) More female than male citizens were in favor of the ratification of the ERA.

Answers are on page 400.

Judging the Adequacy of Facts in Illustrations

There are many ways to represent facts in social studies. You have evaluated the adequacy of facts given in written materials. Now you will do much the same thing with maps and other illustrations.

Maps are used to represent information visually. "One picture is worth a thousand words," says the old expression. Of course, different kinds of maps are used to illustrate different kinds of facts.

- *Topographical* maps show geographic land features of an area.

- *Population* maps explain the distribution of people in an area.

- *Political* maps can outline borders between countries or states, show trade relationships among countries, and indicate systems of government.

- *Weather* maps can show current or forecasted weather as well as climate.

- *World* maps include all of the world's continents in a single picture.

Study the geographical map below and see how adequately it shows facts about the continent of Asia. Then read the statement following the map. Place an X in the space below to indicate whether the map is adequate or inadequate to support the fact. If the information is not adequate, write what kind of map from the list above would best show the kind of information needed.

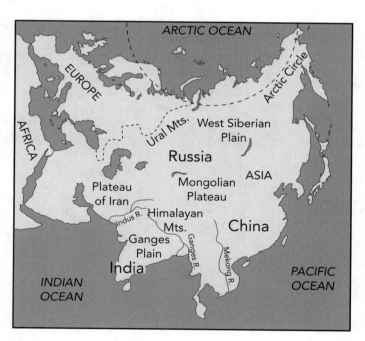

Asia is the world's largest continent and covers over one-third of the earth's surface.

_____ adequate

_____ inadequate: a _____ map would show this.

You should have marked that the information on the map was *inadequate* and that a *world* map would be more appropriate.

EXERCISE 6

Directions: Use the map of Asia on the preceding page. Answer the following questions in the same way as in the preceding exercise.

(1) The continent of Asia extends north and south of the Arctic Circle.

_____ adequate

_____ inadequate: a_____ map would show this better.

(2) Asia contains many mountains, plains, plateaus, and river basins.

_____ adequate

_____ inadequate: a_____ map would show this better.

(3) Some parts of Asia receive more than 80 inches of rain a year.

_____ adequate

_____ inadequate: a_____ map would show this better.

(4) Asia is bordered by three oceans.

_____ adequate

_____ inadequate: a_____ map would show this better.

(5) The countries that have the largest population and the greatest land masses are in Asia.

_____ adequate

_____ inadequate: a_____ map would show this better.

(6) China is the largest Communist country in Asia.

_____ adequate

_____ inadequate: a_____ map would show this better.

Answers are on page 400.

GED PRACTICE

EXERCISE 7

Questions 1 and 2 are based on the picture below.

The U.S. Federal Dollar —Fiscal Year 2001: Where the Money Comes From

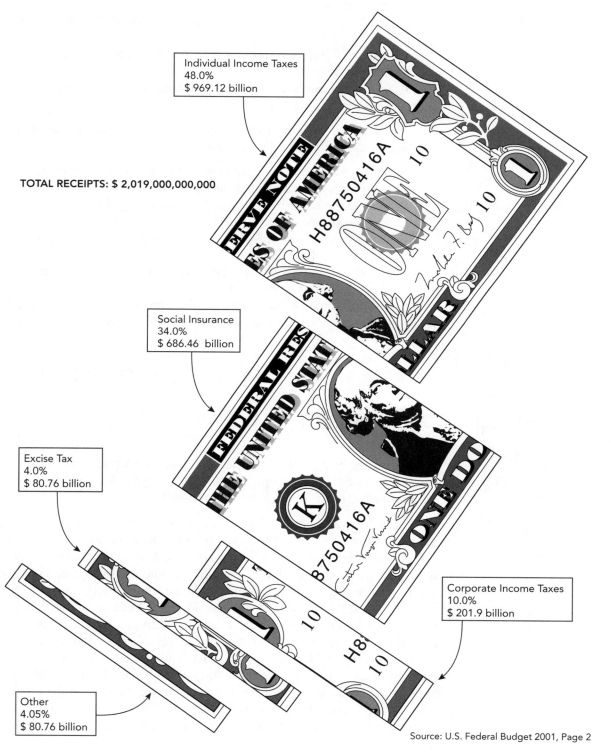

Individual Income Taxes
48.0%
$ 969.12 billion

TOTAL RECEIPTS: $ 2,019,000,000,000

Social Insurance
34.0%
$ 686.46 billion

Excise Tax
4.0%
$ 80.76 billion

Corporate Income Taxes
10.0%
$ 201.9 billion

Other
4.05%
$ 80.76 billion

Source: U.S. Federal Budget 2001, Page 2

1. Which of the following aspects of federal revenue is *not* shown adequately in this illustration?

   (1) There were five major sources of money for the federal government in 2001.
   (2) There are three types of taxes that help to support the federal government.
   (3) The largest single source of money for the federal government is individual income taxes.
   (4) The U.S. Congress decides how much money comes from each revenue source.
   (5) Social insurance accounts for approximately one-third of government money.

2. Which of the following statements is supported adequately by the data provided by the illustration?

   (1) Most of U.S. government revenue comes from corporate taxes, excise taxes, and other sources.
   (2) Individuals contribute as much to the budget as corporations and social insurance put together.
   (3) There is a strong anti-tax movement that is trying to give individual taxpayers a break.
   (4) The U.S. government is looking for additional sources of revenue, since it currently does not have enough.
   (5) The corporate lobby pressures Congress to keep corporate taxes low by saying that the economy will do better that way.

Answers are on page 400.

Comparing and Contrasting Different Viewpoints

Have you ever been startled to hear someone who witnessed the same event as you did describe it in a completely different way? In such moments you may ask yourself, Did we just see the same thing?

Earlier in this chapter you encountered the term *criteria* as it related to judging information. It is important to understand that the viewpoint and subsequent opinion someone has about something is often determined by the set of criteria that person has consciously or unconsciously set. For example, maybe you once went with a friend to see a movie. Afterwards you shared your opinions. You thought it was a good movie because it was the kind you liked. It made you laugh and you found it exciting. Your friend, however, gave it a "thumbs down" review because the acting was poor and the editing was unsophisticated and lacking in creativity. The two evaluations of the movie were completely different because you and your friend were judging it on the basis of different sets of criteria. Your criteria were based on the movie's entertainment value for you as someone who likes the type of movie it was. Your friend's criteria, on the other hand, involved the artistic qualities of the film.

Everyone perceives things differently, whether on the basis of criteria or because a person's background and culture have such a powerful impact on how a person interprets the world and its events. Whenever you read or hear about a historical event, it is essential to keep this fact in mind.

We can learn about events of history in two ways: First, there are the accounts of people who experienced them. In this case we need to be aware of what the political and cultural environment was at the time of the event because that context influenced the way the event was both perceived and documented. Take, for example, the events concerning Native Americans during the course of European settlement in America.

Over a period of 200 years the native peoples of this country were routinely dispossessed of their land and ways of life. The U.S. government and white settlers frequently justified this treatment by portraying Indians as dangerous, uncivilized savages. Their desire for control of more and more land within the white culture of exploration and expansion established this perspective. The Indians, on the other hand, were of cultures that sought harmony with the natural world and had no ambitions for dominance, over either nature or over their new neighbors.

If you were an Iroquois tribesman existing peacefully in the northeastern forests, what would be your concern if you witnessed white trappers looting the woods of the animals on which your survival depended?

_____

_____

If you were a white frontiersman with a spirit of adventure and a belief that the seemingly endless expanses of forests, mountains, and plains were yours for the taking, how would you view the clusters of Indians, with their mysterious languages and customs, you continually encountered in your journey?

_____

_____

Clearly the perspective you would have as each of these people would be different from the other, although there might be a feeling of mistrust held in common. Which person would be likely to label the subsequent events of frontier expansion "heroic" and which one "devastating"? Which one would call it "progress" and which one "exploitation"?

_____

_____

_____

Pontiac, Chief of the Ottawa people in the mid 1700s, led an armed struggle for Indian independence.

Francis Parkman judged Pontiac's efforts as a "conspiracy" and created a generalized portrait of Indians as savage and treacherous.

EXERCISE 8

Each of the quotations in the following items is from someone commenting on the Vietnam War in the late 1960s and represents a different view and set of concerns. Identify the likely speaker from the list below.

Possible Speakers:

(a) an African American who refused the draft

(b) an anti-war Vietnam veteran

(c) a U.S. army officer

(d) an American political leader

(e) a soldier's widow

1. _____ "How do you ask a man to be the last man to die for a mistake?"

2. _____ "America wants peace with victory."

3. _____ "No Viet Cong ever enslaved me or my family."

4. _____ "It became necessary to destroy the town to save it."

Answers are on page 400.

Recognizing Logical Fallacies and Identifying Faulty Reasoning

You have practiced distinguishing conclusions from supporting details in a passage. An extension of that skill is the ability to identify logical fallacies in arguments or conclusions. People often draw illogical conclusions from the information they receive. Look at the following example.

Neighbor #1: What kind of trouble have you gotten yourself into?

Neighbor #2: I'm not in any trouble. What gave you that idea?

Neighbor #1: Come on, tell the truth! I saw the cops at your door last night.

Neighbor #2: Oh, those police officers. They weren't after me. I called them because it looks like some stuff has been stolen out of my garage.

Obviously, Neighbor #1 assumes that if police officers are talking to someone, that person has probably done something wrong. He does not consider that there could be other reasons for the officers' presence at his neighbor's door.

Read the following story. Find two logical fallacies in Marlena and Donnell's thinking.

Marlena Jackson is a working wife and mother. She works because she needs to help support her family financially. Her days are very hectic because she has to keep up with both work and home schedules. Marlena shops primarily at one chain grocery store because it sponsors games with prizes for customers. The prizes provide extras for the house, such as towels, cookware, and small appliances.

The food at this grocery store generally costs more than the food at a discount store a few miles away. This fact, however, just proves to Marlena that the more expensive store has better food.

Marlena drives an old, gas-guzzling car that is always in need of repair. Her husband, Donnell, knows how to fix it, though, so the repair costs are low. Insurance costs on the car are not high either, so Marlena assumes that the car is safe.

Despite all the money they spend on gas and repairs for the old car, it is still cheaper to keep it than it would be to buy a newer, smaller, more fuel-efficient car.

What logical fallacies did you find in the passage?

_____

_____

_____

_____

In the second paragraph above, the logical fallacy is concluding that *a more expensive store is a better store*. The cost of food can be affected by quality, but it can also be affected by other things, such as more lavish surroundings, higher-paid clerks, or more games and gimmicks that draw in customers.

In the third paragraph, it is not a logical argument that *lower insurance costs indicate safer cars*. That could be a reason for the lower premiums, but other factors such as low book value or lower replacement cost on the vehicle could also keep the cost low.

GED PRACTICE

EXERCISE 9

Questions 1 and 2 refer to the following passage.

Some African Americans can claim ancestors who arrived on the continent before the Pilgrims landed at Plymouth Rock. Unfortunately, this just means that racial bias has always existed in the Americas, for most of the first African arrivals were slaves.

Slavery and indentured servitude were both employed initially because of an acute shortage of labor in the Americas. But there were glaring differences between the two systems from the beginning. Most indentured servants were white, and most served only four or five years. Most slaves were black, and most served for their entire lives. Intermarriage between slaves and white servants, considered risky for the slave owner, was prohibited. The few free Negroes living in those early years had their liberties severely restricted, a practice sanctioned by the law. If it had not been for such laws, white Europeans immigrating to the United States would not have become so biased against blacks.

1. Which of the following is an illogical conclusion that is contained in the passage?

   (1) Laws restricting the freedoms of the non-slave blacks in the early years of this country fostered the bias against them by the European immigrants.
   (2) Some American blacks can claim ancestry on the continent for many more generations than many American whites can.
   (3) Slavery and indentured servitude were both reactions to an economic need in the early development of the United States.
   (4) The most glaring difference between indentured servants and slaves is that the servants usually served for just four or five years, whereas slaves served for a lifetime.
   (5) Intermarriage between blacks and whites was made illegal in the early years of the country because of a fear that slaves might run away and claim their freedom.

2. Why is the conclusion at the end of the passage illogical?

   Because it
   (1) is the opposite of what is shown to be true
   (2) compares events of different generations
   (3) is not based on supporting facts
   (4) is unrelated to the topic being developed
   (5) is true for only a limited number of cases

Answers are on page 401.

PART II

Themes in Social Studies

Chapter 5

Time, Continuity, and Change

History is the great story of humanity that unfolds over time. This story can be understood as the interaction of continuity and change. New events are affected by conditions that have continued from the past. In turn, unfolding events will affect the future. Geography, government, and economics can provide lenses to broaden and illuminate this story.

On the GED Social Studies Test, you will be tested on many aspects of world and U.S. history. You will also need to work with concepts from geography, government and civics, and economics. In the chapters in this section, you will work with elements from all of these areas, and will be asked to respond to questions that use all of the reading and reasoning skills presented in the first four chapters of this book.

Reading Political Maps

There are many ways to look at continuity and change over time. One useful method is to look at political maps from different points in history. Look at the following maps of Europe.

EUROPE IN THE YEAR 1000

EUROPE, EARLY 14TH CENTURY

As you look at these two maps, what do you notice stayed the same?

_____

_____

What changed during that time?

_____

_____

A number of place names remained the same, such as the kingdoms of France, Denmark, Sweden, Norway, Poland, and Hungary and the Holy Roman and Byzantine empires.

Almost all the national boundaries shifted. Some place names disappeared, such as Leon, the Principality of Kiev, and the Caliphate of Cordoba. New countries appeared such as Lithuania and the kingdoms of Portugal and Naples.

GED PRACTICE

EXERCISE 1

The following questions are based on the two maps of Europe on pages xxx, plus the map of Europe in the year 2000 below.

EUROPE IN THE YEAR 2000

1. Based on the information in the maps, which of the following countries had the most stable political boundaries over the past 1,000 years?

    (1) France
    (2) Byzantine Empire
    (3) Hungary
    (4) Portugal
    (5) Spain

2. Which ethnic group had its nation moved almost entirely from its original territory to a completely new location?

    (1) English
    (2) Spanish
    (3) French
    (4) Hungarians
    (5) Bulgarians

3. What was the most important political development that affected the names of countries in Europe over the past 1,000 years?

    (1) the spread of Christianity
    (2) waves of emigration
    (3) the decline of monarchies
    (4) the Reformation
    (5) the end of the Cold War

Answers are on page 401.

Physical Changes

While political boundaries have changed frequently over time, the earth has seen physical changes as well. The following map shows Europe during the Ice Age. How was Europe physically different then than it is today?

_____

_____

THE GREAT GLACIATION

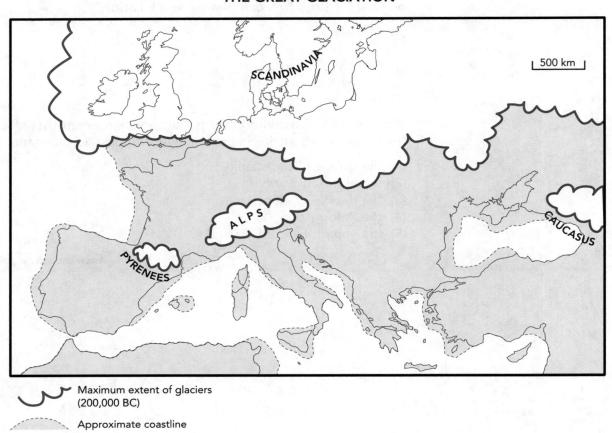

〰️ Maximum extent of glaciers
(200,000 BC)

⌒ Approximate coastline

You should have noted that glaciers covered Northern Europe and the Alps. Sea levels were also lower, so there was more dry land than there is today.

While physical changes during historical times, or the period for which written records exist, may not seem as dramatic as the changes from the Ice Age to today, many significant changes have, nevertheless, taken place, and more continue to happen. Industrialization, the population explosion, global warming, and urbanization have had and continue to have a massive impact on our planet.

EXERCISE 2

Questions 1–3 are based on the following passage.

The Aral [Sea] began to recede in the early 1960s after the Union of Soviet Socialist Republics (USSR)—which included Kazakhstan and Uzbekistan—initiated a drive to expand agriculture, particularly cotton crops, in the area. The dry climate made it necessary to divert water from the Amu Darya and Syr Darya [rivers], and their inflow to the Aral decreased accordingly. During the 1980s inflow was only 10 percent of what it had been in the 1950s. The loss of inflow, combined with evaporation and little rainfall, caused the shoreline to recede, and in 1987 the sea's southern and northern portions separated, although they are still connected at times by a channel.

Severe and wide-ranging impacts on the environment, economy, and human population have accompanied the drying of the Aral Sea. A region of 400,000 sq km (154,441 sq mi) around the sea, where nearly 4 million people live, has been officially recognized as an ecological disaster zone. The deltas of the Amu Darya and Syr Darya have been severely degraded by desertification (the process of becoming desert), accompanied by simplification of native plant and animal communities due to the extinction of some species. Lakes and wetlands in the deltas have been reduced by 85 percent. This reduction, coupled with increasing pollution of remaining water bodies (primarily from irrigation runoff containing fertilizers, pesticides, and herbicides), has caused the number of nesting bird species in the Syr Darya delta to fall from 173 to 38. Irrigated agriculture in the deltas has suffered from a limited water supply due to greatly reduced river flow and the increased salinity of available water. Commercial fishing ceased in the early 1980s as native species, unable to survive in the increased salinity, disappeared. Shipping also stopped as the sea retreated many kilometers from . . . major ports.

—Philip P. Micklin, Microsoft Encarta '99

1. According to the passage, what has been the major cause of the catastrophe at the Aral Sea?

   (1) the incompetence of government officials
   (2) water diverted for agricultural irrigation
   (3) the collapse of commercial fishing
   (4) desertification of the river deltas
   (5) decrease in the amount of rainfall

2. In the dry southwestern United States, water from the Colorado River has been diverted to such an extent that it usually no longer reaches the Gulf of California. Given the information in the passage on the Aral Sea, what important impact of the water diversion should be monitored?

   (1) the amount of new population growth made possible by the diversion
   (2) the amount of new agricultural production made possible by the diversion
   (3) the amount of protests from environmentalists who oppose development
   (4) the degradation of the Gulf of California due to lack of fresh water flow
   (5) the number of species found in the Grand Canyon of the Colorado River

3. What is the main idea of this passage?

   (1) Diverting water for irrigation created an ecological catastrophe at the Aral Sea.
   (2) Large irrigation projects often have unintended negative consequences.
   (3) The Aral Sea, shrinking since the 1960s, is now divided into two sections.
   (4) The Aral Sea has been officially recognized as an ecological disaster zone.
   (5) A major international effort will be needed to save and restore the Aral Sea.

Questions 4 and 5 are based on the following passage.

Once that landscape stretched from Ohio to eastern Kansas and the Dakotas, and from Texas into Canada, a great triangle beneath an empty sky. Once it was wild land; try to imagine it as it must have been.

There were wild flowers, hundreds of kinds of wild flowers, blooming in their place and season. There were elk and shaggy bison, and prairie chickens booming out their mating call on brisk April mornings. Great trees hugged the stream channels and floated like islands on distant horizons. And there was grass in abundance, dozens of kinds of grass. Eight feet tall on favored sites, belt high in most places, it was green and bronze and wine and gold, rippling and shining in the sunlight.

It's almost gone now, that shining, swirling landscape. Other prairie survives, characterized by shorter grasses, on the dry, thinly populated Great Plains to the west. But the tallgrass prairie, the king of prairies, became the corn belt. Became Chicago, became Des Moines, became home for 25 million people. As the homesteaders' steel plows sliced through its matted roots, it all but vanished in a ringing, tearing sound.

—"The Tallgrass Prairie," Microsoft Encarta Encyclopedia '99

4. Which of the following would the writer of this passage most likely support?

(1) the establishment of a tallgrass prairie national park
(2) price supports for corn and other grains to help family farmers
(3) legislation for preserving the farms of the Midwest
(4) anti-growth legislation to limit the growth of Des Moines
(5) an urban revitalization program to help growth in Chicago

5. Which of the following did *not* contribute to the loss of the tallgrass prairie?

(1) the spread of large farms specialized for growing grains
(2) the building of numerous railroads across the region
(3) the growth of cities such as Des Moines and Chicago
(4) increased soil erosion due to overexploited farmland
(5) migration of thousands of homesteaders to the region

Answers are on page 401.

Evolution of Language and Culture

The physical and political landscapes are not the only places where the interplay of continuity and change can be observed. Culture also evolves through time, keeping connections to the past while constantly changing.

A crucial component of a culture is the language of its people. Many languages are spoken throughout the world. It seems that many of these languages are related, and there is strong evidence that many languages have common origins.

One of the largest language families is the Indo-European language family. Look at the following chart that shows the different Indo-European words for mother. All of the languages listed use the Latin alphabet except Greek, which has its own alphabet. Given the information in the chart, what sound would you expect the Greek word for mother to start with?

The word *mother* in various European languages

Sanskrit	*matar*	French	*mère*
Latin	*mater*	Italian	*madre*
Armenian	*magr*	Spanish	*madre*
Irish	*moder*	Greek	μητηϑ
German	*Mutter*		

It is reasonable to expect the initial sound for the Greek word for mother to be /m/.

GED PRACTICE

EXERCISE 3

Questions 1 and 2 are based on the following passage.

With more than 4,000 years of recorded history, China is one of the few existing countries that also flourished economically and culturally in the earliest stages of world civilization. Indeed, despite the political and social upheavals that frequently have ravaged the country, China is unique among nations in its longevity and resilience as a discrete politico-cultural unit. Much of China's cultural development has been accomplished with relatively little outside influence, the introduction of Buddhism from India constituting a major exception. Even when the country was penetrated by such "barbarian" peoples as the Manchus, these groups soon became largely absorbed into the fabric of Han Chinese culture.

This relative isolation from the outside world made possible over the centuries the flowering and refinement of the Chinese culture, but it also left China ill prepared to cope with that world when, from the mid-19th century, it was confronted by technologically superior foreign nations. There followed a century of decline and decrepitude, as China found itself relatively helpless in the face of a foreign onslaught. The trauma of this external challenge became the catalyst for a revolution that began in the early 20th century against the old regime and culminated in the establishment of a Communist government in 1949. This event reshaped global political geography, and China has since come to rank among the most influential countries in the world.

Central to China's long-enduring identity as a unitary country is the province, or *sheng* ("secretariat"). The provinces are traceable in their current form to the T'ang dynasty (A.D. 618–907). Over the centuries, provinces gained in importance as centres of political and economic authority and increasingly became the focus of regional identification and loyalty. Provincial power reached its peak in the first two decades of the 20th century, but since the establishment of Communist rule in China this power has been curtailed by a strong central leadership in Peking. Nonetheless, while the Chinese state has remained unitary in form, the vast size and population of China's provinces—which are comparable to large and midsize nations—dictate their continuing importance as a level of subnational administration.

—Excerpted from Encyclopedia Britannica On-line

1. Which of the following conclusions *cannot* be drawn from the passage?

   (1) Barbarians were not a catalyst for change.
   (2) Buddhism had a strong influence on Chinese culture.
   (3) Chinese painting changed little until the mid 19th century.
   (4) Communism led to changes in the power structure.
   (5) Provinces continue to be important in China.

2. Based on the passage, what is a Chinese *sheng* most similar to?

   (1) a European nation-state
   (2) a state of the United States
   (3) a country created from the former Soviet Union
   (4) a major American metropolitan area
   (5) a county of an American state

Answers are on page 401.

The Growth of Urbanization

The archeological record shows that the first towns arose in the Middle East about 10,000 years ago. Since then, urban areas have gone through periods of growth and decline. However, since the Industrial Revolution began over 200 years ago, urban areas around the world have experienced unprecedented growth.

Look at the following table, which shows the growth and decline of certain cities around the world over the past 1,000 years.

GED PRACTICE

EXERCISE 4

The following questions are based on this table of the largest cities in the world in 900, 1600, 1700, 1800, 1900, and 2000.

900			1600		
City	**Continent**	**Population**	**City**	**Continent**	**Population**
Baghdad	Asia	900,000	Beijing	Asia	706,000
Changan (modern-day Xian)	Asia	750,000	Constantinople (modern-day Istanbul)	Asia	700,000
Constantinople (modern-day Istanbul)	Asia	300,000	Agra	Asia	500,000
Kyoto	Asia	225,000	Cairo	Africa	400,000
Hangchow (modern-day Hangzhow)	Asia	220,000	Osaka	Asia	400,000
1700			**1800**		
Constantinople (modern-day Istanbul)	Asia	700,000	Beijing	Asia	1,100,000
Beijing	Asia	700,000	London	Europe	861,000
Isfahan (modern-day Esfahan)	Asia	600,000	Canton (modern-day Guangzhow)	Asia	800,000
London	Europe	550,000	Constantinople (modern-day Istanbul)	Asia	570,000
Paris	Europe	530,000	Paris	Europe	547,000
1900			**2000**		
London	Europe	6,480,000	Tokyo	Asia	28,000,000
New York City	North America	4,242,000	New York City	North America	20,100,000
Paris	Europe	3,330,000	Mexico City	North America	18,100,000
Berlin	Europe	2,424,000	Bombay	Asia	18,000,000
Chicago	North America	1,717,000	São Paulo	South America	17,700,000

1. According to the information given in the chart, which continent was the first to experience major urbanization?

   (1) Africa
   (2) Asia
   (3) Europe
   (4) North America
   (5) South America

2. Looking at the chart, what part of the world was most favorable for urban growth in the 1800s?

   (1) tropical regions near major waterways
   (2) countries surrounding the North Atlantic
   (3) sites of the earliest civilizations
   (4) areas richest in natural resources
   (5) the Western Hemisphere

3. Changan, Hangchow, Beijing, and Canton are all cities in China. Which of the following statements about China is *not* supported by the information in the chart?

   (1) China had major cities for many centuries before the Industrial Revolution.
   (2) The nineteenth century was a difficult period of decline for China.
   (3) The centers of power and commerce in China have remained constant.
   (4) The modern city of Xian is not the commercial center its predecessor was.
   (5) When the Ming Dynasty made Beijing their capital in 1420, they encouraged its growth.

4. While there have been major cities for thousands of years, the Industrial Revolution allowed cities to reach an unprecedented size. According to the information on the chart, during which century is there the first major evidence of the impact of the Industrial Revolution?

   (1) sixteenth century
   (2) seventeenth century
   (3) eighteenth century
   (4) nineteenth century
   (5) twentieth century

5. Before the Industrial Revolution, which of the following probably contributed least to urban growth?

   (1) long-distance trade
   (2) the administration of empires
   (3) military power
   (4) religious importance
   (5) tourism

Questions 6 and 7 are based on the following graph.

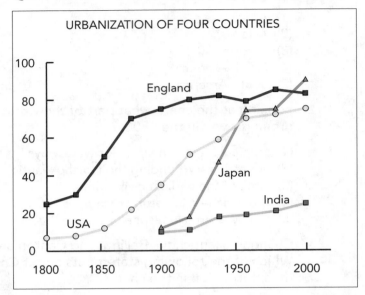

URBANIZATION OF FOUR COUNTRIES

6. Over the past 200 years, there has been a direct correlation between urbanization and industrialization. According to the evidence in the chart, which country or countries had the most rapid period of industrialization?

   (1) England
   (2) United States
   (3) Japan
   (4) India
   (5) United Kingdom and Japan

7. In order for India to approach the urbanization rates of the other countries, what changes would have to take place there?

   (1) India would have to encourage the continued health of its democracy.
   (2) India would have to resolve its dispute with Pakistan over Kashmir.
   (3) India would have to improve the terrible environmental conditions in its cities.
   (4) India would have to have rapid growth in its non-agricultural economy.
   (5) India would have to raise tariffs to protect local industry from competition.

Answers are on pages 401–402.

Implications of Growth

For many years, the dominant philosophy in the United States was that growth was good. We developed the largest economy in the world, and our citizens enjoyed the highest standard of living of any nation. Even though many Americans have been left out of the American dream, as a nation we still consume more natural resources than any other country on earth. In recent years, however, we have become aware of some negative implications of growth, such as acid rain and global warming.

The graph below shows changes in global temperature since 1880, when reliable temperature records became available worldwide. Each vertical bar represents the global average temperature for that year.

The curved line shows the overall trend. The global average temperature has risen nearly 2°F (1°C) since 1880.

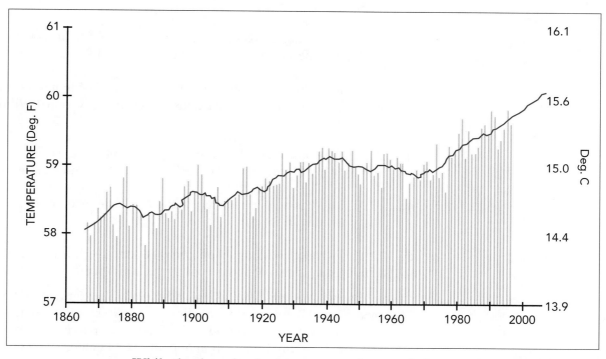

While the data clearly shows a warming trend, there are two very different hypotheses being proposed as an explanation. One hypothesis is that the warming trend is a result of human activity such as the growing use of fossil fuels and the destruction of forests over the past 200 years. Another hypothesis is that this is just a normal fluctuation in world temperatures. For each statement below, place an **H** in the blank if it supports the human activity hypothesis, or place an **F** in the blank if it supports the normal fluctuation hypothesis.

_____ In the past there have been many periods warmer than today.

_____ There has been a major increase in the use of fossil fuels during the period that temperatures have been rising.

_____ Most of the world's forests have been cut over the past 150 years.

The first statement supports the normal fluctuation hypothesis, while the other two statements support the human activity hypothesis.

Looking at all the arguments, what do you think is the correct interpretation of the data?

_____

_____

_____

_____

The debate over these two hypotheses is important because they lead to very different public policy recommendations. For each of the following recommendations, place an **H** in the blank if it is based on the human activity hypothesis, or place an **F** in the blank if it is based on the normal fluctuation hypothesis.

1. _____ Recycling needs to be encouraged since it reduces the need for energy, and therefore reduces the need for fossil fuels.

2. _____ In order to maintain our current standard of living, we need to develop new oil fields in such areas as the Arctic National Wildlife Refuge.

3. _____ We need to develop more fuel-efficient vehicles such as the hybrid vehicle, which runs on a combination of gasoline and electricity.

4. _____ There is no need to change the American way of life, which is the most desirable in the world.

5. _____ We need to maintain and protect our old-growth forests since they keep large amounts of carbon out of the atmosphere.

Statements 1, 3, and 5 are all based on the human activity hypothesis. Statements 1 and 3 are recommendations to use less energy. Statement 5 recommends a way to keep carbon out of the atmosphere. Statements 2 and 4 are based on the normal fluctuation hypothesis. Statement 2 recommends increasing our use of energy in order to maintain our standard of living. Statement 4 recommends keeping to the status quo. Both of these recommendations can be considered reasonable if human activity is not resulting in global warming, but they are dangerous recommendations if the warming is caused by human activity.

EXERCISE 5

Questions 1 and 2 are based on the following passage.

Scientists have discovered that air pollution from the burning of fossil fuels is the major cause of acid rain. Acidic deposition, or acid rain as it is commonly known, occurs when emissions of sulfur dioxide (SO_2) and oxides of nitrogen (NO_x) react in the atmosphere with water, oxygen, and oxidants to form various acidic compounds. This mixture forms a mild solution of sulfuric acid and nitric acid. Sunlight increases the rate of most of these reactions.

Electric utility plants account for about 70 percent of annual SO_2 emissions and 30 percent of NO_x emissions in the United States. Mobile sources (transportation) also contribute significantly to NO_x emissions. Overall, over 20 million tons of SO_2 and NO_x are emitted into the atmosphere each year.

Acid rain causes acidification of lakes and streams and contributes to damage of trees at high elevations (for example, red spruce trees above 2,000 feet in elevation). In addition, acid rain accelerates the decay of building materials and paints, including irreplaceable buildings, statues, and sculptures that are part of our nation's cultural heritage. Prior to falling to the earth, SO_2 and NO_x gases and their particulate matter derivatives, sulfates and nitrates, contribute to visibility degradation and impact public health.

Implementation of the Acid Rain Program under the 1990 Clean Air Act Amendments will confer significant benefits on the nation. By reducing SO_2 and NO_x, many acidified lakes and streams will improve substantially so that they can once again support fish life. Visibility will improve, allowing for increased enjoyment of scenic vistas across our country, particularly in national parks. Stress to our forests that populate the ridges of mountains from Maine to Georgia will be reduced. Deterioration of our historic buildings and monuments will be slowed. Finally, reductions in SO_2 and NO_x will reduce sulfates, nitrates, and ground level ozone (smog), leading to improvements in public health.

1. According to information given in the passage, what would be the best method of reducing the impact of acid rain?

   (1) building newer, more efficient power plants to handle increased electrical needs due to economic growth
   (2) harvesting trees at higher elevations so that fewer trees would be affected by acid rain
   (3) developing more fuel-efficient cars that would need less fuel per mile and would use less gasoline
   (4) promoting energy conservation in industry, business, and homes so fewer electrical plants are needed
   (5) expanding historical preservation efforts that can repair the damage done to buildings

2. Which of the following points in the passage is not meant to persuade the reader of the need to reduce SO_2 and No_x emissions?

   (1) Acidified lakes and streams are unable to support fish life.
   (2) Sunlight can increase the rate at which SO_2 and NO_x reacts with substances in the atmosphere to form acids.
   (3) Acid rain contributes to damage of trees at high elevations and damages lakes and streams.
   (4) Acid rain accelerates the decay of building materials and paints, damaging buildings, statues, and sculptures.
   (5) SO_2 and NO_x contribute to smog, reducing visibility and negatively impacting public health.

Questions 3 and 4 are based on the following passage.

States, territories, and tribes identify nonpoint source (NPS) pollution as the nation's leading source of surface water and ground water quality impairments. When properly managed, wetlands can help prevent NPS pollution from degrading water quality. Wetlands include swamps, marshes, fens, and bogs. Properly managed wetlands can intercept runoff and transform and store NPS pollutants like sediment, nutrients, and certain heavy metals without being degraded. In addition, wetlands vegetation can keep stream channels intact by slowing runoff and by evenly distributing the energy in runoff. Wetlands vegetation also regulates stream temperature by providing streamside shading. Some cities have started to experiment with wetlands as an effective tool to control runoff and protect urban streams.

Improper development or excessive pollutant loads can damage wetlands. The degraded wetlands can no longer provide water quality benefits and become significant sources of NPS pollution. Excessive amounts of decaying wetlands vegetation, for example, can increase biochemical oxygen demand, making habitat unsuitable for fish and other aquatic life. Degraded wetlands also release stored nutrients and other chemicals into surface water and ground water. The U.S. Environmental Protection Agency (EPA) recommends three management strategies to maintain the water quality benefits provided by wetlands: preservation, restoration, and construction of engineered systems that pretreat runoff before it reaches receiving waters and wetlands.

Healthy wetlands benefit fish, wildlife, and humans because they protect many natural resources, only one of which is clean water. Unfortunately, over half of the wetlands in the lower 48 states were lost between the late 1700s and the mid-1980s, and undisturbed wetlands still face threats from development. To help prevent NPS pollution from further degrading the nation's waters and to protect many other natural resources, wetlands protection must remain a focal point for national education campaigns, watershed protection plans, and local conservation efforts.

3. Of the following five statements from the preceding passage, which is a conclusion based on the other supporting statements?

   (1) Nonpoint source (NPS) pollution is the nation's leading source of surface water and ground water quality impairments.
   (2) Improper development or excessive pollutant loads can damage wetlands, which become sources of NPS pollution.
   (3) Excessive amounts of decaying vegetation make a habitat unsuitable for fish and other aquatic life.
   (4) Preservation, restoration, and pretreatment of runoff can maintain the water quality benefits provided by wetlands.
   (5) Healthy wetlands benefit fish, wildlife, and humans because they protect many natural resources such as clean water.

4. Which of the following is an unstated assumption in this passage?

   (1) It is the government's responsibility to protect the environment.
   (2) Protecting wetlands should be the government's top priority.
   (3) Polluters must be caught and punished by the federal government.
   (4) Protecting the environment can lead to economic growth.
   (5) A wetland can produce pollution if it is not kept healthy.

Answers are on page 402.

Violent vs. Nonviolent Change

Over the centuries, the world has changed considerably and in many different ways. There have been both violent and nonviolent changes. The agricultural revolution, which led to the beginning of growing grains for food and domesticating animals, was a nonviolent process. But the wealth created by farming became a desirable target for others, so from an early period we see evidence of violence both in the appearance of walled towns and cities and in the apparent destruction of these towns and cities.

Below are examples of major changes. In each case, describe whether the change was mostly violent or nonviolent.

1. _____ the invention of the internal combustion engine, making possible motorized vehicles such as automobiles and trucks

2. _____ the growth of ancient Assyria as a result of the conquests of its armies, the destruction of the cities of its opponents, and the forced relocation of conquered populations

3. _____ the growth of the European Union in modern times as a result of nations applying for admission and making economic reforms to qualify

4. _____ ending the institution of slavery as a result of the Union's victory in the Civil War

5. _____ ending segregation in the South through boycotts, demonstrations, and litigation

The invention of the internal combustion engine (1) and the growth of the European Union (3) are both examples of nonviolent change. While the civil rights workers sometimes encountered violent opposition, their movement to end segregation (5) used nonviolent tactics. Both the growth of ancient Assyria (2) and the end of slavery as a result of the American Civil War (4) are examples of violent change.

A radical change in a culture, society, or nation is often called a revolution. Revolutions can be violent or nonviolent, or they can have both violent and nonviolent elements.

GED PRACTICE

EXERCISE 6

Questions 1–4 are based on the following passage.

War is expensive. So, soon after the end of the French and Indian War in 1763, England needed to finance its huge war debt. As a result, the British Parliament and King George III passed the Stamp Act of 1765 and the Townshend Acts of 1767. The Stamp Act required all official documents in the colonies to bear a purchased British stamp. The Townshend Acts placed large duties on glass, lead, and tea.

By September 1774, the colonists had had enough. However, the First Continental Congress did not ask Britain for independence for the colonists; it demanded only their rights as British subjects. The purpose of the Congress was to demand representation in the Parliament so that colonists could have a say in what taxes they would have to pay. But by the time of the Second Continental Congress in May 1775, hostile encounters had already taken place between the English soldiers and the colonists.

In the battles of Lexington and Concord, British soldiers had been surprised by the diligence and unorthodox tactics of the American militia. George Washington was named commander-in-chief of the colonists' army, and he immediately began reorganizing and strengthening his troops.

On July 4, 1776, the Second Continental Congress adopted the Declaration of Independence, and thereafter the Americans fought as citizens of a sovereign nation who were expelling a foreign power, not as British rebels against their own king. This was important not only to boost their own morale but also to elicit the sympathetic support of the world for their fight.

1. What was the purpose of the First Continental Congress?

    (1) to ask the British king for the colonies' independence
    (2) to demand the colonists' rights as British citizens
    (3) to form a citizens' militia to fight the British soldiers
    (4) to name George Washington as head of the militia
    (5) to write the Declaration of Independence from Great Britain

2. When did the actual battles between the British and the colonists begin?

    (1) after George Washington was named commander-in-chief
    (2) before the Second Continental Congress was convened
    (3) after the Declaration of Independence was written
    (4) in response to the passage of the Stamp Act in Great Britain
    (5) as a result of George III becoming king of Great Britain

3. The fight of the American colonists against Great Britain can be compared to which anticolonialist event of the twentieth century?

    (1) the attempted takeover by force of Europe by Hitler
    (2) the struggle of India for its independence from Great Britain
    (3) the attack on Pearl Harbor by the Japanese in 1941
    (4) the return of the Panama Canal to the country of Panama
    (5) the growth of communism in Latin America

4. What was the purpose of the Stamp Act of 1765 and the Townshend Acts of 1767?

    (1) to stop the effectiveness of the unorthodox tactics of the American militia
    (2) to expel hostile foreign powers from all English-controlled territories
    (3) to supply needed money to Great Britain after the French and Indian War
    (4) to stop all hostile encounters between colonists and British soldiers
    (5) to give North American colonists representation in the British Parliament

Questions 5 and 6 refer to the passage and maps below.

The United States emerged from the Civil War only to experience another major upheaval in the nation's way of life. America and the rest of the Western world entered an industrial revolution in which the economy relied less on human and animal power and more on machinery to produce goods.

As industries were founded, cities grew up around them. Mechanization of farming caused some people to lose their jobs and move from farm to town. However, more commonly, the potential to earn more money and obtain modern conveniences lured workers to the cities. Jobs in industry paid much higher wages than farm work, and these wages bought luxuries never before dreamed of on the farm.

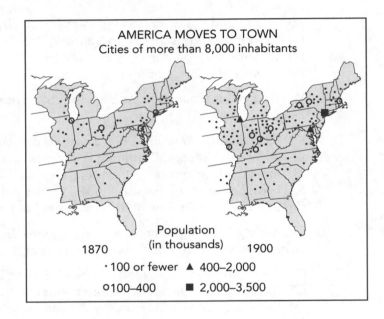

AMERICA MOVES TO TOWN
Cities of more than 8,000 inhabitants

1870   1900

Population
(in thousands)

· 100 or fewer   ▲ 400–2,000
○ 100–400   ■ 2,000–3,500

5. With regard to the period 1870–1900, which of the following statements is supported by the data provided in the passage and the maps?

    (1) The United States experienced the loss of much of its prime farming areas.
    (2) There was more industry in the northern states than in the southern states.
    (3) There was a great influx of immigrants to the northeastern United States.
    (4) There was a population loss in many rural areas in both the north and south.
    (5) There was a bigger move to the South than in any other direction.

Chapter 5 ~ *Time, Continuity, and Change* **139**

6. From the maps, where does it appear that industries and the big cities that grew up around them were usually established?

    (1) in the middle of the country
    (2) near national boundaries
    (3) on mountains and hills
    (4) near bodies of water
    (5) in farming areas

Question 7 is based on the all the passages and maps in the exercise.

7. According to the evidence in the passages and maps, what was the major difference between the Revolutionary War and the Industrial Revolution?

    (1) The Revolutionary War created change violently while the Industrial Revolution created change nonviolently.
    (2) The Industrial Revolution had a greater impact on the daily lives of Americans than did the Revolutionary War.
    (3) The Industrial Revolution impacted a greater part of the country than did the Revolutionary War.
    (4) While the Revolutionary War had its greatest impact on the U.S. government, the Industrial Revolution affected the economy.
    (5) While few Americans moved as a result of the Revolutionary War, many more moved as a result of the Industrial Revolution.

Answers are on page 402.

Continuity and Change in the United States

 Over the past four hundred years, there have been enormous changes in the ways Americans live. Look at the following five pictures and then match them to the appropriate descriptions and year. What helped you decide on each match?

Descriptions	Dates
An Indian Village	about 1900
Levittown, the First Planned Suburban Community	about 1800
Pearl and Maiden Streets in Albany, NY	in 2000
Tallest Residential Building in the World, Manhattan, NY	about 1600
Lower East Side of Manhattan, NY	in 1948

The first picture shows an Indian village in about 1600. The picture clearly shows Indians. From their dress, you should be able to determine that this picture dates from about 1600. The next picture shows the tallest residential building in the world in Manhattan, New York, in the year 2000. This is clearly a photo of a modern skyscraper. The next picture is of the Lower East Side of Manhattan, New York, in about 1900. This picture was taken at the peak of the eastern and southern European immigration to New York and the rest of the United States. The fourth picture shows Levittown, the first planned suburban community, in 1948. The clothes being worn by the family date the picture to the mid-twentieth century. The last picture is of Pearl and Maiden Streets in Albany, New York, in about 1800. The buildings appear to date to near the colonial period.

Despite the enormous changes evident in these pictures, each of them is distinctly American and contributes an important chapter to the American story, which is a story of continuity as well as change.

EXERCISE 7

Questions 1 and 2 are based on the following poster and passage.

Franklin Roosevelt enumerated the Four Freedoms—Freedom from Want and Fear, Freedom of Speech and Worship—in a 1941 speech to Congress. Later he stated that "The declaration of the four freedoms . . . is not a promise of a gift, which under certain conditions, the people will receive; it is a declaration of a design which the people themselves may execute." Norman Rockwell, one of America's most beloved artists, intended to donate his painted interpretations of FDR's words to the War Department, but receiving no response, offered them to the *Saturday Evening Post*, where they were published in 1942. Their immense popularity led the Office of War Information (OWI) to reproduce them as posters in 1943, and more than 2.5 million copies were ultimately printed for the war bond effort.

1. Which of the following probably did not contribute to the popularity of the *Save Freedom of Worship* poster?

   (1) the importance of freedom of worship to most Americans
   (2) the popularity of the artist, Norman Rockwell
   (3) Rockwell's ability to capture the essence of the message
   (4) its potential resale value as a collectible
   (5) patriotic enthusiasm for the war effort

2. With the Constitution guaranteeing the separation of church and state, why might Roosevelt have included Freedom of Worship as one of the Four Freedoms?

   (1) He was concerned that Americans were losing their faith in God.
   (2) He decided it was time to end the separation of church and state.
   (3) The Nazis threatened the American guarantee of freedom of religion.
   (4) He wanted churches and religious leaders to support the war effort.
   (5) He was influenced by Rockwell's inspirational poster to include it.

Questions 3 and 4 are based on the following passage.

Between the American Revolution and the Civil War, so many elements of American society were changing—the growth of population, the movement westward, the development of the factory system, expansion of political rights for white men, educational growth to match the new economic needs—that changes were bound to take place in the situation of women. In preindustrial America, the practical need for women in a frontier society had produced some measure of equality; women worked at important jobs—publishing newspapers, managing tanneries, keeping taverns, engaging in skilled work. In certain professions, like midwifery, they had a monopoly. Nancy Cott tells of a grandmother, Martha Moore Ballard, on a farm in Maine in 1795, who "baked and brewed, pickled and preserved, spun and sewed, made soap and dipped candles" and who, in 25 years as a midwife, delivered more than a thousand babies. Since education took place inside the family, women had a special role there.

There was complex movement in different directions. Now, women were being pulled out of the house and into industrial life, while at the same time there was pressure for women to stay home where they were more easily controlled. The outside world, breaking into the solid cubicle of the home, created fears and tensions in the dominant male world, and brought forth ideological controls to replace the loosening family controls: the idea of "the woman's place," promulgated by men, was accepted by many women.

As the economy developed, men dominated as mechanics and tradesmen, and aggressiveness became more and more defined as a male trait. Women, perhaps precisely because more of them were moving into the dangerous world outside, were told to be passive. Clothing styles developed—for the rich and middle-class of course, but, as always, there was the intimidation of style even for the poor—in which the weight of women's clothes, corsets, and petticoats, emphasized female separation from the world of activity.

3. Given the information in the article, what was the most important source of the Women's Rights movement in the United States in the nineteenth century?

    (1) the important role women played in preindustrial America
    (2) the pulling of women into important economic roles outside the home
    (3) the expansion of political rights and economic opportunities for white males
    (4) the development of new clothing such as corsets and petticoats
    (5) the educational and economic needs created by the Industrial Revolution

4. In 1851, Amelia Bloomer suggested that women wear a kind of short skirt and pants that became known as bloomers. Her proposal and the adoption of bloomers by many feminist American women supports which assertion in the passage?

   (1) As the economy developed, aggressiveness became defined as a male trait.
   (2) With so many elements of America changing, clothing changed as well.
   (3) With so many other changes happening, the status of women had to change.
   (4) Women had a monopoly in certain professions such as midwifery.
   (5) Women's clothing emphasized female separation from the world of activity.

Answers are on page 403.

Continuity and Change in the United States Constitution

As the world's leading industrial country, the United States has long prided itself on being the nation of change. Many innovations started in the United States have swept the world. Yet the United States is also distinguished by examples of continuity. None has been as significant to the world as the continuity of the government of the United States. The cornerstone of that continuity and the foundation of our government is the Constitution of the United States.

The United States Constitution, along with the Declaration of Independence, is considered one of the two most important documents in American history. The Constitution is the basis of our laws. Though it was written over two hundred years ago, it has had only 27 changes, or amendments, added to it, and ten of those changes were added right away and became known as the Bill of Rights.

While other nations have constitutions, none is as old as the United States Constitution. Article I of the Constitution focuses on the legislative powers of the Congress. Look at the following excerpts from Section 8 of Article 1 of the Constitution, and think about how well each of them has stood the test of time. Then in the blank following each excerpt, describe how you think the importance of the excerpt has changed over time.

Section 8. The Congress shall have power:

paragraph 2: To borrow Money on the credit of the United States.

_____

_____

paragraph 8: To promote the Progress of Science and useful Arts, by securing for limited Times to Authors and Inventors the exclusive Right to their respective Writings and Discoveries;

_____

_____

paragraph 12: To raise and Support Armies, but no Appropriation of Money to that Use shall be for a longer Term than two years;

_____

_____

paragraph 15: To provide for calling forth the Militia to execute the Laws of the Union, suppress Insurrections and repel Invasions;

_____

_____

paragraph 18: To make all Laws which shall be necessary and proper for carrying into Execution the foregoing Powers, and all other Powers vested by this Constitution in the Government of the United States, or in any Department or Officer thereof.

_____

_____

For paragraph 2, you could have written that throughout our history, it has been important for Congress to be able to borrow money for the United States. For paragraph 8, you could have written that this paragraph is much more important today. In 1787, the United States was a new and small nation, and most authors and inventors were from Europe. Today, the United States is the world center for authors and inventors. For paragraph 12, you could have written that instead of the part-time army envisaged in the Constitution, we now have the most powerful permanent army on earth. For paragraph 15, you could have written that the need to suppress insurrections or repel invasions has turned out to be much less than envisaged in the Constitution. For paragraph 18, you could have written that this was one of the most visionary sections of the Constitution. It gave Congress the power to pass laws in areas not foreseen by the writers of the Constitution.

EXERCISE 8

The questions in this exercise are all based on Section 8 of Article 1 of the Constitution.

1. Paragraph 1 of Section 8 of the Constitution states that the Congress shall have the power: To lay and collect Taxes, Duties, Imposts and Excises, to pay the Debts and provide for the common Defence and general Welfare of the United States; but all duties, imposts and excises shall be uniform throughout the United States.

   In this paragraph, what is the most likely meaning of *impost*?

   (1) a tax
   (2) a loan
   (3) an obligation
   (4) a seizure
   (5) a building

2. Paragraph 11 of Section 8 of the Constitution states that the Congress shall have the power: To declare War, grant Letters of Marque and Reprisal, and make Rules concerning captures on Land and Water.

   A Letter of Marque is a license granted to a private person to fit out an armed ship to plunder the enemy. Even though Letters of Marque have not been issued in many years, the right of Congress to grant them is still in the Constitution. What is the best explanation for not amending the Constitution to remove the Letters of Marque?

   (1) A situation might arise where it is either necessary or convenient to hire a private individual to attack an enemy of the United States.
   (2) There would be a lot of opposition to removing a section of the Constitution that has never before been challenged.
   (3) If this paragraph were revoked, Congress would no longer have the authority to declare war.
   (4) The amendment process is far too difficult to be used just to remove an anachronism that does no harm.
   (5) It would show disrespect to the Congress to amend the Constitution to remove one of their powers.

3. Paragraph 17 of Section 8 of the Constitution states that the Congress shall have the power: To exercise exclusive Legislation in all Cases whatsoever, over such District (not exceeding ten Miles square) as may, by Session of particular States, and the Acceptance of Congress, become the Seat of the Government of the United States, and to exercise like Authority over all Places purchased by the Consent of the Legislature of the State in which the Same shall be, for the erection of Forts, Magazines, Arsenals, dock-Yards and other needful Buildings.

   What is the best explanation for the omission of air bases from the list of "needful buildings" in paragraph 17?

   (1) States were reluctant to give up the large amount of land needed.
   (2) Air bases are under the control of the individual states, not the federal government.
   (3) The invention of the airplane was over 100 years in the future.
   (4) It was an oversight that should have been caught and corrected.
   (5) The air force was so small that it didn't need its own bases.

Questions 4 and 5 are based on the following excerpts from Section 8 of the U.S. Constitution.

Section 8. The Congress shall have power:

paragraph 3: To regulate Commerce with Foreign Nations, and among the several States, and with the Indian Tribes;

paragraph 5: To coin Money, regulate the Value thereof, and of foreign Coin, and fix the Standard of Weights and Measures;

paragraph 8: To promote the Progress of Science and useful Arts, by securing for limited Times to Authors and Inventors the exclusive Right to their respective Writings and Discoveries;

paragraph 10: To define and punish Piracies and Felonies committed on the high Seas, and Offenses against the Law of Nations;

paragraph 18: To make all Laws which shall be necessary and proper for carrying into Execution the foregoing Powers, and all other Powers vested by this Constitution in the Government of the United States, or in any Department or Officer thereof.

4. Which paragraph of Section 8 gives Congress the authority to regulate the Internet?

   (1) paragraph 3
   (2) paragraph 5
   (3) paragraph 8
   (4) paragraph 10
   (5) paragraph 18

5. Which paragraph of Section 8 gives Congress the authority to approve action against Serbia when it was committing massive human rights abuses against Albanians in the province of Kosovo?

   (1) paragraph 3
   (2) paragraph 5
   (3) paragraph 8
   (4) paragraph 10
   (5) paragraph 18

Answers are on page 403.

Continuity and Change in American Culture

Whenever there has been a major change in American culture, there have been those who were very troubled by that change while other Americans embraced it. In the following passage we can see the opinion of one writer of the Jazz Age, the period also known as the Roaring Twenties. The writer expresses strong opinions about the changes of this time and the reaction of America's top writers, many of whom moved to Paris and became known as the "lost generation."

A new breed of Americans is emerging in our cities. Were I not so frightened by this phenomenon, I might be amused.

Young people are throwing all caution to the wind; their only interest seems to be outdoing one another in outlandish behavior, dress, and dance. The so-called "flappers"—women whose outrageous antics exceed the men's—are the worst offenders.

"Jazz" seems to be the "music" for this younger generation, and it certainly expresses a disdain for American conventions. It is sensuous, spontaneous, and startling. Some are blaming it for an increase in sexual promiscuity, an increase in divorce rates, and a breakup of families.

In reaction to this obvious breakdown in the American moral fabric, our best writers are retreating to Paris to escape their social responsibility for decrying this ugly aspect of American life. As if the Jazz Age's scornful sneering at American ideals were not enough, we are being deprived of our most imaginative minds when we need them the most.

Place a check next to each of the following statements that reflects assumptions by the writer of the piece.

1. _____ The "lost generation" could have reversed the negative effects of the Jazz Age if it had chosen to do so.

2. _____ Its art was more important to the "lost generation" than concern about its country's moral climate.

3. _____ When young artists and writers flocked to Paris, they benefited American society.

4. _____ Young people's striving for individuality and self-expression is a positive sign for our society.

5. _____ Writers have a social responsibility that outweighs their responsibility to themselves as creative artists.

The statements that reflect assumptions by this writer are: (1), (2), and (5). Choice (3) is not an assumption by the writer because the writer felt that American society was hurt by its young artists and writers flocking to Paris. Choice (4) is the opposite of the writer's belief that young people's striving for individuality and self-expression represented a breakdown in America's moral fabric.

While doing the following exercise, think about the balance of continuity and change that keeps us linked to the past while allowing us to move forward.

GED PRACTICE

EXERCISE 9

Questions 1 and 2 are based on the following passage.

"It is clear enough that the Civil War was a watershed experience for America. . . . To understand that part of our past we need to understand the present, because today we are grappling with the commitment that was made for us a century ago. The ultimate meaning of that war depends on what we do now. We are still involved in it. When we move to make a living reality out of the great ideal of the equality of all Americans; when we take our stand anywhere in the world for freedom, and for just dealing between all races and conditions of man; when we work for an enduring unity among human beings, whether at home or abroad—when we do any of these things we are simply trying to meet the obligation that was laid upon us a century ago at a price higher than any other price we ever paid."

—Bruce Catton, Civil War historian

1. Based on the quote, it is likely that Bruce Catton would support the actions of which of the following groups?

(1) the Ku Klux Klan of the fifties
(2) the civil rights workers of the sixties
(3) the anti-ERA demonstrators of the seventies
(4) the Vietnam War protestors of the seventies
(5) the anti-abortion activists of the eighties

2. Based on the quote, which of the following expresses Bruce Catton's opinion?

   (1) the Civil War was the most important event in U.S. history, so it deserves to be written about
   (2) the Civil War experience obligates us to promote freedom throughout the world
   (3) the cost of the Civil War in lives and money was too high, and should not be repeated
   (4) the Civil War could and should have been avoided if the leaders had adhered to the rule of law
   (5) writing about the Civil War is his obligation, so that people can learn about it

 Questions 3 and 4 are based on the following passage.

Those captured from Africa were not people without history and culture. They were mothers and fathers, sons and daughters, and descendants of ancestors; they were religious specialists and supplicants, chiefs and commoners, cooks, musicians, metalworkers, scribes, farmers, and [entertainers]; they belonged to states, clans, lineages, age grades, men's and women's associations, artisan guilds, and secret societies. Their memories of how life should be lived, of womanhood and manhood, of beauty and aesthetics, of worship and spirituality were not annihilated by the Middle Passage. But what they could do with these memories was very much constrained by the conditions in which they found themselves—the racial and class structure of enslavement. To paraphrase a well-known observation, African Americans created themselves, but not just as they pleased, not under circumstances chosen by themselves, but under circumstances directly encountered, given, and transmitted from the past. It was in the context of their African history and the prevailing social and economic relationships that African Americans created culture, religion, family, art forms, political institutions, and social and political theory.

—Excerpted from *Let Nobody Turn Us Around Voices of Resistance, Reform, and Renewal*, ed. by Manning Marable and Leith Mullings

3. What is the main idea of this passage?

   (1) African Americans had their African heritage and cultural memories destroyed by slavery.
   (2) African Americans are a product of their African heritage shaped by the oppression of slavery.
   (3) African American culture emerged unscathed from the oppressive period of slavery.
   (4) African Americans have been able to break with their past and create a new culture, institutions, and art forms.
   (5) Current African American culture is rooted in Africa with little contributed by the American experience.

4. Which of the following were the Africans captured as slaves not constrained by?

   (1) circumstances they did not choose
   (2) their pre-existing roles
   (3) the racial structure of enslavement
   (4) prevailing economic conditions
   (5) the class structure in America

Questions 5 and 6 are based on the following two graphics.

5. Long-distance travel has been a central part of the American experience ever since the ancestors of the Native Americans made their way across the land bridge from Asia during the last Ice Age. What is the most important difference between the two types of travel depicted in these illustrations?

   (1) One depicts travel by boat while the other depicts travel by airplane.
   (2) One depicts travel for survival while the other depicts travel for pleasure.
   (3) One depicts travel across the Atlantic while the other depicts travel across the Pacific.
   (4) One depicts travel in the nineteenth century while the other depicts travel in the twentieth century.
   (5) One depicts tropical conditions while the other depicts cold conditions.

6. In the 1930s planes that carried airmail began to carry passengers. What can you assume from the Pan American poster advertising its mail-carrying flying boat?

   (1) Travelers on flying boats had to cope with long flights and many stopovers.
   (2) The Clipper is the largest and most luxurious flying boat ever built.
   (3) The Hawaiians who are greeting the passengers could not afford to travel.
   (4) The Clipper could carry passengers as well as letters to exotic places.
   (5) Clippers were the largest commercial planes to fly until the arrival of jumbo jets.

Answers are on page 403.

Chapter Review

Questions 1–3 are based on the following map.

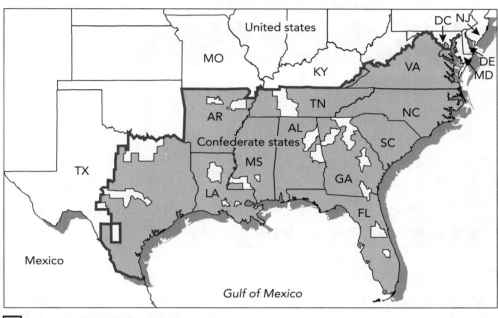

VOTE ON SECESSION IN THE SOUTH

Overwhelmingly for secession

Overwhelmingly against secession

1. Which state split in two over the issue of secession, with the western part remaining loyal to the Union?

    (1) Virginia
    (2) Texas
    (3) Kentucky
    (4) Mississippi
    (5) Maryland

2. Which state seceded from the Union despite the fact that only its eastern part voted to do so?

    (1) Virginia
    (2) Texas
    (3) Kentucky
    (4) Mississippi
    (5) Maryland

3. Which state, being a "border state," remained in the Union despite being a slave state?

    (1) Texas
    (2) Virginia
    (3) Missouri
    (4) New Jersey
    (5) Tennessee

Question 4 is based on the following table.

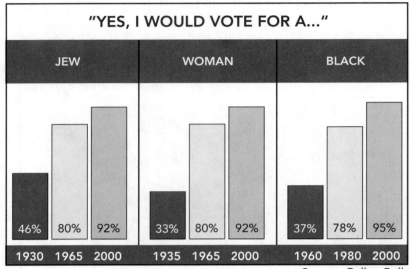

"YES, I WOULD VOTE FOR A..."

JEW			WOMAN			BLACK		
46%	80%	92%	33%	80%	92%	37%	78%	95%
1930	1965	2000	1935	1965	2000	1960	1980	2000

Source: Gallup Polls

4. In the elections of 2000, Al Gore's running mate, Joe Lieberman, was the first Jewish person to run for President or Vice-President from a major party. When Lieberman was first chosen to the ticket, Gore's standing in the polls increased. On election day, the Gore-Lieberman ticket won the most votes, even though they eventually did not win the election. What do these events say about the validity of the 70 years of Gallup Polls?

(1) The votes for Gore-Lieberman confirmed the finding that most Americans in 2000 would vote for a Jewish candidate.

(2) One piece of information, such as the votes given to Gore-Lieberman, is insufficient to have any bearing on the validity of the findings.

(3) The fact that the Gore-Lieberman ticket lost the election is proof that the Gallup polls are invalid.

(4) Even though the Gore-Lieberman ticket had the most votes, it was only 49%, not 92%.

(5) Since there was no black or woman candidate in 2000, there was no way to confirm all the Gallup Poll's findings.

Questions 5 and 6 are based on the following passage.

When most people think of the impact of technology on globalization, they think of computers and telephones. Arguably, much more mundane inventions have had even greater effects: Few things have done more to allow people to escape from the tyranny of place, for example, than the air conditioner. Although the first air-conditioned home was built by a Minneapolis millionaire in 1914, the gadget did not begin to have a real effect on society till after the Second World War. In the United States, several people have claimed that air-conditioning had as much impact on integration in the South as the civil rights movement did. As history professor Raymond Arsenault has put it, "General Electric has proved a more devastating invader than General Sherman."

And what is true for Savannah is also true for São Paulo, Seville, and Shanghai. "Historically, advanced civilizations have flourished in the cooler climates," argues Lee Kwan Yew, Singapore's senior minister. "Now lifestyles have become comparable to those in temperate zones and civilization in the tropical zones need no longer lag behind." Air-conditioning is the reason why offices and hotel rooms—those two staples of business life—feel pretty much the same everywhere. Meanwhile, air-conditioning also paved the way for the much derided theater of placelessness, the shopping mall. Stand in Pacific Place in Hong Kong or the Metrocentre at Gatehead, and it is not just the names of the shops—Benetton, The Body Shop—that are the same, but also that cool, dry, slightly lifeless atmosphere.

—Excerpted from *A Future Perfect: The Challenge and Hidden Promise of Globalization* by Micklethwait & Woolridge

5. Many of the oldest and largest cities of the ancient world were in hot regions. How best could the theory of the importance of air-conditioning be modified to take that fact into consideration?

   (1) Air-conditioning made modern industrial and commercial life possible in the tropical zones.
   (2) Even though it hasn't been discovered yet, it is likely that air-conditioning existed in the ancient world.
   (3) Air-conditioning has allowed tropical cities to develop new types of shopping malls.
   (4) The impact of air-conditioning on the development of tropical areas has been greatly overestimated.
   (5) Hotels could not survive in tropical areas before the development of air-conditioning.

6. How might the United States be different today if air-conditioning had not been invented?

   (1) The South and West might still be underdeveloped.
   (2) Vacation patterns would be very different.
   (3) Large superstores would never have developed.
   (4) The Interstate Highway system might never have been built.
   (5) The development of computers would have been delayed.

Questions 7 and 8 are based on the following passage.

It comes down to who is doing the telling. In North America, native peoples have made some progress challenging inaccurate histories about themselves. But in the Caribbean, the Tainos are, at least according to the official history books, extinct.

Thousands of history books carry the assertion. Millions of references to these books have been made. Meantime, people like myself noticed that my *abuelo*, or grandfather, Juan T. Morales from Puerto Rico, looked "Indian" and so did his sisters, my *tias*, or aunts, who were all born in this century. And then there was the matter of the many Indian-looking people of Puerto Rican descent on the island and up here in North America. Many also mention the Indian ways in the farming communities and the belief system known as *Espiritismo* or Spiritism. Then, too, in the mountains of eastern Cuba, substantial documentation speaks of small communities of the Taino and other Indians and *mestizaje*, or mixed-blooded peoples.

How could this be? Well, I had already learned about lies told in other cultural and ethnic histories, so I assumed the full story had yet to be told. My own Taino blood became a sort of open secret—something I didn't mention to many people. Then, I started hearing about Tainos in Manhattan. They were getting together, demonstrating old ways and telling their own stories within the last few years. I, like many others, began to feel that it was time to reclaim the truth about our heritage. We call our effort the Taino Restoration, and it will be a long process.

—Excerpted from "Taino Restoration" by Rick Kearns, *Native Peoples Magazine*

7. Major historians have long claimed that the Spanish wiped out the native peoples of the Caribbean, the Caribs and Taino, in the sixteenth century. Yet the writer claims not only that the Taino survived, but that he is one of their descendants. When trying to evaluate the validity of his claim, which of the following would be most helpful?

   (1) looking for Taino archaeological artifacts in Puerto Rico and Cuba
   (2) studying surviving historical records of the Caribbean region from the 16th century
   (3) visiting isolated villages in Puerto Rico and Cuba
   (4) comparing Carib and Taino customs with modern Puerto Rican and Cuban customs
   (5) studying physical characteristics and cultural traditions of those claiming Taino descent

8. What would be a reasonable activity to pursue based on the information given in this passage?

   (1) working to create an independent Taino nation
   (2) looking for descendants of other ancient ethnic groups
   (3) removing Spanish descendents from Taino lands
   (4) banning authors who declared the Taino extinct
   (5) replacing all history textbooks that contain inaccurate information

Answers are on page 404.

Chapter 6

Places and People

In 1977 the U.S. spacecraft *Voyager 1* traveled to the outer solar system and sent back pictures of Earth. It was the first time that human beings had had the chance to view our planet as a whole. We had, of course, some idea of what it would look like, but actually seeing it offered many a new perspective. There it was, a mere dot amidst the vastness of the universe, a tiny but perfect blue-green marble. While some have called this vision "beautiful," even "breath-taking," many others, by now, take it for granted. But the one point on which everyone agrees is that it is, indeed, home.

This home is a space within space, that can be identified by locations, shapes, and arrangements, and through distance, directions, and patterns. It is a physical object that human beings have learned how to measure and describe for the purpose of understanding better our own experience on it. Social Studies, most specifically within the field of *geography*, regards the world as a human environment, where people and places interact and impact one another. In this section we will explore this environment and those interactions by considering the following:

- regional organization
- physical systems and how human actions affect them
- human systems and their relationship to environments
- places made by humans

First, however, let's further accustom ourselves to the spatial viewpoint. We can begin by looking at maps. Oceans, seas, and seven continents comprise our planet. On a map these bodies are identified within *hemispheres*. In Chapter 4 on Evaluation Skills, you became familiar with some of the different types of maps. Below is an example of a world map. View A displays the *latitudinal* lines that measure location in the Northern and Southern hemispheres. (Note that the equator serves as the dividing line and is labeled 0°.) In View B you can observe the *longitudinal* lines that measure location east and west of the prime meridian (0°). The lines of longitude and latitude cross each other to form a grid. To locate a particular place on the globe, you identify its point of longitudinal and latitudinal intersection on the grid. In View C, for example, you can pinpoint the country of Spain when you are told that it is located at approximately 40° north latitude and 0° longitude.

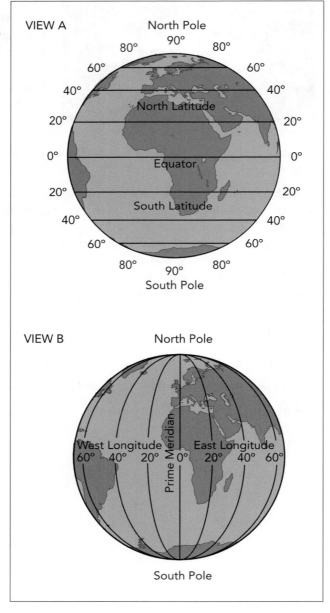

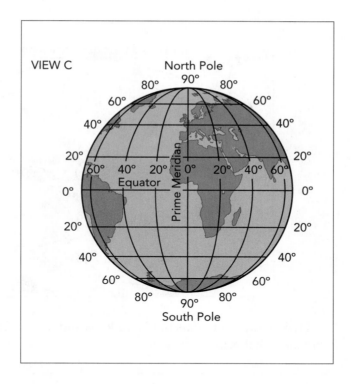

VIEW C

Looking at View C, name the continent that includes the point 20° south and 60° west. _____

You should have written South America. The point where the 20° south line of latitude meets the 60° west line of longitude is in South America.

Both the maps you have just used and the photo on page 157 enhance our current understanding of the world and have been made possible by technological advancements. Technology has enabled us to stand back and see our world from afar and with greater accuracy. On the next page, you will see a world map that dates back to the fifth century B.C.E. At the time he drew this, Herodotus, a Greek *cartographer*, or mapmaker, considered himself to be well-traveled and well-read. He believed he knew much about the world, but his view was limited.

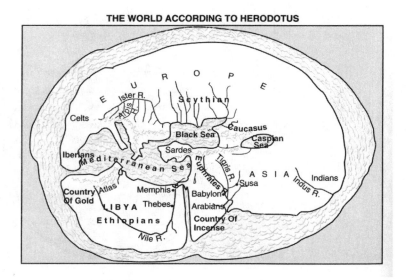

THE WORLD ACCORDING TO HERODOTUS

How many continents did Herodotus and the ancient Greeks think there were and what were their names?

_____

_____

Since the continents are written in all capital letters you can see that Herodotus and the ancient Greeks thought there were three continents: Europe, Asia, and Libya.

GED PRACTICE

EXERCISE 1

Questions 1–4 are based on Herodotus's map.

1. During Herodotus's day, explorers believed that the center of the world existed where they lived. On this basis, in which country could you infer that Herodotus lived?

    (1) Thebes
    (2) Sardes
    (3) Caucasus
    (4) Babylon
    (5) Euphrates

2. On this map there are few lines or labels in the northern and eastern areas. What is the most likely reason for this?

    (1) Herodotus had visited those areas and found few people there.
    (2) The political enemies of the Greeks lived in those areas.
    (3) The Indians and Celts who lived in those regions had their own maps.
    (4) Herodotus had not been able to travel that far north and east.
    (5) There are no rivers, mountains, or people there.

3. The ancient Greeks thought that the flat world of land and seas was completely surrounded by a mysterious, unnamed ocean. Which of the following inventions could have helped them to adjust their perspective?

   (1) telescope
   (2) printing press
   (3) compass
   (4) automobile
   (5) telephone

4. What is the continent that Herodotus called Libya called today?

   (1) Africa
   (2) Australia
   (3) Antarctica
   (4) South America
   (5) Oceania

Answers are on page 404.

While there is an obvious and significant difference between Herodotus's world map and the maps we used on pages 158 and 159 to practice location, there is no single map that can accurately depict all of earth's qualities—distance, direction, or size and shape of land and water bodies. Maps are limited because they are flat surfaces projecting a round earth. Therefore, when you look at a map, you need to be aware of which qualities are being distorted for the sake of other qualities. For a fully accurate picture of the earth, a globe may be preferable to a map. Graphs, diagrams, aerial and other photographs, and satellite-produced images can also be helpful in offering spatial information.

Regional Organization

Every location on earth has its own distinct set of characteristics that defines it as a place. Initially, places are shaped by physical processes like weather and tectonics (activity within the earth that alters the surface, like volcanoes and earthquakes) and can be identified by such natural elements as climate, land forms, soil, vegetation, and wildlife. Rain forests, plains, tundras, mountain ranges, and river valleys are all examples of environments characterized by the physical processes that developed them. The map of North America on the following page describes the continent in terms of its **physiographic,** or natural, areas. The various shades represent different kinds of terrain. What would you predict the landscape of each section to be? Clearly, mountain areas differ significantly from interior plains, which are, in turn, different from coastal plains and highlands.

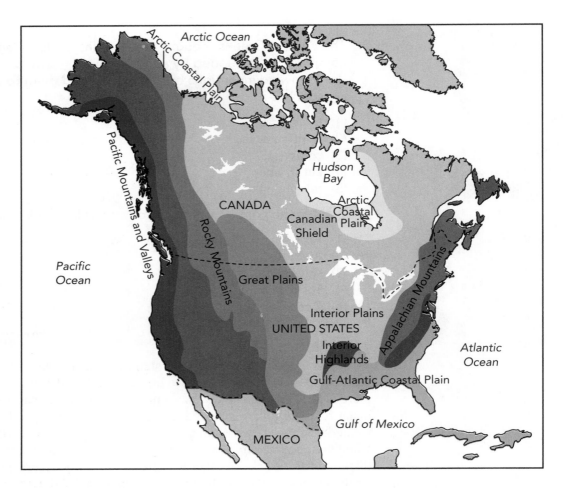

On the basis of their unique physiographic features, each section in the map above may be referred to as a **region.** A region can be any area with one or more common characteristics. Within a region there is a degree of similarity that distinguishes it from the surrounding areas. When we need to consider a particular topic or problem, making regional distinctions can help to focus our view.

Look at MAP A on the next page. It has also regionalized the United States and Canada, but not only according to physiography. Instead it views this part of the continent through a lens that considers a range of cultural, topographic, and economic attributes. Rather than just the natural landscape, the map and its regions ask the viewer to consider history, industry, even ways of speaking.

Compare MAP A to MAP B, a traditional political map of North America. Approximately how many states in the United States are parts of more than one of the nine "nations"? What seems strange or interesting to you as you make your comparison?

_____

_____

_____

_____

MAP A

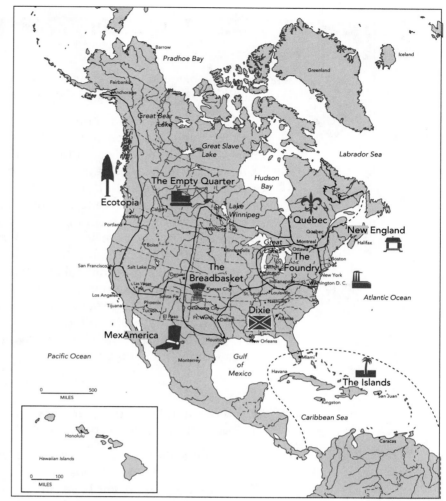

MAP B

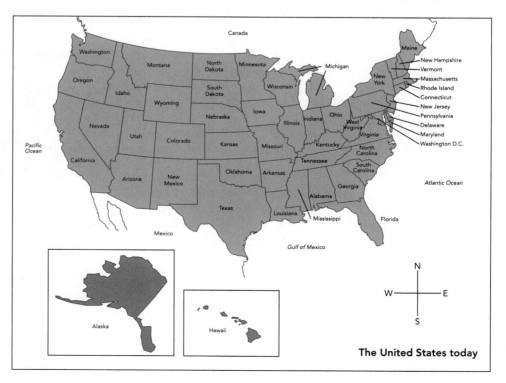

The United States today

EXERCISE 2

The paragraph below refers to the maps on the previous page. Read the paragraph and look at the maps to answer questions 1–3.

Consider . . . the way North America really works. It is Nine Nations. Each has its capital and its distinctive web of power and influence. A few are allies, but many are adversaries. Several have readily acknowledged national poets, and many have characteristic dialects and mannerisms. Some are close to being raw frontiers; others have four centuries of history. Each has a peculiar economy; each commands a certain emotional allegiance from its citizens. These nations look different, feel different, and sound different from each other, and few of their boundaries match the political lines drawn on current maps. Some are clearly divided topographically by mountains, deserts, and rivers. Others are separated by architecture, music, language, and ways of making a living. Each nation has its own list of desires. Each nation knows how it plans to get what it needs from whoever's got it.

—Excerpted from *The Nine Nations of North America* by Joel Garreau

1. Which of the following statements is most consistent with the point of view of the author of the passage?

   (1) Current state boundaries within the United States don't make much economic and cultural sense.
   (2) Most North Americans have similar values and attitudes toward state government.
   (3) A revolution would be the best way to divide the continent in the way it should be divided.
   (4) All of the "nine nations" have approximately the same number of people and square miles.
   (5) Topography should play no role in characterizing the "nine nations" and marking their boundaries.

2. Which of the following characteristics would *not* likely be a factor in determining whether or not a region qualifies as a "nation"?

   (1) climate
   (2) natural resources
   (3) employment opportunities
   (4) political clout in Washington
   (5) predominant ethnic group

3. Which of the following conclusions can you draw from the "Nine Nations" model?

(1) The Empty Quarter is the most powerful because it is the biggest.
(2) You have to speak Spanish if you live in MexAmerica.
(3) Each "nation" exists completely independently from the others.
(4) People are discouraged from moving from one "nation" to another.
(5) Many aspects of life are different from "nation" to "nation."

Answers are on page 404.

Physical Systems and How Humans Affect Them

Based upon what we have considered earlier in this chapter, places can be characterized both in terms of their natural environments and the impact human beings have had on them. Look at the two photographs below. Both pictures show the same street in Los Angeles, California. The picture on the left was taken in 1922, when Wilshire Boulevard was surrounded by barley fields. By 1965 the area had become a fully developed retail district.

These pictures tell a story about a place and the impact human settlement has had on it. Choose three words to describe the distinctive aspects of each picture.

1922

_____

_____

_____

1965

_____

_____

_____

For the first picture, you may have used terms like *rural*, *spacious*, *clean*, *quiet*, or *slow*. For the second picture, however, words like *crowded*, *dense*, *urban*, *dirty*, *loud*, or *fast* may have seemed more appropriate. To fully understand the reasons for the changes over 43 years, you would need to examine the history of the Los Angeles area. Such a study would probably offer information about dramatic increases of population as California in general and Los Angeles in particular drew increasing numbers of residents from across the United States and from other countries searching for economic opportunities and a comfortable climate.

Look at the following illustration of the numerous influences that human activity has on the physical world. Read each of the following short passages and decide which influences are being described.

INFLUENCES ON THE ENVIRONMENT

1. During the twentieth century, the level of carbon dioxide in the atmosphere has risen dramatically, causing what some call a 'greenhouse effect.' Sources of excess carbon dioxide include emissions from automobiles, factories and power plants that are powered by fossil fuels like coal and oil.

    —Excerpted from *Current Issues*, 2001 Edition, Closeup Foundation

2. By 2050, population experts predict 8.9 billion people will inhabit Earth, straining the water, soil, and other natural resources that are key to human survival.

    —Excerpted from *Current Issues*, 2001 Edition, Closeup Foundation

3. EPA (Environmental Protection Agency) has indicated that Rockwell's Rocky Flats, CO. nuclear weapons manufacturing facility may be the nation's most polluted site. EDP documented 166 separate hazardous waste dumps at Rocky Flats. Studies have linked plutonium exposure to cancer among workers and residents living near Rocky Flats.

    —Excerpted from "Large Corporations Are Serious Polluters" by Colin Crawford, in *Pollution*

For 1, the "greenhouse effect" can be attributed most directly to uncontrolled industrialization, energy consumption, and technological development.

For 2, population growth is clearly the biggest influence referred to here. But accompanying it are food needs and therefore, food production, energy consumption, and consumption of natural resources.

For 3, industrial waste, together with technological development, are the harmful agents in this situation.

EXERCISE 3

Read the following passage and answer the questions below.

Deserts, while entirely natural, can also be of anthropogenic origin—a consequence of human actions. It's not altogether certain whether the Sahara itself is an early consequence of human action; the evidence is very thin, though it hasn't stopped extravagant speculation. But even if humans had nothing to do with "causing" the Sahara, they certainly contributed to its spread and the degradation of the surrounding land in the Sahel. As vegetation is stripped from the land, the surface dries out and reflects more of the sun's heat. This condition in turn alters the thermal dynamics of the atmosphere in ways that suppress rainfall. Other experts suspect that increased dust or other atmospheric pollutants could be causing changes in the climate. The process is called desertification.

—Excerpted from *Water: The Fate of Our Most Precious Resource* by Marq DeVilliers

1. Which of the following conclusions can be drawn from this passage?

   (1) Human actions have probably had nothing to do with the increasing size of the Sahara.
   (2) Experts can't tell why the Sahara has continued to get bigger.
   (3) When people try to live on or near a desert they can have a negative impact on it.
   (4) If there were no humans, the Sahara probably wouldn't exist.
   (5) Desertification is beneficial in places that receive too much rain.

2. Which of the following most likely describes the author of this passage?

   (1) a political scientist who is trying to understand the causes of war in desert civilizations
   (2) a sociologist who is trying to explain recent large migrations of people out of the Sahara region
   (3) a biologist who is studying the shrinking variety of plant and animal life in the Sahara region
   (4) an industrialist who is assessing the advantages of developing the Sahara for commercial purposes
   (5) an environmentalist who is concerned with the causes and implications of the increased size of deserts

3. Which of the following natural resources is least likely to be affected by desertification?

   (1) oil
   (2) water
   (3) plant life
   (4) animal life
   (5) top soil

Answers are on page 404.

Human Systems and Their Relationship to Environments

While humans clearly have a significant, and often negative, impact on natural environments, those same environments have played an equally significant role in determining the way in which people live and survive. The challenges and resources that any particular physical location offers the group that inhabits it test that group's problem-solving ability and capacity for innovation. The result is a group character and set of customs and beliefs that reflect both the challenge and the ingenuity demanded.

When we talk about a group of people who share a way of life that has been created and learned over time, we are referring to a **culture.** Culture includes a group's set of beliefs, language, social relationships, institutions and organizations, and material goods—food, clothing, buildings, tools, and machines. The origins of most cultures date back many centuries to a time when groups of people lived in much greater geographic isolation than they do now. When we speak of cultural groups today we are often referring to people whose way of life was a response to the environments in which they lived, be they deserts, mountains, islands, tundras, or tropical forests. A group that derives its identity from places such as these is called **indigenous.**

Consider, for example, the BaMbuti, or pygmies, of the central African rain forest. Read the following paragraph.

> The BaMbuti are the real people of the forest. Whereas the other tribes are relatively recent arrivals, the Pygmies have been in the forest for many thousands of years. It is their world, and in return for their affection and trust it supplies them with all their needs. They do not have to cut the forest down to build plantations, for they know how to hunt the game of the region and gather the wild fruits that grow in abundance there, though hidden to outsiders . . . They know the secret language that is denied all outsiders and without which life in the forest is an impossibility.
>
> The BaMbuti roam the forest at will, in small isolated bands or hunting groups. They have no fear, because for them there is no danger. For them there is little hardship, so they have no need for belief in evil spirits. For them it is a good world.

—Excerpted from *The Forest People: A Study of the Pygmies of the Congo* by Colin M. Turnbull

The BaMbuti are clearly people whose lives, and therefore culture, are defined by the forest. Fortunately for them, the forest is a friendly environment. By contrast the Inuit (also known as Eskimos) of coastal Greenland, Arctic North America, and extreme northeastern Siberia, are a people who have had to forge a way of life within a hostile environment. Obtaining food and warmth is a daily challenge.

EXERCISE 4

Next to each statement below write the number that indicates to whom the statement refers. Base your decision upon the information provided in the two paragraphs above.

I.   the BaMbuti

II. the Inuit

III. both the BaMbuti and the Inuit

IV. neither the BaMbuti nor the Inuit

1. _____ Their myths and rituals reflect a preoccupation with survival.

2. _____ Their language includes dozens of versions of the word "snow."

3. _____ They tend not to worry about how to survive.

4. _____ They are sensitive to even the most subtle changes in their environment.

5. _____ They don't have to move around much in search of food.

Answers are on page 404.

In the 21st century it is increasingly difficult to find people who remain truly indigenous since human history has largely been a history of **migrations,** or movements of groups from one location to another. Initially, people migrated in search of plentiful food supplies. Later, political upheaval and cultural persecution played significant roles in instigating large movements.

Consider this description of migration patterns in Europe during the Industrial Revolution:

At first the urbanization after 1850 had a circular character. In the harvest season, people worked in the countryside and the rest of the time in the cities. However, because of the increasing population, more and more people could not fall back on the countryside. That is when circle migration became chain migration. Cities with textile or heavy industry attracted laborers, just like commercial and administrative centers. People from all over Europe and even from other continents moved toward the new industry centers in England, France, and Germany.

From what the passage says, what do you think the difference is between circle migration and chain migration?

_____

_____

While circle migration involves people moving from one location to another and then back to the original location, chain migration describes the permanent movement of a group to a new place as a result of a change or lack of accommodation in the original location. Most migrations in today's world are chain migrations.

A look at the influx of the U.S. population over the past 300 years can illustrate the nature and impact of various chain migrations. In the 1700s, for example, following the conquest and colonization of the "New World," the slave trade forcibly removed hundred of thousands of Africans from their homelands. In the 1800s, as slavery continued, large numbers of Europeans sought new economic opportunities in America. And finally, in the last century, within a world embroiled in conflict and genocides, the United States became the refuge of political and cultural exiles.

In the graph below are statistics regarding the number and origin of refugees to the United States in a two-year period. On the basis of the graph it is possible to deduce where upheaval has been occurring. For example, the large number of refugees from Europe and the former Soviet Union correctly indicates the presence of conflict in many of those countries.

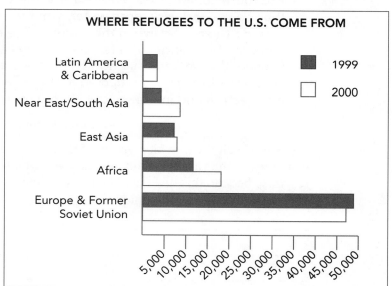

In which geographical area was there likely the largest change in conditions between 1999 and 2000? In which the least change?

_____

_____

The largest change in conditions probably occurred in Africa as evidenced by the biggest difference between the blue and white bars. The least change was probably in Latin America and the Caribbean since the two bars are of the same length.

From this graph we can also estimate the total number of refugees admitted to the United States in these two years by adding the numbers represented by each bar. In which year were there more refugees? A brief glance will tell you that more refugees came in 2000. Closer examination will reveal that in 2000 the total new refugee population reached approximately 100,000.

Places Made by People

For four and a half billion years, all of life on earth evolved according to the laws of nature. Humans, too, were participants in the interdependent chain of survival; our activity was limited to that of hunter-gatherer, continually in search of food. By about 7000 B.C.E., however, people began to settle in places where the land was fertile and a farming lifestyle was possible. Not surprisingly, these early villages coincided with the mastery of the domestication of crops and animals. It was not until cities began to flourish, though, that **civilizations** started to take root. A civilization, or sophisticated level of social development, is a purely human construct. The term derives from the Latin word referring to life in cities.

As you read the following paragraph, reflect on a city with which you are familiar.

The essential catalyst for the beginning of cities everywhere is variety. It is what makes urban civilization possible. Compared to non-urban life, urban life in any culture is always more varied and more complicated. Within a city, the people vary among themselves and vary more widely from the norm in their society than do those who live in the country. The extremes are found here: the best singer, the fastest pickpocket, the wizard of finance, the wasted drug addict. Such variety in the human contents of the city is reflected in the differing forms of urban architecture and in the special history of each city.

—Excerpted from *Cities: The Forces That Shape Them*

Name a city with which you are familiar and describe at least three examples of the variety and extremes you have observed there. What has your response been to this diversity? What are some of the landmarks or historical events that make this city unique?

_____

_____

_____

_____

If a visitor from another planet who knows nothing about human beings visited this city, what is one positive generalization and one negative generalization that visitor would likely make about our species?

_____

_____

_____

_____

Most of the world's earliest cities grew in the Middle East or near the Mediterranean Sea. The oldest, Ur and Uruk of ancient Sumeria, date back about 5 thousand years. Ur and Uruk are now only ruins, but some early cities are very much alive, such as Damascus, currently in Syria. To survive time and the challenges of history, ancient cities have, of course, had to change. The two basic principles that cities have followed in order to remain viable centers for commerce and cultural life are extension and remodeling. So, while Damascus may retain some of its essence as a "city of old," it is a bigger place now with a much altered appearance.

GED PRACTICE

EXERCISE 5

Questions 1 and 2 refer to the photograph of a scene in Rome, Italy. Three distinct historical periods of this ancient city are evident in the photograph: imperial, medieval, and contemporary.

1. Which of the following aspects of the picture would not be of interest to the historian or archaeologist?

    (1) the Corinthian columns
    (2) the large church
    (3) the grassy areas
    (4) the person walking
    (5) the apartment houses

2. Which concept does this photograph most clearly illustrate?

    (1) production
    (2) interpretation
    (3) power
    (4) conflict
    (5) change

Answers are on page 405.

While cities can serve as dazzling and fascinating examples of places made by people, there have been environments that, though constructed by humans, seem to defy humanity. An example is places called concentration, or death, camps, and their creation and purpose is a horrifying testament to the existence of evil in our world. Usually, they have been tools of **genocide,** the systematic destruction of an entire cultural or ethnic group. The last half of the twentieth century has witnessed efforts at genocide and the presence of camps in locations as diverse as Cambodia (Asia), Rwanda (Africa), and the former Yugoslavia (Europe). The camps that first gained international attention and became symbols of hatred and suffering were those established by the Nazi regime that began in Germany in 1933 under the leadership of Adolf Hitler.

The following words were written by Pastor Martin Niemöller. Shortly after writing them, Niemöller was killed by the Nazis.

> They came for the communists, and I did not speak up because I wasn't a communist.
>
> They came for the socialist union leaders, and I did not speak up because I wasn't a socialist union leader.
>
> They came for the Jews, and I did not speak up because I wasn't a Jew.
>
> Then they came for me, and there was no one left to speak up for me.

On the basis of the passage, whom did the Nazis target as victims? What do you know about the Nazis' rise to power? What was their goal? Have you heard the term *holocaust*? What is your understanding of its meaning?

_____

_____

_____

_____

_____

Holocaust refers to the wholesale sacrifice and destruction of a people. The period of Nazi power has been named The Holocaust by Jews because of the unprecedented systematized fashion in which at least six million Jews were slaughtered by the Nazis and their coconspirators.

When the Nazis "came for" those referenced by Pastor Niemöller they sent them to one of the 15,000 camps established throughout Germany and German-occupied countries. The purpose of the camps was to imprison "enemies of the state." These "enemies" included undesirable ethnic groups, such as Jews and Gypsies, members of the political opposition, dissenting clergy, homosexuals, the mentally and physically disabled, and numerous others classified simply as "antisocials." Some camps forced their prisoners to labor under brutal and backbreaking conditions, while others simply exterminated their victims upon arrival. Among the largest and most notorious of the camps, which had both forced-labor and death-factory components, was Auschwitz-Birkenau in Poland. About 4.5 million people of twenty nationalities passed through its gates from 1940 to 1945 and never left.

GED PRACTICE

EXERCISE 6

Questions 1–3 are based on the following photographs from Auschwitz-Birkenau and a statement from an anonymous survivor.

Originally Polish cavalry stables intended for 52 horses, each building held as many as 1,000 prisoners in three-tiered bunks.

Most people deported to Auschwitz-Birkenau were gassed upon arrival without identification or registration.

Statement:

"The S.S. personnel who ran the camp felt secure in the knowledge that all the inmates, whether prisoners of war or internees or whatever, and of whatever nationality—Russians, Ukranian, Polish, White Russians, Jews, French, Greeks, etc.— would sooner or later be killed and that no one who knew what happened would ever live to tell it. This certainty applied especially to those who controlled the behavior of the guards and who decided on which methods of extermination were to be employed. The dead are mute and can tell nothing. And details can be neither imparted nor confirmed through documents alone. Therefore, no one would ever have tangible proof, and that was what mattered most to the Germans."

—Excerpted from *Inside the Concentration Camps: Eyewitness Accounts of Life in Hitler's Death Camps*, compiled by Eugene Aroneanu

1. The pictures dispute which piece of information from the passage?

   (1) The camps were brutally run by German S.S. officers.
   (2) Many groups besides the Jews were victims of the Nazis.
   (3) There is no tangible proof of the horrors of Auschwitz-Birkenau.
   (4) The S.S. used more than one method of extermination.
   (5) The Germans did not want the rest of the world to know what they had done.

2. After more than half a century, what can be said with certainty about the Auschwitz-Birkenau concentration camps?

   (1) There were survivors and witnesses.
   (2) Historians now know exactly how many people died there.
   (3) Something similar will never be replicated.
   (4) Its commanders were insane.
   (5) Their horrors have been forgotten.

3. Who among the following people could *not* be held responsible for the atrocities at Auschwitz-Birkenau?

   (1) the architect who designed the camp
   (2) the train engineer who transported its victims there
   (3) the S.S. officer who was only taking orders
   (4) Hitler and his assistants who never actually killed anyone
   (5) the Jews and others who were deported there

Answers are on page 405.

Chapter Review

Question 1 refers to the following map.

CENTERS OF ORIGINS OF FOOD PRODUCTION

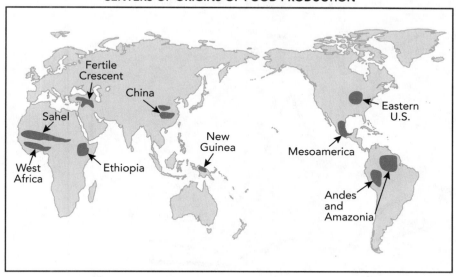

1. On the basis of the information in the map, which of the following statements is least likely to be true?

    (1) Many cultures developed around the areas marked on the map.
    (2) Civilization first developed in what is now Northern Europe.
    (3) The climate and resources in the marked areas could help cultures thrive.
    (4) The BaMbuti culture (Africa) probably developed before the Inuit (Northern Canada).
    (5) All major landmasses had the potential to sustain human communities.

Question 2 refers to the graph below.

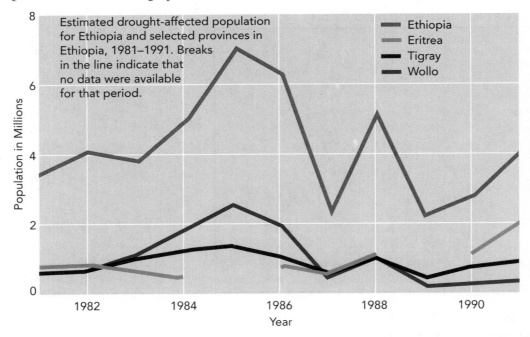

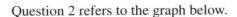

2. Which of the following is an inference that you can make from the graph?

(1) The dramatic drop in the drought-affected population in Ethiopia in 1987 was due to the migration of people out of the country.

(2) The dramatic drop in the drought-affected population in Ethiopia in 1987 was due to the large number of deaths by starvation.

(3) Eritrea, Tigray, and Wollo did not experience the same pattern of fluctuations in the drought-affected population as Ethiopia between 1981 and 1991.

(4) If other countries had offered aid to Ethiopia and its provinces, the shifts in the drought-affected population would not have been so dramatic.

(5) Ethiopia and its provinces experienced dramatic increases and decreases within their populations during a time of extended drought.

Question 3 refers to the photograph below.

3. Which of the following statements does *not* support the need for this sign?

   (1) One animal species becomes extinct about every eight hours, mostly because of human actions.
   (2) All species of animals are important to maintaining a sustaining environment on this globe.
   (3) Even a small action like driving on a beach can have an impact on the earth's ecological balance.
   (4) If beach visitors disturb just a few nests and eggs, the turtles will probably still survive.
   (5) By protecting the turtles we are protecting the whole ecological system of which the turtle is a part.

Questions 4 and 5 refer to the paragraphs below.

People, and especially businesses, dump waste where they think they can get away with it, where they think the community or the powers-that-be don't care. I was not the least bit surprised to learn that most toxic waste sites are located in poor communities, especially poor communities of color. Race is nationally the most significant variable in relation to the location of hazardous waste facilities. Pick a poor community or neighborhood where people of color reside, and you are likely to find hazardous waste sites, incinerators, trash transfer stations, and petrochemical plants, with the resulting bad quality air and water. Studies show that African-Americans are more likely than whites to live within a mile and a half of an uncontrolled hazardous waste site or a polluting factory (74% to 50%). These problems are not unique to poor African-American communities. One of San Diego's poorest Mexican-American neighborhoods has one of the biggest toxic waste generators in the country and many Indian reservations house toxic waste sites.

—Excerpted from "Poor Communities: Everyone's Favorite Dumping Ground" by Silja Kallenbach in *The Change Agent*, March 2000

4. On the basis of this paragraph, what can you infer about the author?

   She is
   (1) either African American or Mexican American
   (2) a resident of a low-income, polluted neighborhood
   (3) a resident of a clean, affluent community
   (4) a manager of a company that dumps waste
   (5) an advocate for improving low-income communities

5. Which of the following statements is the most likely explanation for poor communities being "dumping grounds?"

   (1) The residents of the communities do not speak enough English to protest.
   (2) Businesses often count on poor people to be ignorant and disinterested.
   (3) There's more space for dumping in poor communities than in wealthy ones.
   (4) African, Mexican, and Native Americans do not work well together.
   (5) Poor people do not care as much about clean air and water as rich ones.

Questions 6 and 7 refer to the paragraph below about the Irish potato famine.

   Hunger, poverty and even famine were not strangers to the Irish poor in the first half of the 19th century, particularly in the rural south and west of the country. But by the time the 1845 potato blight hit, there were no other resources left for these people. They had no other means of making a living, and farmers and landlords who depended on receiving rents from them were now vulnerable too. There was nothing else for the Irish poor to eat, and such absolute dependence on this one commodity resulted in one of the worst disasters in history . . . Between 1841 and 1851, Ireland's population of 8 million had dwindled to 6 million. An estimated half of these people left the country while the other million died.

   —Excerpted from *Irish Emigration* by Mary Johnston.

6. Which of the following conclusions can be drawn from this paragraph?

   (1) Many of the Irish poor starved after 1845 because of bad planning on the part of the Irish government.
   (2) At least one cause of the large migration of Irish out of Ireland in the middle of the 19th century was a lack of food.
   (3) The potato blight of 1845 was the first hardship to affect the Irish in rural areas.
   (4) The destitution of the poor in Ireland did not have much effect on other classes of Irish society.
   (5) The Irish should have known not to depend so much on the cultivation of just one crop.

7. Which of the following was probably *not* a result of the Irish potato famine?

   (1) an increase in the Irish population of the United States
   (2) other problems such as the rapid spread of disease
   (3) an in-depth study of the causes of the famine
   (4) increased rents for blight-affected farmland
   (5) the cultivation of additional food resources

Question 8 refers to the following cartoon.

—Bennett/©1999 *The Christian Science Monitor.* This cartoon first appeared in *The Christian Science Monitor* on October 12, 1999 and is reproduced with permission. Copyright © 1999 *The Christian Science Monitor.* All rights reserved. Online at csmonitor. com.

8. What is the concern expressed in this cartoon?

(1) Many birds may become extinct if the human population isn't controlled.

(2) In 1999 too many babies were born in English-speaking countries.

(3) All of the world's regions are contributing to overpopulation.

(4) The world needs to strengthen and increase its resources.

(5) There may not be enough resources to support the human population.

Answers are on page 405.

Chapter 7

Power, Authority, and Governance

A woman breaks up with her abusive boyfriend and seeks protection from the police even though she doesn't think she can support herself and her children without the boyfriend. The employees of a company with unfair pay and promotion policies organize a strike to protest and press for change. Three countries negotiate a complicated agreement to remove the trade barriers between them.

Power. Each of the examples above involves it. Try to define the term *power*. It's one of those words that we have a sense of and can describe through example but whose definition is elusive. We know or can imagine what it feels like to have power, and we know or can imagine what it feels like to be without it. Scholars who study social interactions often claim that any relationship in the world—whether between individuals, groups, or nations—can be viewed in terms of the balance or imbalance of power within it.

Think of a time in your life when you experienced being either powerful or powerless. In relationship to what or to whom did you have that feeling? Was it another person or group of people, a system, or an institution? What aspect or elements of that relationship made you feel that way?

On the GED Social Studies Test you will need to think carefully about power, particularly as it is delegated by and organized within nations. The delegation of power is **authority,** and its organization can be found in **government.**

Some of the earliest thinking about power, authority, and governance was done in the ancient city-states of Greece more than two thousand years ago by such philosophers as Plato and Aristotle. Their thoughts are still relevant today. For example, Aristotle classified governments this way:

- A good government serves the general welfare of the people.

- A bad government subordinates the general good to the good of the individuals in power.

From your reading of the newspaper or watching of the television news, can you give an example of a situation in which a government in the world has acted in a good way, as defined by Aristotle? in a bad way?

Aristotle also offered definitions of various types of governments. This list has expanded over the centuries. Below are some of the categories currently used to describe governments around the world.

- **Monarchy:** A system of government in which a single person (a king or queen) rules by inherited power. His or her power may be absolute, or other elements within the government, such as a constitution, may limit that power.

- **Dictatorship:** a system of government in which one person has absolute authority, including complete domination of the citizens' lives. The most basic of citizens' rights are taken away in order to guarantee the leader's hold on power. Violence generally characterizes the beginning and end of a dictatorship.

- **Oligarchy:** a system of government in which a small group of people exercises total control.

- **Theocracy:** a system of government in which a religion establishes the principles of laws and religious leaders interpret and enforce those laws.

- **Democracy:** a system of government in which "the will of the majority" rules and citizens choose representatives in free elections. The equality of all citizens is a basic principle.

EXERCISE 1

Write the name of the type of government described in each of the examples below.

1. _____ During the period of apartheid the white population of South Africa, which comprised only about 25% of the people, commanded the power and the majority of the wealth of the entire nation.

2. _____ The chief governmental and religious official of Saudi Arabia is chosen from among the Saudi royal family. As king, he usually also serves as Saudi Arabia's prime minister.

3. _____ In 1964 Francois Duvalier declared himself president of Haiti for life. His regime oversaw military and governmental purges, mass executions, and the institution of curfews.

4. _____ In Australia more than 90% of registered voters participate in the election of a representative government.

Answers are on page 405.

In the rest of this chapter we will explore a *case study* in power, authority, and governance. When a scientist or social scientist wants to understand how something really works, he or she will take a specific example and study it in depth. From this example, or case study, he or she will not only understand that single example very well, but will also be able to hypothesize on some general truths about the subject. Our case study will be of the democracy of the United States of America. In our investigation we will pay special attention to:

- the creation of a democracy

- the challenges of a democracy

- the role and influence of citizens in a democracy

The Creation of a Democracy

Democracy was not invented in the United States. The democratic principle of a "free" government "by and for the people" dates back to pre-Christian classical Greece and Rome, where citizens were encouraged to speak and vote in public assemblies. Only men who were not slaves were considered citizens. Slaves and women had no political rights. The concepts of equal political and social rights were not refined until much later, in the Renaissance (1400–1600), with an increased interest in the arts and humanities, and in the Reformation (1500–1700) with the end of the dominance of the Catholic theocracy.

Why do you think the Renaissance and the Reformation contributed toward a greater emphasis on the equality of all people?

_____

_____

_____

_____

By knowing that the Renaissance celebrated human talents and potential, it stands to reason that greater regard was held for the larger "family" of humanity, rather than simply a privileged few. In terms of the Reformation, with its struggles for religious freedom and the breaking away of groups such as the Lutherans from the Catholic church, some people likely found new appreciation for the attitudes of tolerance and respect.

By the time the thirteen American colonies had announced their independence from the king of England (1776) and first organized as a nation (1781), their leaders had absorbed the examples from history and benefited from the thinking and writings of centuries of philosophers and statesmen. Even so, there was a sense of adventure about this undertaking and a boldness, because never had there been a country so new and so determined from the start to embody democracy.

The first attempt at designing a democratic government did not go well for the United States. For six years the new country tried to operate under the Articles of Confederation, which gave each state a lot of power but the national government very little. It was as if there were thirteen small countries, each with its own money system and law enforcement policy. Something else was needed.

In 1787 the decision was made to create a new constitution. This was not an easy task. A split soon developed between the Federalists, who wanted a strong central government with authoritative control over the states, and the Anti-Federalists, who were afraid that the individual person and the individual states would lose their freedom and flexibility under one central government.

Read the following quotes. Write **F** if the speaker favors federalism and **A** if the speaker is an Anti-Federalist and advocates states' rights.

_____ **1.** "The territories themselves should determine whether slavery should exist."

_____ **2.** "I need assurance that my money will have value in Georgia as well as in New Jersey."

_____ **3.** "If this nation is to prosper, trade among states must be regulated uniformly."

_____ **4.** "We need our own local standing militia to put down uprisings in the states' own territories."

_____ **5.** "What right does Massachusetts have to make treaties with other nations?"

You should have identified 1 and 4 as Anti-Federalist statements because they represent the view that states should have sovereignty, whether to decide on supporting slavery or to raise their own militia. Items 2, 3, and 5 represent the Federalist perspective, which held that the national government should have the power to coin money, regulate trade, and make treaties with other countries.

In addition to the disagreement over the strength of individual states, the men at the Constitutional Convention also disputed the structure of representation within the Congress and whether slaves should count as part of a state's population. These arguments and the compromises that settled them are highlighted in the following chart.

EXERCISE 2

Use the chart below to select the best answer to questions 1–4.

COMPROMISES AT THE CONSTITUTIONAL CONVENTION

Dispute: Should the states be governed by a strong central government (Federalists' view)?
or
Should the new government be based on the sovereignty of the states (Anti-Federalists' view)?

Compromise: 1. President is elected by electoral college, the Senate by the state legislatures (this was later changed by the Twelfth Amendment, adopted in 1804), and House of Representatives by the people.
2. Bill of Rights—first ten amendments were added to the Constitution later to guarantee individual rights.

Dispute: Should the makeup of Congress be based on each state's population (large states' view)?
or
Should all states have equal representation (small states' view)?

Compromise: Bicameral legislature (two houses in Congress)
1. Members of House of Representatives are based on each state's population.
2. Senate consists of two delegates from each state. This was called the Great Compromise.

Dispute: Should slaves be counted in the population (southern slave states' view)?
or
Should slaves be excluded from the population count (northern industrialized states' view)?

Compromise: 1. Slave importation would be allowed until at least 1808.
2. Slaves would be counted as three-fifths of the population only for the purposes of representation and for assessing taxes: however they were not permitted to vote.

1. What did the Great Compromise of the Constitutional Convention involve?

   (1) the negotiation of complicated trade agreements between small and large states
   (2) the agreement between Northern and Southern states on how to count slaves
   (3) the addition of a bill of rights to guarantee personal freedoms for the states' citizens
   (4) the creation of a two-house federal legislature to allow for fairness in state representation
   (5) the establishment of an electoral college to select the president more efficiently

2. How did counting only three-fifths of the slave population penalize the southern states?

   (1) in determining the number of seats for the House of Representatives
   (2) in deciding on the number of senators to represent those states
   (3) in the amounts of annual property and income taxes citizens owe
   (4) in establishing trade laws between the North and the South.
   (5) in efforts to postpone setting a date to abolish slavery across the nation

3. Why was the Bill of Rights such an important addition to the Constitution, especially for the Anti-Federalists?

   (1) It guaranteed the end of slavery and the opportunity for women to vote by a certain date.
   (2) It set the rules for the process of making amendments to the Constitution.
   (3) It would end the abuse of personal liberties that many colonists had experienced.
   (4) It determined a fair process under which the president of the United States would be elected.
   (5) It gave the states supreme rights over the federal government on the issue of taxes.

4. Which of the following can be implied from the chart?

   (1) The eagerness of the participants in the Constitutional Convention made the compromise process relatively easy.
   (2) There was a deep hostility between the Federalists and the Anti-Federalists that made compromise difficult.
   (3) The participants in the Constitutional Convention must have been creative problem solvers.
   (4) The issue of slavery should have been resolved once and for all by the Constitution.
   (5) The Southern states and the larger states were the most stubborn in the process of reaching compromise.

Answers are on page 405.

Despite the numerous disagreements, all of the states eventually approved the Constitution, and the new government started operating with George Washington as its first president in the spring of 1789.

The Constitution

This document of seven articles and twenty-seven amendments calls itself the "supreme law of the land" and sets the foundation of American democracy. Its purpose, as stated in its preamble, is "to form a more perfect Union, establish Justice, insure domestic Tranquility, provide for the common defence, promote the general Welfare, and secure the Blessings of Liberty to ourselves and our Posterity."

In your own words, how might you restate the intention of the Constitution?

_____

_____

_____

_____

_____

Within the Constitution is the blueprint for a government consisting of three branches, with power balanced between them. The first article describes the legislative branch (with its two houses) as the maker of laws. The second article portrays the executive branch (the presidency) as the enforcer of the laws. And the third article outlines the judicial branch as the interpreter of the laws.

The Constitution is quite specific on many aspects of the branches, their roles, and their responsibilities. In some areas, however, the Constitution does not specifically spell out the authority of a branch, and those powers have had to be implied. Sometimes the implication of power is controversial. The continual effort required to understand and maintain democracy is evident in these controversies.

Take, for example, the actions that some presidents have taken in executing the nation's laws. None of them is outlined in the Constitution, but because these presidents acted as they did and were not found to be contradicting the Constitution, they set a trend, or precedent, that could be followed by subsequent presidents.

(a) George Washington set up a cabinet of advisors.

(b) Thomas Jefferson entered into the Louisiana Purchase.

(c) James Polk ordered U.S. troops into action before Congress had declared war against Mexico.

(d) Abraham Lincoln freed the slaves during the Civil War.

(e) Theodore Roosevelt mediated labor and international disputes.

(f) Richard Nixon authorized support for the violent overthrow of the socialist-inclined but democratically elected president of Chile.

EXERCISE 3

Match the presidential precedent from the previous page with the subsequent action of a later president by writing the correct letter in the space provided.

_____ 1. Jimmy Carter's mediation efforts in the Camp David accords between Egypt and Israel

_____ 2. George W. Bush's choice of Colin Powell as Secretary of State

_____ 3. Lyndon Johnson's military buildup in the undeclared Vietnam War

_____ 4. Ronald Reagan's invasion of the Caribbean country of Grenada when a Marxist government assumed power there

_____ 5. Franklin Delano Roosevelt's establishment of agencies during the emergencies brought on by the Depression and World War II

Answers are on page 405.

Another indication that the U.S. Constitution is a living document that requires constant examination and interpretation is the performance of the judicial system, specifically the Supreme Court, which can and does reverse itself. For example, in 1896 the Supreme Court ruled that separate but equal facilities for blacks in the South were correct and legal. In 1954, however, the court reversed the earlier decision and ruled the opposite because it decided that "separate but equal" was not consistent with the spirit of the Constitution.

What do you think might have been the reasons that the Supreme Court viewed the "separate but equal" policy differently 58 years after it first ruled on it?

_____

_____

_____

_____

The change in people's perceptions of other people over time is difficult to explain precisely or briefly. We can note, however, that 1896 was not long after the end of slavery, and many whites still regarded African Americans as intellectually and morally inferior on the basis of the color difference. There was, therefore, willingness on the part of many to turn a blind eye to the blatant inequality between the services and facilities offered to African Americans and those offered to whites. Shifts in the political, economic, and social fabric of the country, however, made it more difficult to ignore the injustice of separateness in 1954, and fewer whites were willing to do so.

The federal court system consists of the Supreme Court, eleven circuit courts of appeal scattered throughout the country, and approximately ninety federal district courts. In addition to the federal system of courts, each state has its own system.

The Supreme Court is composed of nine justices appointed for life by the president. Some of the powers vested in the Supreme Court are the powers to rule on:

- cases involving a state and citizens of another state

- controversies between two or more states

- cases between citizens of different states

- cases between a state and a foreign state

The Supreme Court does not have the last word on all legal cases in the country. Only when a revision of the Constitution, an act of Congress, or a right by federal law is involved does the Supreme Court have the authority to rule on a state court's decision. Appellate (appeals) court cases are reviewed only when they involve the national interest. The case of *Miranda* v. *Arizona* was such a case.

In 1966, Ernesto Miranda appealed his case to the Supreme Court. Mr. Miranda had been arrested in Phoenix, Arizona, and interrogated by two police officers in a special interrogation room without being informed of his right to remain silent and his right to a lawyer. Mr. Miranda confessed orally to a charge of kidnapping and rape. The Court, under the leadership of Chief Justice Earl Warren, heard the case because it involved a national interest; namely, the rights of criminal suspects.

GED PRACTICE

EXERCISE 4

Read the following statement by Chief Justice Warren on the Supreme Court's judgment in the Miranda case. Choose the best answer to questions 1–3.

"The cases before us raised questions which go to the roots of our concept of American criminal jurisprudence: the restraints society must observe must be consistent with the Federal Constitution in prosecuting individuals for crime. More specifically, we deal with the admissibility of statements obtained from an individual who is subjected to custodial police interrogation and the necessity for procedures which assure that the individual is accorded his privilege under the Fifth Amendment to the Constitution not to be impelled to incriminate himself . . .

"We have concluded that without proper safeguards the process of in-custody interrogation of persons suspected or accused of crime contains inherently compelling pressures which work to undermine the individual's will to resist and that compel him to speak where he would not otherwise do so freely and to permit a full opportunity to exercise the privilege against self-incrimination, the accused must be adequately and effectively apprised of his rights and the exercise of those rights must be fully honored."

1. From this statement, what can we infer about the Supreme Court's ruling in this case?

   The court ruled
   (1) in favor of Miranda on the grounds that he was not informed of his Fifth Amendment rights
   (2) in favor of Miranda on the grounds he probably didn't commit the crime of which he was accused
   (3) in favor of Miranda on the grounds that the Constitution is wrong on how to prosecute crime
   (4) against Miranda on the grounds that he should have been able to resist the pressures of interrogation if he was innocent
   (5) against Miranda on the grounds that the case should not have gone to the Supreme Court

2. Who did the Miranda decision most likely affect the least?

   (1) trial lawyers
   (2) accused criminals
   (3) police officers
   (4) Ernesto Miranda
   (5) prison guards

3. Why did the Supreme Court consider this case seriously?

   (1) It was clear that Miranda was innocent.
   (2) It had implications for all of criminal law.
   (3) The Constitution was clearly wrong about suspects' rights.
   (4) All other courts refused to hear it.
   (5) The Fifth Amendment needed further changes.

Answers are on page 405.

The Constitution describes a system for balancing the power between the three branches of the government called **checks and balances.** It is an element of this democracy that is much admired by aspiring governments in other countries since it makes sure that no one center of power dominates the other two. If one branch holds more power, the government is no longer a functioning democracy.

An example of how checks and balances work is the law making process. The Congress writes a bill and sends it to the president for approval. If the president doesn't like it, he can **veto,** or refuse to sign, it. Congress, however, can still pass the bill into law by a two-thirds majority vote of its members. This procedure is called **overriding a veto.** Finally, if an individual or group believes that the law is wrong, it can bring the law to the Supreme Court. If the justices agree that the law contradicts the principles of the Constitution, the Court can declare it unconstitutional and the law will be erased.

EXERCISE 5

Below is a list of some governmental powers. In column I write the branch of government, *executive*, *legislative*, or *judicial*, that exercises the power described on the left. In column II, write the branch of government that is checked by the use of the power. The first one is done for you.

Power	I Who exercises power?	II Who is checked?
1. to appoint federal judges	executive	judicial
2. to impeach the president		
3. to approve appointment of judges		
4. to override a veto		
5. to rule a law unconstitutional		
6. to veto a bill		

Answers are on page 406.

The Challenges of a Democracy

Many people around the world regard the United States with awe and yearn to benefit from some of the fruits of this democracy, most especially personal freedom and economic opportunity. As many citizens know and as many immigrants learn, however, the American model is far from perfect. The challenge of maintaining a democracy is evident on a daily basis.

More than 280 million people live in the United States. Within this population is an enormous variety of ethnic, language, and religious groups. Individuals with differing skin colors, genders, and incomes all look for equal regard and consideration under the law. Unfortunately, though, there are many gaps between democratic ideals and reality. Can you point to a situation in which you think some people have had more opportunity to succeed than others? What are the circumstances that contribute to this situation? To what degree do you think the government is responsible for causing and/or righting it?

The U.S. Constitution is referred to as a living document because of its ability to adapt to shifting needs in American society. It is constantly read, interpreted, and sometimes changed. The means by which the Constitution is changed is the **amendment** process. It is not easy. After more than 200 years there are only 27 amendments. The steps for passing an amendment, described in Article Five of the Constitution, are the following:

1. An amendment must first be proposed by either two-thirds of both houses of Congress or by a national convention requested by the legislatures of two-thirds of the states.

2. It must be ratified (approved) by three-fourths of the state legislatures.

The first ten amendments to the Constitution are called the **Bill of Rights.** The authors of the Constitution added these guarantees of personal liberties after it became obvious that the states would not ratify the Constitution without them. The Bill of Rights reassured those who were afraid that the new government would threaten individual freedoms. The following ten amendments are included in the Bill of Rights:

Amendment 1: guarantees the freedom of religion, speech, the press, and assembly

Amendment 2: guarantees the right to belong to a state militia and keep weapons

Amendment 3: prohibits the government from housing soldiers in civilian homes without the owners' permission

Amendment 4: requires a warrant before property can be searched or seized

Amendment 5: guarantees the right to remain silent; establishes a grand jury to hand down indictments for a crime; safeguards individuals from having to testify against themselves; and forbids government seizure of property without compensation

Amendment 6: guarantees the right to a trial by an impartial jury after being informed of charges against oneself, the right to hear and see witnesses against oneself, and the right to a lawyer

Amendment 7: permits the privilege of a jury trial in most lawsuits

Amendment 8: forbids excessive bail or cruel and unusual punishment

Amendment 9: requires the government to increase the list of personal liberties if necessary

Amendment 10: gives the states and the people any rights not specifically denied them by the Constitution

GED PRACTICE

EXERCISE 6

Questions 1–4 refer to the Bill of Rights as described above.

1. When an arresting officer reads an accused man his "rights" and gives him the chance to make one telephone call, which amendments is the police officer upholding?

   (1) the Seventh and Eighth Amendments
   (2) the First and Second Amendments
   (3) the Fourth and Fifth Amendments
   (4) the Fifth and Sixth Amendments
   (5) the Sixth and Seventh Amendments

2. A neo-Nazi group applies for a permit to rally in a public park. Although many people are appalled by the beliefs and intentions of this group, the city government grants the permit on the basis of which amendment?

   (1) Tenth
   (2) Second
   (3) First
   (4) Sixth
   (5) Ninth

3. Some states authorize the death penalty and others do not. The terms of which amendment remain unclarified?

   (1) Eighth
   (2) Tenth
   (3) First
   (4) Fifth
   (5) Sixth

4. There was a delay to the start of the murder trial of a celebrity because few jurors could be found who had not heard of the crime or formed an opinion of the accused. The court was under obligation to comply with which amendment?

   (1) Ninth
   (2) Second
   (3) Fourth
   (4) Sixth
   (5) Eighth

Answers are on page 406.

The struggle for civil rights for minorities is an excellent illustration of the continuing tension between the ideals of the Bill of Rights and the reality of human behavior. Nearly 150 years ago the Thirteenth Amendment to the Constitution ended slavery, although by today's understanding slavery would have been assumed to be unconstitutional from the start on the basis of the Bill of Rights. The Fourteenth Amendment was then approved to grant citizenship to former slaves, followed by the Fifteenth Amendment, which granted African American males (but not females) the right to vote. Discriminatory practices continued, however, despite the law, not only against African Americans but Native Americans, Mexicans, Puerto Ricans, homosexuals, and women. Not until the 1960s was significant progress made in the enforcement of civil rights practices.

Look at the following photograph of drinking fountains taken in the South in the early 1960s.

Which of the following conclusions can you draw from the photo?

(a) Progress had been made since the late 1800s in securing civil rights for all Americans.

(b) Many people supported the separation of facilities.

(c) Facilities for colored people were still greatly inferior to those for whites as late as the 1960s.

(d) Many people were protesting the inequalities apparent in this picture.

The only statement that is supported by the picture is (c). It is clear that these water fountains are not the same and are, thus, symbolic of a large range of civil rights violations directed at African Americans until at least the 1960s. This contradicts statement (a). Neither statement (b) or (d) is supported by the picture. A better piece of evidence of the involvement of various people in this issue would be the photograph below of an African American student entering a formerly all-white Little Rock, Arkansas, high school. Look at the faces of the people in the picture. What do they reveal about the struggle for civil rights?

_____

_____

_____

_____

_____

_____

EXERCISE 7

Questions 1 and 2 are based on the political cartoon below.

1. What message is the cartoon conveying?

    (1) Civil rights violations in this period are more along economic than race lines.
    (2) The civil rights of African Americans are no longer a concern today.
    (3) The poor in 2000 can't vote with computers because they don't know how.
    (4) In 2000 everyone has the right to vote while in the 1930s not everyone did.
    (5) The quality of voting machines is more important than that of water fountains.

2. Which of the following most likely describes the artist who drew this cartoon?

    The artist is
    (1) comfortable with the 2000 election and its results
    (2) an activist who worked for civil rights in the 1960s
    (3) dismayed by a new and different civil rights disparity
    (4) encouraged by the progress of the United States since the 1930s
    (5) either African American, low income, or both

Answers are on page 406.

As a democracy the United States is constantly struggling to achieve and maintain the balance between individual freedom and general order. There is a wide variety of opinion on what that balance should look like.

Political views vary in extremes and moderations. Whatever the particular issue, however, it is argued among elected officials, or officials appointed by the elected officials. This is what it means to have a representative government. The average citizen does not usually engage directly in decision making, except in the voting booth when he or she chooses a representative. As Henry Clay, a nineteenth century statesman, said, "Government is a trust, and the officers of the government are trustees; and both the trust and the trustees are created for the benefit of the people." What two inferences can you make from Clay's statement about both the officers of the government and the people if the government is to live up to its name as a trust?

1. _____

2. _____

If you wrote something along the lines of the people needing to participate with care in the selection of the officers and the officers needing to respond with integrity to the voters' wishes, you were correct. In addition to the challenge of prejudice to a democracy, there are the challenges of a disinterested electorate and of corruptible representatives.

In 2000 an estimated 52 to 53 percent of Americans old enough to vote cast ballots in the presidential election. In 1996, about 49 percent of those old enough to vote did so—the lowest turnout since 1924.

EXERCISE 8

Questions 1 and 2 are based on the information on the previous page and the following graph.

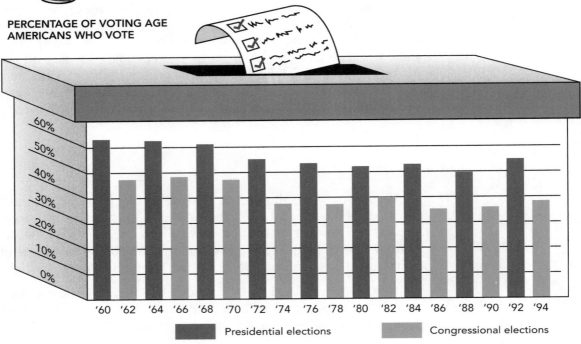

PERCENTAGE OF VOTING AGE AMERICANS WHO VOTE

1. Which of the following statements does the graph support?

   (1) More people vote in congressional elections than in presidential ones.
   (2) The lack of voter participation is not a new issue in American politics.
   (3) The president has consistently been elected by a majority of registered voters.
   (4) The United States has the lowest rate of voter participation of any democracy in the world.
   (5) One cause of low voter turnout is that elections occur too frequently.

2. Which of the following is not a likely explanation for the level of voter disinterest evident in the graph?

   (1) Voter outreach programs have been established and bilingual ballots introduced.
   (2) There are so many elections involving the various levels of government that people become tired and confused.
   (3) Politics seems to be characterized by poor public leadership and increasingly complex issues.
   (4) Campaign politics tend to be negative, urging votes *against* one candidate rather than *for* another.
   (5) The two main political parties are increasingly similar to one another and do not present voters with fresh alternatives.

Answers are on page 406.

Corruption in politics is certainly one of the things that accounts for voter cynicism. It is difficult to believe that there are any good choices in the voting booth when talk about government scandal is everywhere. Citizens are disgusted by the contempt for the law that is demonstrated by those chosen to uphold it.

Scandal is nothing new in America, or anywhere else for that matter. The cumulative effect, however, is highly apparent. In the recent past there have been the Watergate, Iran-Contra, and Whitewater scandals. The unexemplary personal lives of candidates are front-page news, rather than their ideas on important issues. Greed seems to have replaced service as an inspiration for running for public office.

The following paragraphs present two views on one proposal for limiting corruption: term limits. There is a limit on the amount of time a president can stay in the White House (eight years), but not on the terms of senators and members of the House of Representatives. Once someone is elected, it is relatively easy to be re-elected because of the financial support one can muster by virtue of the position. Certainly there are advantages to remaining in office indefinitely that go beyond personal gain. But, clearly, there are also disadvantages.

EXERCISE 9

Questions 1–3 refer to the two paragraphs below.

Speaker A

The concept of term limits, or rotation in office, is nothing new. For centuries, it has been viewed as a necessary component of democratic government. From the city-state of ancient Athens to the early American republic, the virtue of citizen legislators has been universally recognized. Thomas Jefferson, recognizing the corrupting influence of spending too much time in office, stated: "Whenever a man has cast a longing eye on [political office], a rottenness begins in his conduct."

Jefferson's fears couldn't have been more fully realized. Career politicians in modern American politics enjoy advantages that can only be called rotten. From the taxpayer-financed perks and privileges that cannot be matched by any challenger, to massive campaign coffers filled by special interest clients, incumbent members of Congress are able to intimidate potentially qualified opposition and bury any that take on the quixotic crusade of challenging incumbents.

—Excerpted from "Restoring a Democratic Tradition" by Paul Jacob,
Perspectives: Readings on Contemporary American Government

Speaker B

The process of election and reelection, and the drive for reelection, are essentials; the need is to channel them in a positive way. The framers [of the Constitution] recognized this. They did not try to eliminate ambition from the political system, but to transform it into a positive force. The framers rejected the idea of arbitrarily limiting the service of individuals in public office. Frequent elections, checks and balances, the separation of powers, were all elements of their design to channel the ambition of politicians appropriately.

Chances are that if the legislature consisted of amateurs, the real policy decisions and the oversight of financial markets and international affairs would be taken over from an overwhelmed and inexperienced Congress out of its league, and made instead by seasoned bureaucrats, presidential appointees, judges, and the crafty and experienced people not being regulated—those we sometimes call the "special interests."

—Excerpted from "Congress Needs Experienced Lawmakers"
by Norman Ornstein, *Perspectives: Readings on Contemporary American Government*

1. Which of the following statements is accurate?

   (1) Speaker B supports term limits because he believes that the framers of the Constitution would have wanted them.
   (2) Speaker B does not support term limits because if term limits existed, Congress would consist of only inexperienced people.
   (3) Speakers A and B both agree that the personal ambitions of career politicians can be controlled.
   (4) Speaker A supports term limits because even the people of ancient Greece thought they were a good idea.
   (5) Speaker A does not support term limits because they would discourage capable people from entering politics.

2. Which of the following do both speakers want?

   (1) lawmakers that are effective and honest
   (2) changes to the Constitution
   (3) special-interest groups with more influence
   (4) more privileges for incumbent members of Congress
   (5) more opposition candidates

3. Which of the following examples would Speaker A likely cite to support his view?

   (1) A new senator endangered the passage of a bill his constituents supported because of his naiveté about the strategies of lobbying groups.
   (2) A seasoned and influential representative decided to retire, much to the dismay of his constituents who trust him.
   (3) A four-term incumbent speaks out in favor of a bill that three of her major campaign contributors oppose.
   (4) In a year of record-breaking national debt and high unemployment, senior senators took home six-figure salaries.
   (5) Thomas Jefferson never served more than two terms in elected office.

Answers are on page 406.

The Role and Influence of Citizens in a Democracy

 Clearly the first responsibility of a citizen in maintaining a democracy is to vote. In order to vote, one must register, which can be done by filling out a short form at a local city or town hall, through the mail, or over the Internet. Below is a sample voter registration form. Does it look complicated? Why might someone have reservations about filling it out? Which questions are the most challenging?

Voter Registration Application For U.S. Citizens

	You can use this form to: ■ register to vote ■ report that your name or address has changed ■ register with a party Please print in blue or black ink	This space for office use only.

		Last Name	First Name	Middle Name(s)	(Circle one) Jr Sr II III IV
1	Mr. Mrs. Miss Ms.				

	Address (see instructions)–Street (or route and box number)	Apt. or Lot #	City/Town	State	Zip Code
2					

	Address Where You Get Your Mail If Different From Above (see instructions)	City/Town	State	Zip Code
3				

	Date of Birth / / Month Day Year	5	Telephone Number (optional)	6	ID Number (see item 6 in the instructions for your State)
4					

	Choice of Party (see item 7 in the instructions for your State)	8	Race or Ethnic Group (see item 8 in the instructions for your State)
7			

	I swear/affirm that: ■ I am a United States citizen ■ I meet the eligibility requirements of my state and suscribe to any oath required. (See item 9 in the instructions for your state before you sign.) ■ The information I have provided is true to the best of my knowlege under penalty of perjury. If I have provided false information, I may be fined, imprisoned, or (if not a U.S. citizen) deported from or refused entry to the United States.	Please sign full name (or put mark) ↓ Date: / / Month Day Year
9		

	If the applicant is unable to sign, who helped the applicant fill out this application? Give name, address and phone number (phone number optional)
10	

-- Fold here

Please fill out the sections below if they apply to you.

If this application is for a change of name, what was your name before you changed it?

		Last Name	First Name	Middle Name(s)	(Circle one) Jr Sr II III IV
A	Mr. Mrs. Miss Ms.				

If you were registered before but this is the first time you are registering from the address in Box 2, what was your address where you were registered before?

	Street (or route and box number)	Apt. or Lot #	City/Town	State	Zip Code
B					

If you live in a rural area but do not have a street number, or if you have no street address, please show on the map where you live.

	■ Write in the name of the crossroads (or streets) nearest to where you live. ■ Draw an X to show where you live. ■ Use a dot to show any schools, churches, stores, or other landmarks near where you live, and write the name of the landmark.	NORTH ↑
C	Example Route #2 ● Grocery Store Woodchuck Road Public School ● X	

To Mail:
1. Address the back of this application (see address under your state).
2. Remove plastic strip below.
3. Fold form at middle and seal at top.
4. Put on a first-class stamp and mail.

Once you are registered, all you have to do is show up at your neighborhood polling place on election day. On your ballot there is usually more than one issue or office to be decided. Where can you look to find information about the candidates and their stands on issues important to you?

_____

_____

Nonpartisan citizen information groups, or organizations that do not support a particular political party, usually publish voter information guides that come free of charge in the mail to all residents and are available at public libraries as well. Newspapers, of course, can also be good resources, as well as television news. It is important when you read or view something, however, to be aware of the political leanings of the publisher or network. Not all of what you hear is completely objective, and the treatment of issues is often superficial at best.

GED PRACTICE

EXERCISE 10

Critics of television's role in presidential campaigns emphasize what they believe is the triumph of image over issues, personalities over policies. Many media observers say primary elections are shallow popularity contests, and that political conventions are nothing more than very long, staged campaign commercials. Critics also contend television news coverage is too focused on the race and not enough on the important issues. Televised debates, they add, are merely collections of well-rehearsed sound bites in front of a live audience, and political advertisements package the candidate as if he or she were a new car. Many Americans see all of these developments as contributing to the breakdown of the presidential selection process. They argue that television has made it difficult for millions of Americans to cast an informed ballot on election day.

—Excerpted from "Television and Modern Presidential Campaigns" by Tim Walker, *Perspectives: Readings on Contemporary American Government*

1. Which of the following might critics of television's role in elections consider valuable to the electorate?

   (1) A video designed to give voters an "inside look" at a candidate by showing him eating and joking with his children.
   (2) A daily, detailed analysis of what percent of the population support each of the candidates.
   (3) A town meeting with "regular people" asking spontaneous, unrehearsed questions about what concerns them.
   (4) A sordid "scoop" on an extramarital affair that a candidate had fifteen years ago with a much younger person.
   (5) An hour-long interview between a well-known journalist and each of the two main candidates.

Answers are on page 406.

Another responsibility of a person living in a democracy is the payment of taxes. Every working person gives a percentage of his or her income to the federal and state governments to help fund the various programs that help the country as a whole, and the citizens within it. These programs include

- Social Security, Medicare, and other retirement benefits

- national defense, veterans, foreign affairs

- net interest on the debt

- infrastructure (e.g., systems of transportation, power generation, communications, banking, education, and health)

- social aid programs

- law enforcement and general government expenses

The first income tax, back in 1913, was paid only by the richest 5 percent of households. Since then, however, middle- and working-class residents have shouldered more and more of the burden. Every year the Internal Revenue Service (IRS) distributes an instruction book together with the numerous forms on which people must report their incomes and calculate their taxes. The following is a page from the IRS booklet that describes the requirements for filing taxes for the year 2000. Use this information to answer questions 1 and 2.

GED PRACTICE

EXERCISE 11

Filing Requirements–These rules apply to all U.S. citizens, regardless of where they live, and resident aliens.

Do You Have To File?
Use **Chart A, B,** or **C** to see if you must file a return.

Even if you do not otherwise have to file a return, you should file one to get a refund of any Federal income tax withheld. You should also file if you are eligible for the earned income credit or the additional child tax credit.

Exception for Children Under Age 14. If you are planning to file a return for your child who was under age 14 on January 1, 2001, and certain other conditions apply, you may elect to include your child's income on your return. But

you must use Form 1040 and **Form 8814** to do so. If you make this election, your child does not have to file a return. For details, use TeleTax topic 553 (see page 10) or see Form 8814.

Nonresident Aliens and Dual-Status Aliens. These rules also apply to nonresident aliens and dual-status aliens who were married to U.S. citizens or residents at the end of 2000 and who have elected to be taxed as resident aliens. Other nonresident aliens and dual-status aliens have different filing requirements. They may have to file **Form 1040NR** or **Form 1040NR-EZ.** Specific rules apply to determine if you are a resident or nonresident alien. See **Pub. 519** for details, including the rules for students and scholars who are aliens.

Chart A–For Most People		
If your filing status is . . .	AND at the end of 2000 you were* . . .	THEN file a return if your gross income ** was at least . . .
Single	under 65 65 or older	$7,200 8,300
Married filing jointly***	under 65 (both spouses) 65 or older (one spouse) 65 or older (both spouses)	$12,950 13,800 14,650
Married filing separately	any age	$2,800
Head of household (see page 22)	under 65 65 or older	$9,250 10,350
Qualifying widow(er) with dependent child (see page 23)	under 65 65 or older	$10,150 11,000

*   If you turned 65 on January 1, 2001, you are considered to be age 65 at the end of 2000.

** Gross income means all income you received in the form of money, goods, property, and services that is not exempt from tax, including any income from sources outside the United States (even if you may exclude part or all of it). Do not include social security benefits unless you are married filing a separate return and you lived with your spouse at any time in 2000.

*** If you did not live with your spouse at the end of 2000 (or on the date your spouse died) and your gross income was at least $2,800, you must file a return regardless of your age.

1. According to Chart A, which of the following does not have to file a tax return?

    (1) an 80-year-old single man who earns $5000 by selling his paintings
    (2) a 42-year-old head of household who works two jobs, supports three children, and earns $35,000
    (3) a 27-year-old woman who is filing separately from her husband and earns $26,000. Her husband is unemployed.
    (4) a 63-year-old widow whose husband of 71 died before the end of the year with combined earnings of $15,000 last year
    (5) an 18-year old college student who earned $7500 at several part-time jobs

2. Which of the following would not be considered part of your gross income?

    (1) the royalties on a book you published ten years ago
    (2) the rent from the upstairs apartment of a building you own
    (3) Social Security benefits you received after being widowed for two years
    (4) the profit you made by selling some stocks that you inherited many years ago
    (5) the extra spending money you earned by working evenings at Kmart during the holiday season

Answers are on page 406.

Besides voting (which is considered just as much a right as a responsibility) and the payment of taxes (which is considered by most as just a responsibility) a citizen also has the responsibilities of serving on a jury if called to do so and of understanding the legal obligations when entering into a contract. If you are a man, you also have the responsibility of registering for the draft. How many of these responsibilities have you exercised at some point in your life?

In addition to the responsibilities listed above there are many other ways in which people can engage in and enhance American democracy. Commonly called "civic participation," these are the means for building community, acknowledging inequalities, and taking informed action. Examples of these activities include attending meetings to gain information, discuss issues, or lend support; signing a petition; writing letters to elected representatives; campaigning for a candidate; lobbying for laws that are of special interest; and demonstrating through marches, boycotts, sit-ins, or other forms of protest.

Deciding whether to participate in these types of activities and how much time to spend participating is important. To make good decisions, you must think about how important the things discussed in this chapter are to you and how satisfied you are with the way the government is working. You must also think about whether you are working to benefit people at a personal or at an institutional level, and whether your actions will be taken as an individual or collectively (together with a group of similarly minded people).

EXERCISE 12

Identify each of the following four activities with both a letter and a Roman numeral.

A   individual action
B   collective action
I   personal change
II institutional change

1. _____ & _____ You call your elected representatives to express your concern about the high cost of health care.
2. _____ & _____ You organize a group of neighbors to clean up a trashy lot and turn it into a community garden.
3. _____ & _____ You volunteer each week to bring a meal to an ailing and housebound elder.
4. _____ & _____ You join a march to protest the building of a toxic waste site in your region.

Answers are on page 406.

This chapter began with the concept of power and has explored it in numerous ways. Read the following excerpt while continuing to think about power. Then write an answer to the question that follows.

A prominent problem in the North Quabbin area of rural Massachusetts is the lack of public transportation. In a place where facilities and services are far apart and many people cannot afford cars, this means that access to education and employment opportunities is very limited. There is a cab service but the prices are outrageous and the one cab is often unavailable. To address this issue, a group of citizens began to meet together regularly. This is their description of what they did.

We started by looking at the history of transportation—past, present, and future, including trolleys and early buses. We found that if we were going to fight for something we believed in, we would have to know a lot about the subject. We also examined the loss of all forms of public transportation in the area during the last fifteen years. We learned a great deal about transportation and had fun doing it! We wrote letters, made phone calls, and set up meetings with the regional transit officials, selectmen, politicians, and other interested community members. We formed a North Quabbin Transportation Task Force after a community meeting in March. We also did a ten-minute video and aired it on our local cable access television station to make people aware of our problem. After the video, we had a live panel discussion where people could call in with their comments and questions.

During the summer, people from agencies and the community met each Wednesday over lunch to hammer out details concerning a pilot project to bring some form of community-based public transportation to the . . . area. A ten-passenger van with a handicapped lift has been made available from Franklin Regional Transit Authority (FRTA) to the North Quabbin Transportation Co-op. (This is the Task Force that formed after the showing of the video.) The van is going to cost about $3200 a year to cover insurance, upkeep, and other operating costs. Before we get the van on the road, volunteer drivers will be trained. To help raise money, we had a raffle and a walk-a-thon. People continuing to work on this issue are also selling buttons. The button says: "Never doubt that a small group of thoughtful, committed citizens can change the world. Indeed, it's the only thing that ever has!" (Margaret Mead)

With the community van and the ride-share project, we are starting small with a simple plan so we can handle problems. We also plan to continue working with the FRTA to build a permanent public bus service for this area. Hopefully, in a year or two, we can get regular bus service, but that's going to take longer than anything.

—Excerpted from "Getting Involved in Community Issues: Yes, You Can Make a Difference" by Cynthia Rodriguez, Jennifer Savage, Caridad Santiago, Lisa Willard, and Donna Swain, *The Change Agent*, February 1998

As you read the story in what ways did you observe the exercise of power? How did the group's experience reflect the concepts of authority and governance? How did the Constitution support the group's project? In what ways were the group members contributing towards democracy? Write your thoughts on a separate sheet of paper.

Chapter Review

Questions 1–3 are based on the following passage.

The Declaration of Independence states, "We hold these truths to be self-evident, that all men are created equal, that they are endowed by their Creator with certain inalienable Rights, that among these are Life, Liberty and the pursuit of Happiness. That to secure these rights, Governments are instituted among Men, deriving their just Powers from the consent of the governed. That Whenever any Form of Government becomes destructive of these ends, it is the Right of the People to alter or to abolish it, and to institute new Government, laying its foundation on such principles and organizing its Powers in such form, as to them shall seem most likely to effect their Safety and Happiness."

When Thomas Jefferson wrote these words in 1776, he made one of the most powerful political statements of all time. The principles outlined in the Declaration of Independence shaped the American political structure and became embedded in the U.S. Constitution.

1. Which of the following is an opinion expressed by the author of the second paragraph?

    (1) The quotation is from the Declaration of Independence.
    (2) Thomas Jefferson was the author of the quotation.
    (3) The Declaration of Independence is a powerful document.
    (4) The Declaration of Independence was written in 1776.
    (5) The Constitution was derived from the Declaration of Independence.

2. According to the Declaration of Independence, which of the following principles did Jefferson most value?

    (1) the survival of the fittest
    (2) the natural rights of the individual
    (3) the power of government
    (4) freedom of religion
    (5) telling the truth

3. Which part of the Constitution did this section of the Declaration of Independence clearly influence?

    (1) Article One, which describes the two houses of Congress
    (2) Article Two, which describes the executive branch
    (3) Article Three, which describes the judiciary
    (4) Article Five, which describes the amendment process
    (5) the First Amendment, which describes four freedoms

Questions 4–8 are based on the following definitions of five political labels and on the paragraph following the definitions.

Radical: advocates sweeping changes in laws and methods of government with the least delay

Liberal: advocates political change in the name of progress, especially social improvement through governmental action

Moderate: believes in avoiding extreme changes and measures in laws and government

Conservative: advocates maintaining the existing social order

Reactionary: resists change and usually advocates a return to an earlier social order or policy

A controversial issue that has dominated American life in recent years is gun control. Handguns seem to be increasingly accessible and are one of the leading causes of death in the United States. Americans have varying opinions about crime and handgun control. Read the quotes below and identify them with the correct label.

4. "Everybody should arm himself with a gun like people did in the Old West. Then you wouldn't have to worry about crime in the streets."

   (1) radical
   (2) liberal
   (3) moderate
   (4) conservative
   (5) reactionary

5. "Congress needs to introduce more legislation to ban the possession and sale of handguns. Only then will senseless handgun deaths cease."

   (1) radical
   (2) liberal
   (3) moderate
   (4) conservative
   (5) reactionary

6. "The Second Amendment gives American citizens the right to bear arms. To deny this basic right is an infringement on our personal liberties. The law should remain the way it is."

   (1) radical
   (2) liberal
   (3) moderate
   (4) conservative
   (5) reactionary

7. "There's no need to enact new laws or to abolish existing laws on gun control. All that's needed is the enforcement of the current laws on the books."

   (1) radical
   (2) liberal
   (3) moderate
   (4) conservative
   (5) reactionary

8. "The time to enforce gun control is *now*. Not one more murder should be committed because guns are so readily available. Let's stop the manufacture of guns *today*."

   (1) radical
   (2) liberal
   (3) moderate
   (4) conservative
   (5) reactionary

Questions 9 and 10 are based on the following excerpt from a speech given by the Chief Justice of the Supreme Court, William H. Rehnquist, in 1996.

> The framers [of the Constitution] came up with two quite original ideas. The first was the idea of a chief executive who was not responsible to the legislature, as a chief executive is under the parliamentary system. The second was the idea of an independent judiciary with authority to declare laws passed by Congress unconstitutional. The first idea—a president not responsible to Congress—has not been widely copied by other nations in the Western world when they have come to review their systems of government. But the second idea—that of an independent judiciary with the final authority to interpret a written constitution—has caught on with many other nations, particularly since the end of the Second World War. It is one of the crown jewels of our system of government today.

> Change is the law of life, and the judiciary will have to change to meet the challenges which will face it in the future. But the independence of the federal judiciary is essential to its proper functioning and must be retained.

9. Which of the following situations is consistent with Rehnquist's assertions?

    (1) A small Central American country emerges from under three decades of dictatorship and forms a new parliamentary-style government.
    (2) The newly-written constitution of a southern African nation provides for a court system that is not responsible to the executive branch.
    (3) What was once one large country in Eastern Europe has divided into four smaller nations, each independently deciding its own form of government.
    (4) The governors of three Midwestern states recently appointed new members to their state supreme courts.
    (5) Before the Constitutional Convention in 1787, the court system of the United States was not respected by other countries.

10. Which of the following best illustrates the independence and authority of the American judiciary?

    (1) A district court judge receives a bribe to decide in favor of a defendant in a lawsuit.
    (2) The jury for a highly publicized trial is sequestered, or held away from the media, for the duration of the trial.
    (3) A judge is appointed for life and is not vulnerable to shifts in controlling political parties.
    (4) Anti-abortion activists gather regularly at the Supreme Court building in Washington to protest *Roe* v. *Wade*.
    (5) Since1981 Supreme Court Justice Sandra Day O'Connor has became more of a centrist than a conservative.

Question 11 refers to the chart below.

THIRD-PARTY PRESIDENTIAL CANDIDATES

Below are some third-party or independent candidates in the twentieth century who received a significant percentage of the vote.

CANDIDATE	PARTY	% OF VOTE
Theodore Roosevelt (1912)	Progressive Party	27
Eugene Debs (1912)	Socialist Party	7
Robert M. LaFollete (1924)	Progressive Party	17
George Wallace (1968)	American Independent Party	14
John B. Anderson (1980)	National Unity Campaign	7
H. Ross Perot (1992)	(independent)	19
H. Ross Perot (1996)	Reform Party	9
Ralph Nader (2000)	Green Party	3

---

11. What generalization would you be tempted to make about third-party candidates on the basis of the information provided in the chart?

    (1) Third parties don't usually provide a significant challenge to the Democrats and Republicans.
    (2) In almost every election third parties are able to garner at least 5 percent of the vote.
    (3) In the first quarter of the last century, the socialists were a threat to democracy.
    (4) Third parties offer voters a welcome alternative to "politics as usual."
    (5) There should be more third-party candidates.

Question 12 refers to the following paragraphs.

The Voting Rights Act of 1965 helped eliminate many of the barriers to the ballot box for African Americans. By the 1980s, Mississippi had more black elected officials than any other state. Unita Blackwell, one of the MFDP) Mississippi Freedom Democratic Party) delegates in 1964, addressed the Democratic National Convention in 1984, this time as mayor of Mayersville, Mississippi.

"I tried not to get too emotional about it, but there was a feeling that it was worth all of it that we had been through. I remember a woman told me one time when I was running for justice of [the] peace, "The reason I won't vote for you is because they going to kill you." The whites had told that they were going to kill me, and she thought she was saving my life. And when I stood in that podium twenty years later, I was standing there for this woman, to understand that she had a right to register to vote for whomever she wanted to, and that we as a people were going to live."

—Excerpted from "'It Was Worth It': Celebrating the Right to Vote" by Unita Blackwell

12. What can you infer about Unita Blackwell from her speech?

(1) She was extremely frustrated by how long it took to get the Voting Rights Act passed.
(2) She was new to politics and didn't know what to say at a national convention.
(3) She thought that the woman who told her the whites would kill her was crazy.
(4) She had probably endured many years of personal struggle and discrimination.
(5) She almost decided against running for office because of the threats to her life.

Answers are on pages 406–407.

Chapter 8

Production, Distribution, and Consumption

The Green Thumb is a small company that produces indoor and outdoor plants that it distributes through home parties. Its sales personnel visit people's homes to show them the plants, explain how to grow and care for them, and convince the people to be buyers, or **consumers,** of the plants.

The plants are **goods;** the instruction on how to grow and care for them is a **service.** The people who took the risk to establish the business are **entrepreneurs**. They are attempting to fill a need in society. If they succeed, their activity will pay off, or return a **profit** for the money they invested in the business.

In the production of the plants, raw materials, called **natural resources**, are used. **Human resources,** or labor, are the gardeners, the salespeople, and the office workers of The Green Thumb. **Capital,** which includes the greenhouse, gardening tools, grow lights, and money, is also invested in the effort.

The study of the process of producing and distributing these plants to consumers and how it relates to buying, selling, and making a profit in a society is called **economics.** Economics also explores the role of the government in regulating such business activities, and examines how the government acquires and distributes wealth.

In this chapter we will look at economic systems, with primary emphasis on capitalism, the dominant economic system in the United States and the developed world. We will examine the development of the modern economy, and then look at some of its most important features, including the role of money, supply and demand, and the business cycle. We will then look at the role of government in the economy and at financial institutions and personal finance. Finally we will look at measures of economic activity and wealth, the distribution of wealth, and the challenges of economic development.

EXERCISE 1

Directions: Based on the reading on the previous page, match the terms on the left with the descriptions on the right by writing the correct letter in the space provided.

_____ 1. Producers

_____ 2. Distributors

_____ 3. Consumers

_____ 4. Goods

_____ 5. Service

(a) the interior designers and homemakers who buy The Green Thumb's plants

(b) the different varieties of plants The Green Thumb sells

(c) the trucks that deliver the nursery-grown plants to The Green Thumb outlets

(d) what The Green Thumb salespeople give potential buyers

(e) The Green Thumb and other companies like it that make a product

Answers are on page 407.

Economic Systems

The earliest and most historically numerous economic system has been that of primitive society, where the traditions of the tribe dictate how goods are distributed. So far as is known, all ancient tradition-bound peoples solve their economic problems today much as they did 10,000 years or perhaps 10,000 centuries ago—adapting by migration or movement to changes in season or climate, sustaining themselves by hunting and gathering or by slash-and-burn agriculture, and distributing their output by well-defined social claims, the way it has been done for centuries. In these systems, each person in a tribe or group ends up getting enough to eat.

This kind of economic system is known as a **distributive system.** Although many have believed that primitive economic societies were marked by constant scarcity and want, this turns out not to be the case for groups using a distributive system. According to the anthropologist Marshall Sahlins, several primitive societies could increase their distribution of food if they wanted to. While outside observers would perceive the Bushmen of Africa, for example, to have a scarcity of food, the Bushmen themselves would feel that each had received as much or she or he needed, and would be perfectly satisfied.

Another thing to understand about the distributive system in primitive economic systems is the difficulty of describing any part of their life activities as an "economy." The hunting, gathering, and distribution of food and other resources is a part of their existence as a whole. No special activities or procedures of distribution mark their subsistence activities as "economic."

For each of the following, write **P** if it is typical of a primitive economic system.

_____ **1.** free markets for the exchange of goods

_____ **2.** sharing of materials for clothing and shelter

_____ **3.** opportunities to accumulate private wealth

_____ **4.** adapting to changes in seasons by migrating

_____ **5.** strong communal life

In a typical primitive economic system, there would be sharing of materials for clothing and shelter, migration dictated by the seasons, and a strong communal life.

Questions 1–4 are based on the following definitions of economic systems.

Capitalism—an economic system that is based on the private ownership of property and the resources of production

Socialism—an economic system in which a country's major industries may be owned privately or publicly but are subject to governmental control

Communism—an economic system in which property is owned by the state and all citizens share in the common wealth, more or less according to their need

Command Economy—an economic system in which the means of production are publicly owned and economic activity is controlled by the government, which assigns quantitative production goals and gives raw materials to productive enterprises

Primitive Economy—an economic system in which the acquisition and distribution of goods is completely absorbed within the traditional mode of existence as a whole

1. The basis of Egypt's legendary wealth was the highly productive land, which technically remained in royal ownership. A considerable portion was kept under the control of temples, and the remainder was leased out on a theoretically revocable basis to tenant-farmers. The system could best be described as which of the following economic systems?

    (1) Capitalism
    (2) Socialism
    (3) Communism
    (4) Command Economy
    (5) Primitive Economy

2. Great Britain's economic strength was based on a number of factors including its stable currency, the quality of its products, the fairness of its courts for both its own citizens and foreigners, and its free markets. The system could best be described as which of the following economic systems?

   (1) Capitalism
   (2) Socialism
   (3) Communism
   (4) Command Economy
   (5) Primitive Economy

3. Before the arrival of the Europeans, the Mohegans lived in what is now Connecticut by hunting, fishing, and farming. Maize was the primary staple crop. Each village was mostly self-sufficient. The system could best be described as which of the following economic systems?

   (1) Capitalism
   (2) Socialism
   (3) Communism
   (4) Command Economy
   (5) Primitive Economy

4. Sweden has an urban industrialized economy based primarily on extensive forests, rich iron-ore deposits, and abundant waterpower resources. Although more than 90 percent of Swedish industry is privately owned, the government exercises substantial control over the economy to moderate economic fluctuations. Swedish citizens enjoy an impressive array of social services. The system could best be described as which of the following economic systems?

   (1) Capitalism
   (2) Socialism
   (3) Communism
   (4) Command Economy
   (5) Primitive Economy

Answers are on page 407.

Development of the Modern Economy

The modern economy first developed in Europe during the period now known as the Middle Ages. The collapse of the Roman Empire first resulted in a dramatic economic decline, but later created conditions that allowed for the growth of freedom and the economy.

GED PRACTICE

EXERCISE 3

Questions 1–3 are based on the following passage.

The roles of ideas and ideologies in history is much more difficult to establish than is often believed. Neither freedom nor slavery, for example, was the result of ideas or ideologies. Freedom began to emerge where governments were too fragmented, too poorly organized, or too much in need of voluntary cooperation to prevent its emergence. That was the situation in parts of medieval Europe, where a politically fragmented continent had numerous local rulers who needed the economic resources being produced by prosperous towns and cities in order to finance their own wars of aggrandizement or to protect themselves from others' wars of aggrandizement. In this setting, kings and nobles competed in granting townsmen and city dwellers exemptions from the heavy-handed controls of the feudal world, in order to attract and hold the commerce and industry that meant taxes and the military power which those taxes could buy.

Where a single government held firm and undisputed control over a vast area, as in China for example during the same era, no such concessions were necessary and were not given. But when Europe splintered politically after the collapse of the Roman and Byzantine empires, not only did the numerous kings have to fear each other, they also had to fear their own armed nobles and the nobles had to fear one another as well. The rise of lucrative commerce and industry, especially in Western Europe, provided both local and national despots with incentives to create islands of exemption from their own despotism, in order to serve their own economic and military self-interest by attracting people with commercial and industrial skills.

European rulers at all levels were as devoted to government control of the economy as Chinese rulers were. Not only innumerable government regulations but also a farming out of similar regulatory powers to private groups such as the guilds, as well as the creation of government-sponsored private monopolies in various commodities, clearly indicate a dirigiste mentality among rulers in Europe as well as in Asia. However, medieval Europe's lag behind China in technological innovation was paralleled by its lag behind China in effective governmental control. This, together with smaller and much more numerous governmental units in medieval Europe, permitted artisans, merchants, and other European economic agents to escape into various enclaves beyond the jurisdiction of particular authorities, where they could practice their trades and sell their merchandise under freer conditions. Moreover, the threat of losing such valuable taxpayers made more rulers willing to relax their grip on the economy. Along with economic freedom, political freedom developed, again largely as a way of attracting and keeping economically productive classes.

—Excerpted from *Conquests and Cultures, An International History* by Thomas Sowell

1. Unlike Europe, how was the United States able to stimulate economic development?

    (1) through a strong central government that protected individual rights
    (2) by fragmenting into many autonomous states which vied for business
    (3) by offering special tax breaks for new economic growth and expansion
    (4) by developing trade with nations throughout the world, including China
    (5) by collecting taxes from innovators and entrepreneurs

2. According to the article, what was the main reason that China was unable to maintain its technological lead over Europe?

    (1) the lack of political freedom for the Chinese
    (2) the poor educational system in China
    (3) the stresses caused by overpopulation
    (4) the central government stifling innovation
    (5) an inefficient tax collection system

3. If the Roman Empire had maintained its power and control over Europe until the present, how might the economic history of Europe most likely be different?

    (1) The modern economy would have developed hundreds of years sooner.
    (2) Large companies would have flourished and developed enormous wealth.
    (3) The modern economy might never have developed in Europe at all.
    (4) The Italian peninsula would have led the new economy instead of England.
    (5) Europe would have never lost economic leadership to the United States.

Answers are on page 407.

Supply and Demand

Supply and demand, in economics, are the basic factors that determine price. **Supply** is the quantity of goods and services available for sale. **Demand** is the desire and ability of consumers to buy a product or service. According to the law of supply and demand, the market prices of goods and services are determined by the relationship of supply to demand. Theoretically, when supply exceeds demand, sellers must lower prices to stimulate sales. On the other hand, when demand is greater than supply, sellers can raise prices because the buyers are competing to buy the goods.

Look at the following graph to see an example of the relationship between supply and demand.

GED PRACTICE

EXERCISE 4

Questions 1 and 2 are based on the following graph and passage.

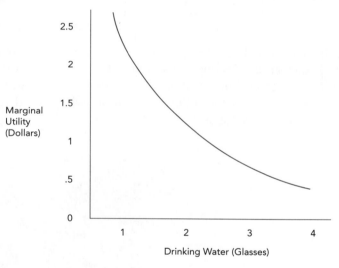

© Microsoft Corporation. All Rights Reserved.

This graph shows the relationship between the value of, or demand for, a glass of water and the quantity available, or the supply. Each additional glass of water has a lower marginal utility; that is, it is worth less than the previous glass. This is because, for a thirsty person, the value of one glass of water is high, and that person would be willing to pay a high price for it. For someone who has already had one or more glasses of water and is no longer so thirsty, the value of another glass of water is less, and the person would not be willing to pay as much for it.

1. According to the graph, how much less is the fourth glass of drinking water worth than the first glass?

   (1) 3 dollars
   (2) 2 dollars
   (3) 1.5 dollars
   (4) 1 dollar
   (5) 0.5 dollar

2. Given the information on the graph, what is the most likely value of a fifth glass of water?

   (1) 5 dollars
   (2) 2.5 dollars
   (3) 1 dollar
   (4) 0.5 dollar
   (5) 0.3 dollar

Answers are on page 407.

Measures of Economic Activity

The Dow Jones Industrial Average is one of the most widely watched measures of economic activity. It measures the value of the stocks of a group of large companies that are considered central to the United States economy. According to the following cartoon, what would you expect to be the behavior of the Dow Jones Average?

"Dow Jonesy enough for you?"

—© The New Yorker collection, 1998, Jack Ziegler.
From cartoonbank.com. All Rights Reserved.

_____

_____

_____

Now look at the following line graph, which measures the actual performance of the Dow Jones Industrial Average. Is the cartoon supported by the graph of the actual performance of the Dow Jones?

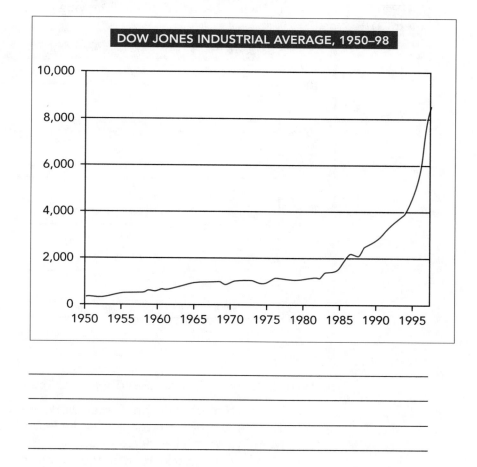

DOW JONES INDUSTRIAL AVERAGE, 1950–98

_____

_____

_____

_____

The cartoon implies that the Dow Jones is constantly going steeply up and down, like a roller coaster. But the line graph shows that after years of relative stability, the Dow has been mostly increasing for the past few decades.

EXERCISE 5

Questions 1 and 2 are based on the following graph.

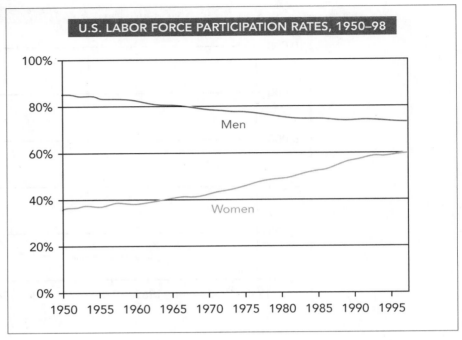

U.S. LABOR FORCE PARTICIPATION RATES, 1950–98

1. Which of the following describes what the graph shows?

   (1) The percent of men and women working has increased since 1950.
   (2) The percent of men working has increased while the percent of women working has decreased.
   (3) Men have been taking on an increasing role in housework.
   (4) The percent of men and women working has leveled off.
   (5) More men now depend on women to help financially support families.

2. Which of the following conclusions can be drawn from the information in this graph?

   (1) The percent of women in the labor force has been steadily increasing for half a century.
   (2) The trends shown in the graph are an indication of a decline in respect for traditional values.
   (3) Within the next half century, the percent of women in the labor force will approach 100 percent.
   (4) Women will soon replace men as the primary wage earners in most American families.
   (5) In order to make ends meet, all the adults in most families must work at a wage-earning job.

Question 3 is based on the following graph.

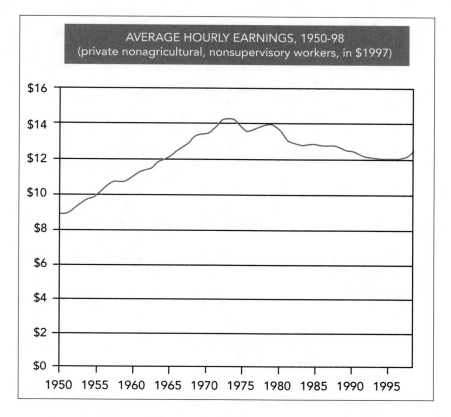

AVERAGE HOURLY EARNINGS, 1950-98
(private nonagricultural, nonsupervisory workers, in $1997)

3. From 1980 to 1992, the Republican Party controlled the White House and the national agenda. Their program to stimulate the economy was called supply-side economics and included a large tax cut. What was the apparent impact of these economic policies on the average hourly earnings of American workers?

(1) Most workers benefited since taxes were reduced.
(2) Wages for the average worker stagnated and declined.
(3) Lower inflation increased workers' real income.
(4) More people were encouraged to seek jobs, stabilizing salaries.
(5) The policies had little impact, since previous wage trends continued.

Answers are on pages 407–408.

The Business Cycle

The amount of goods and services produced by a nation within its borders is called its Gross Domestic Product, or GDP. The total amount of goods and services produced by a nation, both domestically and internationally, is called the Gross National Product, or GNP. Both the GNP and the GDP of a nation tend to fluctuate in a pattern called the **business cycle.** In the business cycle, a period of growth or a boom is followed by a period of slowdown called a recession. If the recession is very severe, it is called a depression. A depression is characterized by high unemployment rates and low business growth. The worst depression in American history, called the Great Depression, occurred in the 1930s.

EXERCISE 6

Questions 1–3 refer to the following definitions of different types of unemployment.

Cyclical unemployment—unemployment caused by a recession or other unstable economic times

Structural unemployment—unemployment caused by a rapid change in the character of the economy

Frictional unemployment—unemployment caused by workers quitting jobs because they are dissatisfied

Seasonal unemployment—unemployment caused by a change from one season or time period to another

Normal unemployment—the level of unemployment that is considered acceptable for a healthy economy (usually less than 4 percent)

1. Construction workers are often out of work for long periods of time during the winter in the North and Midwest of the United States. What kind of unemployment does this represent?

    (1) cyclical unemployment
    (2) structural unemployment
    (3) frictional unemployment
    (4) seasonal unemployment
    (5) normal unemployment

2. Which of the following types of unemployment has most likely been caused by the increasing importance of computers in business and industry?

    (1) cyclical unemployment
    (2) structural unemployment
    (3) frictional unemployment
    (4) seasonal unemployment
    (5) normal unemployment

3. The number of new housing starts is an important indicator of the health of the nation's economy. Under a slow economy, the number of housing starts decreases and construction workers are laid off. When the economy picks up again, these workers are rehired. What kind of unemployment does this represent?

   (1) cyclical unemployment
   (2) structural unemployment
   (3) frictional unemployment
   (4) seasonal unemployment
   (5) normal unemployment

 Questions 4 and 5 are based on the following graph.

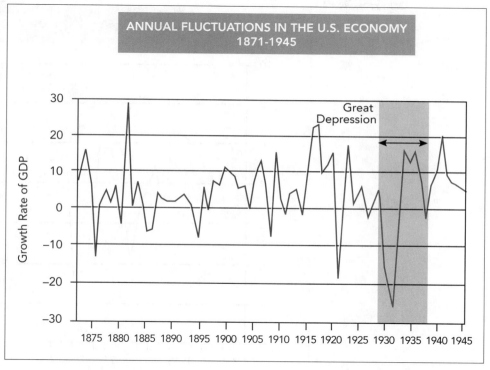

4. According to the graph, which year had the greatest growth rate?
   (1) 1874
   (2) 1882
   (3) 1918
   (4) 1921
   (5) 1932

5. The United States was involved in three wars during the period depicted in the graph. The Spanish American War occurred in 1898. The United States was involved in World War I from 1917 to 1918, and in World War II from 1941 to 1945. According to the graph, what appears to be the impact of these wars on the American GDP?

   (1) The wars had no impact on the GDP.
   (2) The wars made the business cycle fluctuations more extreme.
   (3) The wars all led to growth in the GDP.
   (4) The wars slowed the growth of the GDP.
   (5) War was used to enhance the GDP.

Question 6 is based on the following graph.

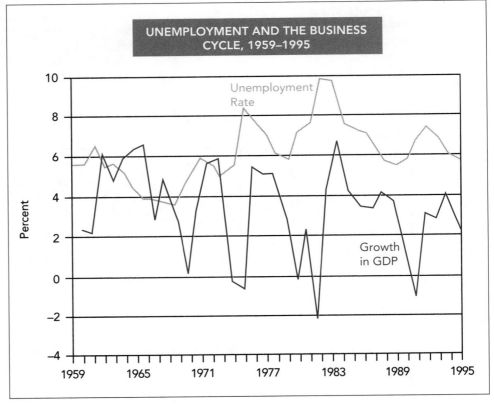

6. Which of the following can be seen by comparing the unemployment rate and the growth in the GDP?

   (1) Unemployment is completely unrelated to the business cycle.
   (2) Unemployment can be predicted by looking at the GDP.
   (3) The GDP and unemployment have a roughly inverse relationship.
   (4) The economic downturn of 1983 was damaging to the economy.
   (5) The economic boom of the 1990s could have been predicted.

Answers are on page 408.

The Role of Government in the Economy

The government has a crucial role to play in the economy. Through their policies and actions, governments can aid an economy or hurt it.

What are some ways that government can help an economy?

_____

_____

_____

_____

What are some ways that government can hurt an economy?

_____

_____

_____

_____

Some of the ways that government can help an economy are by providing security, requiring uniform, dependable standards, providing trustworthy courts, enforcing laws, and maintaining international agreements.

Corruption, such as taking bribes and conducting unfair trials, excessive taxation, oppression and exploitation of residents, and unwise spending are all ways that government can hurt an economy.

EXERCISE 7

Questions 1–3 are based on the following information and quote.

The quote below is from George Washington Plunkitt, who was a ward boss for the corrupt political machine in New York City known as Tammany Hall. He is talking about graft, which is acquiring money in a dishonest or questionable way.

Everybody is talkin' these days about Tammany men growin' rich on graft, but nobody thinks of drawin' the distinction between honest graft and dishonest graft. There's all the difference in the world between the two. Yes, many of our men have grown rich in politics. I have myself. I've made a big fortune out of the game, and I'm gettin' richer every day, but I've not gone in for dishonest graft—blackmailin' gamblers, saloonkeepers, disorderly people, etc.—and neither has any of the men who have made big fortunes in politics.

There's an honest graft, and I'm an example of how it works. I might sum up the whole thing by sayin', 'I seen my opportunities and I took 'em.'

Just let me explain by examples. My party's in power in the city, and it's goin' to undertake a lot of public improvements. Well, I'm tipped off, say that they're going to lay out a new park at a certain place.

I see my opportunity and I take it. I go to that place and I buy up all the land I can in the neighborhood. Then the board of this or that makes its plans public, and there is a rush to get my land, which nobody cared particular for before.

Ain't it perfectly honest to charge a good price and make a profit on my investment and foresight? Of course it is. Well, that's honest graft.

—Excerpted from *Plunkitt of Tammany Hall*

1. Which of the following judgments could be made based on the passage?

    (1) There is a real difference between "honest" and "dishonest" graft.
    (2) Taking advantage of an opportunity is not the same as graft.
    (3) Graft is the "American way" in big-city politics.
    (4) He who does not take advantage of an opportunity is a fool.
    (5) Political bosses appeared to have no sense of right and wrong.

2. What is another name for "honest" graft as described by George Washington Plunkitt?

    (1) accepting bribes of cash or gifts in return for political favors
    (2) appointing friends and relatives to political office
    (3) demanding payoffs from gamblers so they can continue their business
    (4) profiting from inside information on government purchases
    (5) blackmailing tavern owners with information that could shut them down

3. Which of the following does Plunkitt describe as "dishonest" graft?

    (1) rushing to buy land that will soon become valuable
    (2) listening to tip-offs about public improvements
    (3) making a fortune by illegal gambling
    (4) asking for money to ignore illegal activity
    (5) grabbing political power and becoming rich

Questions 4 and 5 are based on the following political cartoon.

4. According to this cartoon from the late nineteenth century, who were the bosses of the Senate?

   (1) the Republicans
   (2) the Democrats
   (3) the common people
   (4) rich businesses
   (5) lobbyists

5. As used in the cartoon, what is the most likely meaning of *trust?*

   (1) a dependable business
   (2) a monopoly
   (3) an honest businessman
   (4) a rich politician
   (5) an overweight person

Questions 6–9 are based on the following information.

Federal, state, and local governments levy taxes to raise money for their operations. Most people in the United States pay at least one of the following taxes:

Income tax—a percentage of wages, profits, and other income paid to federal, state, and local governments

Social Security tax—a percentage of wages paid into a public insurance fund that can be drawn on upon retirement

Capital gains tax—money paid to the federal government out of profits from the sale of land, buildings, stocks, and other capital assets

Property tax—money paid (usually to a local government) by the owners of real estate

Sales tax—money paid to federal, state, or local governments on the purchase of goods or services

6. When people purchase groceries or household goods in most states, they pay an additional percent of the subtotal. What kind of tax are they paying?

    (1) income tax
    (2) Social Security tax
    (3) capital gains tax
    (4) property tax
    (5) sales tax

7. Every year homeowners in Manchester, New Hampshire, have to pay money to the city of Manchester to help pay for local schools, police, fire, and other local services. What kind of tax are they paying?

    (1) income tax
    (2) Social Security tax
    (3) capital gains tax
    (4) property tax
    (5) sales tax

8. Raul Rodriguez's grandfather passed away recently, and in his will he left his house to Raul. Raul sold the house. What kind of tax did he have to pay?

    (1) income tax
    (2) Social Security tax
    (3) capital gains tax
    (4) property tax
    (5) sales tax

9. Manoli Reed retired at age 65. Soon he began to receive monthly checks from the federal government. What kind of tax had Mr. Reed paid that entitled him to this money?

    (1) income tax
    (2) Social Security tax
    (3) capital gains tax
    (4) property tax
    (5) sales tax

Answers are on page 408.

Financial Institutions

Financial institutions are essential to the functioning of the economy. They attract deposits and make money by lending the money deposited for a fee, called interest. These institutions keep part of the interest received and pay part of it to the depositor. In addition to accepting deposits and lending money, they provide the following functions:

- safeguard and transfer funds

- guarantee creditworthiness

- exchange money

Some financial institutions are primarily for individuals to save and borrow money. These institutions include *savings banks*, *savings and loan associations*, and *credit unions*. *Commercial banks* work primarily with businesses. *Central banks* are bankers to the government and other banks. *International financial institutions* provide banking and financial services to governments and nations.

For each of the following examples, in the first blank write what type of banking function is being illustrated. In the second blank, write what type of financial institution is being described.

In the movie *It's a Wonderful Life*, James Stewart plays the owner of a small financial institution that provides loans for building homes, using the money of its depositors. In a scene that takes place at the beginning of the Depression, when panicky depositors are demanding their money, he explains that most of the money has been used to finance mortgages.

_____

_____

In January 2001, when the United States economy was drastically slowing down, Alan Greenspan, chairman of the Federal Reserve Board of Governors, announced a cut in interest rates of 0.5%. This cut the rate of interest that banks had to pay when they borrowed from the Federal Reserve.

_____

_____

Francisco and Jacqueline were going to visit relatives in the Dominican Republic. Before leaving, they went to their local bank and exchanged $500 for 6,000 Dominican pesos.

_____

_____

The Russian government announced on July 13, 1998, that it had negotiated an agreement with the International Monetary Fund (IMF) and other lenders on a multibillion-dollar emergency-assistance package aimed at stabilizing the nation's troubled financial markets.

Russian officials said the $22.6-billion bailout package, to be distributed during the second half of 1998 and in 1999, was needed to make payments on foreign debts and bolster the ruble, Russia's currency. Russia will receive just over $15 billion from the IMF through the end of 1999, a figure that includes $3.5 billion in previously arranged IMF loans. The package also includes $6 billion in loans from the World Bank and $1.5 billion lent from Japan.

The IMF, a specialized agency of the United Nations (UN), asked the Russian government to enact a series of economic reforms in exchange for the new loans.

—Excerpted from *Russia: International Monetary Fund Agrees to Rescue Package*, Microsoft Encarta Encyclopedia

James Stewart is trying to explain how lending works for a savings and loan association.

The Federal Reserve is the central bank of the United States. It helps to stabilize the economy by regulating the supply of money and credit. By setting the interest rate, the Board of Governors was regulating the lending of money to banks.

Francisco and Jacqueline have gone to their local bank to exchange money. Today, most savings banks can handle this function.

The International Monetary Fund is an international financial institution. The IMF is lending money to Russia and guaranteeing Russia's creditworthiness.

GED PRACTICE

EXERCISE 8

Questions 1–3 are based on the following passage.

The International Development Association, IDA, [is the agency of the World Bank that] provides long-term loans at zero interest to the poorest of the developing countries. The mission of IDA is to support efficient and effective programs to reduce poverty and improve the quality of life in its poorest member countries. IDA helps build the human capital, policies, institutions, and physical infrastructure needed to bring about equitable and sustainable growth. IDA's goal is to reduce the disparities across and within countries, to bring more people into the mainstream, and to promote equitable access to the benefits of development. . . . IDA lends only to those countries that have a per capita income in 1999 of less than $885 and lack the financial ability to borrow from [other financial institutions].

At present, 78 countries are eligible to borrow from IDA. Together these countries are home to 2.3 billion people, comprising 53 percent of the total population of the developing countries. Today, 1.5 billion of these people survive on incomes of $2 or less a day.

Since 1960, IDA has lent $120 billion to 106 countries. It lends, on average, about $5–6 billion a year for different types of development projects, especially those that address peoples' basic needs, such as primary education, basic health services, and clean water and sanitation. IDA also funds projects that protect the environment, improve conditions for private business, build needed infrastructure, and support reforms aimed at liberalizing countries' economies. All these projects pave the way toward economic growth, job creation, higher incomes, and a better quality of life.

IDA funds are allocated to the borrowing countries in relation to their income level and track record of success in managing their economies and their ongoing IDA projects. In the [year 2000], a total of $4.4 billion was committed to IDA borrowers. These new credits comprised 126 new operations in 52 countries. Forty-seven percent of new commitments went to Sub-Saharan Africa, 27 percent went to South Asia, 11 percent to East Asia and the Pacific, 7 percent to Eastern Europe and Central Asia (ECA), and the remainder to poor countries in North Africa and in Latin America.

—Excerpted from the World Bank web site, www.worldbank.org

1. Given the information in this passage, which region(s) of the world can you conclude is the poorest?

   (1) Sub-Saharan Africa
   (2) South Asia
   (3) East Asia and the Pacific
   (4) Eastern Europe and Central Asia
   (5) North Africa and Latin America

2. Since this passage comes from the official web site of the World Bank, the parent organization of the IDA, what information would you most likely *not* find on this web site?

   (1) major donors of funds to the IDA
   (2) major recipients of IDA funding
   (3) types of projects funded by IDA
   (4) failures of projects funded by IDA
   (5) mission and goals of the IDA

3. What is the main idea of this passage?

   (1) The IDA provides long-term loans at zero interest to the poorest of developing countries.
   (2) The IDA supports programs to reduce poverty and improve the quality of life of its poorest member countries.
   (3) The 78 countries that are eligible to borrow from IDA are home to 2.3 billion people.
   (4) IDA development projects include primary education, basic health services, and clean water and sanitation.
   (5) IDA funds are allocated to the borrowing countries in relation to their income level and track record of success.

Answers are on page 408.

Personal Finances

Every one of us has to learn to handle our own personal finances. However, there never seems to be enough money to meet all of our needs. One way of borrowing money for a short time is to use a credit card. Credit cards let you obtain goods and services just by providing your card number and signing a receipt. At the end of the month, you receive a bill from the credit card company for all your purchases.

The conditions and features of different credit cards can vary greatly, even among cards issued by the same company. Look at the following list of features from three different credit cards all being offered by the same company and then decide which card would be best for each person described.

Mileage Unlimited Platinum VISA

Annual Percentage Rate for purchases	A fixed rate of 9.9%. Rate will be changed to 19.8% if your account is 30 or more days past due.
Grace period for repayment of the balance for purchases	You will have a minimum of 25 days without a finance charge on new purchases if the total New Balance is paid in full each month by the following statement closing date.
Method of computing the balance used in calculating finance charges for purchases	Average daily balance (including new purchases)
Annual membership fee	$19
Minimum finance charge	For each Billing Period that your Account is subject to a finance charge, a minimum total Finance Charge of $0.50 will be imposed.
Miscellaneous fees	Cash advance fee: 3% of amount of the cash advance, but not less than $5.00 Late Payment fee: $29 Over-the-credit-limit fee: $29 Returned check fee: $29
Additional benefits	Earn 1 mile for every $1 in purchases. Minimum miles for free flight: 18,000 in zone, 25,000 in Continental U.S. Maximum 60,000 miles can be earned.

No-Annual-Fee Platinum VISA

Annual Percentage Rate for purchases	A fixed rate of 9.9%. Rate will be changed to 22% if your account is 30 or more days past due.
Grace period for repayment of the balance for purchases	You will have a minimum of 25 days without a finance charge on new purchases if the total New Balance is paid in full each month by the following statement closing date.
Method of computing the balance used in calculating finance charges for purchases	Average daily balance (including new purchases)
Annual membership fee	NONE
Minimum finance charge	For each Billing Period that your Account is subject to a finance charge, a minimum total Finance Charge of $0.50 will be imposed.
Miscellaneous fees	Cash advance fee: NONE Late Payment fee: $20 Over-the-credit-limit fee: $20 Returned check fee: NONE

Gold VISA

Annual Percentage Rate for purchases	A fixed rate of 0.0%. Beginning with your September billing period, a variable rate currently equal to 19.8% rate will be charged if your account is 30 or more days past due.
Grace period for repayment of the balance for purchases	You will have a minimum of 25 days without a finance charge on new purchases if the total New Balance is paid in full each month by the following statement closing date.
Method of computing the balance used in calculating finance charges for purchases	Average daily balance (including new purchases)
Annual membership fee	$15
Minimum finance charge	For each Billing Period that your Account is subject to a finance charge, a minimum total Finance Charge of $0.50 will be imposed.
Miscellaneous fees	Cash advance fee: 3% of amount of the cash advance, but not less than $5.00 Late Payment fee: $29 Over-the-credit-limit fee: $29 Returned check fee: $29

Mira flies frequently to visit family and friends. She is very careful about paying her bills on time, and never has had to pay a penalty fee. Which credit card is best for Mira?

Tanya loves to buy new things. Though she always intends to pay her credit card bill in full, she often loses track of how much she has spent and cannot pay the entire balance. She has even occasionally spent over her credit limit. Which credit card is best for Tanya?

Because Mira flies frequently and pays her bills on time, the Mileage Unlimited Platinum VISA would be best for her. She would benefit from the miles and would be unaffected by the higher fees.

Since Tanya has more trouble managing her money, she would be better off with No-Annual-Fee Platinum VISA since it has the lowest fees of the three cards listed.

GED PRACTICE

EXERCISE 9

Question 1 is based on the following cartoon.

"I don't suppose you remembered the tax-deduction forms that I asked you to bring last year, did you?"

1. What might the man in the cartoon want to do with tax-deduction forms from trick-or-treaters?

   (1) claim a child care credit
   (2) claim a charitable contribution
   (3) avoid paying taxes
   (4) prove his generosity
   (5) discourage trick-or-treaters from returning

Questions 2 and 3 are based on the following passage.

In a report about consumer debt, one magazine included information about a special type of charge card called a *debit card*. When a customer makes a purchase with a debit card, the money is immediately deducted from the customer's checking account.

According to *U.S. News and World Report*, "The retailer gets an immediate OK, through an electronic terminal at the checkout counter, that the cardholder's bank account can cover the purchase. Older cards, like credit cards, involve only a signed receipt. And anyone with a checking account at a participating bank can get one.

2. Which of the following is implied about debit cards?

   Debit cards
   (1) are harder to get than credit cards
   (2) can help consumers stay out of debt
   (3) are more popular than credit cards
   (4) are difficult to use
   (5) are not accepted by many retailers

3. Which of the following would be the most likely result if the federal government was required to spend as if it were using only a debit card?

   (1) Government spending would be limited.
   (2) Government spending would increase.
   (3) The national debt would be eliminated.
   (4) The national debt would increase.
   (5) The government wouldn't have to repay the national debt.

Answers are on page 408.

Distribution of Wealth

What do you think is the key point of the photo above?

_____

_____

_____

You might have said that there are huge differences in the lives of different people, or you might have said that this photo illustrates the unequal distribution of wealth in the world. The distribution of wealth is the way that money is divided among the people in a group, country, or the world. The graphics and passages in the following exercise help show the distribution of wealth in the world.

EXERCISE 10

Question 1 is based on the following passage.

As the rich get richer, it becomes hard to imagine what the wealth of the ultra-rich actually means.

- The cost of providing basic education and health care, as well as adequate food and safe water for all the people of earth, is estimated to be $40 billion—less than the net worth of Bill Gates.
- The three richest people in the world have assets that exceed the combined GDP of the 48 poorest countries.
- The combined wealth of the 32 richest people exceeds the total GDP of South Asia.
- The wealth of the 225 richest people is equal to the annual incomes of the poorest 47 percent of the world's population (over 2.5 billion people).

1. What can you conclude from the information in this passage?

   (1) Estate taxes in the United States need to be abolished.
   (2) Bill Gates gained his enormous wealth unfairly.
   (3) Too much wealth is in the hands of too few people.
   (4) The poor have not done a good job of managing money.
   (5) The cost of education, health care, food, and safe water is too high.

Question 2 is based on the following line graph.

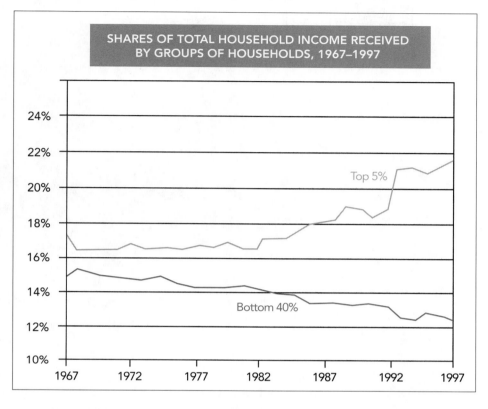

SHARES OF TOTAL HOUSEHOLD INCOME RECEIVED BY GROUPS OF HOUSEHOLDS, 1967–1997

2. Which policy recommendation is best supported by the evidence from this line graph?

   (1) The United States needs to drastically reduce taxes for the richest Americans so they can create jobs.
   (2) Companies should receive tax breaks to establish more minimum-wage jobs to cut unemployment.
   (3) A tax cut should concentrate its benefits on households in the bottom 40% of income received.
   (4) Taxes should be increased for the bottom 40% since they are already so unproductive.
   (5) The United States should rely on the free market to lower the unequal distribution of income.

Question 3 is based on the following cartoon.

"What a delightful surprise. I always thought it just trickled down to the poor."

3. What economic theory is this cartoon ridiculing?

    (1) Giving more money to the rich is the best way to benefit the poor.
    (2) As the rich become wealthier, the poor also benefit.
    (3) If we reduce regulation of business, they will create wealth.
    (4) Lowering taxes is the best way to stimulate the economy.
    (5) In order to promote economic growth, we need to invest in infrastructure.

Answers are on page 409.

Economic Development

These capable young African American women welders helped change the face of the American workforce during World War II. The memory of the contribution of these women and others like them helped to lay the groundwork for the hard-won advances in employment opportunities for women and minorities in the more than half century since this photo was taken.

Before the war these young women and others like them had rarely been equal participants in the economic development of America. The work of minorities and women had frequently been exploited. A paradoxical result of that exploitation was a loss of productivity, since workers who are abused and mistreated cannot work up to full capacity.

Even though modern economic development and the Industrial Revolution had begun in Europe, by the end of the twentieth century, the United States had become the largest and most productive economy in the world.

Read the following passage about economic development in Great Britain in the 19th century.

EXERCISE 11

Questions 1 and 2 are based on the following passage.

Great Britain, and more especially the Midlands, saw the birth of the Industrial Revolution. This incited British inventors to feats of ingenuity. The inventions of James Hargreaves, Richard Arkwright and Samuel Crompton led to the mechanization of the cotton industry. Factories used steam power provided by James Watt's rotary steam engine. By concentrating production in factories, manufacturers were able to economize on transport costs, apply new working methods, use more powerful machinery and impose discipline and punctuality. By about 1850, British steam engines were producing the equivalent of 1.2 million horsepower, more than half of Europe's total energy output, while 2.5 million tons of iron ore were being smelted in Britain, more than ten times the German figure. Nicknamed 'the workshop of the world,' Great Britain enjoyed a period of exceptional economic growth and became the richest nation on earth: it accounted for half the world market of manufactured goods and about a third of the world's industrial production.

—Excerpted from *Illustrated History of Europe*, Frederic Delouche, ed.

1. What is the main point of this passage?

   (1) By being the first nation to industrialize, Great Britain became the richest nation on earth.
   (2) The best way for a nation to become wealthy is to industrialize and modernize its economy.
   (3) British inventions led to the mechanization of the cotton industry and the use of steam engines for power.
   (4) Great Britain smelted 2.5 million tons of iron ore, more than ten times the German amount.
   (5) Great Britain accounted for half the world's manufactured goods and about a third of its industrial production.

2. What was the most significant difference between the economic development of Great Britain in the nineteenth century and the economic development of the United States in the twentieth century?

   (1) American inventors made more significant discoveries than the British had.
   (2) Petroleum and electricity replaced steam and coal as the main sources of energy.
   (3) Both the British and the Americans built on economic growth that had started the century before.
   (4) Great Britain dominated the nineteenth century economically more than the Americans did the twentieth.
   (5) The United States was unable to match Great Britain's gains in productivity.

Question 3 is based on the following passage.

> I had a recommendation to a famous factory. I had never been so well paid. My only wish was to have fine clothes. I wanted no one to know I was a factory girl when I went to church on Sunday, because I was ashamed of my position. When I was still an apprentice, I was always hearing people say that factory girls were loose-living and corrupt. They only talked about them scornfully. All I felt was that I was no longer poor. Our magnificent Sunday dinner seemed to me to be fit for a king. For 20 kreuzer we bought meat and when my salary went up we added a small glass of sweet wine.

—Excerpted from "A Young Working Girl" by A. Popp, *Illustrated History of Europe*

3. What can you infer about factory girls from the evidence given in this passage?

(1) Factory girls were cruelly exploited and abused.
(2) Factory girls were very seductive and wild.
(3) Factory work helped young women out of poverty.
(4) Factory workers saved what they could from their earnings.
(5) Townspeople knew the truth about the behavior of others.

Question 4 is based on the following cartoon.

"On the one hand, eliminating the middleman would result in lower costs, increased sales, and greater consumer satisfaction; on the other hand, we're the middleman."

—©The New Yorker Collection, 1997, Robert Mankoff.
From cartoonbank.com. All Rights Reserved.

4. What would be the most likely decision to be made at this meeting?

(1) to eliminate the middleman
(2) to keep the status quo
(3) to lower costs by making overall cuts
(4) to share these conclusions with clients
(5) to devise better sales strategies

Answers are on page 409.

Chapter Review

Question 1 is based on the following passage.

Industrialization transformed human history as profoundly as the emergence of agriculture in Neolithic times, eight millennia earlier. Never had Europe undergone such sudden and intense change.

Between 1880 and 1914 Europe was swept by a wind of modernism with an optimistic tinge. Europeans believed in progress and had no fear of the future. European civilization at that time had unprecedented enterprise, adaptability and self-confidence. As a result its technology soon spread throughout the world. Indeed, industrialization created ideal conditions for overseas ventures. The European nations were able to increase their supremacy by commercial, cultural and diplomatic means. In the last quarter of the 19th century they incorporated new territory into their existing empires, either by conquest or by discovery, mainly in Africa.

—Excerpted from *Illustrated History of Europe*, Frederic Delouche, ed.

1. Despite Europe's early lead over the United States in the nineteenth century, by the middle of the twentieth century, the United States had become the leading economic power. Which of the following probably had the greatest impact in causing Europe to fall behind?

    (1) Overconfidence probably led to the Europeans not seriously reacting to American growth.
    (2) Overextension into Africa and other areas diverted European resources from increasing productivity.
    (3) The two world wars were centered in Europe and devastated the continent, damaging the economy.
    (4) American inventors were creating many more new products than were developed in Europe.
    (5) The early industry was inefficient and polluting compared to industries built later.

Question 2 is based on the following passage.

The ancient world had left in the Mediterranean basin a model of urban and rural civilization and an agriculture combining grain-growing, market-gardening, vine-growing and olive-growing, all of which needed simply to be revived. The mainland regions of Europe, however, had to find completely new solutions, using relatively novel and largely untried techniques. Three such elements may be singled out. One was iron-working, which made it possible to produce basic tools and accessories such as metal parts for ploughs, horseshoes, nails and forestry equipment. A second was the heavy plough with a coulter and mould-board, capable of turning over low-lying land which was more fertile but harder to plough. The third was three-year crop rotation, which reduced fallow land from 50 percent to 30 percent of the total and made it possible to grow spring crops such as oats.

—Excerpted from *Illustrated History of Europe*, Frederic Delouche, ed.

2. According to the passage, what was the crucial element in the economic development of mainland Europe?

    (1) a revival of the ancient Roman economy in areas once under Roman control
    (2) a discovery of fertile lands throughout the region for agriculture
    (3) the development of iron-working for making tools and metal parts
    (4) the invention of original and effective means to advance agriculture
    (5) the decision to move from a two-crop to a three-crop rotation

Question 3 is based on the following cartoon.

"We got a great buy on the apartment but, unfortunately, it didn't include the mineral rights."

— ©The New Yorker Collection, 1991, Robert Weber. From cartoonbank.com. All Rights Reserved.

3. What was the artist most likely trying to illustrate?

   (1) You should not be willing to give away your rights.
   (2) We need to exploit every possibility to increase energy supplies.
   (3) Oil rigs are now so environmentally friendly, they can be in your living room.
   (4) Apartments are getting much too expensive for most people.
   (5) Always expect the unexpected when visiting someone for the first time.

Question 4 is based on the following graph.

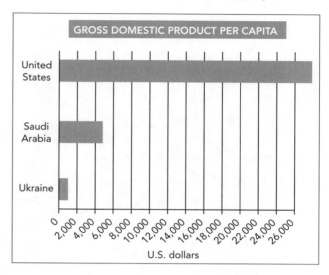

4. Which assertion is best supported by the information in this graph?

   (1) Because of Saudi Arabia's enormous oil wealth, Saudi Arabians are better off than Americans.
   (2) The United States could afford to pay its workers higher wages than Ukraine can pay its workers.
   (3) The United States provides the highest standard of living of any country on earth.
   (4) The citizens of Ukraine are among the poorest people in the Northern Hemisphere.
   (5) Because there is so much room for growth, Ukraine is a better place for investment than the United States.

Question 5 is based on the following cartoon.

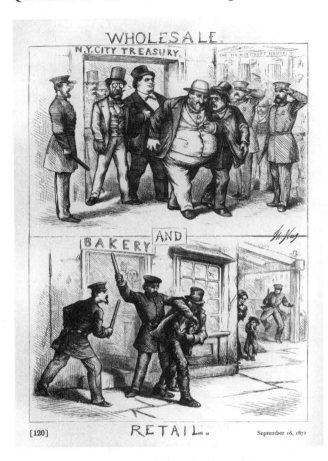

5. What is the best explanation of the titles "Wholesale" and "Retail" in this cartoon?

    (1) Small retail businesses such as bakeries had a much more serious crime problem than banks.
    (2) Because of the success of large companies such as banks, cities could afford to fight street crime.
    (3) People who steal millions are honored while small thieves are punished.
    (4) The upper level organization of the police force helps make it effective in fighting crime.
    (5) The New York City Treasury handles much larger amounts of money than neighborhood businesses.

Questions 6 and 7 are based on the following passage from President Dwight Eisenhower's farewell address.

"The conjunction of an immense military establishment and a large arms industry is new in the American experience. In the councils of government, we must guard against the acquisition of unwarranted influence, whether sought or unsought, by the military-industrial complex. The potential for the disastrous rise of misplaced power exists and will persist."

6. What was President Eisenhower trying to warn the American people about?

    (1) We need to keep the military strong in order to combat Communism.
    (2) The military and the arms industry could become too influential.
    (3) Our military and our industry were becoming too complex.
    (4) We need to watch out for the rise of new dangerous military powers.
    (5) We must maintain our military power to deal with the threat of terrorism.

7. Which of the following is an example of what President Eisenhower was trying to warn the American people about?

    (1) Despite the end of the Cold War, President George W. Bush wanted a large increase in military spending.
    (2) Committing hundreds of thousands of troops in Vietnam led to widespread opposition and protests.
    (3) In Bosnia, Serbs pushed aside United Nations peacekeepers, and murdered hundreds of Bosnian Muslims.
    (4) The United States today sells more weapons and other military equipment than any other nation.
    (5) Many veterans of the Vietnam War became ill due to the effects of Agent Orange, a defoliant used in the war.

Questions 8 and 9 refer to the following chart.

U.S. Department Of Labor, Bureau of Labor Statistics		
Consumer Price Index		
All Urban Consumers		
1982–84=100 (Something that cost $100 in 1982–84 would have cost the amount in the CPI column in that year.)		
YEAR	**CPI**	**Inflation rate for year (%)**
1915	10.1	1.0
1920	20.0	15.6
1925	17.5	2.3
1930	16.7	−2.3
1935	13.7	2.2
1940	14.0	0.7
1945	18.0	2.3
1950	24.1	1.3
1955	26.8	−0.4
1960	29.6	1.7
1965	31.5	1.6
1970	38.8	5.7
1975	53.8	9.1
1980	82.4	13.5
1985	107.6	3.6
1990	130.7	5.4
1995	152.4	2.8
2000	172.2	3.4

8. Over what 20-year period was there an actual decrease in average prices in urban America?

   (1) 1915–1935
   (2) 1920–1940
   (3) 1925–1945
   (4) 1935–1955
   (5) 1980–2000

9. After World War I, the American economy was hit by severe inflation. What other period shown on this chart experienced serious inflation?

   (1) the Depression of the 1930s
   (2) the period right after the Second World War
   (3) the peak of the Civil Rights movement
   (4) the oil crisis of the late 1970s to early 1980s
   (5) the unprecedented economic expansion of the 1990s

   Answers are on page 409.

Chapter 9

Science, Technology, and Society

We are who we are as a species, in part, because we can make and use tools. Those tools, in turn, determine how we live. Look at where you are right now. Has any part of the room in which you are sitting not been influenced by human invention? To what degree does the work you do, the food you eat, and the activities you enjoy derive from human inventions?

To be inventive means to be able to adapt discoveries to practical use. Innovation is the action of putting an invention into practice. At the time of the earliest inventions (about one million years ago) "practical" meant addressing the most basic survival needs. Look at the following list and consider the ways in which each invention or inventive development enhanced people's chances for survival: stone tools, the ability to produce and control fire, spoken language, the wheel.

Technology and Science

When we think about invention and progress, the term **technology** often comes to mind. In some ways invention and technology may appear synonymous. After all, at the heart of technology is the ability to recognize a human need or desire and then to devise a means—an invention—to satisfy it economically. By "economically" we mean in a way that enables it to be reproduced and used by many people. But technology also brings to mind a relationship to **science**, or systematic knowledge. The difference between invention and technology, then, is that invention does not necessarily grow out of the principles of science, but technology does. Science may advance technology, and technology may advance science. Inventions are always a part of that relationship but may also exist outside of it. This is certainly true of the earliest inventions listed above, since systematic organizations of thinking (science) did not begin until about 600 B.C.E

To many of us the word "technology" brings to mind something that is recent and changing, forcing us to leave behind more familiar and sometimes more comfortable options. Think of the first time, for example, that you had to use something connected to a computer. Maybe it was an automated teller machine at a bank, an electronic passkey for a building or room, or a computer itself. You may have felt nervous and unsure of yourself. Maybe you wished that you had chosen to use a human teller or had access to an old-fashioned metal key.

The "newness" in technology depends on one's point of view. Consider the topic of windows—glass ones, not the software that Microsoft© produces. The glass window was a new technology, or invention, in the Middle Ages. In churches, its purpose was to give light, to create a particular, prayerful ambiance, and more practically, to tell religious stories. From that point windows evolved so that they could help control temperature in homes, workplaces, and vehicles. If our starting point for investigating the technology of windows were 1970, "new" technology might be the kinds of switches that control the rates by which windows are raised and lowered in our cars, or improved weather resistance. The rule this example illustrates is that after the technology has been used in one form, it continues to evolve or becomes irrelevant.

Look at the two pictures in the following exercise. Both show spinning machines, a tool that has proven critical to the economies of many cultures over time. The top picture depicts an early version of the spinning wheel in China, where many of the world's inventions were born. The picture on the bottom shows a computer-controlled textile spinning machine.

GED PRACTICE

EXERCISE 1

Questions 1 and 2 are based on the following two pictures.

1. Which of the following implications about the evolution of the spinning wheel *cannot* be made on the basis of these pictures and your understanding of innovation?

   (1) The fibers spun from the modern machine are of higher quality than those spun from the older version.
   (2) There has been a continual need to transform natural fibers of finite length into long, continuous lengths of thread or yarn.
   (3) Early spinning machines were labor intensive while more contemporary versions require little human attention or skill.
   (4) The basic engineering principles of the spinning machine are not likely to have changed despite increased mechanization.
   (5) The forms of the spinning wheel that were developed in the time between these two were increasingly more efficient.

2. Who would be least likely to welcome the innovation of the machine on the bottom?

   (1) The owner of the company that manufactures the textiles produced by this machine.
   (2) The factory worker who operated the noncomputerized version that preceded this one.
   (3) The consumer purchasing clothing made from material that was more cheaply produced than before.
   (4) The technician recently hired to maintain the machines and ensure smooth operation.
   (5) The clothing manufacturer who has just agreed to sell his products to five new stores.

Answers are on page 410.

What do you think has been the most important invention or technological advancement in human history? This is a complicated question. It becomes slightly easier to answer when you can consider history in terms of periods. For example, what has been the most significant invention of the past five hundred years? Even with this breakdown, though, the task is difficult since many inventions can be traced back to others. So, do you identify the initial invention or its most advanced form? And on the basis of what criteria do you make your choice: on how the invention has positively impacted human life, negatively impacted human life, or could potentially impact human life but hasn't yet done so?

In the rest of this chapter we will discuss inventions within the context of particular arenas and the ways in which those inventions have impacted human life, both positively and negatively. The arenas we will consider are:

- community life

- work

- health

- communication

Community Life

Cities, one of the most complex creations of humankind, began to evolve relatively soon after the shift from nomadic life to farming life. With the advent of farming, nomads who had always relied on hunting and gathering were now staying in one place, cultivating crops and domesticating animals. The city itself is a technological phenomenon, an invention with many facets, containing networks of transportation, communication, and trade systems. People live in close proximity to one another, the result being new forms of social conduct.

How do you think city life impacts people's behavior? How does that behavior differ from that of people who live in a more rural environment?

_____

_____

_____

Jacob Bronowski, a noted scientist, inventor, historian, and humanist, wrote the following: "A city is stones and a city is people; but it is not a heap of stones, and it is not a jostle of people. In the step from the village to the city, a new community organization is built, based on the division of labor and on chains of command."

What do you think Bronowski means by "new community organization"? What are examples of "division of labor" and "chains of command"?

_____

_____

_____

_____

_____

The emergence of the city made possible a surplus of food and an abundance of material wealth never before experienced in human communities. Since there was more than enough food, not everyone had to be involved in food production. People assumed different roles (division of labor) according to their talents and capabilities. In other words, specialists evolved and markets developed in which artisans could exchange their specialties for other types of goods. But because people's skills varied and the demand for some goods and services was higher than for others, the society became stratified (chains of command). Leaders emerged and rules of order were established. Temples, tombs, and citadels were constructed. Thus the development of some of humanity's major institutions (government, religion, and social class) was set in motion.

EXERCISE 2

Read the following paragraph about the ancient city of Babylon and answer questions 1 and 2.

Four thousand years ago Hammurabi, who ruled a small territory in Babylon, expanded his kingdom into a large state and created a comprehensive system of laws—the Code of Hammurabi. It can be said that this system of laws, which attempted to establish balance in society and to ensure that differences were settled by rational procedures applicable to all people, was the origin of civilized society. Furthermore, Babylonian clay tablets have revealed a remarkable skill in arithmetic and astronomy. From generation to generation the motions of the heavenly bodies were recorded by astronomers and numerical methods of prediction developed. In addition the development of settled agriculture necessitated the division of and the buying and selling of land. This, in turn, required the art of the surveyor and the making of charts, diagrams, or maps showing the areas of land involved in transactions. Some clay tablets carry beautifully drawn diagrams showing the division of land and calculations of the dimensions involved.

—Adapted from *The Norton History of Technology* by Donald Cardwell

1. Which of the following modern objects or institutions cannot be traced to the developments initiated by Babylon?

    (1) property plot maps
    (2) deeds of property and sale
    (3) the U.S. Constitution
    (4) calculators
    (5) calendars

2. Which of the following conclusions does the archaeological evidence that has been gathered at the site of ancient Babylon support?

    (1) Cities require strong leaders to thrive.
    (2) Babylon was an exceptional city.
    (3) Cities nurture innovation.
    (4) Babylon beat the odds for success.
    (5) People welcome systems of law.

Answers are on page 410.

Consider a more recent example of an urban environment: the industrial city of Manchester, England, in the 19th century. In the early 1770s Manchester numbered only 25,000 inhabitants. By 1850, after it had become a center of cotton manufacturing, its population had grown to more than 350,000. The inventions that made this transformation possible included such devices as the flying shuttle and the spinning jenny. Powered by water or steam, row upon row of these innovative, highly productive machines filled large, new mills and factories.

Besides new machinery, the industrial city also forwarded the concept of the division of labor. In division of labor, each worker is assigned to a different task, or step, in the manufacturing process, and as a result, total production increases. For example, if five tasks are required to manufacture a product and a different person specializes in each of the tasks, many more products can be made than if a single person performed all five tasks alone.

The marvel of rising productivity, initiated by the division of labor, was the central economic achievement that made the Industrial Revolution such a milestone in human history. It was not without its drawbacks, however. It significantly changed the daily lives of many men, women, and children for the worse. By the mid-1800s millions of British people lived in crowded, grim industrial cities, and reformers began to speak of the mills and factories as dark, evil places.

GED PRACTICE

EXERCISE 3

Questions 1–3 refer to the following passage.

Women in households who had earned income from spinning found the new factories taking away their source of income. Traditional handloom weavers could no longer compete with the mechanized production of cloth. Skilled laborers sometimes lost their jobs as new machines replaced them.

In the factories the jobs were repetitive and boring. People had to work long hours, often more than 12 hours a day, six days a week. They faced strict rules and close supervision by managers and overseers. Factory owners paid them the minimum amount necessary, frequently recruiting women and children to tend the machines because they could be hired for even lower wages.

1. Which of the following would *not* likely have been part of the experience of factory workers in industrial England?

    (1) low literacy rates
    (2) regular increases in wages
    (3) poor health conditions
    (4) crippling machine accidents
    (5) growing anger and discontent

2. Factories similar to those in England were constructed in the United States. The working conditions were also similar. Who among the following would have least likely been a factory worker in the American mills?

    (1) young single women
    (2) recent immigrants
    (3) university students
    (4) school-aged children
    (5) former craftspeople

3. Based on the information in the passage, which social movement most likely grew out of the Industrial Revolution?

    (1) the Environmental movement
    (2) the Women's Suffrage movement
    (3) the Labor Organizing movement
    (4) the Antiwar movement
    (5) the Antislavery movement

Answers are on page 410.

As cities continued to be centers for industry and technology well into the 1900s, an alternative to urban living started to evolve in the United States: the suburb. It was generally considered a sign of an individual's success when he could move his family to a home outside of the city. The invention of the trolley car contributed to the creation of suburbs around American cities at the beginning of the 20th century. In 1902, Charles Skinner, a magazine essayist, made the following observations and comments:

> On one point the American is determined: he will not live near his work. You shall see him in the morning, one of sixty people in a car built for twenty-four, reading his paper, clinging to a strap, trodden, jostled, smirched, thrown into harrowing relations with men who drink whiskey, chew tobacco, eat raw onions, and incontinently breathe; and after thirty minutes of this contact, with the roar of the streets in his ears, with languid clerks and pinguid market women leaning against him, he arrives at his office. The problems of his homeward journey in the evening will be still more difficult, because, in addition to the workers, the cars must carry the multitude of demoiselles who shop and go to matinees. To many men and women of business a seat is an undreamed luxury. Yet, they would be insulted if one were to ask why they did not live over their shops, as Frenchmen do, or back of them, like Englishmen. It is this uneasy instinct of Americans, this desire of their families to separate industrial and social life, that makes the use of the trolley car imperative, and the street railway in this manner widens the life and dominion of the people; it enables them to distribute themselves over wider spaces and unwittingly to symbolize the expansiveness of the nation.

—Excerpted from "The American Will Not Live Near His Work" by Charles M. Skinner, *Visions of Technology*

EXERCISE 4

Questions 1–3 refer to the preceding passage.

1. Which of the following of the author's assertions is a fact?

    (1) No Americans in 1902 lived near their workplaces.
    (2) People who commuted by trolley cars in 1902 were miserable.
    (3) Some Americans commuted to work by trolley car in 1902.
    (4) In 1902 commuters to the suburbs were national symbols.
    (5) The newly invented trolley car was a luxury in 1902.

2. The author makes which of the following assumptions?

    (1) Many Americans do not live far from their workplaces.
    (2) The trolley car was a temporary solution for people who commuted.
    (3) Most riders of trolley cars are pleasant and polite people.
    (4) Americans work for city businesses and live in the suburbs.
    (5) The English and French like to live apart from their jobs.

3. If an essay about the trolley car, or its evolved counterpart, the subway, were to be published today, how might it differ from Mr. Skinner's essay?

    (1) There would probably be no reference to the wide diversity of people who ride it.
    (2) There would probably be no reference to how loud, smelly, and crowded it tends to be.
    (3) There would probably be no reference to the separation of people's work and social lives.
    (4) There would probably be no reference to symbolizing the expansiveness of the nation.
    (5) There would probably be no reference to the necessity for this kind of transportation.

Answers are on page 410.

Work

It is clear that invention and technology influence where people live (cities, suburbs, countryside), and how, in turn, those communities impact people's quality of life. From the examples above, however, it is also clear that invention and technology have a profound impact on how people work and what that work is.

When we first described what we meant by invention, innovation, and technology, we emphasized their relationship to practical use. One of the most significant ways that something can be practical is if it saves physical energy or lessens the work people need to do. Running through the history of inventions is the linking thread of the economy of energy.

With this understanding we can see that the development of agriculture, one of the basic but most historically important innovations, is one of a sustained drive to lessen the work required to provide a food supply. First came the cultivation of crops like wheat and the understanding of the conditions under which those crops best grow. Then came the hand plow, followed by the horse harness, and, finally, the specialized engine-driven machines like harvest combines and wheat threshers. Use of agricultural machinery substantially reduced the amount of human labor needed for raising crops. In the United States, for example, the average amount of labor required to produce and harvest corn, hay, and cereal crops has fallen to less than a fourth of what was required only a few decades ago. Mechanization, together with improved crop varieties, better techniques, and more efficient food processing, has enabled the small percentage of the U.S. population living on farms to produce enough food to feed the nation.

Inventions designed to conserve human energy certainly deserve praise. One now-familiar concept that developed out of the wide application of labor-saving technology is that of "leisure." While the creation of art appears to have always been a human activity, the notion of entertainment began evolving once it was no longer necessary for people to use all of their time and energy for basic survival. In the early urban societies there were those whose work it became to help others relax and have fun when their work was over. Before that, work was never over. Entertainers, therefore, became part of a civilized economy.

Today many of us work so that we can "play." We buy televisions with the money we earn, and tickets to movies, sporting events, concerts, and plays. We go shopping at malls that display not so much the things that we need, but those that we might want. The invention of leisure, then, can be seen as having spurred many other inventions and created many whole new fields of work.

Consider the movie industry. How many people, machines, and innovations are involved in the creation and distribution of the film playing at the theater nearest you? Read the following passage about some of the work involved in bringing a movie to you.

After films have been produced, they must be distributed to individual movie houses and theater chains. This is accomplished through distributors, who lease motion pictures from the producer or production company. They then pay for the making of prints; arrange screenings so theaters can bid on the rights to show the film; promote and advertise the film; distribute copies of the film to the theaters; arrange for release on cable and broadcast television; coordinate distribution of videotapes, laser discs, and digital video discs to stores; and keep records of the income and expenses for all aspects of film distribution. Distributors bill theaters at the end of engagements, upon receipt of attendance reports.

—Excerpted from "Motion Picture," Microsoft Encarta

Can you get an idea from this passage about how much work is required to entertain you? Remember, this does not include any of the details about the incredibly complex filming and editing processes! On the basis of this example, what hypothesis can you make about the labor that is saved through invention?

_____

_____

_____

What may be saved in one area usually gets applied to another. People need to earn a living, and if one sector can't supply it, the society will create others that can.

The creation of new kinds of work does not happen immediately, however, and the transition time is usually difficult for societies. As certain kinds of jobs phase out due to advances in technology, the economy suffers. The unemployment rate is high and because many people have lost their jobs and don't have the income they used to, they do not buy or invest as they did before. This can be viewed as the downside of invention.

The graphs on the next page show three periods within the 20th century in which dramatic shifts in employment were taking place.

EXERCISE 5

Questions 1–3 refer to the following graphs.

U.S. Employment by Sector

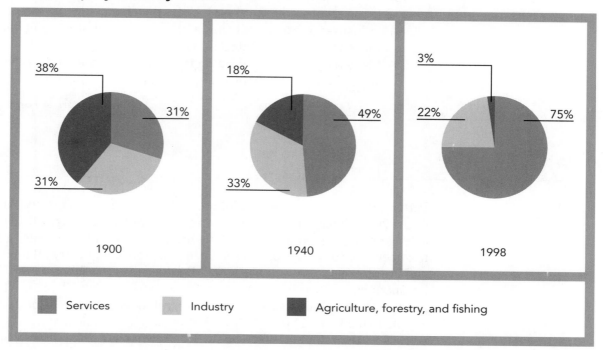

1. **What do the graphs indicate about the labor force in 1900 compared to the labor force in 1998?**

   It was
   (1) composed mostly of factory workers
   (2) almost equally balanced among job types
   (3) eager to get off the farms and into the cities
   (4) not very oriented to providing essential services
   (5) less financially secure and well off

2. **Which of the following inventions or events probably had the least impact on the changes shown in the graphs?**

   (1) the wheat threshing machine
   (2) the computer
   (3) the Second World War
   (4) the farming crisis of the 1980s
   (5) the airplane

3. Which of the following has probably *not* been a result of the changes reflected in the graphs?

    (1) There are fewer but larger and more heavily equipped farms to produce the agricultural products needed by a growing population.
    (2) There has been a slow down in the computer industry due to a decrease in the number of factories that produce them.
    (3) There are more social programs funded by the government to help those displaced from their jobs by the changes.
    (4) Industries in other countries make products that compete with those made in the United States.
    (5) Many more people are being trained to maintain and fix machines since there are so many more machines.

Answers are on page 410.

Health

Perhaps the greatest innovation of recent times has been longevity. At the turn of the 20th century, many men and women were feeble by age 40. The average American born in 1900 had a life expectancy of 47.3 years. Effective treatments for disease were so scarce that doctors could carry all their drugs and instruments in a small black bag. By the end of the 20th century, medical advances had caused life expectancy to increase to about 77 years. Modern health-care practitioners can prevent, control, or cure hundreds of diseases. People in the United States today often remain independent and physically active into their 80s and 90s. The fastest-growing age group in the population now consists of people aged 85 and over.

The capacity to stay alive longer and in better health has been the result of centuries upon centuries of research, invention, and determination. If there is one thing all human beings have in common it is the vulnerability of our bodies to sickness and disease. All the accomplishments of human activity seem of little consequence when we cannot prevent ourselves from becoming ill or, upon becoming ill, we cannot cure ourselves. And thus a large part of inventive energy and skill has been applied to the advancement of medical science.

As with many things, the Chinese were the first to make headway in medicine. In the second century B.C.E. they discovered that blood circulated and that hormones could be extracted and used to treat a number of conditions. Perhaps the most significant contribution of the Chinese was made in the 10th century C.E. with an understanding of immunity and the development of an inoculation against smallpox. To prevent an infectious virus like smallpox, the Chinese invented a way to extract a sample of the virus and then inject it into a healthy person. If the body could survive the exposure, it developed a resistance to the virus and could not be infected in the future.

Inoculation appears to fly in the face of reason. To prevent a disease by giving it was deemed a risky business at best by other cultures. But in the late 1700s an Englishman, Edward Jenner, made an innovation on the Chinese development by using a less potent strain of smallpox as a vaccine. The strain was called "cowpox" and at first the public was extremely skeptical. Smallpox epidemics were common in 18th-century Europe, however, and a leading cause of death. Although fearful and dubious, people began to seek Jenner out. The cartoon below depicts people's reactions to the smallpox vaccine.

GED PRACTICE

EXERCISE 6

Questions 1 and 2 refer to the following cartoon.

The Cow Pock — or — the Wonderful Effects of the New Inoculation! — vide the Publications of ye Anti Vaccine Society

1. What can you infer about life in late-18th-century England on the basis of this cartoon?

   (1) The practice of medicine was not as advanced as it is today.
   (2) Doctors tended to have ridiculous ideas that were not respected.
   (3) People became easily hysterical when confronted with a new idea.
   (4) Doctors didn't care much about the concerns of their patients.
   (5) There was a serious problem of overcrowding in towns and cities.

2. What was the purpose of this cartoon?

   (1) to show how ridiculous Jenner's theory was
   (2) to demonstrate how deadly a disease smallpox was
   (3) to satirize people's anxieties about the vaccine
   (4) to protest the unethical nature of this approach
   (5) to express concern for the cows from which the virus was taken

Answers are on page 410.

Vaccines have been one of the major medical advances. Others have included anesthesia, antiseptics, antibiotics, and the simple sterilization of surgical implements. Even as discoveries were made and inventions developed, however, they needed to be perfected.

Below is a description of the work of the Mayo family (father and two sons) at their now-famous clinic in Minnesota.

GED PRACTICE

EXERCISE 7

Questions 1 and 2 are based on the following passage.

The Mayo brothers didn't often originate the new surgical procedures. What they usually did was refine them, perfect them, perform them in incredible numbers and with observant care and reduce their mortality until finally they became routine. Ten gallbladder operations in 1895 became 75 in 1900 and 324 in 1905. In 1905 the Mayos performed 2,157 abdominal operations in all. They were boyish-looking men when they were young, dressed in country suitings. When they showed up at Eastern medical meetings with their careful reports, claiming to have performed hundreds of operations in a town of six thousand souls (in 1904 they reported jointly on 1,000 gallbladder procedures when many surgeons had not yet performed ten), they were sometimes taken for charlatans. They evolved a stock answer for doubters: "Come and see." Eventually the doubters did, and went away convinced.

—Excerpted from "A Reservoir of Suffering Humanity"
by Richard Rhodes, *Visions of Technology*

1. What is the point of this paragraph?

   (1) to prove that country doctors are as good as city ones
   (2) to emphasize the importance of seeing for oneself
   (3) to point out how widespread abdominal problems were in the Midwest
   (4) to emphasize the importance of practice and refinement
   (5) to raise questions and doubts about the Mayos' surgical record

2. Which of the following would have been a likely result of the Mayos'
    work as it is described here?

    (1) Scandal detracted from the impact of the Mayos' work as imposters
        posed as the Mayos in order to get more patients.
    (2) Skepticism on the part of both the public and other doctors
        prevented the Mayos from expanding the services of their clinic.
    (3) Other doctors learned from the Mayos, and successful abdominal
        surgery became much more commonplace around the country.
    (4) Malpractice suits soared as patients whose surgery was
        unsuccessful pressed charges against the Mayos and other doctors.
    (5) The Mayos went on to develop treatments for lung and bone cancer
        as well as numerous other afflictions.

Answers are on page 410.

While new treatments and approaches to illness are eventually praised
with great fanfare and their inventors awarded prestigious prizes, initial doubt
and worry often accompany the announcement of advances, as the previous
examples illustrate. This is also true for new things in fields beyond medicine,
even when the positive potential of a new invention is enormous. People can
be fearful, not only of the implications of the new thing for their personal
lives, but for society as a whole. Cloning is a recent major breakthrough that
was received with a less-than-enthusiastic response.

To clone an organism is to create from it another organism by an asexual
(nonsexual) reproductive process. Usually clones are identical in their
inherited characteristics—that is, in their genes. The purpose behind the
current cloning experiments has been to develop a cost-effective method of
producing medicines to treat such conditions in humans as cystic fibrosis and
hemophilia.

EXERCISE 8

Read the following paragraph about Dolly, a cloned sheep (pictured below), and answer questions 1 and 2.

But Dolly the cloned sheep was not heralded as a glorious piece of innovative science. Aghast, the newspapers of the world responded to this sensational scientific advance with a clamor of moral outrage. Driven blindly by the search for the new, we were told, the Scottish scientists were careening towards disaster along that sinister path to damnation notoriously embarked upon by the demonic hero of Mary Shelley's famous novel, Dr. Frankenstein. In no time at all we would face the nightmare scenario of genetically engineered armies of identical soldiers, bred to exterminate with ruthless efficiency. Parents would shortly decide exactly what mental and physical characteristics they wanted for their offspring and order them tailor-made, off the shelf. Worst of all, with no further need for sperm in order to beget children, men would be sidelined or cut out of the reproductive cycle altogether, consigned to the scrap heap of history.

—Excerpted from *Building the Scientific Revolution: Ingenious Pursuits* by Lisa Jardine

1. What does the tone of this paragraph suggest?

(1) The response of the press to the cloning of Dolly is exaggerated and ridiculous.

(2) While Dolly may not exactly be Frankenstein's monster, there is sufficient cause to be worried.

(3) New child-planning services are likely to be offered soon for those who can afford them.

(4) Concerns about how armies will be formed and wars fought in the future are not overblown.

(5) The cloning of Dolly is not such a big deal and no one should pay attention to it.

2. Which of the following would *not* be an example of something resulting from "the search for the new"?

(1) American democracy
(2) laser surgery
(3) frozen dinners
(4) chimpanzee language
(5) trash recycling

Answers are on page 410.

Communication

Communication is the process of sharing ideas, information, and messages with others in a particular time and place. Communication includes writing and speaking, as well as nonverbal communication (such as facial expressions, body language, or gestures), visual communication (the use of images or pictures, such as painting, photography, video, or film), and electronic communication (telephone calls, electronic mail, cable television, and satellite broadcasts). Communication is a vital part of personal life and is also important in business, education, and any other situation where people encounter each other.

Since the beginning of writing, inventions and innovations in communication have had a major influence on society. Some scholars believe that evolving means of communication were the key elements in the development of all the great ancient societies: Egypt was transformed by papyrus and written hieroglyphics; ancient Babylonia used cuneiform writing (a mode of writing utilizing wedge-shaped strokes, inscribed mainly on clay) to develop a sophisticated economic system; the ancient Greeks' love of the spoken word led them to perfect public speaking, persuasive rhetoric, drama, and philosophy; for administering their empire, the Romans developed an unparalleled system of government that depended on the Roman alphabet.

The developments just described occurred over several thousand years. Advancements in communication really began to speed up, however, in the 1400s with the invention of the printing press by Johannes Gutenberg. What distinguished Gutenberg's machine from other printing mechanisms that had preceded it was that it had movable type. With movable type, a raised, reversed image of each letter can be hand-set, word by word, into a frame that holds the pieces together. The raised letters are inked, a sheet of paper laid over them and pressed down on the letters with a screw-driven press, creating a correct image of the text. When enough copies are printed, the letters can be taken apart and reused. The technique made printing numerous copies of textual material much easier.

It has been estimated that more books were published in the first fifty years following Gutenberg's invention than had been produced in the previous thousand years. And what happened when books were published and more easily available to the public? People became inspired to learn to read. Reading, in turn, led to thinking about what had been read, to further publication, and to communication between people. The result of that communication was the rapid dissemination of knowledge and ideas. The first "World Wide Web" had arrived!

What are some of the important ideas and knowledge that you think may have begun to be disseminated with the widespread availability of print? When you think about the years 1500 to 1800 B.C.E., what historical events come to mind? Perhaps you remember that the exploration and settlement of the "New World" occurred during this period. Or that there were major changes in religious and scientific thinking. Or that people began to demand more of a voice in how they were governed and the concept of democracy was born. How do you think communication contributed to these significant changes?

_____

_____

_____

_____

_____

Many kinds of messages can be communicated between human beings: messages about feelings, messages about ideas and thoughts, and messages about information. The messages that are transforming the world today are those concerning information because of the abundance of them made possible by electronic technology, also called the "information marketplace."

GED PRACTICE

EXERCISE 9

Read the following passage about the World Wide Web and answer questions 1–3.

[In the mid-1990s] the Web had shed its techie aura and become a major cultural movement involving millions of people. The tens of millions of Web users, from homeowners to CEOs, were growing in number at an incredible rate, adding daily to the cumulative web of information by posting their own 'home pages' that described their interests and needs and included writings and other offerings. The [computer] mouse links of all these people, like twists on millions of door handles, were opening countless doors to information, fun, adventure, commerce, knowledge, and all kinds of surprises at millions of sites—down the street or a continent away.

Clearly the new world of information was already affecting everyone's lives.

In a quiet, relentless way information technology had begun to change the world so profoundly that it has claimed its place in history as a socioeconomic revolution equal in scale and impact to two industrial revolutions.

—Adapted from *What Will Be* by Michael Dertouzos

1. Which of the following is *not* stated or implied in this passage?

    (1) Before the mid-1990s, the Web was assumed to be something only for people with technological expertise.
    (2) "Home pages" can be made and used by anyone, no matter who they are or what they do.
    (3) Access to the Web is limited to those who can afford both a phone line and a computer.
    (4) A person's physical location does not affect his or her ability to reach any site on the Web.
    (5) The Industrial Revolution was important in history and caused great change in the world.

2. On the basis of this passage what generalization can you make about information technology?

    (1) It is easier to use if you are a homemaker or a CEO.
    (2) There are limits to how many people can use it.
    (3) Nobody could have predicted its impact prior to the mid-1900s.
    (4) The potential for it to further impact our society remains great.
    (5) Computers offer the best possibilities for fun and learning.

3. Which of the following statements is an assumption that the author is making in this paragraph?

    (1) Everyone has been impacted by information technology.
    (2) Many people use the Web and have "home pages."
    (3) There are lots of ways to have fun with a computer.
    (4) There are big socioeconomic changes under way.
    (5) You don't have to be an expert to use a computer.

Answers are on page 411.

Information technology can change how we receive health care, how we learn, how the elderly remain connected to society, how governments conduct their affairs, how ethnic groups preserve their heritage, and how goods are produced and marketed. Considering, anticipating, and participating in bringing about these changes can be exciting. However, it is important as well not to lose sight of the challenges such innovations pose. Two challenges that command particular attention are

- maintaining individual privacy

- ensuring information equity

Privacy

New communication and information technologies have enabled many organizations and people to collect, organize, and sell information about other people and organizations quickly and cheaply. The easy availability of personal information makes banking, education, health care, and sales much more convenient for both consumers and sellers. Credit card and automated teller machine (ATM) systems would be impossible without large databases of information available on demand. Scanners in the supermarket rapidly and accurately record every item that passes over them, making grocery checkouts faster and more error-free. Companies maintain huge mailing lists of customers that record not only their names, addresses, and phone numbers, but also major recent purchases, credit ratings, and demographic information (such as sex, age, income, and educational level) that helps the companies identify target markets for specific products.

The negative side to all this shared information is that there is little control over who sees or uses this personal information. Medical records are not only shared by doctors' offices and hospitals but are regularly made available to insurance companies as well. Auto insurance companies obtain information about traffic violations from state and local police departments. Credit report errors occur often and can be very damaging to a person's financial situation. Many Americans worry that having so much of their personal information available to so many others endangers their privacy.

Information Equity

Another concern among researchers studying changes in society is the growing gap between the information-rich (people with easy access to information) and the information-poor (people with less access to information). As new technologies and communication services emerge, the service companies would like to find receptive—and paying—audiences. Newspapers, radio, and television were for many years the major sources of day-to-day information, and they were very inexpensive for the audience. Broadcast signals could be received free of charge, and daily newspapers supported themselves mainly with advertising so that per-copy prices stayed low. AT&T provided "universal service at affordable prices" so that most people could afford local telephone service.

The media today, however, are charging more than ever for their products and services. More households pay for cable television rather than settle for over-the-air, or free, television. Local telephone rates have gone up since the breakup of AT&T in the 1980s (although long-distance services, with many competing providers, have become cheaper). Newspaper circulation has declined, and magazine subscriptions and book prices have increased sharply. On-line services (Internet service providers) charge customers to connect to their networks. Communication equipment is more sophisticated, and costs more, than in the past; even the prices of computers, which have become vastly more powerful in the past few years, have stayed about level. In short, people who can afford more and better services may become more informed than people who cannot afford them. Some researchers think that the differences between the information-rich and -poor may have negative social consequences and refer to the issue as the "digital divide." In the most basic sense, the digital divide is the ever-growing gap between those people and communities who have access to information technology and those who do not.

Consider the following statistics. Remember that a developing country is a place where the standard of living for most people is very low because of limited capital (goods and monies from which income can be derived).

- Fewer than 1 percent of on-line users live in Africa, and the number drops dramatically when South Africa is excluded. The United States and Canada account for nearly three-fifths of Internet users.

- The developed world has nearly 50 phone lines for every 100 people, compared to 1.4 phones per 100 people in low-income countries. Tokyo has more phone lines than all of Africa, while more than half of the world's population has yet to make a phone call.

- Less than 5 percent of computers connected to the Internet are in developing countries.

—From the *World Employment Report 2001: Life at Work in the Information Economy* by the International Labour Organization, Geneva

What point do these statistics make?

_____

_____

_____

_____

One thing that this information makes clear is that there are huge differences between what people in the developed world have in terms of electronic and communication technology and what people in developing countries have. This means that much of the world has little access to information in an age when information is the driving economic, political, and social force. We can expect, therefore, that the poor may become poorer and the rich richer.

EXERCISE 10

 Refer to the graph and chart below to answer questions 1–3.

PERCENT OF U.S. HOUSEHOLDS WITH A COMPUTER BY INCOME BY RACE/ORIGIN, 1998

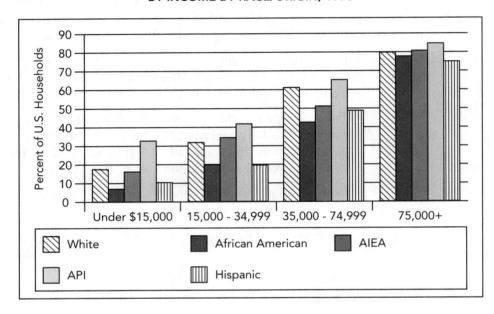

PERCENT OF U.S. HOUSEHOLDS WITH A COMPUTER BY INCOME AND ORIGIN, 1998

	Under $15,000	$15,000 - $34,999	$35,000 - $74,999	$75,000+
White	17.5	32.5	60.4	80.0
African-American	6.6	19.4	43.7	78.0
AIEA	16.8	35.3	50.9	80.5
API	32.6	42.7	65.6	85.0
Hispanic	9.4	19.8	49.0	74.8

API refers to Asian or Pacific Islander

AIEA refers to American Indian, Eskimo, or Aleut

1. According to the graph and chart, who among the following was least likely to own a computer in 1998?

    (1) White
    (2) African American
    (3) AIEA
    (4) API
    (5) Hispanic

2. What generalization can be made on the basis of this graph?

    (1) The more money you earn, the more likely you are to own a computer.
    (2) An African American is not likely to own a computer.
    (3) Only people who earn a lot of money can afford to buy a computer.
    (4) Hispanics and African Americans earn almost the same amount of money.
    (5) API people enjoy using computers more than anyone else.

3. To whom would the information in this chart and graph be most useful?

    (1) a civil rights lawyer protesting discriminatory employment practices by computer manufacturers
    (2) a computer retailer interested in promoting a newly developed, expensive home computer system
    (3) a community advocate requesting funds for computers and skills training in a low-income neighborhood
    (4) a Peace Corps volunteer preparing to go to a developing African country to help strengthen its village industries
    (5) a professor of statistical analysis in an undergraduate degree program

Answers are on page 411.

Progress

While we have investigated invention and technology in numerous contexts and from a number of perspectives, we have almost never mentioned the term *progress*. We have waited until the end so that we can consider it in relationship to what we have learned.

Progress can be defined as a series of improvements in human life marked by inventions and discoveries. The most important word in this definition is *improvement*. There is no doubt, as we have seen, that inventions and discoveries cause change. The question, however, concerns whether or not that change is good, whether it brings us to a better condition than we were in before. The 20th-century philosopher Bertrand Russell wrote that "change is indubitable, whereas progress is a matter of controversy." When we think about some of the enormous changes caused by such things as agriculture, cities, printing, and computers it is easy to see that the effects are a mixed bag and that whether or not there has been progress is, indeed, controversial. As civil rights leader Martin Luther King, Jr. said, "All progress is precarious, and the solution of one problem brings us face to face with another problem."

Read the following paragraph as you continue to think about the new problems created by solutions to the old.

Man sometimes fears his own machines; they seem to take on inhuman qualities and are regarded as divorced from the essence of humanity; indeed, some of man's infernal machines— for example, nuclear bombs—threaten to destroy all mankind, and his use—or misuse—of technology appears to threaten the quality of human life, as well as the life of all creatures, by environmental changes which disturb the ecological balance. What is more, man fears that some of the monster automatons which he has recently created will make him expendable as a worker—and even deprive him of his humanity.

—Excerpted from "Man and Machines," *Technology and Culture*, ed. by Melvin Kranzberg and William Davenport

The two chief concerns mentioned in the passage are environmental destruction and the loss of what it means to be human. To describe the first involves reference to the sobering phenomena of global warming, chemical pollution, the extinction of species, and human overpopulation of the planet. The second can't be quite so specifically exemplified but its essence lies in the fear of becoming both completely flooded with the words and ideas of others and at the same time completely isolated from genuine contact.

Chapter Review

Questions 1 and 2 are based on the following graph and paragraph.

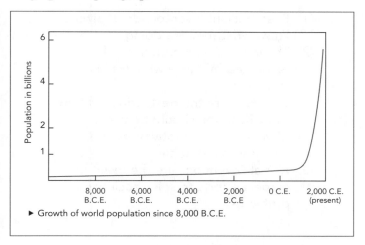

► Growth of world population since 8,000 B.C.E.

By the time of the Bronze Age, the different human societies on every continent had long since made a number of technological advances. They had developed barbed spears, the bow and arrow, animal-oil lamps, and bone needles for making containers and clothing. They had also begun a major cultural revolution—the shift from nomadic hunting and herding societies to the more settled agricultural way of life.

1. Which of the following innovations would have been least likely to contribute to the major cultural revolution referred to in the paragraph?

   (1) sickle
   (2) irrigation
   (3) cultivation of plants
   (4) bows and arrows
   (5) domestication of animals

2. Which explanation of the shift in the line of the graph is most likely given the information from the paragraph?

   (1) The human population increased dramatically once people could make warmer clothing and survive cold winters.
   (2) The human population increased dramatically once hunters had better tools and were able to kill more and bigger animals.
   (3) The human population increased dramatically once people began to stay in one place and grow their own food.
   (4) The human population continues to increase dramatically up to the present because of abundant food supplies.
   (5) The human population didn't increase until it had stopped living in caves and had developed a way to communicate.

Question 3 is based on the following passage.

The prime example of tinker-driven inventing is Thomas Edison's phonograph, widely considered to be the most brilliant invention of America's most brilliant inventor. When Edison built his first phonograph in 1877, it was not in response to a growing national clamor to hear Beethoven's symphonies at home. Instead, Edison was intrigued by the challenge of building something that could capture sound. Having built it, he wasn't sure what to do with it, so he drew up a list of ten possible uses. High on his list were recording the last words of dying people, announcing clock time, and teaching spelling. When entrepreneurs instead incorporated his invention into a machine to play music, Edison objected to this debasement of his idea.

—Excerpted from "Afterword" by Jared Diamond, *The Greatest Inventions of the Past 2,000 Years*

3. Which of the following assertions does this story illustrate?

(1) Even brilliant inventors don't always know what they are doing.
(2) The inventor's intention should be respected by those who use his invention.
(3) Inventors are the best judges of how their invention should be used.
(4) Most inventors' motivations are a mystery to the public.
(5) Not all inventions are the result of earnest efforts to solve society's problems.

Questions 4 and 5 are based on the following passage.

It is a widespread misunderstanding that necessity is the mother of invention. Actually, invention is the mother of necessity, by creating needs that we never felt before. (Be honest: did you really feel a need for your Walkman CD player long before it existed?) Far from welcoming solutions to our supposed needs, society's entrenched interests commonly resist inventions. In Gutenberg's time, no one was pleading for a new way to churn out book copies: there were hordes of copyists, whose desire not to be put out of business led to local bans on printing. For many decades after the first internal combustion engine was built in 1866, motor vehicles continued to languish unneeded, because the public was happy with horses and railroads, neither of which were in short supply. Transistors were invented in the United States, but the American electronics industry ignored them to protect its big investment in vacuum tube products; it was left to Sony in bombed-out postwar Japan to adapt transistors to consumer electronics products.

—Excerpted from "Afterword" by Jared Diamond, *The Greatest Inventions of the Past 2,000 Years*

4. According to the author of this passage, which of the following is an example of societal resistance to inventions?

   (1) parents educating their children at home instead of sending them to a school.
   (2) people buying cars instead of bigger trucks which can carry more people
   (3) the Japanese continuing to use their complex writing system instead of an alphabet
   (4) drug users remaining addicted rather than participating in rehabilitation programs
   (5) people continuing to use phones with cords although cordless and cell phones are available

5. Which of the following examples challenges the author's assertion that "invention is the mother of necessity"?

   (1) the achievement of the polio vaccine
   (2) the production of the cellular telephone
   (3) the institution of the "long weekend"
   (4) the availability of cable television access
   (5) the development of the telescope

Question 6 is based on the following photograph.

6. Which of the following has probably *not* resulted from the use of the robots pictured in this photograph?

   (1) increased business at the local shopping mall
   (2) high unemployment in the auto industry
   (3) improved production efficiency and quality control
   (4) fewer dangerous tasks performed by people
   (5) more training centers for service-related jobs

Questions 7 and 8 are based on the following passage.

Thirteenth-century Europe invented the sonnet as a poetic form and the functional button as a means of making civilized life more nearly possible in boreal climes. Since most of us are educated in terms of traditional humanistic presuppositions, we value the sonnet but think that a button is just a button. It is doubtful whether the chilly northerner who invented the button could have invented the sonnet then being produced by his contemporaries in Sicily. It is equally doubtful whether the type of talent required to invent the rhythmic and phonic relationships of the sonnet pattern is the type of talent needed to perceive the spatial relationships of button and buttonhole . . . The billion or more mothers who, since the 13th century, have buttoned their children snuggly against winter weather might perceive as much of spirituality in the button as in the sonnet and feel more personal gratitude to the inventor of the former than of the latter.

—Excerpted from "The Act of Invention: Causes, Contexts, Continuities, and Consequences" by Lynn White, Jr., *Technology and Culture*

7. Which of the following assumptions does the author make?

   (1) His readers know what sonnets are and value them more than buttons.
   (2) Sicilians think that poetry is better than buttons.
   (3) Buttons should be more deeply appreciated by everyone.
   (4) His readers don't know the difference between a button and a sonnet.
   (5) Northern Europeans don't write poetry because it's too cold.

8. What is the point of this passage?

   To emphasize that
   (1) everyone should read sonnets because so much talent goes into writing them
   (2) it is still difficult to determine whether the sonnet or the button is the more important contribution
   (3) the value of an invention depends upon the concerns and conditions of the person utilizing it
   (4) if a billion mothers appreciate buttons more than sonnets, then buttons are more important
   (5) the spiritual nature of many inventions in history has long been underestimated

Question 9 is based on the following cartoon.

—DILBERT, reprinted by permission of United Feature Syndicate, Inc.

9. Which of the following phrases would most accurately summarize the view presented by this cartoon?

(1) What I Wouldn't Give for a Chip
(2) Man's Best Friend
(3) The Race Is On
(4) Monkey See, Monkey Do
(5) Here Today, Gone Tomorrow

Question 10 is based on the following passage.

Slaves living in Texas celebrated in 1865 upon receiving the word that they were free. There were some mixed feelings, however, when they learned that their bondage had lasted more than two years longer than necessary. President Abraham Lincoln had issued the Emancipation Proclamation back in 1863, but inefficiencies in communication had prevented transmission of the news.

10. Which of the following would have been the most likely purpose for telling this story?

   (1) to emphasize the injustice of slavery in the United States
   (2) to praise Abraham Lincoln for his moral convictions
   (3) to illustrate the importance of information access
   (4) to criticize Texas for being behind the times
   (5) to express sympathy for the slaves in Texas

Answers are on page 411.

Chapter 10

Global Connections

In a speech at Harvard University in 1998, then President Nelson Mandela of South Africa said:

> The greatest single challenge facing our globalized world is to combat and eradicate its disparities. While in all parts of the world progress is being made in entrenching democratic forms of governance, we constantly need to remind ourselves that the freedoms which democracy brings will remain empty shells if they are not accompanied by real and tangible improvements in the material lives of the millions of ordinary citizens of those countries.
>
> Where men and women and children go burdened with hunger, suffering from preventable diseases, languishing in ignorance and illiteracy, or finding themselves bereft of decent shelter, talk of democracy and freedom that does not recognize the material aspect can ring hollow and erode confidence exactly in those values we seek to promote. Hence our universal obligation towards the building of a world in which there shall be greater equality among nations and among citizens of nations.

—Nelson Mandela, excerpted from *Harvard Magazine*, November/December 1998

President Mandela recognized the interdependence of the various parts of the world. He saw that the greatest challenges facing us are global challenges. In this chapter we will be looking at various aspects of the global connections that link all of us. We will look at the spread of civilization around the globe, the diffusion of cultures beyond their original borders, and the spread of agriculture and the origins of some of our common agricultural products. We will examine trade as a vehicle of global connection, both historically and today. We will look at the influence of worldwide religions in transmitting values as they spread religious practices and beliefs. We will then consider various modern political and economic philosophies that have had a worldwide impact. Finally, we will look at some of the modern worldwide political and economic institutions such as the United Nations and the World Bank, and some of the environmental, humanitarian, economic, and political problems they are trying to deal with in the modern world.

Spread of Civilization

For thousands of years, technological and cultural developments that occurred in one place had a tendency to spread. Art, architecture, social structures, and customs that originated in one region often had an influence in other regions. Two cultures that had enormous influence on the rest of the world were the Greek and Chinese cultures. Below are examples of ancient Greek and Chinese architecture. Following are examples of architecture from other regions and times. For each of these examples, state whether they are primarily influenced by the Greeks, the Chinese, or neither.

Parthenon in Greece

Forbidden City in China

1.

_____

2.

_____

3.

_____

4.

_____

Picture 1, the Colosseum in Rome, was influenced by the Greeks. The Amida Byodoin Temple in Japan (picture 2) and the Gandan Monastery in Mongolia (picture 4) were influenced by the Chinese. The Mayan Ruins in Tikal, Guatemala (picture 3), were not influenced by either. The Mayans at that time had no knowledge of the existence of either the Greeks or the Chinese.

GED PRACTICE

EXERCISE 1

Questions 1–3 are based on the following passage.

Cities first emerged as complex forms of social and political organization in the [river] valleys of the Euphrates and the Tigris, the Nile, the Huang Ho, and the Yangtze. These early cities broke dramatically with the patterns of primitive life and the rural societies from which they sprang. Kinship as the basis of society was replaced by status determined by class and occupation; the primitive magical leaders of the tribe were displaced by temple priesthoods presiding over highly developed religious institutions and functioning as important agencies of social control; earlier systems of rule by the tribal chieftains and the simple forms of communal leadership gave way to kingships endowed with magical powers and important religious functions; and specialized functionaries in the royal courts became responsible for supervising new kinds of governmental activity. Many other developments contributed to the growing centralization of power in these city civilizations. Barter was replaced by more effective systems of exchange, and the wealth generated in commerce and the specialized city trades became both an object of taxation and an instrument of power. Class distinctions emerged as the result of a division of labour and advances in technical development. A military order and a professional soldiery were created and trained in new techniques of warfare, and a slave class provided the work force for large-scale projects of irrigation, fortification, and royal architecture. As these developments proceeded, the city was able to project its power even further into the surrounding countryside, to establish its rule over villages and other cities in its sphere, and finally to become the centre of such early empires as those of Sumeria, Egypt, China, Babylonia, Assyria, and Persia.

—Excerpted from "Cities," *Encyclopedia Britannica*

1. **Though not specifically mentioned in the passage, which of the following most likely developed in the cities?**

    (1) domestication of animals
    (2) use of plow in agriculture
    (3) tools made from metal
    (4) development of writing
    (5) building of first boats

2. Of all the features of the ancient city, which of the following functions is still centered in modern cities?

   (1) the central importance of kinship in daily communal life
   (2) kingships based on magical powers and religious functions
   (3) housing, training, and development of military personnel
   (4) central locations for conducting major financial activities
   (5) a slave class providing the labor for major building projects

3. What was the most likely reason that kinship as the basis of society was replaced by status determined by class and occupation?

   (1) When people move from farms to cities, they stop caring about their extended families.
   (2) People felt that determining status based on family relationships was too old-fashioned.
   (3) People felt that determining status by class and occupation was more democratic.
   (4) Kings and priests maintained their power more effectively when class and occupation were most important.
   (5) Cities became too large and complex for kinship bonds to remain the basis of society.

 Questions 4–6 are based on the following passage.

Although Greece never formed a unitary state, Greek culture was so original and so striking that it became the basis of Western culture as a whole. The Greeks learned from Oriental civilizations, from which they adopted the alphabet, mathematics, and astronomy; but in a large number of fields the Greeks were themselves the creators.

Greece was the first country in the world where citizens could take part in public affairs. The preconditions for such democracy were liberty and equality, including freedom of expression, which made possible criticism of existing situations and the emergence of new forms of thought. The gift of withdrawing from the real world and proposing utopias is characteristic of Greek civilization.

Greek thought freed itself from old mythological explanations in order to explore the unknown and explain it by the known and by logical reasoning. The Greeks were thus the originators of experimental science, which the West later developed.

Education had an important role in the city, for without it there could be no way to take part in political life. The concept of the school is of Greek origin: at first it meant free time, then studies and educational establishments. The Greeks espoused a number of scholarly subjects: mathematics, natural sciences, grammar, logic, rhetoric, and the social sciences. Their curriculum underlies many later educational systems in Europe.

For the Greeks opposition was very important as a challenge and an incentive, in the stadia as on the battlefield. In the People's Assemblies dialogue was also an essential element if the city was to maintain the interests of its citizens—just as debate was vital for philosophers and scientists seeking knowledge. Even dramatists took part in an annual competition for a first prize awarded to the best play.

Theatre, with its double aspect of tragedy, and comedy, was a Greek invention. It was not merely for entertainment: it also had a religious purpose, venerating the gods, and a political function, exposing problems and involving the people in the affairs of the city.

In literature, too, the Greeks were innovators. It is significant that the words *epic*, *drama*, *tragedy* and *lyric* are much the same in different European languages and they all derive from Greek. Greek architecture, as exemplified in theatres, temples, and stadia, has also become a model, not only for the Romans but also, through the Renaissance, for architects down to the present day.

—Excerpted from "The Legacy of Greece,"
Illustrated History of Europe, Frederic Delouche, ed.

4. The Greeks were responsible for all except which of the following innovations?

   (1) the development of democracy
   (2) the development of theater
   (3) the creation of the alphabet
   (4) the beginning of experimental science
   (5) the establishment of the first schools

5. Over the past one hundred years, which nation has filled a role in world culture most similar to the role of the ancient Greeks?

   (1) the United States
   (2) the United Kingdom
   (3) France
   (4) Japan
   (5) India

6. Looking at the tremendous accomplishments of the ancient Greeks, it can be concluded that they were more intelligent and creative than any other people in history.

   Which of the following does *not* point out a logical fallacy in the preceding argument?

   (1) The paragraph does not include the failures and shortcomings of the ancient Greeks.
   (2) The accomplishments of other groups and societies are not described in the passage.
   (3) It is not possible to compare levels of intelligence and creativity over different times and places.
   (4) There are many accomplishments more important than those listed in the passage.
   (5) The failures and shortcomings of other groups and societies are not described in the passage.

Answers are on page 411.

The Importance of Trade

The lifeblood of global connections is world trade. There is evidence of human trading from prehistoric times. Before the modern era, the bulk of world trade took place along established trade routes. One of the most famous and important of these routes was the Silk Road, which linked China with the Middle East and Europe. One of the first Europeans to travel this route and leave an account of his journey was Marco Polo. When he wrote of his journey during the late 13th century, the Silk Road was already over 1,400 years old.

Following is a list of items that were traded on the Silk Road. Of the items on this list, one item came from China while the others came from the West. Check the item that came from China.

_____ Silk

_____ Wool

_____ Gold

_____ Silver

Silk was the one item on the list that came from China. The trade route was called the Silk Road because this was the only way that the West could obtain silk until the 15th century, when Europeans were first able to sail around Africa and on to Asia.

EXERCISE 2

Questions 1–2 are based on the following passage.

The expansion of Europe also brought about great changes in the agricultural field. European techniques were introduced into the New World and plants and animals were exchanged between continents. This made a decisive contribution to surmounting or attenuating food crises.

Plants introduced and grown in Europe improved people's diet, curbed famine, and helped increase the population. Particularly important in this respect were maize and potatoes, both from America. Beans, tomatoes, and pumpkins also made for a more varied diet, as did imported products such as cocoa, vanilla, tea and spices.

At the same time the Europeans profoundly changed the American economy by introducing horses, sheep, cattle, cereals, vines, olives, sugar canes, coffee, and rice.

In Africa the Europeans acclimatized wheat, cassava, beans, cashews, passion fruit, yams, rice, and tea. In China they introduced American species such as groundnuts and maize. Large-scale production of maize, indeed, partly explains the growth of population there from the 16th century onwards.

—Excerpted from *Illustrated History of Europe*, Frederic Delouche, ed.

1. Given the information given in this passage, which of the following is a valid conclusion about the Americas at the time that they were discovered by the Europeans?

    (1) Native Americans were mainly hunters and gatherers.
    (2) Native Americans had domesticated many plants.
    (3) Europeans were looking to bring back new foods.
    (4) Native Americans were eager to adopt the European diet.
    (5) Europeans introduced french fries and Italian marinara sauce to America.

2. Which of the following is an unstated assumption from the passage?

    (1) The exchange of foods benefited all the peoples involved.
    (2) Europeans were eager to help other, more primitive peoples.
    (3) Native Americans mainly profited from contact with Europeans.
    (4) Europeans forced other peoples to adopt their foods and diet.
    (5) Increased trade was an important and valuable goal.

Questions 3–4 are based on the following map.

COLONIAL EMPIRES AND TRIANGULAR TRADE PATTERNS, 1750 ONWARD

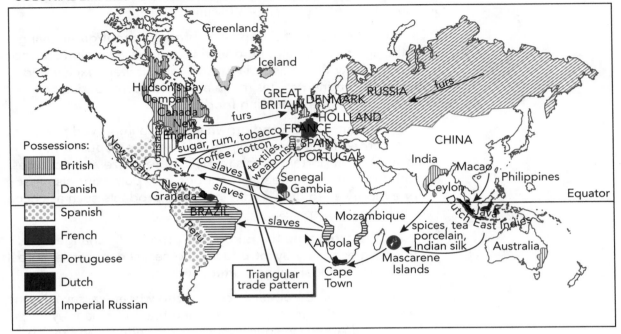

3. What part of the earth was most disrupted by the triangular trade?

   (1) North America
   (2) Western Europe
   (3) Western Africa
   (4) South Asia
   (5) South America

4. Of the nations shown on this map, which nation's expansion was most similar to the expansion of the United States?

   (1) Great Britain
   (2) Russia
   (3) China
   (4) India
   (5) Peru

Question 5 is based on the following passage.

By making known European painting, engraving, and sculpture, and training local artists, missionaries played an essential role in spreading the techniques and tastes of the 'Old World.' In this way themes treated by African, Asian, and Native American artists were linked with Europe.

But the traffic was not all one way. Oriental artistic creations inspired, in Europe, the multicoloured decoration of porcelain and furniture, the building of Chinese pavilions and gardens.

—Excerpted from *Illustrated History of Europe*, Frederic Delouche, ed.

5. Which of the following does *not* describe what missionaries did?

(1) shared their European culture and tastes with others
(2) converted local people to Christianity
(3) influenced the themes of African, Asian, and Native American artists
(4) introduced Oriental creations in Europe
(5) introduced the religions of native peoples to Europe

Questions 6 and 7 are based on the following table.

**Leading Exporters and Importers in World Merchandise Trade, 1999
(Billion dollars and percentage)**

Rank	Exporters	Value	Share	Annual Percentage Change	Rank	Importers	Value	Share	Annual Percentage Change
1	United States	695.2	12.4	2	1	United States	1059.1	18.0	12
2	Germany	541.5	9.6	0	2	Germany	472.5	8.0	0
3	Japan	419.4	7.5	8	3	United Kingdom	320.3	5.4	2
4	France	300.4	5.3	-2	4	Japan	311.3	5.3	11
5	United Kingdom	269.0	4.8	-1	5	France	290.1	4.9	0
6	Canada	238.4	4.2	11	6	Canada	220.2	3.7	7
7	Italy	230.6	4.1	-6	7	Italy	216.9	3.7	-1
8	Netherlands	200.4	3.6	0	8	Netherlands	187.6	3.2	0
9	China	195.2	3.5	6	9	Hong Kong, China	180.7	3.1	-3
10	Belgium	176.3	3.1	-		retained imports	28.7	0.5	-21
					10	China	165.8	2.8	18
11	Hong Kong, China	174.4	3.1	0	11	Belgium	160.9	2.7	-
	domestic exports	22.4	0.4	-9	12	Mexico	148.7	2.5	14
	re-exports	152.0	2.7	1	13	Spain	144.8	2.5	9
12	Korea, Rep. of	144.7	2.6	9	14	Korea, Rep. of	119.8	2.0	28
13	Mexico	136.7	2.4	16	15	Singapore	111.1	1.9	9
20	Russian Fed.	74.3	1.3	0	28	Russian Fed.	41.1	0.7	-30
	World	5625.0	100.0	3		World	5881.0	100.0	4

6. The predecessor of the Russian Federation, the Soviet Union, was considered the world's second superpower. Given the information on the chart, which of the following is the most reasonable conclusion?

    (1) The Soviet Union had been a master at deceiving the world as to its true strength.
    (2) The level of imports and exports for the Russian Federation has declined precipitously.
    (3) The power of the Soviet Union was not based on its economic strength and productivity.
    (4) The Russian Federation has a strong and vibrant internal economy.
    (5) Germany will most likely develop into the world's new second superpower.

7. China is the world's most populous country and one of the largest countries in the world. Belgium is one of the smallest nations, both in land area and population. Yet the level of imports and exports of these two nations is very similar. What does this information demonstrate?

    (1) Geographic location is a major determinant of the economy of a nation.
    (2) There is a direct correlation between the size of a nation and the size of its national economy.
    (3) There is an inverse correlation between the population of a nation and its level of economic prosperity.
    (4) The economic strength of a nation is not necessarily tied to its amount of territory or population.
    (5) A capitalist, free-market economy, such as exists in Belgium, creates the highest standard of living.

Answers are on pages 411–412.

War and Conquest

While trade usually involves mutually beneficial and voluntary contact between peoples and cultures, not all interaction between people is peaceful. Much of recorded history is a chronicle of repeated wars and conquests. In addition to the enormous destruction caused by war, cultural change often comes about as a result of conflict.

Time and again, ethnic groups rise from modest beginnings to become the dominant group in a major nation or empire. After a period of domination, even the most powerful empires appear to inevitably decline.

For nearly five hundred years, the nations of Europe were the most powerful in the world. But their long domination was not inevitable. In the century following the founding of Islam, the Arabs threatened to conquer Europe.

THE ISLAMIC-ARAB ATTACKS ON EUROPE (7th–8th CENTURIES)

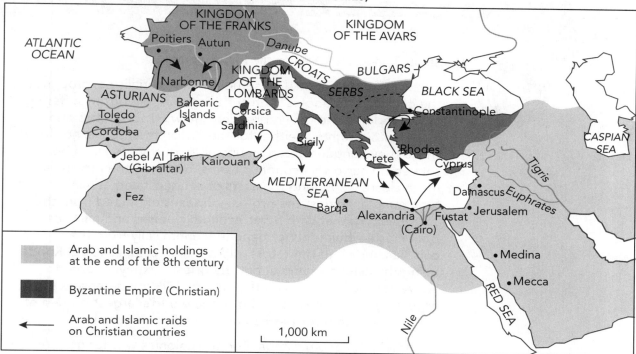

Conflict between Christians and Muslims continued through the period of the Crusades, and through the expansion of the Turks into Europe. Only at the start of the Age of Exploration did Christian Europe start to gain the upper hand. Today, both Islam and Christianity have expanded their areas of influence, but the boundaries of the areas where their cultures dominate have shifted. For each area listed below, write whether its dominant religion was Christianity or Islam in the 8th century and today.

	Eighth Century	**Twenty-first Century**
France		
Spain		
Italy		
Egypt		
Turkey		
Algeria		

In the eighth century, France, Italy, and Turkey were Christian, while Spain, Egypt, and Algeria were Islamic countries. Today, France, Spain, and Italy are Christian countries, while Egypt, Turkey, and Algeria are Islamic.

EXERCISE 3

Questions 1 and 2 are based on the following passage.

British imperialism, like some other imperialisms, brought to the conquered peoples both suffering and relief from suffering, new freedoms and new repressions, new opportunities and losses of old rights. Neither for the British themselves nor for those they conquered can an unambiguous net balance be totaled. In narrowly economic terms, however, the picture is much clearer. Counting the costs of conquest and administration, for example, against the profits and taxes extracted from the colonies, together with other economic pluses and minuses, Britain as a whole did not benefit economically from the colonies. Individual investors might make fortunes (Cecil Rhodes being the classic example) but the British taxpayers bore the heavy costs of maintaining the empire. Military defense was an especially heavy drain, leading to the world's largest burden of military expenditures per capita on the British people.

Britain's economic impact on the colonies was far greater than the colonies' impact on the British economy. It was not simply that the conqueror brought more advanced technology to the conquered lands. The conquered peoples themselves were able to use the existing land, with existing technology, more effectively because food, for example, could now be grown in fertile but militarily indefensible areas where it would have been foolhardy to plant before. Such situations had existed in medieval Scotland, as well as later in Africa, in British dominions and in those of many other nations. More generally, confidence that an investment of labor and resources could claim its reward—whether at harvest time or when dividends were issued years later—has been crucial to the economic efforts which create national prosperity. The security and stability provided by British colonial governments also made possible large-scale immigrations of foreign peoples, bringing new skills, talents and energies—the Chinese immigration to Malaya, the Indians to East Africa, and the Lebanese to West Africa, for example—as well as similar internal migrations, such as those of the Marawis in India and Ibos in Nigeria.

—Excerpted from *Conquests and Cultures* by Thomas Sowell

1. What is the main idea of this passage?

   (1) The British Empire was created and maintained to economically exploit weaker countries.
   (2) Britain had a far greater economic impact on its colonies than the colonies had on Britain.
   (3) The stability provided by the British made possible economic growth and prosperity in the colonies.
   (4) The benefits of British imperial rule far outweighed the drawbacks for its colonies.
   (5) The British encouraged the immigration of foreign peoples, who strengthened the empire.

2. Despite the advantages described in the passage of being a colony of the British, most areas under British control eventually won their independence. What might have motivated these countries to break away from British rule?

   (1) a belief that economically they would be better off as independent nations
   (2) a desire to abandon the declining British Empire because it was becoming less powerful
   (3) a desire for self-determination and the affirmation and rebirth of local culture
   (4) a disbelief that British rule had actually economically benefited their countries
   (5) a desire to embrace the political system and culture of the United States

Questions 3 and 4 are based on the following map and passage.

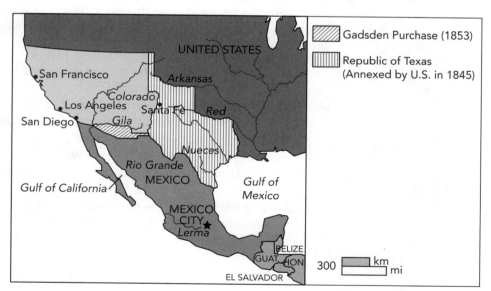

Texas was once a province of Mexico, though by the 1830s most of its inhabitants were from the United States. These settlers successfully revolted against Mexico and created the Republic of Texas, which joined the United States in 1845. Even though the Nueces River had been considered the southern boundary of Texas, the United States claimed that the Rio Grande was the southern boundary. When United States troops entered the area between the rivers and the Mexicans resisted, the Mexican War began.

3. When planning the American transcontinental railroads, industrialists decided that the best route for the Southern Pacific Railroad would be along a route partially still in Mexico. As a result, the United States government negotiated the Gadsden Purchase, which brought the proposed train route totally within the United States. The city of Phoenix, which lies on the Gila River in Arizona, began as a stop on the railroad.

   If the Gadsden Purchase had never taken place, which of the following is likely?

   (1) Phoenix today would be a major Mexican city.
   (2) The railroad would have been built farther north.
   (3) The Mexicans would have built the railroad.
   (4) Los Angeles would not have developed into a major city.
   (5) Phoenix today would be a major border city.

4. Before the Mexican War, the United States sent a negotiator to Mexico City with an offer to purchase California and New Mexico. The Mexicans, not wanting to have their country dismembered, refused to meet with the negotiator. This information, along with the map and the passage, most strongly supports which of the following hypotheses?

   (1) The Mexican War was provoked by the United States as a pretext for an imperialist land grab.
   (2) The Mexicans brought the Mexican War on themselves by being unwilling to negotiate with the United States.
   (3) The main motive of the United States in the Mexican War was to bring democracy to the Southwest.
   (4) The United States realized that California would someday become our richest and most populous state.
   (5) If the United States had not fought the Mexican War, today Mexico would be the world's most powerful country.

Questions 5 and 6 are based on the following passage.

When the Roman conquerors withdrew from Britain, the Britons' standard of living declined by all indications—the cruder products, crumbling infrastructure, wilderness growing back into human settlements, and people being buried in shallower graves and without coffins, for example. Later, in the last half of the 20th century, the withdrawal of European imperialists from Sub-Saharan Africa likewise left much of that region with lower per capita incomes 20 years later than they had had when living under the domination of the imperialists. It was much the same story in Central Asia, after the dissolution of the Soviet Union made it independent of the Russians for the first time in centuries—but also left it with shortages of the skills that many of the departed Russians had supplied.

Such facts are far more consistent with the economic consequences of differences in productivity, based on differences in cultural capital, than with theories of exploitation. Even economically motivated imperialism—and economic motives have by no means been the sole motives for conquest—has not always sought to acquire existing wealth but often, especially in modern times, to acquire resources that would produce wealth with the technology of the conqueror, even if these same resources had not made their current owners wealthy. Thus gold in South Africa and oil in the Middle East brought on the conquest of people whose own developed wealth and standards of living were modest at best.

—Excerpted from *Conquests and Cultures* by Thomas Sowell

5. Which of the following supports the exploitation theory of imperialism?

   (1) the conquest of Great Britain by the Romans
   (2) the conquest of Central Asia by the Russians
   (3) the conquest of Australia by Great Britain
   (4) the conquest of the Incas by the Spanish
   (5) the conquest of Hawaii by the United States

6. What is the key point that the author is trying to make in the passage?

   (1) The productivity of the ruling culture helps to determine the standard of living of an area.
   (2) Great Britain was better off under Roman rule than it was for centuries after the Romans left.
   (3) The Europeans did a poor job preparing their former African colonies for independence.
   (4) After independence, Central Asia needed the skills that had been provided by the Russians.
   (5) Imperialists often seek to acquire resources that, combined with their technology, can produce wealth.

Answers are on page 412.

Age of Exploration

WORLD MAP SHOWING WINDS AND CURRENTS

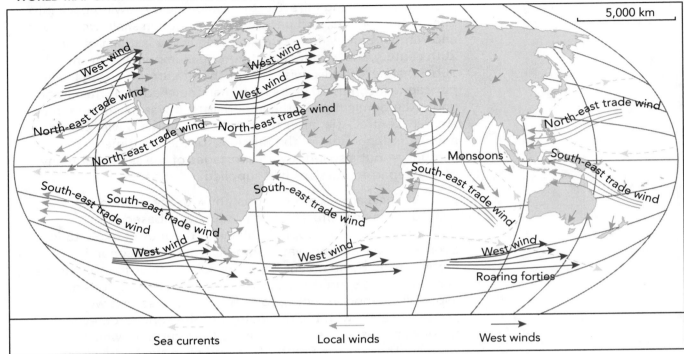

The map above shows the major winds and currents around the globe. When ocean-going ships used wind power in order to travel, these patterns were very important. While the Norsemen were the first Europeans to reach America, they left no permanent settlements, and their contact with America had no influence on later events. It was a few hundred years before the Portuguese developed ships that could sail long distances in the Atlantic. They tried for many years before they successfully sailed around Africa. From the map, why do you think they had such a problem making this journey?

_____

_____

After the Norsemen, the Spanish and Portuguese were the first to sail to the New World. Looking at the map, what was the route they probably took? As a result of this route, what parts of the Americas did they first discover?

_____

_____

The best route was to go southwest along the coast of Africa until the ships could pick up the northeast trade wind to America. To return, they would travel northeast until they picked up the west wind that would take them home.

EXERCISE 4

Questions 1 and 2 are based on the following passage.

Between 1500 and 1620 the average level of prices in Europe rose by 300 to 400 percent. This revolutionary price-rise was caused by the expansion of trade, the increase in the money supply owing to the influx of precious metals from overseas, the increase in demand for agricultural products which suppliers could not satisfy, the rise in the standard of living and the development of industry in northern Europe. Profits from trade and increased income led to greater investment, which in turn stimulated economic growth. Gold and silver, while contributing to international trade, encouraged Europe to live beyond its means and to spend more than it saved. This was why, given the growing demand for money, all the Antwerp banking institutions, leaders in their field in Europe, lent only at high rates of interest.

The 16th century seemed to be a golden age, especially for Spain, which received fabulous quantities of gold and silver from the Americas. More than Portugal, which had been unable to organize trading companies, Spain had the opportunity of becoming, in the 17th century, a great economic centre. It let slip the chance by failing to modernize its industry. The bourgeoisie preferred to buy land, while the aristocracy squandered its capital on luxury. As a result Spanish gold and silver were invested elsewhere in Europe, to the benefit of French, English and Dutch industries. North-west Europe became the nerve centre of the economy, with Amsterdam its capital. The Netherlands, England and northern France, which had real economic, cultural and technological dynamism, suffered less from the depression that struck Spain and Portugal in the 17th century.

—Excerpted from *Illustrated History of Europe*, Frederic Delouche, ed.

1. What lesson could the oil-rich nations of the Middle East learn from the experience of Spain and Portugal during the Age of Exploration?

    (1) They should get whatever political advantage from their wealth as they can since it won't last.
    (2) They should invest in developing modern, productive industries in their countries.
    (3) They should maintain the discipline of the OPEC oil cartel in order to maintain their power.
    (4) They should buy land and encourage their citizens to purchase expensive consumer items.
    (5) They need to invest their revenues in those countries where they can get the best return on their investments.

2. The defeat of the Spanish Armada by the English in 1588 is often given as the reason that the English replaced the Spanish as the world's greatest power. Given the information in this passage, what would most likely have occurred if the Armada had not been defeated?

   (1) Spain would have crushed all opposition and remained the most powerful nation on earth for centuries.
   (2) England or another northern European country that was developing its industry would have surpassed Spain anyway.
   (3) Spain would have become the largest world empire by taking over all English colonies in North America.
   (4) The Industrial Revolution would have started in Spain rather than England since Spain was the most powerful nation.
   (5) The industrialization of Europe would have been delayed for many years since no other nation could have replaced England.

Questions 3 and 4 are based on the following painting.

GRANDIBVS EXIGVI SVNT PISCES PISCIBVS ESCA.

3. Flemish painter Pieter Bruegel's *The Big Fish Eat the Little Fish* is said to be an allegory of the Spanish domination of the Low Countries, where Bruegel lived. Which of the following does *not* support this interpretation?

   (1) It would have been risky at the time to obviously attack Spain.
   (2) The imagery would be understood by his contemporaries.
   (3) The Low Countries were fighting for independence from Spain.
   (4) The image appears to be predicting what will happen to Spain.
   (5) Bruegel is famous for depicting groups of common people at work.

4. According to Pieter Bruegel, what is the ultimate fate of the big fish?

   (1) It ends up swallowing all the little fish.
   (2) It dies as a result of its own greed.
   (3) It lives to a healthy ripe old age.
   (4) It stops eating when it has enough.
   (5) It cannot live on dry land out of water.

Questions 5 and 6 are based on the following map.

**LAND CLAIMS IN
THE NEW WORLD 1689**

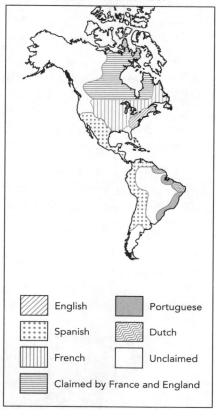

English		Portuguese	
Spanish		Dutch	
French		Unclaimed	
Claimed by France and England			

5. According to this map of the New World, which of the following conclusions can be drawn about the year 1689?

   (1) Spain became uninterested in the resources and possibilities of the New World.
   (2) France and England became rivals in the establishment of some settlements in the New World.
   (3) The Dutch were consistently driven out of areas that they tried to colonize in the New World.
   (4) Portugal's dwindling power led to its being limited to a small coastal area in South America.
   (5) Most of both North and South America was unclaimed by any of the European powers.

6. Which European nation had claimed the largest area of land in the Americas by 1689?

   (1) Spain
   (2) England
   (3) The Netherlands
   (4) France
   (5) Portugal

Answers are on pages 412–413.

Religions and Ideologies

Global connections are created not only by people and objects, but also by ideas. Great religions and political and economic ideologies have spread through large areas. Some are distant memories, while others are still vibrant and powerful today.

While many religions exist in today's world, only four—Christianity, Islam, Buddhism, and Hinduism—are dominant across large areas. Other religions, such as Judaism, Sikhism, Taoism, Shinto, and the religions of many indigenous peoples, still have millions of believers. Even within the four largest religions there are various sects.

Political and economic ideologies have also swept the world. One of the most controversial of these ideologies is Communism, in which a country is run by one political party which controls the entire government and economy. The following two cartoons show two very different viewpoints of this ideology.

Both of these cartoons are meant to persuade their audience. For each cartoon indicate whether it is promoting or attacking Communism and list the elements in each cartoon that back up your conclusion.

_____

_____

_____

_____

_____

_____

   The cartoon of Marx is in favor of Communism. Marx is made to look like Moses about to take his people to the promised land. The cartoon of Stalin opposes Communism. It depicts Stalin as an evil-looking octopus trying to ensnare the entire globe in his tentacles.

EXERCISE 5

Questions 1 and 2 are based on the following passage.

The widespread acceptance of polytheism, or belief in many gods, allowed the ancient world to be more tolerant of pluralism than the Judeo-Christian monotheism that succeeded it. The Middle Eastern religions of their time seemed familiar and acceptable to some Greeks and Romans: They too had a god of the sky, of thunder, a goddess of love; and they too honored the planets and the stars. To others, Middle Eastern religions seemed violent and sensuous, promoting barbarous and immoral practices. Likewise, to some Israelites, the religions of Syria-Palestine, or Canaan, with their emphasis on nature and fertility, seemed natural and attractive. To others, the religions of Canaan were false superstitions to be driven from the community by violence. Monotheism, with its principles of revelation and conversion, ultimately brought new identities to peoples of the ancient world and left the old religions to die out.

Since Judaism, Christianity, and Islam developed in the Middle East, they inevitably drew on existing Middle Eastern religions both for content and forms of expression. At the same time, these religions changed and reinterpreted what they had taken from others. For example, beliefs such as an original paradise, a universal deluge, prophecy, divine grace, purification, and holiness are known in ancient Middle Eastern religions. Morality and ethics, like that found in the biblical commandments, were taught by many ancient Middle Eastern religions. Hopes for the future, such as resurrection and afterlife, are found as well. Study of ancient Middle Eastern religions can therefore shed light on the origins of modern religions and on the world in which they developed.

—Excerpted from "Ancient Middle Eastern Religions" by Benjamin R. Foster, Microsoft Encarta Encyclopedia '99

1. Which of the following five choices is a conclusion based on the other four choices?

   (1) The modern monotheist religions adopted important beliefs, morality, and ethics from ancient Middle Eastern religions.
   (2) Beliefs such as an original paradise, a universal deluge, and prophecy all existed in ancient Middle Eastern religions.
   (3) Morality and ethics, like those found in the biblical commandments, were taught by many ancient Middle Eastern religions.
   (4) The Bible contains accounts of an original paradise, a universal deluge, and prophecy.
   (5) The concepts of divine grace, purification, and holiness are common to the monotheist religions and the ancient religions.

2. What might account for the hostility of the monotheistic religions to the polytheistic religions they encountered?

   (1) They thought that worship of gods and goddesses was primitive and ridiculous.
   (2) They felt that the emphasis on nature and fertility made the polytheistic religions attractive.
   (3) They did not want it known that they had borrowed many stories, beliefs, practices, and ideas from the old religions.
   (4) They felt that the polytheistic gods were strong competition for their one God and needed to be eliminated.
   (5) They felt that the polytheistic religions were violent and sensuous, promoting barbarous and immoral practices.

Question 3 is based on the following picture.

To the right in the engraving are the Calvinist theologians; to the left, the pope, the cardinals, the bishops, and monks and nuns at prayer.

3. Most likely, what was the point of view of the creator of this engraving?

   (1) The Protestant Reformation was returning the Bible to its true importance.
   (2) The leaders of the Church were being taken too lightly and shown disrespect.
   (3) Only the pope should be interpreting the Bible for all Christians.
   (4) Mass printings of the Bible had given people the opportunity to study it.
   (5) The Calvinist theologians were the only ones capable of interpreting the Bible.

Questions 4 and 5 are based on the following passage.

The usurper Napoleon had been a product of the Revolution, lasting from 1789 to 1815. In France, by contrast, people preferred to emphasize that he had betrayed the revolutionary ideas of liberty—as others had done before him. Yet by bringing about long-term stability in France he had made permanent the essential core of the Revolution. Thanks to him, the restoration of the monarchy in 1814–15 was not a return to 1789.

The French Revolution had had great repercussions in Europe. Early on it had spread the new ideas of the time, which awakened echoes in the 'patriotic' movements in many countries. Thus, for example, the Irish republicans sang the *Marseillaise* when they attacked the British. With Napoleon there was an attempt to unite Europe by force—a French Europe very different from that of the Enlightenment philosophers.

The attempt was a failure because it aroused against it an upsurge of nationalism. Yet it had its successes. Its uniform system of weights and measures and its codification of the law in many cases survived. Political debates, too, now gave an important place to the notions of motherland, nation and individual liberty. Traditional social ties may have suffered, but their decline paved the way for capitalism and industrialization.

The invasion of the Iberian Peninsula even led, outside Europe, to some first steps in decolonization. The King of Portugal took refuge in Brazil, which in 1822 proclaimed its independence and was granted it in 1825. The Spanish colonies remained loyal to the Bourbons and refused to recognize Joseph Bonaparte. Their loyalty was hardly rewarded when Ferdinand VII returned in 1813. It took only three years for the colonies to revolt again and declare their independence.

North America, France, Latin America: all witnessed revolutions, on both sides of the Atlantic, which confirmed that history was now developing on a world scale.

—Excerpted from *Illustrated History of Europe*, Frederic Delouche, ed.

4. In the 19th century, Napoleon unsuccessfully tried to unite Europe. Today nations are clamoring to join the European Union. What is the main difference between Napoleon's failure and the success of the European Union today?

    (1) The European Union arose after a huge war, World War II, while Napoleon had come to power in peaceful times.
    (2) Napoleon tried to introduce a uniform system of weights and measures, which the European Union downplayed.
    (3) Napoleon developed a codification of the law, while the European Union has established a continental government.
    (4) Napoleon tried to promote French culture, while the European Union encourages cultural diversity.
    (5) Napoleon used force to try to unite Europe, while nations apply to join the European Union.

5. Given the information in the passage, which of the following probably describes the Bourbons?

    (1) influential producers of alcoholic beverages
    (2) allies and supporters of Napoleon
    (3) the former royal family of Spain
    (4) Spanish patriots who rebelled against Joseph Bonaparte
    (5) leaders who promoted democracy

 Question 6 is based on the following passage about Andrew Jackson.

[Andrew] Jackson himself enjoyed widespread support that ranged across all classes and sections of the country. He attracted farmers, mechanics, laborers, professionals and even businessmen. And all this without Jackson being clearly pro- or antilabor, pro- or antibusiness, pro- or anti-lower, middle or upper class. It has been demonstrated that he was a strikebreaker [Jackson sent troops to control rebellious workers on the Chesapeake and Ohio Canal], yet at different times . . . he and the Democrats received the backing of organized labor.

It was the new politics of ambiguity—speaking for the lower and middle classes to get their support in times of rapid growth and potential turmoil. The two-party system came into its own in this time. To give people a choice between two different parties and allow them, in a period of rebellion, to choose the slightly more democratic one was an ingenious mode of control. Like so much in the American system, it was not devilishly contrived by some master plotters; it developed naturally out of the needs of the situation. Remini compares the Jacksonian Democrat Martin Van Buren, who succeeded Jackson as president, with the Austrian conservative statesman Metternich: "like Metternich, who was seeking to thwart revolutionary discontent in Europe, Van Buren and similar politicians were attempting to banish political disorder from the United States by a balance of power achieved through two well-organized and active parties."

—Excerpted from *A People's History of the United States* by Howard Zinn

6. According to Howard Zinn, how was the two-party system in the United States developed?

   (1) almost by accident to respond to political needs in the United States
   (2) deliberately as an ingenious mode of control of a ruling class over the people
   (3) by Andrew Jackson, with assistance from Martin Van Buren
   (4) with the assistance of the Austrian conservative statesman, Metternich
   (5) in order to maintain a balance of power and keep order in the United States

Answers are on page 413.

Globalization

We live in an era of globalization. The media allows us to see images and hear stories from around the world almost instantaneously. There are giant multinational corporations that do business in many countries around the globe. Worldwide organizations such as the United Nations (U.N.) and its components work with governments, organizations, and individuals. Documents such as the Universal Declaration of Human Rights and the Universal Test Ban Treaty set new standards for international law and behavior. And nongovernmental organizations such as Amnesty International, Oxfam, Doctors Without Borders, and the World Wildlife Fund have become the conscience of the world. As we become organized on a worldwide scale, we also face worldwide problems including environmental degradation such as the ozone hole and global warming, overpopulation, poverty, human rights abuses, and health crises such as the AIDS epidemic.

Following is an organizational chart that shows some of the more prominent parts of the United Nations. Following the chart is a list of issues. For each of these issues, list the parts of the U.N. that would most likely be working on that issue.

United Nations					
General Assembly	**Trusteeship Council**	**Security Council**	**International Court of Justice**	**Economic and Social Council**	**Secretariat**

UNICEF—U.N. Children's Fund	**U.N. Peacekeeping Forces**	**GATT**—General Agreement on Tariffs and Trade
UNHCR—U.N. High Commission for Refugees		**UNESCO**—U.N. Educational, Scientific and and Cultural Organization
UNEP—U.N. Environmental Program		**WHO**—World Health Organization
INSTRAW—International Research and Training Institute for the Advancement of Women		**IMF**—International Monetary Fund

Human rights abuses and genocide in Rwanda

_____

Economic development in Bangladesh

_____

Distribution of vaccines around the world

_____

Debt relief for the poorest countries

_____

Global warming

_____

The U.N. High Commission for Refugees, or UNHCR, would most likely be working to end human rights abuses and genocide in Rwanda. The IMF would most likely be working on economic development in Bangladesh and debt relief. The WHO would work to distribute vaccines around the world, and UNEP would likely be looking at the issue of global warming.

EXERCISE 6

Question 1 is based on the following passage.

The participating states recognize the territorial integrity of each of the other participating states. . . . In the same way the participating states each abstain from making the territory of any of them the subject of military occupation or of other measures involving a direct or indirect recourse to force contrary to international law, or the threat of such measures. No occupation or acquisition of this kind shall be recognized as legal. The participating states respect human rights and fundamental freedoms, including freedom of thought, conscience, religion or conviction for everyone without distinction of race, sex, language or religion.

—Excerpted from "The Helsinki Agreements (1 August 1975)," *Illustrated History of Europe*

1. The signers of the Helsinki Agreements included the NATO countries, the Soviet Bloc, and most of the other European nations. Why was it considered important that the Soviet Union signed this agreement?

   By signing, it committed itself to
   (1) reducing the size of its army
   (2) giving up control in Eastern Europe
   (3) promoting the growth of religious practices
   (4) free trade with the other signers of the agreement
   (5) respecting the freedom and rights of individuals

Questions 2 and 3 are based on the following passage.

The most common mistake of those who talk about globalization as a fact has been exaggeration. Capital slips around the world ever more easily but not in the frictionless way that Asian dictators fear. Most labor markets remain stubbornly national. Even in the richest countries, many markets for products still stop at a national border: A Canadian province trades twelve times as many goods and forty times as many services with another Canadian province than it does with an American state of similar size and proximity. In the supposedly open European Union, people are still six times more likely to trade with their fellow nationals. Industries have an irksome but entirely sensible reason for sticking to certain areas: For example, there are plenty of cheaper places to locate a film industry than Hollywood, but none of them has the same people. And a surprising number of basic products come from local sources. Nearly all of America's lightbulbs are still made inside the country, largely because the transport costs are too high to justify moving the factories elsewhere.

No matter how many times American politicians summon up images of a world that has slipped out of their control, macroeconomic statistics tell a different story. Events overseas usually have only small direct bearings on jobs and growth in the United States. If, for example, Japan gave up buying American products entirely, it would knock just 1 percent off America's gross domestic product (GDP); indeed, exports to the whole of Asia account for just 2.5 percent of America's economy.

—Excerpted from *A Future Perfect: The Challenge and Hidden Promise of Globalization* by John Micklethwait and Adrian Woolridge

2. During the late 1990s a number of Asian economies, including Thailand, Indonesia, and Korea, collapsed while Japan went through a deep recession. Many were surprised when the United States economy weathered the storm and kept on growing. What is the most reasonable explanation of the ability of the United States to withstand the pressures of the Asian economic crisis?

   (1) Only a small part of the American economy was directly tied to Asia.
   (2) The United States was able to expand its economy at the expense of Asia.
   (3) Since Asia is so far away from the United States, it couldn't affect the U.S. economy.
   (4) The Asian economic crisis ended before it had enough time to affect the U.S. economy.
   (5) Since the Asian economies are so small compared to the U.S. economy, they couldn't affect it.

3. Given the information in this passage, with which of the following is it likely that the Canadian province of Quebec does the most trading?

   (1) New York State, which is directly south of Quebec
   (2) Greenland, which lies to the northeast of Quebec
   (3) the province of Ontario, Quebec's neighbor to the west
   (4) the province of Alberta, over a thousand miles to the west
   (5) the state of Florida, a popular winter tourist destination

Questions 4 and 5 are based on the following bar graph and cartoon.

**HOURLY LABOR COSTS IN U.S. AND
MAJOR TRADING PARTNERS IN 1997**

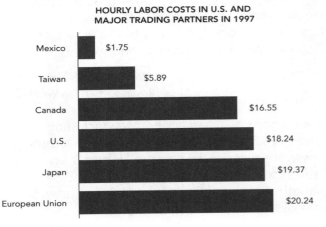

Mexico	$1.75
Taiwan	$5.89
Canada	$16.55
U.S.	$18.24
Japan	$19.37
European Union	$20.24

—©2001 Norman Dog

4. With which of the following opinions would the cartoonist most likely agree?

   (1) It always makes sense to look for the best price.
   (2) Family relationships are not as important as they used to be.
   (3) There is no limit to the selfishness of Americans.
   (4) Lowest price is not the only consideration in making decisions.
   (5) Jobs will continue to move to Mexico because of its lower labor costs.

5. Even though the United States and Mexico are neighbors, their labor costs are very different. Ross Perot predicted that if the United States signed NAFTA, the North American Free Trade Agreement, there would be a "great sucking sound" as American jobs moved south to Mexico. Instead, in the first years after NAFTA was implemented, the United States experienced job growth.

   What may explain the resilience of the U.S. economy despite having much higher labor costs?

   (1) Most employers in the United States are unaware that labor costs in Mexico are so low.
   (2) The U.S. economy produced enough new jobs to offset all the jobs that went to Mexico.
   (3) The difference in labor costs is a result of making more complex items in the United States.
   (4) The patriotic movement to produce and buy American goods outweighed the cost advantage.
   (5) The skills, education, and work ethic of the American labor force justify its high cost.

Answers are on page 413.

Addressing Worldwide Problems

The United Nations is not the only organization dedicated to addressing worldwide problems. Many nongovernmental organizations exist that work on a wide range of issues. Following is a list of some nongovernmental organizations. Match the organization to some problems that might be a priority for it. Some organizations may have more than one priority, and some problems might be addressed by more than one nongovernmental organization.

Amnesty International—deals with human rights abuses by governments

Oxfam—deals with the problem of world hunger

Doctors Without Borders—deals with world health problems

Cousteau Society—deals with environmental issues impacting bodies of water

World Wildlife Fund—works for the survival and protection of animals

Greenpeace—works on various environmental issues

Red Cross—deals with health emergencies

Nature Conservancy—works on protecting habitats

CARE (Cooperative for Assistance and Relief Everywhere)—works on disaster relief

Saving the whales _____

Global warming_____

AIDS epidemic_____

Women's genital mutilation in Africa_____

Government-sponsored imprisonment and torture in Turkey _____

Drought and crop failure in Ethiopia _____

Saving the Giant Panda from extinction_____

Destruction of the Amazon rain forest _____

Major earthquake in India _____

The Cousteau Society, World Wildlife Fund, and Greenpeace are all working on saving the whales. The Cousteau Society and the Nature Conservancy are concerned with global warming. Doctors Without Borders and the Red Cross are combating the AIDS epidemic. Amnesty International addresses women's genital mutilation in Africa and government-sponsored imprisonment and torture in Turkey. Oxfam and CARE would respond to drought and crop failure in Ethiopia. Saving the Giant Panda from extinction is a core project of the World Wildlife Fund. The Nature Conservancy is working to save the Amazon rain forest. The Red Cross, Doctors Without Borders, Oxfam, and CARE would all respond to aid the victims of a major earthquake.

EXERCISE 7

Questions 1 and 2 are based on the following passage and map.

A number of factors combined to bring about catastrophe: famines, illness (smallpox, influenza) and war. The grain crisis in the 14th century affected the poorest people in Europe. The plague, when it came, hit an underfed and hence vulnerable population. The coastal regions of the Low Countries, where more fish than grain was eaten, saw far fewer deaths.

For four years, from 1347 to 1351, the plague ravaged Europe. It took two forms: bubonic, with 80 percent mortality, and pulmonary, with 100 percent. It reached Europe from Asia and the Orient, where it was a frequent occurrence, onboard a Genoese ship. The Genoese had had warehouses on the shores of the Black Sea since the 11th century; and in 1346 one of them, Kaffa, was besieged by the Mongols. They were decimated by an epidemic of plague and got rid of the corpses by catapulting them into the besieged city. Its panic-stricken inhabitants fled in galleys to Sicily, bringing the disease with them. It spread like wildfire. By the end of 1347 it had reached northern Italy and Provence, and from there went up the Rhone Valley to Paris. In 1348 it was raging in Portugal and Britain, and the following year in Flanders and Germany. It then reached Scandinavia and entered Russia from the north. Europe was united, as it were, by disease.

Panic among the people became frenzied when bubonic plague turned into pulmonary plague. In bubonic plague the rat's bite was visible; but pulmonary plague was spread by invisible microbes. The Black Death was one of the greatest tragedies in the history of Europe. In a few months it killed a third of the population.

—Excerpted from *Illustrated History of Europe*, Frederic Delouche, ed.

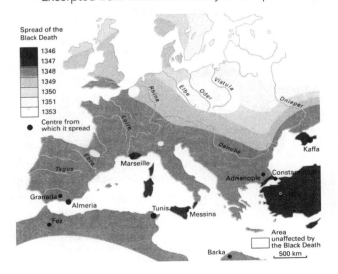

1. The author attributes the source of the plague in Europe to which of the following?

    (1) the Genoese who owned warehouses on the shores of the Black Sea
    (2) the grain crisis in the 14th century that affected poor people
    (3) pulmonary disease that was spread by invisible microbes
    (4) catastrophes including famine, smallpox, influenza, and war
    (5) a Genoese ship that landed in Sicily whose passengers were escaping the plague

2. According to the map, in which direction did the Black Death spread?

    (1) from the cities to the countryside
    (2) from Africa to Europe
    (3) from coastal areas inland
    (4) from south to north
    (5) from west to east

Questions 3 and 4 are based on the following passage and chart.

A persistent killer continues to stalk people in communities around the world. While AIDS can strike anyone, it mostly infects the young and the poor. Sub-Saharan Africa has been hit the worst, with an estimated 22.5 million adults and children living with HIV/AIDS. Cumulative deaths worldwide as of December 1998 totaled almost 14 million.

Since the disease strikes people in their most productive years, the economic consequences of HIV/AIDS are potentially enormous. For example, in Botswana, average life expectancy has been reduced by 20 years. This loss of life is devastating on a number of levels. It cripples a country's productive potential and raises the question of who will raise the next generation. In 1997 alone, AIDS orphaned 1.6 million children.

Poor countries bear a disproportionate burden of the epidemic. Expensive treatments allow people in rich nations to live longer, but the annual costs of medication for one person exceed the per-capita GDP of most developing countries.

—Excerpted from *The Ultimate Field Guide to the U.S. Economy*

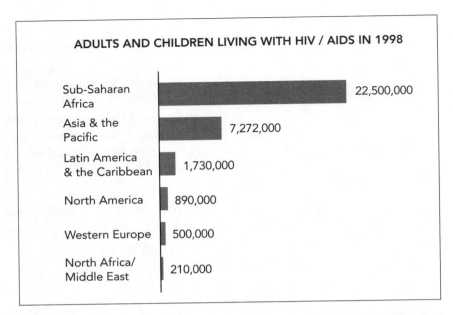

ADULTS AND CHILDREN LIVING WITH HIV / AIDS IN 1998

Sub-Saharan Africa	22,500,000
Asia & the Pacific	7,272,000
Latin America & the Caribbean	1,730,000
North America	890,000
Western Europe	500,000
North Africa/ Middle East	210,000

3. According to the passage and the chart, on which of the following has AIDS had the greatest impact?

   (1) the world economy
   (2) the poor
   (3) Africans south of the Sahara
   (4) orphaned children
   (5) the costs of drug treatments

4. Which of the following policies might have the greatest impact in helping the areas most affected by the AIDS epidemic?

   (1) increasing aid for industrial development so that the countries affected might become wealthier
   (2) providing AIDS drug treatment at an affordable price to people who test HIV positive
   (3) promoting public relations "Just Say No to Sex and Illegal Drugs" campaigns
   (4) expanding adoption programs so that the orphaned children can all be cared for
   (5) distributing free condoms and hypodermic needles through local clinics

Question 5 is based on the following passage.

W.E.B. Du Bois gave the keynote address, "To the Nations of the World." In this speech Du Bois, who is often called the father of Pan-Africanism, made his well-known prophecy: "The problem of the 20th century is the problem of the colour line, the question as to how far differences of race, which show themselves chiefly in the colour of the skin and the texture of the hair, are going to be made, hereafter, the basis of denying to over half the world the right of sharing to their utmost ability the opportunities and privileges of modern civilisation." The conference called for European countries to administer their African colonies justly and in preparation for independence. The conference also aimed at institutionalizing the Pan-African Association, but the appropriate conditions did not yet exist in Africa. Nonetheless, after July 1900, the word "Pan-African" had been coined and was used.

—Excerpted from *Encarta Africana*

5. Of which of the following do you think W.E.B. DuBois would *not* have approved?

(1) the actions of Martin Luther King in leading the civil rights struggle in the United States

(2) the actions of Nelson Mandela in ending the era of apartheid in South Africa

(3) the civil war in the Congo that involved many of its neighboring countries

(4) the Freedom Riders in the 1950s and 1960s who desegregated public areas in the United States

(5) the decision of the French government to grant independence to all its African colonies

Question 6 is based on the following passage.

President Harry Truman, in late 1946, appointed a Committee on Civil Rights, which recommended that the civil rights section of the Department of Justice be expanded, that there be a permanent Commission on Civil Rights, that Congress pass laws against lynching and to stop voting discrimination, and suggested new laws to end racial discrimination in jobs.

Truman's Committee was blunt about its motivation in making these recommendations. Yes, it said, there was "moral reason:" a matter of conscience. But there was also an "economic reason"—discrimination was costly to the country, wasteful of its talent. And, perhaps most important, there was an international reason:

"Our position in the post-war world is so vital to the future that our smallest actions have far-reaching effects. . . . We cannot escape the fact that our civil rights record has been an issue in world politics. The world's press and radio are full of it. . . . Those with competing philosophies have stressed—and are shamelessly distorting—our shortcomings. . . . They have tried to prove our democracy an empty fraud, and our nation a consistent oppressor of underprivileged people. This may seem ludicrous to Americans, but it is sufficiently important to worry our friends. The United States is not so strong, the final triumph of the democratic ideal is not so inevitable that we can ignore what the world thinks of us or our record."

—Excerpted from *A People's History of the United States* by Howard Zinn

6. From the information given in this passage, what was the most likely motivation for President Truman's civil rights policy?

   (1) concern about the threat of Communism
   (2) the economic costs of discrimination
   (3) a desire to do what was morally correct
   (4) an interest in deluding the people of the world
   (5) an understanding of the future Civil Rights movement

 Questions 7 and 8 are based on the following passage.

The genius of our black foremothers and forefathers was to create powerful buffers to ward off the nihilistic threat, to equip black folk with cultural armor to beat back the demons of hopelessness, meaninglessness, and lovelessness. These buffers consisted of cultural structures of meaning and feeling that created and sustained communities; this armor constituted ways of life and struggle that embodied values of service and sacrifice, love and care, discipline and excellence. In other words, traditions for blacks surviving and thriving under usually adverse New World conditions were major barriers against the nihilistic threat. These traditions consist primarily of black religious and civic institutions that sustained familial and communal networks of support. If cultures are, in part, what human beings create (out of antecedent fragments of other cultures) in order to convince themselves not to commit suicide, then black foremothers and forefathers are to be applauded. In fact, until the early seventies black Americans had the lowest suicide rate in the United States. But now young black people lead the nation in suicides.

What has changed? What went wrong? The bitter irony of integration? The cumulative effects of a genocidal conspiracy? The virtual collapse of rising expectations after the optimistic sixties? None of us fully understands why the nihilistic threat is more powerful now than ever before. I believe that the commodification of black life and the crisis of black leadership are two basic reasons. The recent shattering of black civil society—black families, neighborhoods, schools, churches, mosques—leaves more and more black people vulnerable to the nihilistic threat. This shattering spawns a deracinated and denuded people with little sense of self and few existential moorings.

—Excerpted from "Race Matters" by Cornel West.

7. Given the analysis of Cornel West, what change in America might have the greatest impact in reducing the suicide rate among young black people?

    (1) requiring high stakes annual standardized testing in all the nation's public schools
    (2) re-segregating the United States, so black people can create their own institutions
    (3) capturing and prosecute those responsible for the conspiracy to undermine the black community
    (4) trying to rebuild black religious and civic institutions by having them reach out to young people
    (5) setting up government funded education, housing, job training, and youth counseling programs

8. According to the article, which of the following did *not* help Black people survive centuries of oppression and discrimination?

    (1) the support of family members
    (2) the development of black churches
    (3) an identifiable oppressor
    (4) civic organizations such as the NAACP
    (5) the Civil Rights movement

Question 9 is based on the following passage.

It was a gripping human-interest story tailor-made for television: the inadvertent switching of newborn babies by hospital employees, whose carelessness came to light by pure chance three years later. Both families involved in the incident had grown attached to their babies, and the little boys themselves were by now happily and securely settled in their homes. During the legal proceeding to determine custody, a judge heard testimony from the two sets of parents, who agonized over their predicament, and from neighbors who supported the status quo. The judge ruled that each youngster be turned over to his natural parents, who would have the right to visit the child they had given up only after a six-month period of adjustment. TV news programs milked every dollop of pathos from the exchange, as those touched by the incident expressed their unrestrained dismay.

In the course of the reportage, no one saw fit to remark on the evident fact that one of the boys was black and had been accepted at birth without question by white parents; while the other was white and had been raised unhesitatingly by dark-skinned parents.

It is unlikely that this could have happened anywhere else but in Brazil, where miscegenation has been a common and accepted practice dating back to the arrival of the first Portuguese explorers.

—Excerpted from *The Brazilians* by Joseph H. Page

9. Based on the information in the passage, what does *miscegenation* most likely mean?

   (1) a mixture of races
   (2) ignoring the obvious
   (3) a love of children
   (4) an acceptance of authority
   (5) a promotion of tolerance

Answers are on pages 413–414.

Chapter Review

Questions 1 and 2 are based on the following cartoon.

Mikhail Gorbachev, having dug the grave of Soviet totalitarianism, is at once attacked by the resurgent ghost of nationalism.

1. **What is the most likely explanation for the image of a ghost escaping from a grave?**

    (1) like a ghost, nationalism is extremely frightening
    (2) it emphasizes Gorbachev's inability to control events
    (3) the end of Communism would increase Russian power
    (4) with Communism buried, nationalism reemerged as a threat
    (5) nationalists were angry at Gorbachev for weakening Russia

2. **What is the overall mood of the cartoon?**

    (1) celebration over the death of Communism
    (2) surprise over the unexpected return of nationalism
    (3) humorous since the ghost is a comical figure
    (4) apprehension at the return of an old threat
    (5) confidence that nationalism can be controlled

Questions 3 and 4 are based on the following graph.

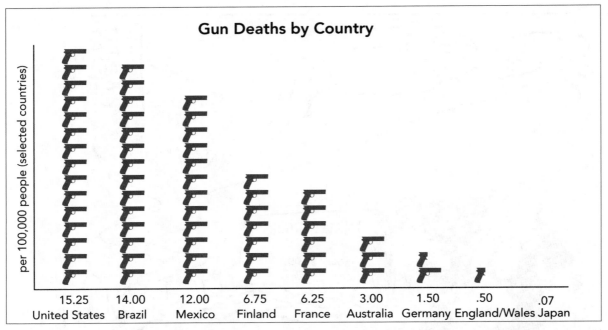

The United States and Finland have the two highest rates of per capita gun ownership, and the two highest rates of gun suicide, in the world.

3. This pictograph and caption most strongly support which of the following policies?

(1) promoting the ownership and carrying of loaded guns to reduce crime
(2) increasing mandatory sentences of those using guns in their crimes
(3) promoting export of American-made guns and ammunition to other countries
(4) increasing the use of the death penalty to deter crime and protect citizens
(5) decreasing the private ownership of guns as a means of reducing gun deaths

4. According to this graph, in which country it is least likely that someone would die from a gun wound?

(1) United States
(2) Mexico
(3) France
(4) England/Wales
(5) Japan

Questions 5 and 6 are based on the following passage.

    Finally, black politics was deeply affected by another development within the U.S. state—the rapid expansion of what was later termed the "prison-industrial complex." With the decline of the Cold War and the reduction of expenditures for both the military arms race and social-welfare programs, massive resources were reallocated toward prison construction and the expansion of security personnel. The death penalty, which had been abolished in 1972, was reinstated; by 1999 there were over 3,500 people waiting execution, about 45 percent of them African Americans. The number of Americans incarcerated in federal and state prisons and jails soared from 650,000 in 1983 to 1.8 million in 1998. By the end of the century, the United States had about 350,000 prison guards and over 600,000 police officers, possessed the highest penal-incarceration rate in the world, and yet continued to build an average of a hundred new prison cells every day. The growth of this prison-industrial complex had disastrous consequences for the entire society, but particularly for young African Americans. By 1999, more than one-third of all black males in their twenties were either in jail, on probation, on parole, or awaiting trial. In the context of global proliferation of arms and illegal drugs, between the thousands of deaths produced by the illegal-drug gang wars and the massive rates of imprisonment, many urban communities were largely depopulated of their young black men.

    —Excerpted from *Let Nobody Turn Us Around: Voices of Resistance, Reform, and Renewal* by Marable Manning and Leith Mullings

5. What is the main idea of this passage?

  (1) Young black men have been targeted by the "prison-industrial complex."
  (2) The United States is turning to prisons to solve its social problems.
  (3) The number of incarcerated Americans has nearly tripled over twenty years.
  (4) Over one-third of young black males are in jail, on probation, on parole, or awaiting trial.
  (5) Forty-five percent of those on death row awaiting execution are African Americans.

6. With which of the following would the writer most likely agree?

  (1) The growth in prisons and the prison population is solving the crime problem.
  (2) Prisons are a very expensive, but effective, way to control crime.
  (3) It is detrimental to the Black community to keep building prisons.
  (4) There are many excellent job opportunities opening up in the law enforcement field.
  (5) Investing in prisons is a good alternative to military spending, which has been reduced.

Questions 7 and 8 are based on the following passage.

A number of elements are needed if a country is to become industrialized: larger units of production, greater division of labour and the replacement of people or animals by machines. The expression 'Industrial Revolution' was first used by a Frenchman at the beginning of the 19th century to describe the economic and social changes under way.

But why did modern industrialization first affect Western Europe? The principle of the steam engine had been known for a long time, but to make its development possible required economic structures and technological resources. Until the Middle Ages, countries such as China had been technologically ahead of Europe. Then in the 18th century, Europe began to catch up and overtake them. By directing its trade overseas, it was able to enjoy greater resources, enlarge its markets, profit from its technological advantages and export capital. Rapidly expanding industry was easily able to absorb the growing number of workers leaving the land.

While industrialization shared common features throughout Europe, every country and especially every region developed in its own way. As iron-smelting technology progressed, industrialization tended to concentrate in areas rich in coal and iron ore, notably a belt stretching from Wales to the Donets basin and encompassing the Midlands and north of England, north-eastern France and Belgium, the Ruhr and Silesia. Steam soon became the key source of energy in the Industrial Revolution, even if water power still played a major role in many industries for much of the 19th century.

—Excerpted from *Illustrated History of Europe,*
Frederic Delouche, ed.

7. Which of the following was one of the key reasons that the Industrial Revolution began in Europe?

(1) Europe had long led the world in technical innovation and natural resources.
(2) Europe had built up economic structures that encouraged development.
(3) Europe had a climate that was most conducive to hard work.
(4) Europeans invented iron smelting and the use of water power.
(5) The Chinese helped the Europeans develop their first industries.

8. After the Industrial Revolution started in Europe, the next place it took hold was the United States. The United States shared all the conditions leading to industrialization in Europe except which of the following?

(1) sovereignty fragmented among many nations
(2) abundant and accessible natural resources
(3) a system of laws and courts that protected property
(4) a labor force with a strong work ethic and productivity
(5) growing markets for the products of industrialization

Questions 9–11 are based on the following document.

On December 10, 1948, the General Assembly of the United Nations adopted and proclaimed the Universal Declaration of Human Rights. Following are some of the thirty articles of the Declaration.

Article 1.

All human beings are born free and equal in dignity and rights. They are endowed with reason and conscience and should act towards one another in a spirit of brotherhood.

Article 3.

Everyone has the right to life, liberty and security of person.

Article 4.

No one shall be held in slavery or servitude; slavery and the slave trade shall be prohibited in all their forms.

Article 5.

No one shall be subjected to torture or to cruel, inhuman or degrading treatment or punishment.

Article 9.

No one shall be subjected to arbitrary arrest, detention or exile.

Article 12.

No one shall be subjected to arbitrary interference with his privacy, family, home or correspondence, nor to attacks upon his honour and reputation. Everyone has the right to the protection of the law against such interference or attacks.

Article 16.

(1) Men and women of full age, without any limitation due to race, nationality or religion, have the right to marry and to found a family. They are entitled to equal rights as to marriage, during marriage and at its dissolution.

(2) Marriage shall be entered into only with the free and full consent of the intending spouses.

(3) The family is the natural and fundamental group unit of society and is entitled to protection by society and the State.

Article 18.

Everyone has the right to freedom of thought, conscience and religion; this right includes freedom to change his religion or belief, and freedom, either alone or in community with others and in public or private, to manifest his religion or belief in teaching, practice, worship and observance.

Article 19.

Everyone has the right to freedom of opinion and expression; this right includes freedom to hold opinions without interference and to seek, receive and impart information and ideas through any media and regardless of frontiers.

Article 20.

(1) Everyone has the right to freedom of peaceful assembly and association.

(2) No one may be compelled to belong to an association.

9. Taken together, Articles 1 and 3 of the Universal Declaration of Human Rights is most similar to what important American document?

   (1) the Mayflower Compact
   (2) the Declaration of Independence
   (3) the Articles of Confederation
   (4) the Constitution
   (5) the Bill of Rights

10. Articles 18, 19, and 20 make guarantees that are most similar to those contained in which of the following important American documents?

   (1) the Mayflower Compact
   (2) the Declaration of Independence
   (3) the Articles of Confederation
   (4) the Constitution
   (5) the Bill of Rights

11. While the American system of government contains all the protections listed in the Universal Declaration of Human Rights, the Constitution and its amendments do not directly address the issues of which of the following articles?

   (1) Article 4
   (2) Article 5
   (3) Article 9
   (4) Article 16
   (5) Article 18

Answers are on page 414.

Historical Timeline

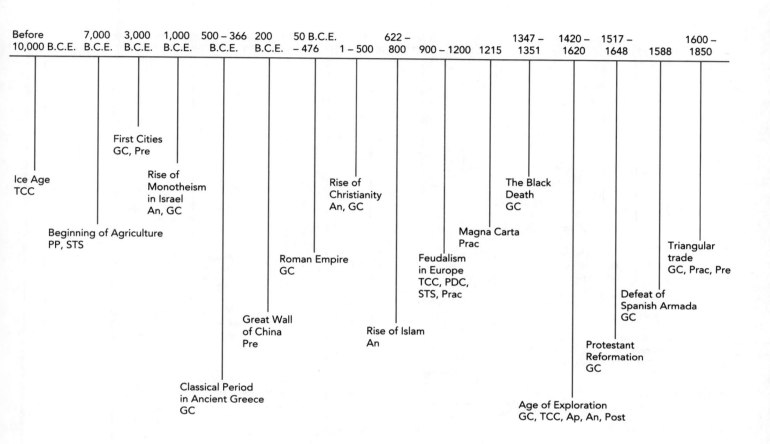

| Before 10,000 B.C.E. | 7,000 B.C.E. | 3,000 B.C.E. | 1,000 B.C.E. | 500 – 366 B.C.E. | 200 B.C.E. | 50 B.C.E. – 476 | 1 – 500 | 622 – 800 | 900 – 1200 | 1215 | 1347 – 1351 | 1420 – 1620 | 1517 – 1648 | 1588 | 1600 – 1850 |

Ice Age
TCC

First Cities
GC, Pre

Rise of Monotheism in Israel
An, GC

Rise of Christianity
An, GC

The Black Death
GC

Beginning of Agriculture
PP, STS

Roman Empire
GC

Magna Carta
Prac

Feudalism in Europe
TCC, PDC, STS, Prac

Triangular trade
GC, Prac, Pre

Defeat of Spanish Armada
GC

Great Wall of China
Pre

Rise of Islam
An

Protestant Reformation
GC

Classical Period in Ancient Greece
GC

Age of Exploration
GC, TCC, Ap, An, Post

Key to Chapter Names

Comp – Comprehension
App – Application
An – Analysis
Ev – Evaluation
TCC – Time, Continuity, and Change
PP – People and Places

PAG – Power, Authority, and Governance
PDC – Production, Distribution, and Consumption
STS – Science, Technology, and Society
GC – Global Connections

Pre – Pre test
Post – Post test
Prac – Practice test

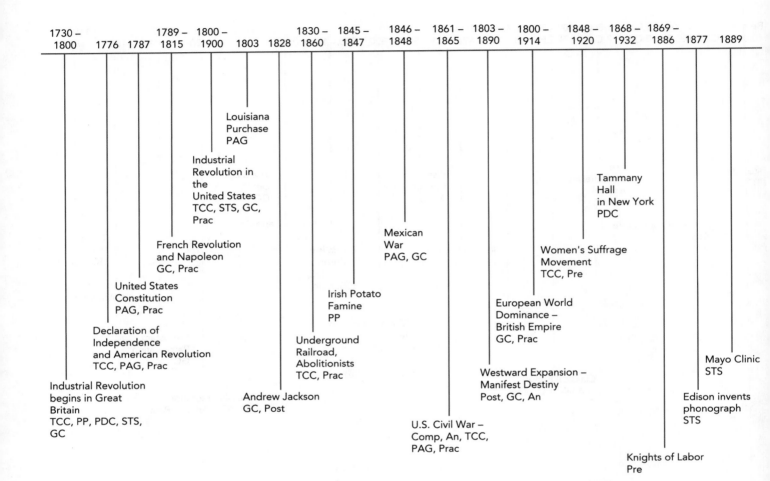

1730 – 1800

1776

1787

1789 – 1815

1800 – 1900

1803

1828

1830 – 1860

1845 – 1847

1846 – 1848

1861 – 1865

1803 – 1890

1800 – 1914

1848 – 1920

1868 – 1932

1869 – 1886

1877

1889

Louisiana
Purchase
PAG

Industrial
Revolution in
the
United States
TCC, STS, GC,
Prac

Tammany
Hall
in New York
PDC

French Revolution
and Napoleon
GC, Prac

Mexican
War
PAG, GC

Women's Suffrage
Movement
TCC, Pre

United States
Constitution
PAG, Prac

Irish Potato
Famine
PP

European World
Dominance –
British Empire
GC, Prac

Declaration of
Independence
and American Revolution
TCC, PAG, Prac

Underground
Railroad,
Abolitionists
TCC, Prac

Westward Expansion –
Manifest Destiny
Post, GC, An

Mayo Clinic
STS

Industrial Revolution
begins in Great
Britain
TCC, PP, PDC, STS,
GC

Andrew Jackson
GC, Post

Edison invents
phonograph
STS

U.S. Civil War –
Comp, An, TCC,
PAG, Prac

Knights of Labor
Pre

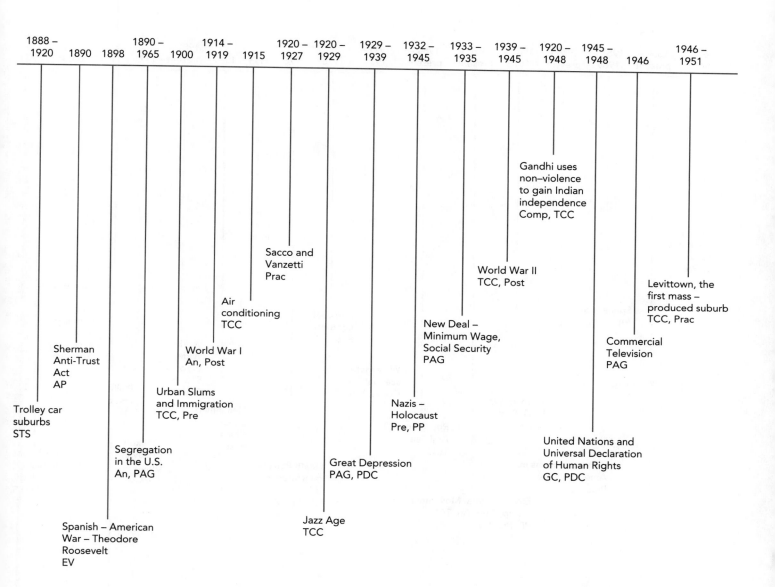

1888 – 1920 | Trolley car suburbs STS

1890 | Sherman Anti-Trust Act AP

1898 | Spanish – American War – Theodore Roosevelt EV

1890 – 1965 | Segregation in the U.S. An, PAG

1900 | Urban Slums and Immigration TCC, Pre

1914 – 1919 | World War I An, Post

1915 | Air conditioning TCC

1920 – 1927 | Sacco and Vanzetti Prac

1920 – 1929 | Jazz Age TCC

1929 – 1939 | Great Depression PAG, PDC

1932 – 1945 | Nazis – Holocaust Pre, PP

1933 – 1935 | New Deal – Minimum Wage, Social Security PAG

1939 – 1945 | World War II TCC, Post

1920 – 1948 | Gandhi uses non–violence to gain Indian independence Comp, TCC

1945 – 1948 | United Nations and Universal Declaration of Human Rights GC, PDC

1946 | Commercial Television PAG

1946 – 1951 | Levittown, the first mass – produced suburb TCC, Prac

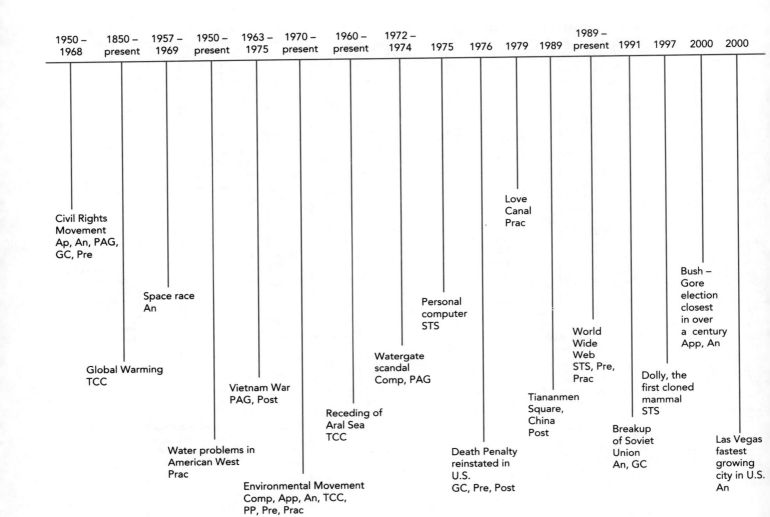

1950 – 1968

Civil Rights
Movement
Ap, An, PAG,
GC, Pre

1850 – present

Global Warming
TCC

1957 – 1969

Space race
An

1950 – present

Water problems in
American West
Prac

1963 – 1975

Vietnam War
PAG, Post

1970 – present

Environmental Movement
Comp, App, An, TCC,
PP, Pre, Prac

1960 – present

Receding of
Aral Sea
TCC

1972 – 1974

Watergate
scandal
Comp, PAG

1975

Personal
computer
STS

1976

Death Penalty
reinstated in
U.S.
GC, Pre, Post

1979

Love
Canal
Prac

1989

Tiananmen
Square,
China
Post

1989 – present

World
Wide
Web
STS, Pre,
Prac

1991

Breakup
of Soviet
Union
An, GC

1997

Dolly, the
first cloned
mammal
STS

2000

Bush –
Gore
election
closest
in over
a century
App, An

2000

Las Vegas
fastest
growing
city in U.S.
An

Directions: This Social Studies Posttest will give you the opportunity to evaluate your readiness for the actual GED Social Studies Test.

This test contains 50 questions. Some of the questions are based on short reading passages, and some of them require you to interpret a chart, map, graph, or political cartoon. The questions are drawn from the areas of U.S. History, World History, Civics and Government, Geography, and Economics.

You should take approximately 70 minutes to complete this test. At the end of 70 minutes, stop and mark your place. Then finish the test. This will give you an idea of whether you can finish the real GED Social Studies Test in the time allowed.

Try to answer as many questions as you can. A blank will count as a wrong answer, so make a reasonable guess for questions you are not sure of. When you are finished with the test, turn to the evaluation chart on page 357. Use the chart to evaluate whether you are ready to take the actual GED Test, and if not, what areas need more work.

Posttest Answer Grid

	①	②	③	④	⑤		①	②	③	④	⑤		①	②	③	④	⑤
1	①	②	③	④	⑤	18	①	②	③	④	⑤	35	①	②	③	④	⑤
2	①	②	③	④	⑤	19	①	②	③	④	⑤	36	①	②	③	④	⑤
3	①	②	③	④	⑤	20	①	②	③	④	⑤	37	①	②	③	④	⑤
4	①	②	③	④	⑤	21	①	②	③	④	⑤	38	①	②	③	④	⑤
5	①	②	③	④	⑤	22	①	②	③	④	⑤	39	①	②	③	④	⑤
6	①	②	③	④	⑤	23	①	②	③	④	⑤	40	①	②	③	④	⑤
7	①	②	③	④	⑤	24	①	②	③	④	⑤	41	①	②	③	④	⑤
8	①	②	③	④	⑤	25	①	②	③	④	⑤	42	①	②	③	④	⑤
9	①	②	③	④	⑤	26	①	②	③	④	⑤	43	①	②	③	④	⑤
10	①	②	③	④	⑤	27	①	②	③	④	⑤	44	①	②	③	④	⑤
11	①	②	③	④	⑤	28	①	②	③	④	⑤	45	①	②	③	④	⑤
12	①	②	③	④	⑤	29	①	②	③	④	⑤	46	①	②	③	④	⑤
13	①	②	③	④	⑤	30	①	②	③	④	⑤	47	①	②	③	④	⑤
14	①	②	③	④	⑤	31	①	②	③	④	⑤	48	①	②	③	④	⑤
15	①	②	③	④	⑤	32	①	②	③	④	⑤	49	①	②	③	④	⑤
16	①	②	③	④	⑤	33	①	②	③	④	⑤	50	①	②	③	④	⑤
17	①	②	③	④	⑤	34	①	②	③	④	⑤						

POSTTEST

Questions 1–3 are based on the following passage.

Two days after Japan attacked Pearl Harbor, FDR made the following statement: "In the past few years and most violently in the past few days, we have learned a terrible lesson. We must begin the great task that is before us by abandoning once and for all the illusion that we can ever again isolate ourselves from the rest of humanity."

1. Roosevelt is expressing the ideas of which of the following?

   (1) an isolationist
   (2) an imperialist
   (3) a jingoist
   (4) an internationalist
   (5) an anti-imperialist

2. By trying to remain neutral while the Allied forces fought against the Axis powers, the United States was following which of these policies?

   (1) progressivism
   (2) imperialism
   (3) jingoism
   (4) internationalism
   (5) isolationism

3. From reading Roosevelt's statements, you can infer that he possessed which of the following traits?

   (1) idealism
   (2) violence
   (3) humanity
   (4) realism
   (5) terror

Questions 4–5 are based on the following passage.

The short-lived American Party had its beginnings as a secret society in the 1840s. Early members were called "Know-Nothings" because when asked about their politics, they said they know nothing. The group had organized in reaction to the large number of German and Irish immigrants entering the United States. The Know-Nothings were sure that these immigrants would accept low wages and take jobs away from Americans. As a political party, the group supported only the candidacies of people who were Protestant and American-born.

Abraham Lincoln said of this group that, "As a nation, we began by declaring that 'all men are created equal' . . . When the Know-Nothings obtain control, it will read: 'All men are created equal except Negroes, foreigners, and Catholics.'"

4. Which of the following effects did President Lincoln foresee if the American party were to come into power?

   (1) Immigrants would be welcomed and offered all the good-paying jobs.
   (2) A Catholic would be able to run for president and be elected.
   (3) The principles of the Declaration of Independence would be undermined.
   (4) All Americans, regardless of national origin, would be able to live as equals.
   (5) African Americans would support the Know-Nothing party in a bid for equality.

POSTTEST

5. If the Know-Nothings were active today, with which of the following statements would they most probably agree?

(1) America is open to all who need help.
(2) Undocumented aliens must be kept out of the country at all costs.
(3) Immigration laws should be relaxed to allow more people to enter the country.
(4) Immigrants should not be turned away just because they are HIV-positive.
(5) America is strong because of its diversity of peoples.

Questions 6–7 are based on the following passage.

Andrew Jackson's election as president in 1828 gave new meaning to the idea of democracy. Jackson, a poor orphan from South Carolina, became a tough soldier and later a self-educated lawyer in Tennessee. To ordinary voters, he represented the common man. He believed in equal economic opportunity and allowing people to make their own decisions. The right to vote had been given to people who did not own property only a few years before Jackson's candidacy. The new Democratic Party drew its strength from the working class and the developing middle class. Jacksonian Democracy was seen as government by and for the "plain people." Its goal was reform based on mass participation.

6. According to the passage, why was Jackson elected?

Because he
(1) followed the party line
(2) was a wealthy, self-made aristocrat
(3) spent a lot of money on his campaign
(4) was a true patriot and war hero
(5) had the support of average Americans

7. Which of the following conclusions is supported by information in the passage?

(1) Jackson was a good president because he was a true "man of the people."
(2) The United States was not a functioning democracy until 1828.
(3) Jacksonian Democracy helped broaden the base of American politics.
(4) Jacksonian Democracy drew strength from the working and middle classes.
(5) Jackson believed in equal economic opportunity for all Americans.

POSTTEST

Questions 8–10 are based on the following map.

NATIVE AMERICAN TRIBES AND CULTURAL AREAS IN 1492

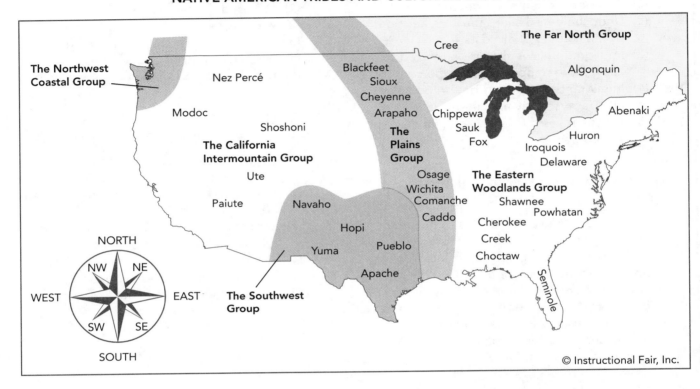

8. Which of the following pieces of information cannot be found on the map?

    (1) the date
    (2) the names of tribes
    (3) the names of cultural areas
    (4) the location of tribes
    (5) population figures

9. According to the map, the Sioux were in which group?

    (1) Far North
    (2) Eastern Woodlands
    (3) Plains
    (4) Southwest
    (5) California Intermountain

10. The information on the map best supports which of the following conclusions about America in 1492?

    (1) The land was heavily settled only where it was forested.
    (2) Most of the land was sparsely settled or unoccupied.
    (3) Native American culture was well established throughout the land.
    (4) Native Americans were primarily hunters and gatherers.
    (5) Native Americans had developed political organization in only a few areas.

POSTTEST

Questions 11–13 are based on the information below.

The world's five climate regions are:

Tundra—land frozen solid most of each year with very short periods of thawing

Rain forest—area of heavy vegetation and almost continual rain and heat

Mediterranean—region of little rain or temperature change, except during the rainy part of the winter

Desert—territory of little rain along with quick evaporation and much heat

Continental—region of extreme seasonal changes and much moisture year-round

11. Southern California has hot, dry summers and mild, wet winters. In which climate region is it located?

    (1) tundra
    (2) rain forest
    (3) mediterranean
    (4) desert
    (5) continental

12. The central Corn Belt of the United States has warm, wet summers and cold, damp winters. In which region is it located?

    (1) tundra
    (2) rain forest
    (3) mediterranean
    (4) desert
    (5) continental

13. The Amazon River basin is hot and rainy and contains an abundance of plants and trees as a result. In which region is it located?

    (1) tundra
    (2) rain forest
    (3) mediterranean
    (4) desert
    (5) continental

Questions 14–16 are based on the paragraph and map below.

"The world must be made safe for democracy." On April 2, 1917, Woodrow Wilson spoke these words to a special session of Congress called by him to ask that they declare war on Germany. Congress did so on April 6, 1917.

THE EUROPEAN POWERS AT WAR

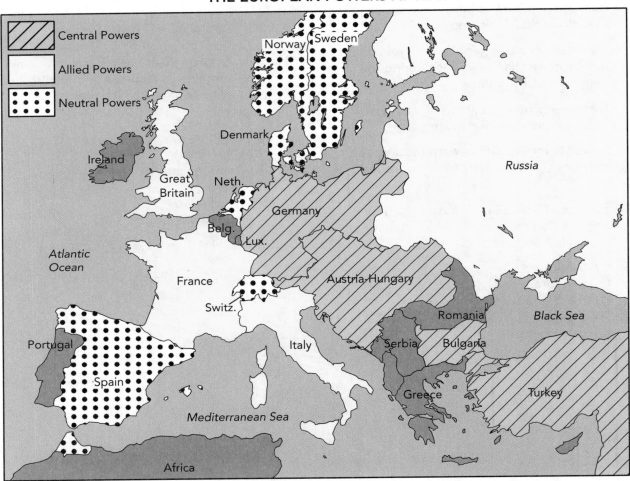

POSTTEST

14. By declaring war on Germany, with what other countries was the United States essentially at war?

(1) Norway, Sweden, and Spain
(2) Russia, France, and Italy
(3) Austria-Hungary, Bulgaria, and Turkey
(4) Italy, Greece, and Turkey
(5) Africa, France, and Russia

15. By declaring war on Germany, the United States was also aligning itself with which major European powers?

(1) Norway, Sweden, and Switzerland
(2) Great Britain, Italy, France, and Russia
(3) Austria-Hungary, Bulgaria, and Turkey
(4) Italy, Greece, and Turkey
(5) Great Britain, Norway, and Sweden

16. Which of the following statements can we assume to be true based on the quote and the map?

(1) Germany and Bulgaria were not democracies in 1917.
(2) Portugal and Ireland were not democracies in 1917.
(3) France and Great Britain were not democracies in 1917.
(4) Democracy existed in almost all of the world's countries in 1917.
(5) Russia was a communist threat to Europe in 1917.

Questions 17 and 18 are based on the following information.

Three well-known federal agencies often get confused in the public mind. The *Central Intelligence Agency,* or CIA, was designed to collect information about the activities of foreign governments. The CIA is responsible only to the president and can keep its operations secret from Congress. The *Federal Bureau of Investigation,* or FBI, is part of the Justice Department and investigates suspected violations of federal laws, including espionage and treason. The *Secret Service* was founded to prevent counterfeiting. Since 1901, this agency has also protected U.S. presidents and, more recently, the vice president, the president's family, and major presidential candidates.

17. Which of the following situations would be investigated by the Secret Service?

(1) the discovery of fake $20 bills circulating in Tampa
(2) a person suspected of selling U.S. military secrets
(3) a revolution in a Central American country
(4) a suspected drug ring operating in St. Louis
(5) the kidnapping of a U.S. senator's son

18. Which of the following situations would be investigated by the CIA?

(1) the discovery of fake $20 dollar bills circulating in Tampa
(2) a person suspected of selling U.S. military secrets
(3) a revolution in a Central American country
(4) a suspected drug ring operating in St. Louis
(5) the kidnapping of a U.S. senator's son

POSTTEST

Questions 19 and 20 are based on the following passage.

Most home buyers finance their purchase with a mortgage and make monthly payments that include interest. When interest rates go down, people often refinance their mortgages in order to make lower monthly payments.

Usually only about 15 percent of loan applications are for refinancing. However, the Mortgage Bankers Association reported that refinancing applications made up to 65 percent of loan applications in 1992.

19. Which of the following is implied in the passage?

(1) Refinancing can save homeowners money.
(2) People apply for refinancing only when mortgage payments are unaffordable.
(3) Mortgage payments automatically change when interest rates change.
(4) Refinancing does not affect interest payments.
(5) Refinancing eliminates interest payments on mortgages.

20. Which of the following conclusions is supported by information in the passage?

(1) Interest rates went down in 1992.
(2) Interest rates went up in 1992.
(3) Interest rates remained stable in 1992.
(4) The number of general loan applications went up in 1992.
(5) The number of general loan applications went down in 1992.

Questions 21 and 22 are based on the following cartoon.

—By Cameron Cardow/Syndicam Productions

21. Which of the following assumptions does the cartoonist make?

The "senseless shooting spree"
(1) could easily have been prevented
(2) is part of the American way of life
(3) is the fault of the gun lobby
(4) is the fault of the U.S. government
(5) represents a fundamental civil right

22. The conflict depicted in this cartoon is most similar to which of the following conflicts?

(1) sexual harassment vs. freedom from gender bias
(2) pro-choice advocates vs. anti-abortion activists
(3) private schools vs. public schools
(4) private insurance vs. public health-care system
(5) school segregation vs. school integration

Questions 23 and 24 are based on the following passage.

Since the early 1900s, Mexico City has tried to reduce its high level of air pollution. Since 1982, due in part to increases in population and industry, the amount of contaminants in the air has more than tripled, to 7 million tons. Because the capital lies 2,240 m (7,347 ft.) above sea level, fossil fuels do not burn efficiently, producing more ozone than normal. During calm winter months, the mountains that encircle the city trap the polluted air close to the ground in atmospheric sandwiches known as thermal inversions.

23. Which of the following conditions does *not* contribute to Mexico City's air pollution problem?

(1) the city's extremely high altitude
(2) the excessive burning of fossil fuels
(3) the proximity of surrounding mountains
(4) the season of the year
(5) Mexico City's inland location

24. Which of the following is *not* stated in the passage?

(1) location of the problem
(2) type of problem
(3) partial causes of the problem
(4) time frame of the problem
(5) solution for the problem

25. In the 1840s hundreds of wagon trains headed west on the Oregon Trail for Oregon and California. Following the doctrine of Manifest Destiny, thousands of migrant pioneers sought to extend U.S. borders to the Pacific, even though much of the land had been claimed by Britain and Mexico. Believers in Manifest Destiny acted on which of the following assumptions?

(1) Americans had the right to claim the land.
(2) Americans would become British or Mexican citizens.
(3) Land would be inexpensive and available for settling.
(4) Americans could create a whole new nation.
(5) The U.S. government wanted to reduce the population.

26. Jeanette Rankin of Montana was the first woman elected to Congress. She voted against U.S. participation in both world wars. In 1968 Rankin led a protest march against the Vietnam War.

Based on this information, on which of the following did Jeanette Rankin place a high value?

(1) public opinion
(2) military intervention
(3) pacifism
(4) civil rights
(5) victory

Questions 27 and 28 are based on the following graph.

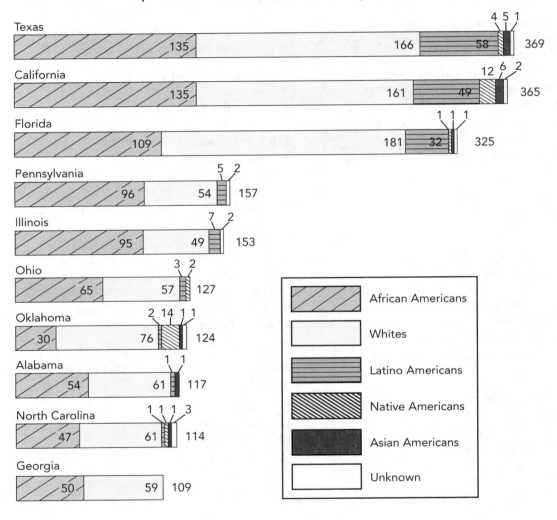

WHO IS ON DEATH ROW
Top 10 States – Number of Inmates by Race

Texas: 135, 166, 58, 4, 5, 1 — 369
California: 135, 161, 49, 12, 6, 2 — 365
Florida: 109, 181, 32, 1, 1, 1 — 325
Pennsylvania: 96, 54, 5, 2 — 157
Illinois: 95, 49, 7, 2 — 153
Ohio: 65, 57, 3, 2 — 127
Oklahoma: 30, 76, 2, 14, 1, 1 — 124
Alabama: 54, 61, 1, 1 — 117
North Carolina: 47, 61, 1, 1, 1, 3 — 114
Georgia: 50, 59 — 109

African Americans
Whites
Latino Americans
Native Americans
Asian Americans
Unknown

POSTTEST

27. Which of the following statements about capital punishment in the ten states cited is best supported by the graph?

    (1) Texas judges have been consistently harsher in sentencing minorities that in sentencing whites.
    (2) A person convicted of a serious crime is more likely to be sentenced to capital punishment in Texas than in any other state.
    (3) Texas is the most dangerous state in the United States.
    (4) Pennsylvania, Illinois, Ohio, and Georgia have very few Asian Americans in their criminal populations.
    (5) Violent crimes are much less common among Latino Americans than among other minority groups.

28. Which of the following groups would most likely use this graph to support its position?

    (1) The U.S. Supreme Court
    (2) The Southern Governors' Conference
    (3) The National Prison Guards Union
    (4) The Texas State Legislature
    (5) The Coalition Against the Death Penalty

POSTTEST

Questions 29–31 are based on the following information.

Workers and employers can't always agree on wages or working conditions. The following terms identify processes involved in labor disputes.

Collective bargaining—meetings in good faith between representatives of employers and employees to discuss and attempt to agree on conditions of employment

Mediation—use of an impartial go-between to help reach an agreement between two sides of a labor dispute when the two sides cannot agree on their own

Picketing—stationing of striking workers in front of a business to protest conditions or to dissuade workers and customers from entering the business

Sit-down strike—planned work stoppage in which employees stop work but do not leave the workplace until an agreement is reached with management

Walk-out strike—planned work stoppage in which employees stay away from the workplace until an agreement is reached with management

29. Metal workers at the Ucan factory want a raise of $1 an hour. Two of their representatives and an attorney meet with Ucan's owners and their attorney. Ucan offers the workers a $.50 raise. Which of the following are the workers and owners engaged in?

   (1) collective bargaining
   (2) mediation
   (3) picketing
   (4) a sit-down strike
   (5) a walk-out strike

30. Coal miners at Old Ben 52 refuse to go back into the mine unless the bosses agree to provide an on-site doctor. Which of the following are the workers engaged in?

   (1) collective bargaining
   (2) mediation
   (3) picketing
   (4) a sit-down strike
   (5) a walk-out strike

31. Representatives of the machine operators at Boxboy have been meeting for a week with company representatives. They have agreed to improved pension benefits, but they cannot agree about which benefits would be affected. Which of the following would most likely be the next step in settling the dispute?

   (1) collective bargaining
   (2) mediation
   (3) picketing
   (4) a sit-down strike
   (5) a walk-out strike

POSTTEST

Questions 32 and 33 are based on the map below.

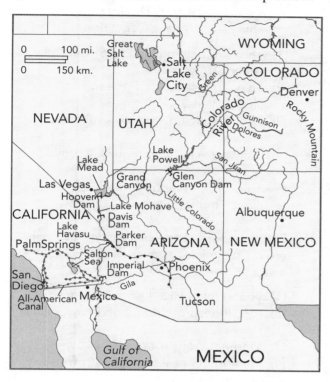

32. According the map, which of the following groups of states receives water from the Colorado River?

(1) Colorado and Utah only
(2) Utah, Nevada, and Arizona only
(3) Arizona and California only
(4) Colorado, Utah, Arizona, and California only
(5) Colorado, Utah, Nevada, Arizona, and California

33. Recently, experts have warned that the Colorado River is in trouble. Its once-raging waters have been reduced to a trickle by the time they reach the Gulf of California. Which of the following situations *best* explains the cause of the problem?

(1) the drying up of part of the Gila River
(2) overuse of Lake Mead and Lake Mohave
(3) drainage into the Little Colorado and San Juan rivers
(4) erosion in the Grand Canyon
(5) drain-off by dams and aqueducts

Questions 34 and 35 are based on the following passage.

In 1953 the U.S. Congress passed the Refugee Relief Act. This act increased the immigration quota for victims of war and disaster. In 1980 Congress raised the total number of persons permitted entry into the United States under the act from 290,000 to 320,000 yearly. The latter act also redefined a refugee as a person fleeing any part of the world, not just communist countries or the Middle East.

Despite the revamping of the law, however, some still find it difficult to enter the United States with refugee status. Many resort to illegal means to enter the country, risking imprisonment and deportation if caught.

Some of the people entering the United States illegally are attempting to escape political persecution or war-torn conditions in their homelands. As the numbers of these people increased during the last decade, so did the number of members in the sanctuary movement in the United States. The sanctuary movement consisted of American citizens and a network of churches who banded together to assist illegals in crossing the border, getting settled, and seeking official recognition as political refugees. Members of the movement defied immigration laws, mostly on behalf of victims of Central American wars, by declaring churches religious sanctuaries immune from the law.

34. Why might members of the sanctuary movement think they should receive immunity from legal prosecution?

(1) They are helping victims of Central American wars.
(2) They are risking their lives to help illegal aliens.
(3) They are doing work of a religious nature.
(4) They are a large and quickly growing group.
(5) They are preventing the deportation of illegal immigrants.

35. The members of the sanctuary movement are most similar to which group in U.S. history?

(1) young men who resisted the draft
(2) the Underground Railroad for runaway slaves
(3) Vietnam War protesters
(4) immigrants seeking religious freedom
(5) civil rights activists

POSTTEST

Questions 36 and 37 refer to the following cartoon.

36. According to the cartoonist, Congress has a reputation for which of the following?

(1) moving too quickly
(2) increasing its spending
(3) cautious driving
(4) wasting time
(5) spending too much time traveling

37. The cartoonist holds which of the following opinions?

(1) Congress will continue to spend wisely.
(2) Congress doesn't spend as much as it should.
(3) Congressional representatives are like used-car salesmen.
(4) Congressional spending should be slowed.
(5) The 103rd Congress will do better than the 102nd Congress.

38. The U.S. Constitution provides for an orderly succession to the presidency. If a president dies or steps down from office, the vice president becomes president. If the vice president dies or steps down, the president can appoint a new vice president. Which of the following can be explained by these provisions?

(1) Vice President George Bush won the 1988 presidential election.
(2) Jimmy Carter's choice for vice president was Walter Mondale.
(3) Gerald Ford became both vice president and president without being elected.
(4) Gerald Ford and Walter Mondale both lost when they ran for president.
(5) It was necessary for Vice President Spiro Agnew to resign.

POSTTEST

Questions 39–42 refer to the passage and two photographs below.

During the spring of 1989 pro-democracy student activists staged a series of demonstrations in Tiananmen Square in Beijing, the capital of China. As a symbol of their protest, demonstrators erected a 10m (33ft) statue called "Goddess of Democracy," modeled after the Statue of Liberty in the United States. Hundreds of protestors died on June 3 and 4, 1989, when the Chinese government ordered the military to crack down on the protest.

39. How would an American government official probably describe the events in these pictures?

    (1) as an irresponsible display of personal desires
    (2) as a brave tribute to the spirit of democracy
    (3) as an ignorant and foolish risk of life and freedom
    (4) as an unrealistic attempt at social change
    (5) as an unforgivable act of treason

40. How would a Chinese government official probably describe the events in these pictures?

(1) as an irresponsible display of personal desires
(2) as a brave tribute to the spirit of democracy
(3) as an ignorant and foolish risk of life and freedom
(4) as an unrealistic attempt at social change
(5) as an unforgivable act of treason

41. By erecting a statue of the "Goddess of Democracy," the protesters were doing which of the following?

(1) making fun of the Statue of Liberty
(2) protesting the prominence of democracy in China
(3) hoping to start a new religious movement
(4) showing their support for democratic ideals
(5) comparing their political leaders to divine figures

42. The situation depicted in the photograph on the right is most similar to which of the following historical events?

(1) Ordinary German citizens hid and protected Jews during the Holocaust. If caught by the Nazis they faced deportation to concentration camps or execution.
(2) Ancient Greek soldiers entered the city of Troy secretly inside a large, wooden horse. They surprised and defeated the citizens of Troy against great odds.
(3) Rosa Parks refused to give up her seat to a white person on a bus in Montgomery, Alabama, in 1955. She was arrested but her courage sparked the beginning of the Civil Rights movement.
(4) American patriots plotted undercover to overthrow British rule of the colonies in the early 1770s. They believed they should have the right to govern themselves.
(5) Palestinians have thrown stones at Israeli army tanks to express their anger and bitterness over the control Israel has over areas the Palestinians consider part of their homeland.

Questions 43 and 44 refer to the graph below.

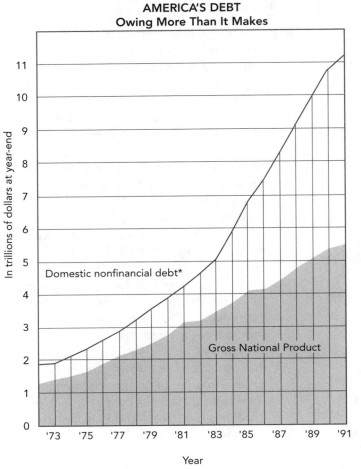

AMERICA'S DEBT
Owing More Than It Makes

In trillions of dollars at year-end

Domestic nonfinancial debt*

Gross National Product

'73 '75 '77 '79 '81 '83 '85 '87 '89 '91

Year

*Federal and state government, households and nonfinancial business

43. Which of the following statements is best supported by the information in the graph?

(1) The domestic debt is normally lower than the Gross National Product.
(2) The domestic debt increases and decreases from year to year.
(3) The domestic debt tends to decrease, while the Gross National Product tends to increase.
(4) The domestic debt tends to increase more slowly than the Gross National Product does.
(5) The domestic debt increases at a faster rate than the increase of the Gross National Product.

44. In which of the following years was the amount of the domestic debt almost twice the amount of the Gross National Product?

(1) 1973
(2) 1978
(3) 1983
(4) 1985
(5) 1991

POSTTEST

Questions 45 and 46 are based on the quote and photo below.

"Please understand that we are not asking for a parade, a movement, or pity. But we do ask you to remember in your own way the 57,661 Americans who died in the war. Perhaps all of them died in vain."

—Al Santoli, Vietnam veteran

45. Santoli's remarks reflect which aspect of the Vietnam War?

(1) There was great disagreement in the United States as to whether America should be involved at all.

(2) The American effort to defeat the Communists of North Vietnam was unsuccessful.

(3) The death toll of Vietnamese civilians was much higher than that of the U.S. military.

(4) The U.S. involvement in Vietnam began at least as far back as the Kennedy administration.

(5) President Richard Nixon was determined to achieve "peace with honor" in Vietnam.

46. Which of the following statements is *not* a value held by either Santoli or the artist who sculpted this statue?

(1) All Americans who died in Vietnam deserve remembrance.

(2) Women as well as men served and suffered in Vietnam.

(3) People who fight in a war that is wrong should not be honored.

(4) War is not a glorious adventure.

(5) Vietnam is an important chapter in U.S. history.

POSTTEST

Question 47 refers to the W-4 tax form below.

When a person is hired for a job in the United States, that person is required to complete a number of forms, including a W-4 tax form, part of which is shown here.

FORM W–4 (2001)

Purpose. Complete Form W–4 so your employer can withhold the correct Federal income tax from your pay. Because your tax situation may change, you may want to refigure your withhold–ing each year.

Exemption from withholding. If you are exempt, complete only lines 1, 2, 3, 4, and 7, and sign the form to validate it. Your exemption for 2001 expires February 18, 2002.

Note: *You cannot claim exemption from withhold–ing if (1) your income exceeds $750 and includes more than $250 of unearned income (e.g. inter–est and dividends) and (2) another person can claim you as a dependent on their tax return.*

Basic instructions. If you are not exempt, com–plete the **Personal Allowances Worksheet** below. The worksheets on page 2 adjust your withholding allowances based on itemized deductions, certain credits, adjustments to income, or two-earner/two-job situations. Com–plete all worksheets that apply. They will help you figure the number of withholding allowances you are entitled to claim. **However, you may claim fewer (or zero) allowances.**

Head of household. Generally, you may claim head of household filing status on your tax return only if you are unmarried and pay more than 50% of the costs of keeping up a home for yourself and your dependent(s) or other qualify–ing individuals. See line **E** below.

Tax credits. You can take projected tax credits into account in figuring your allowable number of withholding allowances. Credits for child or dependent care expenses and the child tax credit may be claimed using the **Personal Allowances Worksheet** below. See **Pub. 919**, How Do I Adjust My Tax Withholding? for infor–mation on converting your other credits into withholding allowances.

Nonwage income. If you have a large amount of nonwage income, such as interest or dividends, consider making estimated tax payments using **Form 1040-ES**, Estimated Tax for Individuals. Otherwise, you may owe additional tax.

Two earners/two jobs. If you have a working spouse or more than one job, figure the total number of allowances you are entitled to claim on all jobs using worksheets from only one Form W-4. Your withholding usually will be most accu–rate when all allowances are claimed on the Form W-4 for the highest paying job and zero allowances are claimed on the others.

Check your withholding. After your Form W-4 takes effect, use Pub. 919 to see how the dollar amount you are having withheld compares to your projected total tax for 2001. Get Pub. 919 especially if you used the **Two-Earner/Two-Job Worksheet** on page 2 and your earnings exceed $150,000 (Single) or $200,000 (Married).

Recent name change? If your name on line 1 dif–fers from that shown on your social security card, call 1-800-772-1213 for a new social security card.

Personal Allowances Worksheet (Keep for your records.)

A Enter "1" for **yourself** if no one else can claim you as a dependent. . . . . A _____

B Enter "1" if: {
- You are single and have only one job; or
- You are married, have only one job, and your spouse does not work; or
- Your wages from a second job or your spouse's wages (or the total of both) are $1,000 or less. } . . B _____

C Enter "1" for your **spouse**. But, you may choose to enter –0– if you are married and have either a working spouse or more than one job. (Entering –0– may help you avoid having too little tax withheld.) . . . . C _____

D Enter number of **dependents** (other than your spouse or yourself) you will claim on your tax return. . . . . . . D _____

E Enter "1" if you will file as **head of household** on your tax return (see conditions under **Head of Household** above) . E _____

F Enter "1" if you have at least $1,500 of **child or dependent care expenses** for which you plan to claim a credit . . F _____
(**Note:** Do **not** include child support payments. See **Pub. 503**, Child and Dependent Care Expenses, for details.)

G **Child Tax Credit** (including additional child tax credit):
If your total income will be between $18,000 and $50,000 ($23,000 and $63,000 if married), enter "1" for each eligible child.
If your total income will be between $50,000 and $80,000 ($63,000 and $115,000 if married), enter "1" if you have two eligible children, enter "2" if you have three or four eligible children, or enter "3" if you have five or more eligible children. G _____

H Add lines A through G and enter total here. (**Note:** This may be different from the number of exemptions you claim on your tax return.) H _____

For accuracy, complete all worksheets that apply. {
- If you plan to **itemize or claim adjustments to income** and want to reduce your withholding, see the **Deductions and Adjustments Worksheet** on page 2.
- If you are **single**, have **more than one job** and your combined earnings from all jobs exceed $35,000, **or** if you are **married** and have a **working spouse or more than one job** and the combined earnings from all jobs exceed $60,000, see the **Two-Earner/Two-Job Worksheet** on page 2 to avoid having too little tax withheld.
- If **neither** of the above situations applies, **stop here** and enter the number from line H on line 5 of Form W-4 below.
}

---

47. A single mother of three children is "head of household" and works one full-time job at which she earns $26,000 a year. Two of her children are in day-care while she works (the other is school-age). The annual cost of that day-care exceeds $1,500. What will be the total number she will enter on line H of the form?

(1) 0
(2) 2
(3) 3
(4) 7
(5) 10

Question 48 refers to the following cartoon.

—©The New Yorker Collection, 1979, Sam Gross. From cartoonbank.com. All Rights Reserved.

48. Which of the following can be concluded from this cartoon?

(1) The artist does not consider it wise to invest in the stock market.
(2) Investing in the stock market is as easy as learning a nursery rhyme.
(3) The stock market often crashes, like Humpty Dumpty.
(4) Most people are suspicious of the reliability of the stock market.
(5) A little humor and wit is needed on Wall Street.

POSTTEST

Questions 49 and 50 refer to the graph below.

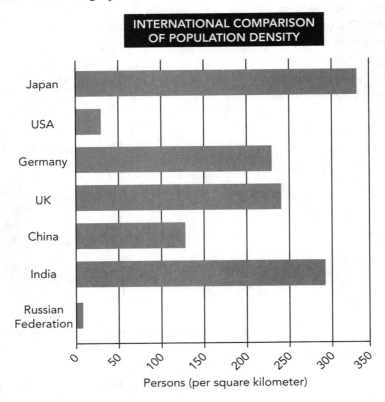

INTERNATIONAL COMPARISON OF POPULATION DENSITY

Persons (per square kilometer)

49. Which of the following would you expect to find in Japan and India?

    (1) large tracts of empty land
    (2) wide, open ranges for grazing
    (3) huge national forests
    (4) widespread poverty
    (5) many big cities

50. Which of the following statements is proved by the information on the graph?

    (1) Japan is densely populated because it is an island.
    (2) Japan, the UK, and India have reached their population limits.
    (3) The growth rate of India is the fastest in the world.
    (4) Compared to Japan, the United States is not very crowded at all.
    (5) The countries on the graph are the most densely populated in the world.

Answer Key

1. **Analysis (4)** Choice (4) is correct because an internationalist believes in maintaining good relations with other nations. Choice (1) is incorrect because Roosevelt says that we can't isolate ourselves from the rest of humanity. Choices (2) and (5) are incorrect because the quote makes no mention of one country controlling or not controlling another. Choice (3) is incorrect because Roosevelt's language is not warlike.

2. **Analysis (5)** Acting on a policy of isolationism, the United States tried to remain neutral, or uninvolved, as the Allies fought against the Axis powers.

3. **Evaluation (4)** Roosevelt showed the trait of realism when he stated that from now on America must no longer be isolated from the rest of the world.

4. **Comprehension (3)** Lincoln's quotation refers to a line in the Declaration of Independence that asserts a basic principle of American political belief. The Know-Nothings did not want to allow any but their own kind to enjoy equality. The other choices are the opposite of what the Know-Nothing party advocated.

5. **Evaluation (2)** Some people believe that immigrants take jobs from Americans because they work for low wages. Just as they had objected to immigrants, the Know-Nothings would want to keep undocumented aliens out of the country. They would not be likely to support any statement that encouraged immigration.

6. **Comprehension (5)** Jackson appealed to the ordinary voter because he seemed, like them, to be from a simple background. His political stance was unlike the party line. The passage doesn't mention the campaign at all and refers only briefly to Jackson's time as a soldier.

7. **Analysis (3)** Before Jackson, the political base of democracy was focused on property owners. By supporting the role of average people, Jackson encouraged a large group to become politically active. This change was welcomed by many people. There is no information in the passage to support choices (1) and (2). Choices (4) and (5) are directly stated in the passage, so they are not conclusions drawn from the information, but instead are supporting information for conclusions that can be drawn.

8. **Comprehension (5)** The date is provided in the map title. The names and locations of tribes and cultural areas are written on the map. No numbers for Native American population are given.

9. **Comprehension (3)** The name of the Sioux is found in the center of the map in the Plains Group.

10. **Analysis (3)** Tribal groups are shown in almost every section of the country. The clear definition of cultural areas supports the conclusion that culture was well established. There is no support for conclusions about forests or Native American occupations or political structures.

11. **Application (3)** Southern California is mild and dry most of the year, which best fits the description of the mediterranean climate.

12. **Application (5)** The temperature changes and the cold winter indicate that the Corn Belt is located in the continental region.

13. **Application (2)** Hot, rainy weather all year is typical of rain forests.

14. **Comprehension (3)** Germany, Austria-Hungary, Bulgaria, and Turkey comprised the Central Powers (represented by diagonal lines).

15. **Comprehension (2)** Great Britain, Italy, France, and Russia made up the major Allied powers (represented in yellow) with which the United States aligned itself.

POSTTEST

16. **Analysis (1)** One can infer from Wilson's statement that the countries against which the U.S. was waging war were a threat to democracy and thus not democracies themselves. According to the map, only Germany and Bulgaria could be identified as such threats.

17. **Application (1)** The fake bills would fall under the Secret Service's function to prevent counterfeiting. Investigation of the other situations would belong to either the CIA or the FBI.

18. **Application (3)** A problem with a foreign government would be looked into by the CIA. The other situations would be investigated by either the Secret Service or the FBI.

19. **Analysis (1)** A reduction in interest payments because of refinancing would save money. No amount of refinancing would get rid of interest payments altogether.

20. **Analysis (1)** The dramatic increase in applications for refinanced loans in 1992 suggests that interest rates went down because refinancing often takes place when interest rates are low. The percentage of loan applications refers only to refinancing, not to the number of general loans.

21. **Comprehension (3)** By including the figure of the gun lobby, the cartoonist indicates that it is the gun lobby's opposition to gun-control laws that allows irresponsible people to have guns. Therefore, the cartoonist is assuming that the fault lies with the gun lobby, not the government.

22. **Application (2)** Some people believe that strict gun-control laws would reduce violent crime. Others feel that gun-control laws violate their right to bear arms. This conflict is like that between the belief in a woman's right to abortion and the belief in an unborn child's right to life. Each side of both issues could possibly be protected by the Constitution.

23. **Comprehension (5)** All but the fact that Mexico City is located inland instead of on a coast are mentioned in the passage as contributing factors.

24. **Analysis (5)** All aspects of the problem except its solution are mentioned in the passage.

25. **Analysis (1)** Despite other countries' claim to the West, believers in Manifest Destiny were not deterred, suggesting they believed it to be their right. There is no question of a change in citizenship or formation of a new nation; they were extending U.S. borders.

26. **Analysis (3)** Rankin opposed three different wars, all fought for different reasons. Her votes against the two world wars went against prevailing public opinion and showed that she was against military action. Her stance on civil rights is not mentioned.

27. **Evaluation (2)** The graph shows that Texas has the most convicted criminals on death row.

28. **Application (5)** The large number of inmates on Death Row could be cited by a group that opposes the death penalty.

29. **Application (1)** Labor and management are negotiating for a wage agreeable to both. This is not a process limited to management or to the union. As both sides seem willing to work out an agreement, there is no need for mediation, a strike, or picketing.

30. **Application (5)** The proposed action by labor means that work will stop because no one will be in the mines. A sit-down strike would require the miners to stay in the mine. There is no mention of discussion between labor and management, or a need for mediation at this point.

31. **Application (2)** While in the process of collective bargaining, labor and management have deadlocked. The advice of a third party (mediation) could help them reach agreement.

32. **Comprehension (5)** The map shows that the Colorado River flows through or along the border of five states, all of which benefit from its water.

POSTTEST

33. **Analysis (5)** The drain-off from the five dams and several aqueducts would divert more water than the natural drainage into the Colorado River and its tributaries. The drying up of the Gila and the erosion of the Grand Canyon are effects, not causes of the problem.

34. **Analysis (3)** The last sentence in the passage tells us that these people have declared their churches to be religious sanctuaries. Therefore, they believe they are immune from prosecution.

35. **Application (2)** The sanctuary movement members break the law to assist illegal aliens who are fleeing persecution and oppression. This activity is similar to that of members of the Underground Railroad who transported and hid slaves.

36. **Comprehension (2)** The car represents Congress's spending (not the tendency for its members to travel). The salesman is assuring the customer that the car can go faster and faster. There is no support for the ideas that Congress acts quickly, drives cautiously, or wastes time.

37. **Analysis (4)** The customer's question about brakes suggests that there should be a way to slow spending. Congress spends too much, not wisely nor too little. No mention is made of the 102nd Congress.

38. **Evaluation (3)** Ford became vice president by appointment, not election, when Spiro Agnew resigned. When President Nixon resigned, Ford became president. Ford's loss of the next election had nothing to do with the constitutional provision. The other choices are not explained by the process for presidential succession.

39. **Evaluation (2)** Because the American government is an institution of democracy, it applauds what it perceives to be efforts towards democracy in other countries. Thus, the Tiananmen Square protest would be viewed as a valiant demonstration of a group's determination to pursue democracy, in spite of oppression and military threat.

40. **Evaluation (5)** Because the Chinese government is Communist and views democracy as a threat to itself and to the well-being of the country, the Tiananmen Square protest called for a drastic response. "Treason," or acts of treachery and betrayal against a government, could be seen as justifying military intervention.

41. **Analysis (4)** Because the protests were pro-democratic, it stands to reason that the statue was intended to serve as a positive symbol of democratic ideals and not as an object of ridicule. Although it was called a "goddess" that title did not indicate a religious tendency on the part of the protesters or of Chinese government officials. Because China is a Communist country the statue would not have been used to protest democracy.

42. **Application (3)** The example of Rosa Parks most closely resembles that of the young man before the tanks because she was a single individual protesting an entire city institution and set of laws. The other examples, while instances of the courage of "underdogs," do not emphasize the determination of one person.

43. **Evaluation (5)** The line for the domestic debt rises much more quickly than the line for the GNP. The rate of increase in both lines does not support the other choices.

44. **Comprehension (5)** In 1991, the GNP was about 5.5 trillion dollars. Domestic debt was slightly over 11 trillion, about twice as much. These amounts were not equaled by any of the earlier years shown.

45. **Analysis (2)** While all of the statements about the war are true, only the one about its failure relates to the concern that more than 57,000 American died for nothing.

46. **Evaluation (3)** Santoli's comment and/or the artist's statue underscore the toll of war (as opposed to its excitement), the contributions of many people, including women, and the need to remember and appreciate sacrifice. Neither suggests that Americans who died in Vietnam should not be honored because the war was unpopular.

47. **Application (5)** This woman will enter "1" on line A, "1" on line B, "3" on line D, "1" on line E, "1" on line F, and "3" on line G.

48. **Evaluation (1)** In this cartoon the artist is expressing his or her feelings of concern about the stability of the stock market and would not consider it a wise investment.

49. **Evaluation (5)** Such dense populations would most likely indicate large numbers of cities but would not necessarily result in poverty. The first three choices would be in countries with much sparser populations.

50. **Evaluation (4)** The graph offers some comparative information, and thus a conclusion can be correctly drawn about Japan and the United States. There is no information in the graph, however, to support any of the other statements.

Evaluation Chart

Use the answer key on pages 353–356 to check your answers to the Posttest. Then find the item number of each question you missed and circle it on the chart below to determine the skills in which you need to do the most work. For each question that you missed, review the skill pages indicated.

Skill Area/ Content Area	Comprehension (pages 27–42)	Application (pages 43–58)	Analysis (pages 59–98)	Evaluation (pages 99–115)
U.S. History	6, 14, 15	35	1, 2, 7, 16, 25, 34, 45	3, 8, 37, 46
World History	23	42	24, 41	39, 40
Civics & Government	4, 21, 27, 36	17, 18, 22, 28	26	5, 38
Geography	8, 9, 32	11, 12, 13	10, 33	49, 50
Economics	44	29, 30, 31, 47	19, 20	43, 48

Directions: This Social Studies Practice Test will give you a second opportunity to evaluate your readiness for the GED Social Studies Test.

This test contains 50 questions. Some of the questions are based on short reading passages, and some of them require you to interpret a chart, map, graph, or political cartoon. The questions are drawn from the areas of U. S. History, World History, Civics and Government, Geography, and Economics.

You should take approximately 70 minutes to complete this test. At the end of 70 minutes, stop and mark your place. Then finish the test. This will give you an idea of whether you can finish the real GED Social Studies Test in the time allowed.

Try to answer as many questions as you can. A blank will count as a wrong answer, so make a reasonable guess for questions you are not sure of. When you are finished with the test, check your answers. Then look at the evaluation chart on page 394. Use the chart to evaluate whether you are ready to take the actual GED Test. If there are areas in which you still need more work, review those sections in the book.

Practice Test Answer Grid

	①	②	③	④	⑤			①	②	③	④	⑤			①	②	③	④	⑤
1	①	②	③	④	⑤		18	①	②	③	④	⑤		35	①	②	③	④	⑤
2	①	②	③	④	⑤		19	①	②	③	④	⑤		36	①	②	③	④	⑤
3	①	②	③	④	⑤		20	①	②	③	④	⑤		37	①	②	③	④	⑤
4	①	②	③	④	⑤		21	①	②	③	④	⑤		38	①	②	③	④	⑤
5	①	②	③	④	⑤		22	①	②	③	④	⑤		39	①	②	③	④	⑤
6	①	②	③	④	⑤		23	①	②	③	④	⑤		40	①	②	③	④	⑤
7	①	②	③	④	⑤		24	①	②	③	④	⑤		41	①	②	③	④	⑤
8	①	②	③	④	⑤		25	①	②	③	④	⑤		42	①	②	③	④	⑤
9	①	②	③	④	⑤		26	①	②	③	④	⑤		43	①	②	③	④	⑤
10	①	②	③	④	⑤		27	①	②	③	④	⑤		44	①	②	③	④	⑤
11	①	②	③	④	⑤		28	①	②	③	④	⑤		45	①	②	③	④	⑤
12	①	②	③	④	⑤		29	①	②	③	④	⑤		46	①	②	③	④	⑤
13	①	②	③	④	⑤		30	①	②	③	④	⑤		47	①	②	③	④	⑤
14	①	②	③	④	⑤		31	①	②	③	④	⑤		48	①	②	③	④	⑤
15	①	②	③	④	⑤		32	①	②	③	④	⑤		49	①	②	③	④	⑤
16	①	②	③	④	⑤		33	①	②	③	④	⑤		50	①	②	③	④	⑤
17	①	②	③	④	⑤		34	①	②	③	④	⑤							

359

Question 1 refers to the following quotation by a Confederate lieutenant after a battle during the Civil War.

> As we lay there watching the bright stars and listening to the twitter of the little birds in their nests, many a soldier asked himself the questions: What is all this about? Why is it that 200,000 men of one blood and one tongue, believing as one man in the fatherhood of God and the universal brotherhood of man, should in the nineteenth century of the Christian era be thus armed with all the improved appliances of modern warfare and seeking one another's lives? We could settle our differences by compromising and all be at home in ten days.

—R. M. Collins in *The American Iliad: The Epic Story of the Civil War as Narrated by Eyewitnesses and Contemporaries*, Otto Eisenschiml and Ralph Newman, eds. 1947.

1. Which value is most important to the writer of this passage?

   (1) loyalty to the Confederate cause
   (2) victory at all costs
   (3) efficient use of modern weapons
   (4) the abolition of slavery
   (5) the common humanity of all people

Questions 2–5 refer to the passage below.

Military service in the field was basic to feudalism, but it was far from all that the vassal owed to his lord. When the lord had a castle, he might require his vassals to guard it. The lord also expected his vassals to attend his court in order to give him advice and to participate in judgments of cases concerning other vassals. If the lord needed money, he might expect his vassals to give him financial aid. During the 12th and 13th centuries many conflicts between lords and their vassals arose over just what services should be rendered. In England it was the Magna Carta that defined the obligations of vassals to the king and the obligations of the king to his vassals.

The Magna Carta included two important legal clauses. One stated that "To no one will we sell, to no one will we deny or delay right or justice." This clause establishes the principle of equal access to the courts for all citizens without high fees. In the second, the king promised that "No free man shall be taken or imprisoned or outlawed or exiled or in any way destroyed, nor will we go or send against him, except by the lawful judgment of his peers or by the law of the land." This clause established that the king would follow legal procedure before he punished someone. Historians have debated at length the meaning in 1215 of "by lawful judgment of his peers or by the law of the land," and who exactly was covered by the term "free man." By the later 14th century, however, statutes interpreting the Magna Carta equated "judgment of peers" with trial by jury (which did not exist in criminal cases in 1215). Other statutes rephrased "by the law of the land" as "by due process of law."

—Adapted from "Feudalism" by Fred A. Cazel

PRACTICE TEST

2. What is the meaning of the word *vassal*?

   (1) a well-built ship
   (2) an uneducated peasant
   (3) a penniless beggar
   (4) a king's brother
   (5) a wealthy aristocrat

3. From the passage, what can be inferred about the relationship between a king and a vassal before the year 1215?

   (1) a vassal did more for the king than the king did for a vassal
   (2) a king did more for a vassal than a vassal did for a king
   (3) kings and vassals had a well-balanced, give-and-take relationship
   (4) there was little argument over who should do what for whom
   (5) vassals most often served the king as military guards

4. From the portion of the Magna Carta described here, what does its emphasis appear to have been?

   (1) what the king owed his vassals and other citizens
   (2) what vassals and other citizens owed the king
   (3) the need for capital punishment for crimes against the king
   (4) a call for elected officials to replace the monarchy
   (5) the need in the future to change the way trials were held

5. The principle of trial by jury would have been familiar to everyone except which of the following?

   (1) a trial lawyer in the United States today
   (2) the framers of the U.S. Constitution
   (3) a 15th-century British magistrate
   (4) a 12th-century vassal
   (5) a 19th-century queen

PRACTICE TEST

Questions 6–8 are based on the text and maps below. The maps show the minority populations of the United States in 1999.

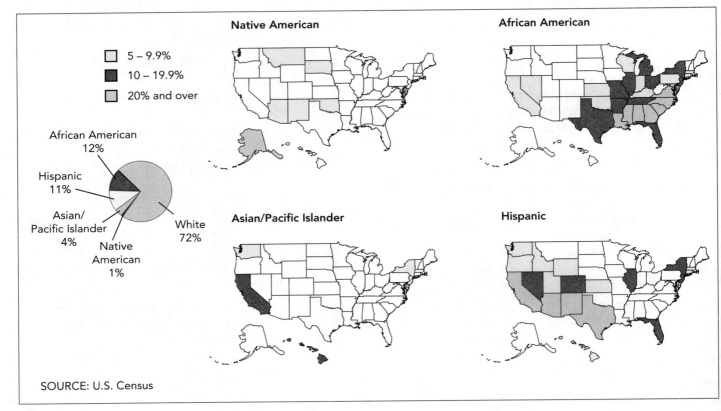

SOURCE: U.S. Census

6. **Which would be the most likely explanation for the settlement of Hispanics in the Southwest?**

   (1) a preference for dry, hot climates
   (2) the proximity of the Southwest to Mexico
   (3) an advertising campaign for new jobs
   (4) the unwelcoming attitudes of northerners
   (5) floods in Colorado that forced people southward

7. **Which of the following is a plausible explanation for the concentration of African Americans in New York and New Jersey?**

   (1) Many other immigrant groups were arriving there from other countries.
   (2) People liked the change of seasons, but not the extreme cold of farther north.
   (3) The industrial cities in New York and New Jersey offered job opportunities.
   (4) Southern plantation owners transported their former slaves to get rid of them.
   (5) The midwest and far west promoted a "no blacks allowed" policy.

8. By giving people the choice in 2000 to identify themselves in more than one racial/ethnic category, what was the U.S. Census Bureau trying to do?

   (1) look for ways to make the population count a more complicated procedure than it had ever been before

   (2) acknowledge that people often come from a variety of backgrounds and don't want to limit themselves to one identity

   (3) prove that minorities make up a much larger portion of the population than the 29 percent previously reported

   (4) limit the number of ethnic holidays likely to be celebrated in the United States by various minorities

   (5) support the movement to make Spanish and Chinese additional official languages in the United States

PRACTICE TEST

Questions 9 and 10 refer to the following information and passage from the Federalist Papers.

The Federalist Papers were written and published during the years 1787 and 1788 in several New York State newspapers to persuade New York voters to ratify the newly proposed constitution. The primary authors were Alexander Hamilton and James Madison with help from John Jay. In total, the Federalist Papers contain 85 essays outlining how this new government would operate and why this type of government was the best choice for the United States of America. Below is a section from the first essay of the Federalist Papers.

"To the People of the State of New York: AFTER an unequivocal experience of the inefficiency of the subsisting federal government, you are called upon to deliberate on a new Constitution for the United States of America. The subject speaks its own importance; comprehending in its consequences nothing less than the existence of the UNION, the safety and welfare of the parts of which it is composed, the fate of an empire in many respects the most interesting in the world. It has been frequently remarked that it seems to have been reserved to the people of this country, by their conduct and example, to decide the important question, whether societies of men are really capable or not of establishing good government from reflection and choice, or whether they are forever destined to depend for their political constitutions on accident and force. If there be any truth in the remark, the crisis at which we are arrived may with propriety be regarded as the era in which that decision is to be made; and a wrong election of the part we shall act may, in this view, deserve to be considered as the general misfortune of mankind. "

9. From these paragraphs, what can we infer about a Federalist?

   A Federalist was someone who
   (1) supported the new Constitution
   (2) opposed the new Constitution
   (3) was undecided about the new Constitution
   (4) had played an active role in the American Revolution
   (5) had sided with the British in the Revolution

10. The first essay of the Federalist Papers states that it is up to the people of the United States to answer an important question. That question can best be rephrased in what way?

    (1) Why does there always have to be violence when a new government is created?
    (2) Hasn't America had long enough to think about the kind of government it wants?
    (3) Can ordinary people form their own governments purposefully and peacefully?
    (4) Is this country going to be interesting to the rest of the world or boring?
    (5) How can the American states make the best of an accidental and threatening situation?

PRACTICE TEST

Questions 11 and 12 are based on the table below.

Estimated Slave Imports by Importing Region, 1451–1870

Importing Region	1451–1600	1601–1700	1701–1810	1811–1870	Total per region
British North America	—	—	348,000	51,000	399,000
Spanish America	75,000	292,000	578,600	606,000	1,552,100
British Caribbean	—	263,700	1,401,300	—	1,665,000
French Caribbean	—	155,800	1,348,400	96,000	1,600,200
Dutch Caribbean	—	40,000	460,000	—	500,000
Brazil	50,000	560,000	1,891,400	1,145,400	3,646,800
Old World	149,900	25,100	—	—	175,000
TOTALS	274,900	1,337,100	6,027,700	1,898,400	9,538,100

11. What does the information in this table indicate?

(1) The Old World continued to import slaves in larger and larger numbers until the end of the 19th century.
(2) Brazil imported almost as many slaves as British North America and the British and French Caribbean put together.
(3) Sugar was one of the biggest crops in the Caribbean and demanded the largest number of slaves.
(4) The largest increases in the slave trade occurred in most regions during the nineteenth century.
(5) British North America didn't start importing slaves until the 1700s because the colonies weren't settled until then.

12. Based on this table, in which of the following places could one expect to find the largest number of people with African ancestry today?

(1) St. Croix
(2) Brazil
(3) Mexico
(4) The United States
(5) England

Question 13 is based on the following passage.

Movement has always been a feature of Caribbean society, and its very basis is caught up in the idea of migration. Planters and colonial officials often saw their Caribbean sojourns as temporary. Enslaved Africans were dragged from their homelands and, being regarded as chattel, were often sold, moving from plantation to plantation and from island to island. Indentured workers came with the intention of returning, but only a small percentage ever did.

After slavery, Caribbean people moved around the region and beyond in search of the few opportunities available. After the Haitian Revolution, white and *mulâtre* planters and their slaves fled to Cuba and to Louisiana. In the 1850s West Indians worked on the Panama railroad. In the 1880s at least 50,000 workers—mostly Jamaicans—were involved in the French attempt to build the Panama Canal, while Cuban cigar workers migrated with their factories to Key West and Tampa, Florida.

13. Which of the following is *not* an example of the importance of movement in Caribbean society?

(1) After Castro's victory, many affluent Cubans relocated to the Miami area in Florida.
(2) Today, Dominicans are one of the largest ethnic groups in Lawrence, Massachusetts.
(3) In the 1990s, many Haitians tried to come to the United States by boat to escape poverty and hopelessness.
(4) Many vacationers consider the Caribbean an ideal place to go on vacation in the winter.
(5) Many Puerto Rican families have repeatedly moved back and forth between New York City and Puerto Rico.

PRACTICE TEST

Question 14 is based on the following document.

Below is a sample of a credit report on Karen Jones. It was prepared by a credit reporting agency for her bank. Karen Jones is a single mother with two children who lives in Iowa City, Iowa.

IDENTIFICATION

APPLICANT'S LAST NAME	FIRST NAME	INITIAL	SOCIAL SECURITY NUMBER	DATE OF BIRTH	NUMBER OF DEPENDENTS INCLUDING SELF
JONES	KAREN	B.	111-22-3333	6/20/63	3

SPOUSE'S LAST NAME	FIRST NAME	INITIAL	SOCIAL SECURITY NUMBER	DATE OF BIRTH	HOME PHONE
N/A					(402) 555-0000

RESIDENCE INFORMATION

CURRENT ADDRESS	CITY	STATE	ZIP CODE
325 MAIN STREET	IOWA CITY	IA	52240

LENGTH OF TIME	RENT
3 YEARS	$500/MO. STEVE JONSEN 733-1800

EMPLOYMENT INFORMATION

CURRENT EMPLOYER	POSITION HELD	ESTIMATED MONTHLY INCOME
GENERAL HOSPITAL	NURSING ASSISTANT	$1,900

LENGTH OF TIME	DATE EMPLOYMENT VERIFIED	VERIFIED BY
2 1/2 YEARS	07/01/97	CATHY BERGER (402) 300-2222

PREVIOUS EMPLOYER	POSITION HELD	ESTIMATED MONTHLY INCOME
FERRIS NURSING HOME	NURSE'S AIDE	$1500

LENGTH OF TIME	DATE EMPLOYMENT VERIFIED	VERIFIED BY
3 YEARS 6 MONTHS	07/01/97	BARB SMITH (402) 300-3333

CREDIT HISTORY

CREDITOR ACCOUNT NO	DATE REPORTED AND METHOD OF REPORTING	DATE LAST ACTIVITY AND DATE OPENED	HIGHEST CREDIT OR LIMIT	BALANCE OWING (PRESENT STATUS)	AMOUNT PAST DUE (PRESENT STATUS)	ECOA ACCT TYPE	NO MOS HIST REVD	30-60 DAYS ONLY	60-80 DAYS ONLY	80 DAYS AND OVER	REVOLVING PAID OR PAYMENT AMOUNT
MARSHALL & CO. 918009819833	06/94A	05/94 11/91	2500	1000	–0–	J – R	30	0	0	0	X$50
STEPHENS MOTOR CO. 467309898	07/94A	05/94 08/91	6500	940	–0–	J – I	36	0	0	0	X$113
CHOICE CREDIT CARD 98713478387	07/94M	05/94 07/90	2000	200	–0–	J – R	46	0	0	0	X$10

14. There is sufficient evidence in this document to support which of the following?

(1) Karen was formerly married.
(2) Karen has two children.
(3) Karen is a good credit risk.
(4) Karen is due for a raise.
(5) Karen likes her apartment.

Question 15 is based on the following passage.

After World War I, labor unrest at home and the spread of communism abroad led many Americans to fear a takeover by communists, or "Reds." During the "Red Scare" of 1919–20, Attorney General A. Mitchell Palmer organized the "Palmer Raids," arresting thousands of innocent people suspected of being communists with little or no evidence of wrongdoing, and deporting hundreds of aliens.

Many of those suspected were of foreign ancestry. In Massachusetts, Italian anarchists Nicola Sacco and Bartolomeo Vanzetti were arrested on charges of robbery and murder in 1920 and eventually executed in 1927. The judge in the case, Judge Webster Thayer, was widely regarded as biased, and many people believed that Sacco and Vanzetti were convicted not because of criminal activity (for which there was insufficient evidence), but because of their political ideas.

—Adapted from "Because I Am a Radical and an Italian," *Ordinary Americans: U.S. History Through the Eyes of Everyday People*

15. According to the information given in this passage, which of the following is most likely?

Judge Webster Thayer
(1) would have approved of Hollywood blacklisting writers suspected of sympathy for the Soviet Union
(2) would have approved of President Franklin D. Roosevelt because his family had lived in the US for generations
(3) would have supported the liberalization of immigration policy in the late 20th century
(4) had a long and distinguished career marked by many wise and thoughtful decisions
(5) considered capital punishment or execution to be cruel and unusual punishment that was unconstitutional

PRACTICE TEST

Questions 16–17 refer to the photograph and passage below.

The Bedouins are Muslim Arabs who have wandered the desert areas of the Middle East since ancient times. Beginning about 1045 and continuing at a decreasing rate for several centuries, these nomads invaded northern Africa, taking over all suitable grazing land and upsetting the balanced agricultural and urban civilization of the resident Berbers, various native, non-Arab tribes. The Bedouin flocks destroyed most of the natural ground cover; by overgrazing, the flocks turned pastureland into semi-desert. Some of this balance has been restored, however, and today many Middle Eastern and North African states have tried to curtail the movement of Bedouin groups from one country to another.

Some Bedouins continue their nomadic and pastoral way of life into the twenty-first century. They live primarily on meat, milk, and dairy products provided by their herds. However, with the rise of oil production in the 1960s and 1970s, many Bedouins have taken jobs in the oil industry. Government programs throughout the Middle East have encouraged the Bedouins to become more settled and urban. Currently, only 5 to 10 percent of Bedouins lead a fully nomadic lifestyle, but many more are seasonal nomads.

—Adapted from "Bedouins", Microsoft Encarta Encyclopedia

16. What is the photographer most likely trying to say with this photograph?

   (1) The Bedouins are ideally suited to work in the oil industry.
   (2) Old and new live side by side in today's Middle East.
   (3) Camels are used to transport supplies to oil workers.
   (4) Oil drilling is a serious environmental threat.
   (5) Modern industry is threatening traditional lifestyles.

17. Given the information in this passage, which is the most plausible prediction?

   (1) The Bedouin way of life will persist long after the oil industry dies out.
   (2) The northern fringe of the Sahara will start to receive more rainfall.
   (3) The Berbers in Morocco will welcome renewed Bedouin immigration.
   (4) The Bedouin nomadic way of life is dying out and might disappear.
   (5) Bedouins are likely to dominate oil drilling and refining in the Middle East.

Question 18 refers to the graph and information below.

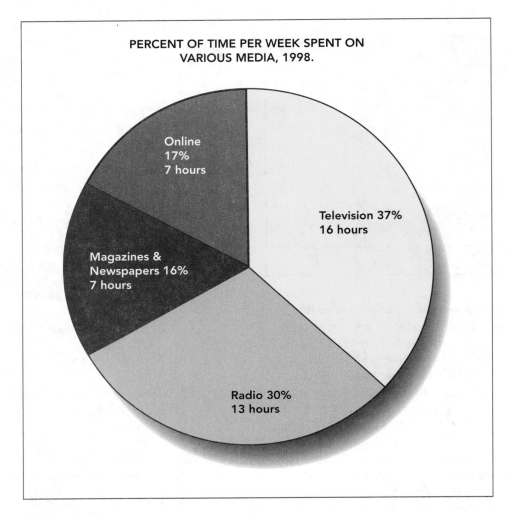

PERCENT OF TIME PER WEEK SPENT ON VARIOUS MEDIA, 1998.

Online
17%
7 hours

Television 37%
16 hours

Magazines &
Newspapers 16%
7 hours

Radio 30%
13 hours

18. By the year 2020, all but which of the following will most likely be true?

(1) At least 60% of adults will enjoy using a PC at home.

(2) On average, online time will exceed 11 hours per week.

(3) The total amount of time spent on various media will stay about the same.

(4) TV viewing will stabilize as stations create compelling new programs.

(5) Computer use will continue to cut into time available for other media.

PRACTICE TEST

Questions 19 and 20 refer to the following poster and passage.

TIME TABLE OF THE LOWELL MILLS,

Arranged to make the working time throughout the year average 11 hours per day,

TO TAKE EFFECT SEPTEMBER 21st., 1853,

The Standard time being that of the meridian of Lowell, as shown by the Regulator Clock of AMOS SANBORN, Post Office Corner, Central Street.

From March 20th to September 19th, inclusive.

COMMENCE WORK, at 6.30 A. M. LEAVE OFF WORK, at 6.30 P. M., except on Saturday Evenings. BREAKFAST at 6 A. M. DINNER, at 12 M. Commence Work, after dinner, 12.45 P.M.

From September 20th to March 19th, inclusive.

COMMENCE WORK, at 7.00 A. M. LEAVE OFF WORK, at 7.00 P. M., except on Saturday Evenings. BREAKFAST at 6.30 A. M. DINNER, at 12.30 P.M. Commence Work, after dinner, 1.15 P.M.

BELLS.

From March 20th to September 19th, inclusive.

Morning Bells.	Dinner Bells.	Evening Bells.
First bell,.............4.30 A. M.	Ring out,..........12.00 M.	Ring out,................6.30 P.M.
Second, 5.30 A. M. ; Third, 6.20	Ring in,............12.35 P. M.	Except on Saturday Evenings

From September 20th to March 19th, inclusive.

Morning Bells.	Dinner Bells.	Evening Bells.
First bell,.............5.00 A. M.	Ring out,..........12.30 P. M.	Ring out,................7.00 P.M.
Second, 6.00 A. M. ; Third, 6.50	Ring in,............1.05 P. M.	Except on Saturday Evenings

In February 1834, more than eight hundred women millworkers in Lowell, Massachusetts, went on strike. Broadsides, or posters, had been posted in the mills with the news of upcoming wage cuts. A mill agent, who operated the mill for the owners, decided to fire a woman who had argued with him during a meeting. "This woman . . . retorted upon me with no little vehemence, & declare that there was no cause for any reduction whatever . . ." he reported to the owners. He fired the woman because she "had great sway over the minds of the other females." As the woman left the mill, she waved her calash (scarf) in the air. Her sister workers who were watching from the window marched out after her. The strike had begun. Marching from mill to mill, the women enlisted other strikers.

According to a newspaper report, one of the leaders gave a "flaming . . . speech on the rights of women and the iniquities of the 'monied aristocracy.'"

—Excerpted from *Strike: The Bitter Struggle of American Workers from Colonial Times to the Present* by Penny Coleman

19. The information on the poster and in the passage shows that which of the following was an important objective of the mill owner?

   (1) concern for the health and safety of the workers
   (2) to maintain a rigorous work schedule and remove opposition to its policies
   (3) to negotiate aggressively and fairly with the union
   (4) to win the support of the public for their position on wages and work hours
   (5) to maintain uniform and fair working conditions for all workers

20. As used by the strike leader, what does the phrase "iniquities of the monied aristocracy" most likely refer to?

   (1) the lavish and extravagant lifestyle of the richest Lowell residents
   (2) the special privileges of people descended from British nobility
   (3) the oppressive working conditions the mill owners imposed on the workers
   (4) the refusal of the rich industrialists to share ownership with the workers
   (5) the degrading and abusive treatment of the poorest people by the wealthy

Questions 21 and 22 are based on the following passage.

Even a small European country like Belgium—a pawn in Europe's power politics—could carve out a huge portion of central Africa as its empire, calling it The Belgian Congo. Portugal, a country both small and relatively backward by European standards, had an even larger colonial empire in Africa. Major European powers like Britain and France took over African territory several times their own size. Not all this was achieved through sheer military power on the battlefield. On the contrary, both the conquerors and the conquered tended to minimize their losses by agreeing to some form of indirect rule, in which local authorities continued in their traditional roles (or in strengthened versions of those roles under European hegemony) while the imperial power made policy through them and influenced, or controlled, who could act as local authorities. However, such abrogations of African sovereignty were not agreed to merely by persuasion, bribery, or trickery. An obvious and enormous military disparity provided the context for such agreements.

—Excerpted from *Conquests and Cultures* by Thomas Sowell

21. According to the information in this passage, what was the main reason that local African authorities continued in their traditional roles?

    (1) the respect of Europeans for African culture and traditions
    (2) the economic benefit of having African rather than European administrators
    (3) to avoid the costs and destruction of armed confrontations
    (4) as a result of European manipulation of African politics
    (5) to gain the support of the African people for European rule

22. In this passage, what does the term *abrogations* mean?

    (1) traditions
    (2) disregard
    (3) advantages
    (4) control
    (5) respect

Question 23 is based on the following map.

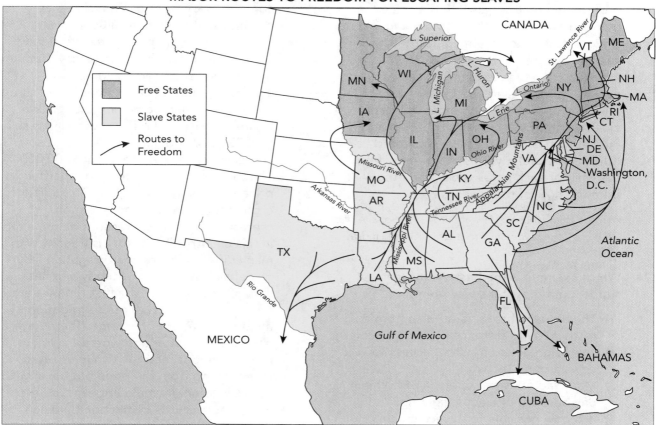

MAJOR ROUTES TO FREEDOM FOR ESCAPING SLAVES

23. According to the information given in the map, which of the following conclusions can be drawn?

(1) Escaped slaves tried to reach the Northern states and Canada.

(2) Escaped slaves left the South in all directions possible.

(3) Mexico closed its borders to refugees from the United States.

(4) Cuba was the main destination of escaped slaves.

(5) Slaves needed the assistance of sympathetic northerners to escape.

Question 24 is based on the following passage.

Frozen foods represent the tail end of a progression that began with the spice trade and moved on through canning and refrigerated boxcars, until at last the culinary arts have been completely unyoked from the seasons. We can eat peas in February and pumpkins in June. This again brings to mind a parallel to the electric light. Both Edison's lightbulb and Birdseye's flash-freezer have separated us from the natural rhythms of life—one from the whirl of each passing day, the other from the flow of the seasons.

—Excerpted from *House of Invention: The Secret Life of Everyday Products* by David Lindsay

24. Which example is the best evidence in support of the writer's viewpoint?

   (1) The airplane has separated us from the restrictions of distance.
   (2) Television gives us instant access to news around the world.
   (3) Many factories can operate 24 hours a day because of electric lighting.
   (4) It is now possible to buy ice cream year-round.
   (5) Gourmet restaurants can use spices and sauces from around the world.

Questions 25–27 are based on the following passage.

There are many characteristics of contemporary suburban housing that distinguish it from its traditional counterpart. Perhaps the strangest and most troubling of these is the way that new housing is distributed. . . . a typical suburban landscape [is] composed of three different housing pods, or *clusters*. One cluster consists entirely of houses that sell for $350,000 and up. The second cluster contains houses costing about $200,000. The third cluster is made up of apartments priced at less than $100,000. This sort of organization, a suburban invention, represents a relatively recent phenomenon in this country. Our history is fraught with many different types of segregation—by race, by class, by how recently one has immigrated—but for the first time we are now experiencing ruthless segregation by minute gradations of income. There have always been better and worse neighborhoods, and the rich have often taken refuge from the poor, but never with such precision. It would appear that, for many, there is little distinction between someone slightly less wealthy than themselves and a Skid Row bum. . . .

The segregation of housing by "market segment" is a phenomenon that was invented by developers who lacking a meaningful way to distinguish their mass-produced merchandise, began selling the concept of exclusivity: *If you live within these gates, you can consider yourself a success.* The real estate business caters to this elitism so relentlessly that even some mobile home parks are marketed in this way. . . .

Moving is a well-established tradition in America, and *moving up* constitutes a significant part of the American dream. Not only is working one's way to a bigger house central to our ethos but it makes sense functionally as families bring children into the world. But why must the move to a larger or more luxurious house bring with it the abandonment of one's neighbors, community groups, and often even schoolmates? Sadly, the suburban pod system causes people to move not just from house to house but from community to community. Only in a traditionally organized neighborhood of varied incomes can a family significantly alter its housing without going very far. In the new suburbs, you can't move up without moving out.

—Excerpted from *Suburban Nation, the Rise of Sprawl and the Decline of the American Dream* by Duany, Plater-Zyberk, and Speck

25. Given the evidence in this passage, what appears to be an important trend in America?

   (1) the end of racial segregation in housing
   (2) segregation based on small variations in wealth
   (3) the growth of new suburban neighborhoods
   (4) a renaissance of interest in living in the city
   (5) moving to new neighborhoods every few years

26. The writers of this passage appear to believe that what value is most important?

   (1) displaying wealth as publicly as possible
   (2) developing and maintaining ties within the community
   (3) associating only with those from your own income bracket
   (4) knowing when to move out to a more affluent neighborhood
   (5) cultivating and maintaining one's social status

27. The developers of modern suburban neighborhoods are trying to exploit what values of their customers?

   The need
   (1) to have a sense of belonging and community
   (2) for people to feel good about themselves
   (3) to contribute to the well-being of others
   (4) to preserve what is best from our past
   (5) to develop and maintain lifelong relationships

Question 28 is based on the following passage.

In the mid-1960's New York City and the federal government took a great gamble. Not only did they throw out the time-honored distinction between the worthy and unworthy poor that the New Deal had clung to, but they refused to recognize that there were many different ways to be poor.

Virtue does not correlate with class, income is not a proxy for character, and hard work is not necessarily an indicator of income, but certain vices, like desertion and violent crime, do have distinct class correlates. In an act of principled ignorance, liberal activists, anxious to erase the invidious distinctions that held poor people back, argued away the essential differences between those who suffered from only a lack of money and those who suffered from far more. Liberals in New York and Washington gambled that what makes people poor is simply a lack of money and that the fastest way to eliminate poverty is to get more people on the welfare rolls while increasing what recipients are entitled to.

—Excerpted from *The Future Once Happened Here: New York, D.C., L.A., and the Fate of America's Big Cities* by Fred Siegel

28. Which recommendation would the author of this passage most likely support?

(1) Vote liberal activists out of office so that they can't do any more damage.
(2) Invest more federal money into drug and alcohol rehabilitation programs.
(3) Make tougher rules about who receives welfare and for how long.
(4) Increase the number of uniformed police officers on city streets.
(5) Require moral development courses for all students in public schools.

Questions 29 and 30 are based on the following cartoon.

— John Chase, Library of Congress.

29. John Chase drew this cartoon of President Truman in 1950, during the Korean War, when Truman was having disagreements with General Douglas MacArthur, who was commanding United Nations troops in Korea. What was Chase trying to accomplish with this cartoon?

(1) He wanted to show that Truman was growing into his job of commander-in-chief.
(2) He wanted his readers to see Truman as a man of peace, who opposed the war.
(3) He wanted readers to see that behind his gentle façade, Truman was a strong military leader.
(4) He wanted to encourage Truman to fire MacArthur, who was undermining Truman's authority.
(5) He was trying to depict Truman as a little boy who could not even wear MacArthur's hat.

30. This cartoon could be seen as a challenge to which principle of American government?

(1) civilian control of the military
(2) freedom of speech
(3) separation of powers
(4) right to bear arms
(5) right to a fair trial

Question 31 is based on the following photograph.

Question 32 is based on the following political cartoon.

JOIN, or DIE.

31. From this photograph of rice paddies in China, which of the following conclusions *cannot* be drawn?

(1) Rice cultivation drastically changes the physical landscape.
(2) Manual labor is still very important in China.
(3) Irrigation is needed to grow rice in this region.
(4) This is an area of heavy rainfall and mild temperatures.
(5) Ancient methods are still used in order to grow rice.

32. This cartoon, created by Benjamin Franklin in 1754, is one of the earliest American political cartoons. What was the message Franklin was trying to communicate?

(1) Anyone who refused to join a united government would be killed.
(2) The enemies of the colonies were like a dangerous snake.
(3) If the colonies united, they would be very powerful.
(4) The colonies needed each other in order to survive.
(5) Leaders from the different colonies needed to follow him.

PRACTICE TEST

Questions 33 and 34 are based on the following passage.

About halfway between Phoenix and Tucson on Interstate 10, not far from where the Hohokam civilization once flourished, is the small, dusty agricultural town of Elroy, whose main distinction is that it is sinking, as is much of the land surrounding it. The U.S. Geological Survey mapped a 4,500-square-mile area in south-central Arizona, where 60 percent of the state's population and a little over half its agricultural lands are located. Here, in the sixty years since 1915, more than 109 million acre-feet of groundwater were extracted. And the land both sank and opened up into jagged fissures. In the 120 square miles surrounding Elroy, the land has dropped more than 7 feet since 1952, reaching a maximum of 12.5 feet south of town. Fissures in the earth opened up, eroded rapidly during infrequent rains, and became trenches more than 1,000 feet long and as much as 10 feet wide and 10 feet deep. One fissure 9 miles long intersects the interstate southeast of Elroy, requiring constant repairs to the highway's surface. Railroads, utilities, irrigation canals, sewage systems, farmland, and private homes have all been damaged—mostly in rural areas. Tucson shifted some of its underground pumping activities to rural areas to avoid subsidence in more populated sections. But the expanding populations of both metropolitan areas were encroaching on the sinking land. The survey's report had little effect in Arizona.

—Excerpted from *A River No More, The Colorado River and the West* by Philip L. Fradhim

33. What is the main idea of this passage?

   (1) Despite alarming evidence of environmental damage, Arizonans are not concerned.
   (2) As a result of groundwater being extracted, Elroy has sunk more than seven feet.
   (3) Removing excessive amounts of groundwater can have a negative environmental impact.
   (4) People traveling from Phoenix to Tucson on Interstate 10 must pass through Elroy.
   (5) There has been extensive damage in Arizona as a result of the removal of groundwater.

34. This passage was written in 1981. According to the evidence given in the passage, which of the following is most likely today?

   (1) Environmental issues are far more important in Arizona.
   (2) Interstate 10 has had to be rerouted around the fissure.
   (3) Phoenix and Tucson now need less water than they used to need.
   (4) Tucson's action to shift underground pumping has solved the problem.
   (5) The town of Elroy and the surrounding area has continued to sink.

PRACTICE TEST

Question 35 is based on the following table.

FAMILIES WITH CHILDREN UNDER 18 BY TYPE: 1960–2010			
	Mother Only with Children Under 18	Father Only with Children Under 18	Married Couples with Children Under 18
1960	8.2	.9	90.9
1970	10.2	1.2	88.6
1980	17.6	2.0	80.4
1990	20.4	3.6	76.0
1998	22.1	5.2	72.7
2010 (est.)	22.3	5.9	71.8

Source: U.S. Bureau of the Census

35. Which of the following trends is *not* documented in this table?

(1) The percent of families with children under 18 headed by a mother only has been steadily increasing.

(2) The percent of families with children under 18 headed by a father only has been steadily increasing.

(3) The percent of families in which a married couple lived with children under 18 has been steadily decreasing.

(4) The percent of families with children under 18 headed by a single parent has been steadily increasing.

(5) The percent of families with children under 18 headed by a never-married parent has been steadily increasing.

PRACTICE TEST

Question 36 is based on the following passage.

Whenever a new technology is born, few see its ultimate place in society. The inventors of radio did not foresee its use for broadcasting entertainment, sports, and news; they saw it as a telegraph without wires. The early builders of automobiles did not see an age of "automobility;" they saw a "horseless carriage." Likewise, the computer's inventors perceived its role in future society in terms of the functions it was specifically replacing in contemporary society. The predictions that they made about potential applications for the new invention had to come from the context of "computing" that they knew. Though they recognized the electronic computer's novelty, they did not see how it would permit operations fundamentally different from those performed by human computers.

—Excerpted from *Imagining Tomorrow, History, Technology, and the American Future*, Joseph J. Corn, ed.

36. Which of the following current uses of computers did its inventors probably foresee?

   (1) Internet chat rooms for finding people to date
   (2) word processing for creating written documents
   (3) following a formula to do long calculations
   (4) beating the world's top chessmaster in chess
   (5) playing arcade-style video games

Questions 37 and 38 are based on the following passage.

The demographic face of APAs [Asian-Pacific Americans] has changed from miners, railroad laborers, farm and factory workers to scientists, business owners, and professionals. As we celebrate the Asian-Pacific American Heritage Month in May each year, all should appreciate the diversity of the APA community and utilize its talents and resources. For every image of sweatshop employees, there is designer Vera Wang. For every image of gardeners and carpenters, there is the famous architect I. M. Pei. For every image of computer programmers, there is the world's most sought-after cellist, Yo-Yo Ma. For every image of martial arts masters, there is ice skater Kristi Yamaguchi and tennis player Michael Chang. For every image of uneducated refugees, there is University of California at Berkeley Chancellor Dr. Tien Chang-Lin. For every image of welfare recipients, there is Elaine Chao, the former Peace Corps director and president of the United Way. And for every image of restaurant owners, there is Governor Gary Locke of Washington.

In conclusion, as the population of Asian-Pacific Americans increases, so does the importance of working with the community at large. Whether we are naturalized or born Americans, it is our desire to share and celebrate our Asian cultures with fellow Americans, to contribute to the economic and social well-being of the United States, and to be recognized for our contributions. To reach these goals, we have to actively participate in American society at the national as well as local levels and in the public as well as private sectors. We also ask all racial and ethnic groups to get to know, and work with, Asian-Pacific Americans. With this cooperation, all Asian-Pacific Americans

in the United States can and will become an equal and integral part of this diverse community.

—Excerpted from "Faces and Activism of the Asian Pacific-American Community," by Alice H. Yang.

37. Who is most likely delivering this speech?

(1) an experienced politician running for office
(2) a thoughtful Asian-Pacific American (APA) leader
(3) a creative public relations professional
(4) a proponent of enacting English First legislation
(5) someone who wants to reach out to the Asian community

38. Why did the author list successful Asian-Pacific Americans?

(1) to show how APAs are the most successful of all ethnic groups
(2) to showcase the diversity and achievements of APAs
(3) to reinforce commonly held stereotypes of APAs
(4) to alert the reader that APAs are taking over in many areas
(5) to encourage other Americans to be more like the APAs

Questions 39 and 40 are based on the following passage.

The new presence of women in the law has prompted many feminist commentators to ask whether women have made a difference to the profession, whether women have different styles, aptitudes, or liabilities. Ironically, the move to ask again the question of whether women are different merely by virtue of being women recalls the old myths we have struggled to put behind us. Undaunted by the historical

PRACTICE TEST

overtones, however, more and more writers have suggested that women practice law differently than men. One author has even concluded that my opinions differ in a peculiarly feminine way from those of my colleagues.

The gender differences cited currently are surprisingly similar to stereotypes from years past. Women attorneys are more likely to seek to mediate disputes than litigate them. Women attorneys are more likely to focus on resolving a client's problem than vindicating a position. Women attorneys are more likely to sacrifice career advancement for family obligations. Women attorneys are more concerned with public service or fostering community than with individual achievement. Women judges are more likely to emphasize context and de-emphasize the general principles. Women judges are more compassionate. And so forth.

This "new" feminism is interesting, but troubling, precisely because it so nearly echoes the Victorian myth of the "true woman" that kept women out of law for so long. It is a little chilling to compare these suggestions to Clarence Darrow's assertions that women are too kind and warmhearted to be shining lights at the bar.

Asking whether women attorneys speak with a "different voice" than men do is a question that is both dangerous and unanswerable. It sets up again the polarity between the feminine virtues of homemaking and the masculine virtues of breadwinning. It threatens, indeed, to establish new categories of "women's work" to which women are confined and from which men are excluded.

Do women judges decide cases differently by virtue of being women? I would echo the answer of my colleague,

Justice Jeanne Coyne of the Supreme Court of Oklahoma, who responded that "a wise old man and a wise old woman reach the same conclusion."

—Excerpted from "Portia's Progress: Women and the Law" by Justice Sandra Day O'Connor, *New York University Law Review*

39. Which of the following lines of reasoning would Justice O'Connor most likely support?

   (1) There must be a black justice on the Supreme Court to represent the way that black people think about justice.
   (2) Affirmative action programs need to be supported for women and minorities to influence the way decisions are made.
   (3) Racial profiling is not acceptable since a person's behavior is not determined by ethnic origin.
   (4) The Taliban in Afghanistan use Islamic law to prohibit women from working outside the home.
   (5) Since women are more conciliatory than men are, they should take the lead in settling international disputes.

40. Which of the following values would be most important for Justice O'Connor when deciding a case before her?

   (1) her relationship with the other justices of the Supreme Court
   (2) consideration of the feelings of those involved in the case
   (3) creating an opinion that would be studied in law schools
   (4) pleasing her supporters who applauded her nomination to the court
   (5) strictly adhering to the law and to the facts of the case

Question 41 and 42 are based on the following table.

HOW BIG IS THE BUREAUCRACY?			
FISCAL YEAR	CIVILIAN EMPLOYEES IN THE EXECUTIVE BRANCH*	TOTAL U.S. POPULATION	EMPLOYEES FOR EVERY 1,000
1965	2,496,000	194,303,000	12.8
1970	2,944,000	205,052,000	14.4
1975	2,848,000	215,973,000	13.2
1980	2,821,000	228,468,000	12.3
1985	2,964,000	239,134,000	12.4
1990	3,067,000	250,726,000	12.2
1995	2,288,000	263,814,000	8.7

*Includes employees of the U.S. Postal Service

Source: Bureau of the Census/Office of Management and Budget

41. Which of the following can be concluded from the evidence in this chart?

(1) The government bureaucracy continues to grow out of control.
(2) The size of the bureaucracy has been proportional to the total population.
(3) The bureaucracy was smaller in 1995 than at any time since 1965.
(4) The bureaucracy was even smaller in 2000 than it was in 1995.
(5) The bloated bureaucracy needs to be drastically cut back.

42. Which year had the highest proportion of bureaucrats compared to the total population?

(1) 1965
(2) 1970
(3) 1983
(4) 1990
(5) 1995

PRACTICE TEST

Questions 43 and 44 are based on the following passage.

For centuries, Native Americans have lived in balance with their natural surroundings. They were the "first" environmentalists. In sharp contrast, their reservations today are the site of some of our country's most severe environmental crises. Strip mining, radioactive and other toxic-waste dumping, deforestation from logging and many other industrial activities have had a profound, lasting impact on land, air and water quality as well as on the health of many families living in affected areas.

Imagine the impact on tribal communities where fishing was once a mainstay of the economy, but where river pollution is now so severe that it is hazardous to eat fish and shellfish. Consider the effects of high doses of radiation on nearby tribal lands after years of dumping radioactive wastes in Washington State rivers. In Montana, the Fort Belknap reservation has been forced to sue the mining company because its chemical processing has poisoned wells and contaminated groundwater. And in many lands, aerial spraying of pesticides on farms is not properly controlled by regulatory agencies.

A new generation of environmentalists is now finding solutions to these crises. As American Indian students become aware of catastrophes on their tribal lands, they also realize they have alternatives. Through training in environmental science programs at tribal colleges, they become directly involved in solving critical community needs. By learning scientific tools in biology, chemistry, and natural resources, and by gaining practical experience through research projects in the field, they will be qualified to tackle environmental crises. Gradually the colleges are building faculty and laboratory resources to cope with the rapidly increasing demand for training qualified environmental specialists.

—Excerpted form "Cleaning up the Land: Tribal colleges train a new generation of Environmentalists," *Mind and Spirit.* October/November 1998.

43. Which of the following conclusions can be drawn from this passage?

(1) Until recently, Native Americans did not have the resources to clean up environmental damage on the reservations.
(2) Industries are no longer dumping radioactive and toxic waste on Native American reservations.
(3) Young Native Americans living on the reservations do not care about the environmental problems on their tribal lands.
(4) Native Americans have only recently become aware that they can do something about environmental damage on the reservations.
(5) Tribal colleges are trying to recruit more students to help solve the environmental problems on the reservations.

44. What is the writer of this passage suggesting?

(1) The federal government created the environmental problems on reservations and must clean them up.
(2) Native American leaders must lobby politicians at all levels for support in fixing environmental problems.
(3) It is important for tribal colleges to train Native Americans to solve the reservations' environmental problems.
(4) Reservations have been permanently damaged by years of mining, dumping, and industrial activities.
(5) Outside experts need to come to work with Native Americans on cleaning up the reservations.

Question 45 is based on the following passage.

Almost everyone has heard about Love Canal, but not many people know what it is all about. The Love Canal story is about a thousand families who lived near the site of an abandoned toxic chemical waste dump. More important, it is a warning of what could happen in any American community. We have very little protection against the toxic chemical wastes that threaten to poison our water, our air, our food. The federal and state governments have agreed to move away everyone who wants to move; but they didn't at first. We had to work to achieve that goal. Love Canal is the story of how government tends to solve a problem, and of how we, ordinary citizens of the United States, can take control of our own lives by insisting that we be heard. . . .

When we moved into our house on 101st Street in 1972, I didn't even know Love Canal was there. It was a lovely neighborhood in a quiet residential area, with lots of trees and lots of children outside playing. It seemed just the place for our family. . . . I liked the idea of my children being able to walk to the 99th Street School. The school's playground was part of a big, open field with houses all around. Our new neighbors told us that the developers who sold them their houses said the city was going to put a park on the field.

It is really something, if you stop and think of it, that underneath that field were poisons, and on top of it was a grade school and a playground. We later found out that the Niagara Falls School Board knew the filled-in canal was a toxic dump site. We also know that they knew it was dangerous because, when the Hooker Chemical Corporation sold it to them for one dollar, Hooker put a clause in the deed declaring that the corporation would not be responsible for any harm that came to anyone from chemicals buried there. That one-dollar school site turned out to be some bargain!

—Excerpted from *Love Canal: My Story*
by Lois Marie Gibbs

45. What does the writer of this article believe?

(1) The government can be trusted to do the right thing.
(2) She was lucky to have lived near Love Canal.
(3) It was the residents' responsibility to investigate Love Canal.
(4) The government knew that the area was dangerous.
(5) The School Board did shrewd bargaining in purchasing the field.

PRACTICE TEST

Question 46 is based on the following passage.

. . . Observe good faith and justice toward all nations. Cultivate peace and harmony with all. . . . It will be worthy of a free, enlightened, and at no distant period a great nation to give to mankind the magnanimous and too novel example of a people always guided by an exalted justice and benevolence. . . .

In the execution of such a plan nothing is more essential than that permanent, inveterate antipathies against particular nations and passionate attachments for others should be excluded, and that in place of them just and amicable feelings toward all should be cultivated. . . . Antipathy in one nation against another disposes each one readily to offer insult and injury, to lay hold of slight causes of umbrage, and to be haughty and intractable when accidental or trifling occasions of dispute occur. . . .

So, likewise, a passionate attachment of one nation for another produces a variety of evils. Sympathy for the favorite nation, facilitating the illusion of an imaginary common interest where no real common interest exists, and infusing into one the enmities of the other, betrays the former into a participation in the quarrels and wars of the latter without adequate inducement or justification. . . . The great rule of conduct for us in regard to foreign nations is, in extending our commercial relations to have with them as little political connection as possible. So far as we have already formed engagements let them be fulfilled with perfect good faith. Here let us stop. . . .

—Excerpted from George Washington's Farewell Address, 1796

46. Which of the following policies was George Washington advocating?

(1) isolationism
(2) protectionism
(3) imperialism
(4) capitalism
(5) internationalism

Question 47 is based on the following graph.

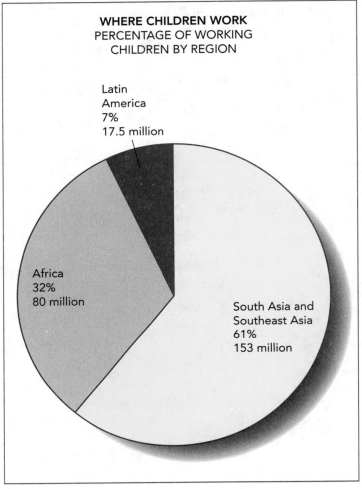

WHERE CHILDREN WORK
PERCENTAGE OF WORKING
CHILDREN BY REGION

Latin
America
7%
17.5 million

Africa
32%
80 million

South Asia and
Southeast Asia
61%
153 million

47. Which of the following is a valid conclusion that can be drawn from the details of this graph?

(1) The greatest child labor problems are in the developing world.
(2) There are 17.5 million child laborers in Latin America.
(3) Thirty-two percent of all child workers live in Africa.
(4) Asia is home to 153 million child workers.
(5) Child labor is a growing problem around the world.

PRACTICE TEST

Question 48 is based on the following painting.

48. By composing this picture as he did, which of the following was the painter able to emphasize?

(1) the difficulties of crossing the Alps
(2) the support Napoleon enjoyed from his troops
(3) the usefulness of horses in combat
(4) Napoleon's dramatic and heroic leadership
(5) the ruthless tyranny of Napoleon's rule

Question 49 is based on the following drawing.

49. The title of this drawing is "Joyously Singing, Our Brave Troops Move to the Front." What can you infer about the artist Daumier?

He was
(1) trying to glorify war and soldiers
(2) emphasizing the importance of officers
(3) contrasting propaganda with reality
(4) admiring of the courage of the soldiers
(5) depicting the soldiers' enthusiasm

PRACTICE TEST

Question 50 is based on the following map and passage.

EUROPEAN POSSESSIONS AT THE END OF THE 19TH CENTURY

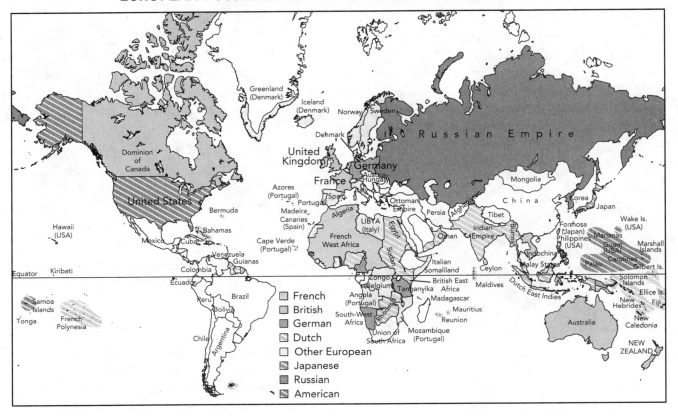

By the end of the nineteenth century, most of the Americas had broken free of European rule. The trend toward independence continued throughout the twentieth century. By the beginning of the twenty-first century, most of Asia and Africa were independent of direct European rule.

50. According to the map and the passage, which of the following conclusions can be drawn?

(1) The world's political boundaries have changed little in the last one hundred years.

(2) Over the past few hundred years, Europe at some time controlled most of the world.

(3) The twentieth century will be remembered as the American century.

(4) Most European nations continue to be influential in the areas they once colonized.

(5) In the twenty-first century, Asia will become the most powerful area on earth.

1. **Evaluation (5)** The soldier values "the fatherhood of God and the universal brotherhood of man."

2. **Comprehension (5)** Not only did the vassal provide military service, he also gave the lord advice and participated in settling disputes. These were the functions of an aristocrat. Since he was also expected to give his lord financial aid if necessary, he needed to have some wealth.

3. **Comprehension (1)** The key clauses of the Magna Carta for the first time limited the absolute power of the king. Since the Magna Carta was signed in 1215, one can infer that before that the king was benefiting more than the vassal was.

4. **Analysis (5)** Both clauses cited refer to the way trials would be held.

5. **Analysis (4)** The concept of trial by jury did not exist before the Magna Carta was signed in 1215, which was in the thirteenth century. Only the 12th century vassal who lived before that time and would not know of trial by jury.

6. **Analysis (2)** Many Mexicans emigrate from Mexico to the states closest to Mexico's border, those in the Southwest.

7. **Analysis (3)** The opportunities for work in the industrial centers of New York and New Jersey have always been a strong draw, both to blacks from the south and immigrants from other nations.

8. **Evaluation (2)** The U.S. Census finally recognized that people identify themselves in a number of ways. The other choices present narrow or inaccurate motivations.

9. **Analysis (1)** The Federalists were trying to convince their readers of the importance of approving the new Constitution.

10. **Comprehension (3)** The passage asks whether societies of men are really capable or not of establishing good government from reflection and choice. Choice (3) is the only choice that rephrases this question.

11. **Comprehension (2)** Added together, British North America and the British and French Caribbean combined imported only a few thousand slaves more than Brazil did on its own.

12. **Evaluation (2)** The evidence in the table is sufficient to expect that Brazil would have the largest number of people with African ancestry, since it received far more African slaves than any of the other places listed.

13. **Application (4)** Vacationers to the Caribbean usually stay only a week, which is too brief a time to be considered a migration. All the other choices are examples of Caribbean peoples migrating.

14. **Evaluation (3)** Since the report shows that Karen has not had any problems with her credit cards or with loans, she can be considered a good credit risk. Even though she has dependents, the report does not state they are her children. It also doesn't state whether or not she was previously married. There is also no information on whether she is due for a raise or whether she likes her apartment, even though she has lived there for a while.

15. **Application (1)** The evidence in the passage indicates that Thayer was biased against Sacco and Vanzetti because of their political ideas. Therefore, it is likely that he would have approved of the blacklisting of writers by Hollywood in the 1950s. Blacklisted writers were unable to find work solely because of their suspected political views.

16. **Analysis (2)** By photographing the camels next to the oil rig, the photographer is dramatizing how old and new live side by side.

17. **Evaluation (4)** With only 5 to 10 percent of Bedouins currently engaged in a fully nomadic lifestyle and continued pressure to become more settled and urban, it is reasonable to predict that the Bedouin nomadic way of life will die out.

18. **Analysis (5)** As the trend toward more online time continues, the time will most likely cut into all the other competing media.

19. **Analysis (2)** Both the passage and the poster give evidence that the mill owners required the workers to work long hours, and did not tolerate opposition to their policies.

20. **Comprehension (3)** Since it is a strike leader speaking, and that leader is trying to rally support for a strike, it is most likely that she is referring to oppressive working conditions for the workers.

21. **Comprehension (3)** The passage emphasizes that both sides wanted to limit the losses they would incur in a military confrontation.

22. **Comprehension (2)** The passage explains that the Europeans let Africans remain in their traditional roles, but the Europeans made the policy and controlled the rulers. In this way, they essentially disregarded African sovereignty.

23. **Analysis (2)** In addition to escaping the South by going north to Canada and the Northern States, slaves also escaped through Texas to Mexico and through Florida to the Caribbean.

24. **Application (3)** Factories operating 24 hours a day because of electric lighting is an example of work being separated from the natural rhythm of the day. The airplane having a similar effect on distance (1) does not actually support the writer's viewpoint. Buying ice cream year round (4) or using gourmet spices (5) does not support the writer's focus on the disruption of the natural rhythms of life. Television giving instant access to the world (2) focuses again on the shrinking of the effects of distance, which is not the writer's main point.

25. **Comprehension (2)** The passage is about the new suburban neighborhoods that are strictly segregated according to the cost of housing.

26. **Analysis (2)** The writers show what they value when they write "Sadly, the suburban pod system causes people to move not just from house to house but from community to community."

27. **Evaluation (2)** Developers are trying to sell the notion "If you live within these gates, you can consider yourself a success." In other words, they are trying to exploit peoples' desire to feel good about themselves.

28. **Evaluation (3)** The author states that the mistake that was made in the 1960s was envisioning that access to welfare would help people escape poverty. Therefore, the author would advocate a reduction in the welfare rolls.

29. **Analysis (5)** In the cartoon, Truman's head is large in proportion to his body, emphasizing that he is being depicted as a young child. The huge hat makes Truman appear even more childlike.

30. **Analysis (1)** By attacking Truman, the President and civilian Commander-in-Chief, as being a child compared to his leading general, the cartoonist was attacking the principle of civilian control of the military.

31. **Analysis (4)** While rice needs mild temperatures and a great deal of water, the extensive use of irrigation leaves it unclear whether the water comes from heavy rainfall or from extensive irrigation.

32. **Analysis (4)** None of the segments of a snake can survive on its own. In the same way, the individual colonies cannot survive on their own.

33. **Comprehension (1)** The main point of this paragraph is that despite all the damage described, the report had little effect in Arizona.

34. **Evaluation (5)** Since the final sentence states that the survey had little effect in Arizona, it is unlikely that the underlying conditions causing the problem have changed. Therefore, it is most likely that Elroy and the surrounding area have continued to sink.

PRACTICE TEST

35. Analysis (5) There is no evidence in the table indicating whether the single parents had ever been married. All other choices are facts that can be directly proven from the data in the table.

36. Application (3) Following a formula to do long calculations was one of the original reasons computers were built.

37. Analysis (2) The speaker says, "it is our desire to share and celebrate our Asian cultures with fellow Americans. . . . " It is clear from this statement that the speaker is an Asian-Pacific American. The whole speech also makes clear that this person is a leader in her community.

38. Analysis (2) The listing shows a tremendous diversity of achievement that goes far beyond common stereotypes. Therefore, the list showcases this diversity and achievement.

39. Application (3) The whole point of Justice O'Connor's article is that her being a woman should have no bearing on her judicial decisions. It is consistent with this reasoning that she would be opposed to racial profiling, which considers a person suspicious of criminal intent solely on the basis of racial origin.

40. Evaluation (5) Justice O'Connor states "a wise old man and a wise old woman reach the same conclusion." In other words, she would adhere to the law and the facts of the case.

41. Comprehension (3) The total number of people in the bureaucracy was smaller in 1995 than for any other year in the table. It is reasonable to conclude that the years in between not shown also had higher numbers of employees than in 1995.

42. Comprehension (2) Of the years listed on the chart, 1970 has the highest proportion of bureaucrats. Even though 1983 is not listed on the chart, we can confidently predict that its employee-to-population ratio was close to the 12.3 of 1980 and 12.4 of 1985, well below the 14.4 ratio of 1970.

43. Analysis (4) The writer states in the passage that "As American Indian students become aware of catastrophes on their tribal lands, they also realize they have alternatives." This contradicts choice (3), which states that young Native Americans are not concerned about the tribal lands. While choices (1), (2), and (5) may be true, there is no evidence supporting them in the passage.

44. Comprehension (3) The writer makes clear that it is Native American environmentalists who are best able to fix the environmental problems on the reservations.

45. Comprehension (4) The writer states, "the Niagara Falls School Board knew the filled-in canal was a toxic dump site." In other words, the government knew that the area was dangerous.

46. Analysis (1) George Washington was advising the United States to avoid political involvement in other nations. This policy later became known as isolationism.

47. Comprehension (1) Latin America, Africa, and South and Southeast Asia are all part of the developing world. Together they make up the vast majority of the child labor problem.

48. Analysis (4) Today this pose would seem over-dramatic, but at the time it was meant to glorify Napoleon as a heroic figure.

49. Analysis (3) The caption contrasts sharply with the image of the officer coercing his terrified soldiers with a whip.

50. Comprehension (2) The areas on the map under European control, plus the areas that the passage states were once under European control, together comprise almost all the land area of the earth.

Evaluation Chart

Use the answer key on pages 391–393 to check your answers to the Practice Test. Then find the item number of each question you missed and circle it on the chart below to determine the skills in which you need to do the most work. For each question that you missed, review the skill pages indicated.

Skill Area/ Content Area	Comprehension (pages 27–42)	Application (pages 43–58)	Analysis (pages 59–98)	Evaluation (pages 99–115)
U.S. History	10, 20, 45	15, 24	9, 19, 29, 30, 37, 38, 46	1
World History	2, 3, 11, 21, 47, 50	13	4, 5, 16, 22, 31, 48, 49	12, 17
Civics & Government	41, 42	39	32, 43	28, 40
Geography	33, 44		6, 7, 23	8, 34
Economics	25	36	18, 26, 35	14, 27

Answer Key

Chapter 1

Exercise 1, pages 28–29

1. **(4)** The main idea is that there was much abuse of power during the Nixon administration, a point stated at the end of the passage. Choices (1) and (3) are neither stated nor supported by the passage. Choices (2) and (5) are ideas that support the main idea.

2. **(3)** The passage refers to John Dean's testimony, which led to formal charges against former President Nixon. The passage neither states nor implies that Nixon was found innocent (1), or was convicted (2). It is obvious that he was not imprisoned. Because the former president resigned from office to escape impeachment proceedings, choice (5) is incorrect.

Exercise 2, pages 31–32

1. **(5)** The focus of the graph is on population growth, not total population (1), (2). Population controls are not mentioned in the graph (3) and (4). What is striking is that just these five countries accounted for almost half of the world's population growth from 1995 to 2000.

2. **(3)** This graph indicates nothing about the steps a country can take or have taken to impact population growth. Choices (1), (2), (4), and (5) are reasonable conclusions to draw from the graph.

3. **(4)** The graph shows an overall decline in the percentage of voter turnout. It does not show how many people were registered or eligible to vote (2), (3), or seem to correlate with the economic situation. While overall voter turnout has declined, there have been a few increases, so it has not been a steady decline.

4. **(1)** The chart gives no information about population or the numbers of people of voting age. All of the other conclusions can be drawn from the graph.

Exercise 3, pages 35–36

1. **(4)** The passage says, ". . . a primary target is the American citizen." Choices (1), (2), (3), and (5) are not stated in the passage.

2. **(2)** The passage says, "sustain communication among hostages as much as possible." This means communicate as often as possible with other hostages. Choices (1), (3), (4), and (5) are all contradicted in the passage.

3. **(2)** The article says that you should not even appear to be capable of providing valuable information to the terrorists. This could put you in danger.

Exercise 4, page 38

1. Answers may vary slightly, but they should be similar to this: Take Midlothian Road north to Peterson Road. Turn right on Peterson Road and drive east until you reach State Highway 45. Turn left on state Highway 45 and drive north to State Route 120. Turn right on State Route 120 and follow it to Wildwood.

2. Answers may vary, but examples of correct restatements could include
   • The cost of a single military item can benefit a large number of people in social programs.
   • Military programs are extremely expensive.
   • Compared to military costs, social programs are inexpensive.

Exercise 5, page 40

1. **(5)** If the middle-income group spends 2 out of every 10 dollars on wants and the upper-income group spends 6 out of every 10 dollars on wants, then the implication is that as one's income goes up, one has more money to spend on wants.

2. **(1)** When the author says, "At best, they have just enough food and shelter to stay alive," he is implying that the poor cannot even provide for their basic needs.

3. **(4)** The upper-income group can most afford to spend money on excess wants (superfluities) and not just on needs.

Exercise 6, page 42

1. **(1)** The graph indicates the increasing gap over time between the tax burden of corporations and individuals. (2) is incorrect since in 1960 corporations were paying over 20% of taxes, while in 1998 they were paying only 10%. (3) is a matter of opinion, and there is no evidence to support (4) and (5).

2. **(4)** There is no information within the graph to support (1), (2), or (5). While (3) is a correct interpretation of the graph, it does not offer a conclusion. (4) is the only choice that considers the implications of the graph on the basis of what is presented.

Chapter 2

Exercise 1, page 44

1. **YES** Busing children would quickly desegregate schools.

2. **NO** African American history courses do not address the problem of separate and unequal facilities.

3. **NO** The United Negro College Fund program provides funding for colleges where the vast majority of students are black.

4. **YES** Making diversity a criterion for admission would help desegregate the universities and colleges.

5. **YES** "Magnet" schools, open to students from all racial backgrounds, can attract students from all parts of the community.

Exercise 2, page 45

1. **No** An anonymous tip is not strong enough evidence to meet the probable cause requirement.

2. **N/A** Looking for a paper clip is not an unreasonable search, and the amendment does not apply to such personal situations. The searches and seizures that the amendment refers to and limits would be conducted by officials of the state.

3. **Yes** The detectives found probable cause before asking for a warrant.

4. **No** Being pulled over for a random test that includes a search of a car would be considered an unreasonable search and seizure.

Exercise 3, pages 46–48

1. **(4)** This is the only choice that involves a violation of the Sherman Anti-Trust Act—price fixing.

2. **(1)** Choice (1) is a government-sanctioned monopoly, whereas the other choices involve price-fixing, eliminating competition, and underproduction of goods.

3. **(3)** The situation with French and English in Canada is similar to the situation with Spanish and English in the United States.

4. **(5)** Europe is an example of a successful, modern region where it is expected that people can speak more than one language. It supports the author's point that Americans should accept the speaking of Spanish.

5. **(3)** This is the only choice based on physical features as described in the passage.

Exercise 4, pages 49–50

1. **(2)** The propaganda technique used is glittering generalities, since the manufacturer speaks in general and vague terms. The statement does not say what is revolutionary and new about the product or what "like magic" really means.

2. **(4)** The propaganda technique used is bandwagoning. The announcer advises the residents to subscribe to the paper because practically everyone else does it.

3. **(3)** The propaganda technique used is transferring. The candidate expected the influence of the leader of the fundamentalist Christians to "rub off" and favorably affect the voters.

4. **(1)** The term "tax-and-spend liberal" is an example of the propaganda technique known as name calling.

Exercise 5, page 52

1. **(4)** Of all the choices, this is the only one that gives a greater benefit to the bottom 90% of the population than it gives to the top 1%.
2. **(2)** A union negotiator fighting for a wage increase for a large group of workers would most likely want to point out that the distribution of wealth in the United States is getting more unequal.

Exercise 6, pages 54–55

1. **(2)** The Great Depression was a period of economic collapse and widespread poverty, most similar to the economic situation in Russia after the fall of Communism.
2. **(2)** By calling the recovery of the gray wolf good news, it is clear that the article assumes the reader knows wolves can be beneficial to their environment.
3. **(1)** Their great success in eliminating the wolf and other large predators shows that the people who wanted to protect livestock a century ago knew how to kill large animals.

Exercise 7, pages 57–58

1. **(2)** In the story of Cinderella, the fairy godmother changes Cinderella's rags into a beautiful evening gown.
2. **(5)** Instead of a beautiful evening gown, our modern Cinderella has a business suit, cell phone, and attaché case.
3. **(5)** Mitsubishi is a Japanese company.
4. **(2)** Since the giant companies' sales are so much larger than the GNP of the smaller countries, those countries are at a disadvantage when dealing with the companies.

Chapter 3

Exercise 1, pages 61–62

1. **(2)** According to the passage, the main source of stress for controllers is poor labor-management relations. Choice (2) is the only one that involves labor-management relations.

2. **(1)** This is the only choice given that can be proved with data. The other choices either are not true or are opinions.
3. **(3)** This answer is based on the quote "Controllers who were interviewed complained that their recommendations for providing safety backups and other measures were not being considered by their employers or the Federal Aviation Administration."
4. **(5)** According to the passage, the more conscientious, or careful, workers were most prone to experience stress.

Exercise 2, pages 63–64

1. **(2)** The house for sale is located on the moon, or out of reach.
2. **(3)** The man in the cartoon is holding a sign that says that new house costs have doubled in 10 years. A doubling in cost is a rise of 100 percent. Ten years is a decade.

Exercise 3, page 64

1. **(1)** The graph shows a strong financial commitment to the Allied Powers getting stronger each year, while the level of imports to the Central Powers drops to a much lower amount.

Exercise 4, page 66

1. **(2)** Since borrowers must choose between higher fixed-interest rates and rates that can fluctuate (go up or down), the conclusion is that the mortgage system has become much more complex.
2. **(2)** Parents have the ultimate responsibility for the proper development of their children (since parental neglect is punishable by the state).

Exercise 5, pages 67–69

1. **(3)** By requiring businesses to give a year's notice before plant closings or layoffs, several community groups have given some employees a chance to plan their futures.
2. **(4)** The company in (4) has been given tax incentives to remain in Vacaville, and yet it is moving out of the area. The other choices do not involve employers subject to the agreement.

3. **(1)** Because the 1920s, like the 1980s, saw a large rise in wealth concentration, they must have been boom years for the rich.

4. **(1)** Since the net worth of the top 1 percent of American households rose from 31 percent in 1983 to 37 percent in 1989, you can infer that the gap widened between the super-rich and the rest of American households.

5. **(5)** Choices (1)–(4) are all facts that support the conclusion that African Americans have largely reshaped and redefined what U.S. life and society are about.

Exercise 6, page 70

(a) X There is nothing in the graph that indicates the nationalities of the immigrants.

(b) F The bar for 1921–30 goes slightly above the 4 million line.

(c) C The two bars for 1931–40 and 1941–50 are the two smallest bars on the graph.

(d) F The bar for 1901–10 is slightly below the 9 million line.

(e) X There is no indication on the graph of what caused changes in immigration.

(f) X The graph alone does not give enough information to give a dependable prediction of the future.

(g) C The bar for 1901–10 is the longest on the entire graph. Therefore, immigration was highest during that period.

(h) C The bar for 1981–90 is longer than any other on the graph except 1901–10, which means that the decade had the highest immigration since the first decade of the twentieth century.

Exercise 7, pages 72–73

1. **(3)** Nixon is completely entangled in the tape, just like an insect would be caught in a spider's web.

2. **(1)** The cartoonist's point is that Nixon had been caught in a lie because of the tapes, and that he had no way to escape.

3. **(5)** The image is one of total devastation.

Exercise 8, pages 74–75

Exact words may vary.

1. The writer assumes that socialism is harmful for developing countries and that capitalism is better.

2. The writer assumes that, before westernization, China was a dreary place to live.

3. The writer assumes that there is usually trouble at a rock concert, but there wouldn't be at a Christian event.

4. The writer assumes that the growth of Las Vegas was due to the actions of government leaders.

5. The writer assumes that without American pressure, the Soviet Union would not have collapsed.

Exercise 9. pages 75–76

1. **(4)** The governor says that private corporations would be good at running prisons because they are running hospitals effectively. The assumption is that privately run prisons would require management skills similar to those needed by privately run hospitals.

2. **(2)** "Doing well" means making a profit. "Doing good" means doing good works for society.

3. **(3)** Alexander believed that if prisons were run like businesses, they would be more efficient and cost-effective.

4. **(5)** Making a profit is one of its chief goals. The other choices are contradicted in the passage.

Exercise 10, pages 78–79

1. **(5)** The cartoonist is assuming that his readers are familiar with the cartoon characters Alfred E. Neuman and Elmer Fudd.

2. **(3)** The foolish appearance of the President indicates that the cartoonist thinks that what he is saying makes no sense.

3. **(4)** The cartoonist is assuming that just as Elmer Fudd cannot be trusted to suddenly stop hunting Bugs Bunny, Senator Ashcroft cannot be trusted to protect those he formerly opposed.

Exercise 11, pages 80–81

1. **(4)** Farmworkers are being exposed to dangerous pesticides as a result of Brazil's importing of dangerous pesticides, not as a result of factory discharges.
2. **(3)** Longer life expectancy would be likely, since the article implies that one of the effects of the pollution is excess mortality.
3. **(2)** Given the information in this passage, Brazil would most likely support miners who have illegally moved onto Indian land. The passage states that Brazilians have an indifference to risk, especially as it might affect people on the lower end of the social scale. Mining is risky for the environment, and Indians are on the lower end of the social scale in present-day Brazil.

Exercise 12, pages 83–84

1. **(4)** The author clearly considers these actions to be harmful, so it is reasonable to expect that they would have a negative impact on the poor.
2. **(2)** While the Civil Rights era was marked by great sacrifice, it was dominated by a dignity and sense of purpose, as well as activism on the part of many African Americans, that was the opposite of victimization.

Exercise 13, pages 86–88

1. **(2)** Malcolm X is trying to encourage blacks to gain control of their own communities.
2. **(3)** Angela Davis is calling for a redistribution of wealth in America and the transformation of the economy from capitalist to Communist.
3. **(5)** The National Alliance is an organized hate group that justifies any action on the basis of its being helpful to whites.
4. **(1)** Martin Luther King's "I Have a Dream" speech is an eloquent appeal for integration and equality.

Exercise 14, pages 90–91

1. **(4)** While today it might seem ridiculous that the different native peoples of the Americas were all called Indians, it might not have seemed so ridiculous 500 years ago when knowledge of the Americas was fragmentary.

2. **(1)** The understanding of the Indian perspective, as well as the acknowledgement of the importance of women and people of non-English descent in the frontier story all point to this article being quite recent. The reference to the next century means that this piece was most likely written at the end of the twentieth century.
3. **(2)** The author still appears to believe that the settlers showed great courage in standing alone against authority. He understands that the whole picture was more complex than that, but that aspect is still unchanged.

Exercise 15, pages 93–94

1. **(4)** If the men want to store nuclear waste in a citizen's garage, it can be inferred that nuclear waste disposal is "getting much too close for comfort."
2. **(3)** Because of the men's protective garb, you can infer that nuclear waste is dangerous to handle.
3. **(4)** The humor of the cartoon is based on the absurd idea that just dumping it in someone's garage could solve the complex problem of nuclear waste disposal.
4. **(3)** According to the passage, only Islam makes an explicit insistence on racial equality. It can be argued that the concept of monotheism has to lead to such a conclusion, but Islam is the only one of the three religions that addresses the issue directly in a single statement.

Exercise 16, pages 97–98

1. **(3)** Overhead includes the costs of doing business—such as rent, insurance, and electricity—that are not part of the actual product sold to the customer, but add to its cost.
2. **(4)** The bar for 1901–1910 shows that the immigration rate was much higher at the beginning of the century. However, since the population of the United States grew so much in the 20th century, we cannot conclude that the actual total number of immigrants was higher at the beginning of the century.

Chapter 4

Exercise 1, page 100

1. No, 5. In this case, there can be no legal contract because illegal activity has taken place.
2. Yes, in this case there is a legal contract. The attorney is a representative of the apartment's owner and accepts the deposit of the two friends who want to lease the apartment. Once all parties have signed the lease, the friends can begin to live there.
3. No, 2. The buyer seems to have made a clear offer, but the seller has not accepted; therefore, no settlement can be made.
4. Yes, the agreement is in writing and the valuable exchanged in the arrangement will be labor for room and board.

Exercise 2, page 101

1. **(3)** Montagu's race has no bearing on the believability of the hypothesis.
2. **(3)** How long Montagu has had the theory adds nothing to its believability.
3. **(2)** The fact that the term *race* is still widely used and accepted tends to dispute Montagu's theory.
4. **(2)** There appear to be valid reasons for classification by race based on physical features.
5. **(1)** Montagu has strong credentials in the anthropological field, which adds validity to his theory.
6. **(1)** Other noted professionals support Montagu's theory, which adds to its believability.

Exercise 3, pages 102–103

1. You should have written *patriotism* or *responsibility to his country*, since he chose to serve his country over getting married and settling down.
2. You should have written something like *principles* over his *career*, since he refused the project despite its prestige.

Exercise 4, pages 103–104

1. **(5)** The value of concern for lives and property after the sinking of the battleship Maine was the deciding factor in the United States' decision to enter the war.

2. **(3)** The passage states that the United States had become a world power. None of the other choices are stated directly or implied in the passage.
3. **(3)** The viewpoint that the United States is an imperialist nation would be held by someone who believed that the invasion of Grenada was an act of aggression.
4. **(4)** The fact that the United States had an isolationist policy did not contribute to the start of the Spanish-American War. All the other choices cite factors that did play a role.

Exercise 5, page 106

1. **(3)** The statement to the effect that the ERA was not given enough time is the conclusion made, but there are no facts to support that conclusion.
2. **(1)** The last sentence of the passage says that a majority of American citizens supported the ERA. Since feminist organizations supported the amendment heavily, and since the government failed to pass the ERA, we can infer that organizations working for the ERA have more popular than governmental support.

Exercise 6, page 108

1. adequate
2. adequate
3. inadequate; a weather map would show this better.
4. adequate
5. inadequate; a population and world map would show this better.
6. inadequate; a political map would show this better.

Exercise 7, pages 109–110

1. **(4)** The illustration indicates nothing about how the sources are determined.
2. **(2)** The illustration either refutes or provides no evidence for the other options.

Exercise 8, page 113

1. b
2. d
3. a
4. c

Exercise 9, page 115

1. **(1)** There is no logical connection made by the writer between laws restricting the freedom of blacks and the bias shown against them by European immigrants.

2. **(3)** There is no logical reason to believe that if these laws did not exist, there would not be racial bias.

Chapter 5

Exercise 1, pages 120–121

1. **Analysis (1)** The Byzantine Empire no longer exists. Spain and Portugal did not exist in 1000. France and Hungary are the only two nations that have existed the entire 1000 years. Of the two, France has had more stable boundaries.

2. **Comprehension (5)** Almost all of the Bulgarians' entire current nation was not part of the area under Bulgar control in 1000. Spain did not exist as a nation in the first two maps. The Anglo-Saxon kingdoms were the predecessors of England and occupied its current location. While the French and Hungarians have modified their borders, most of their current territory has been under their control for the 1,000 years covered in the maps.

3. **Analysis (3)** The decline of monarchies has had the greatest impact on the names of nations. Prior to the rise of democracy in Europe, most states were kingdoms or empires. Now only a few states in Europe are still officially called kingdoms.

Exercise 2, pages 123–125

1. **Analysis (2)** The diversion of water for agricultural irrigation was the main cause for the crisis at the Aral Sea. The incompetence of officials could be seen as contributing to the decisions to divert the water, but the diversion itself is the main cause of the catastrophe. The collapse of commercial fishing and desertification of the river deltas are effects, not causes, of the catastrophe at the Aral Sea. There is no mention in the article of changes in the amount of rainfall.

2. **Application (4)** The degradation of the Gulf of California due to lack of fresh water flow would be the problem that most closely parallels the problem at the Aral Sea.

3. **Comprehension (1)** The passage explains the cause, the irrigation project, and the effects of the disaster at the Aral Sea.

4. **Evaluation (1)** Given the writer's clear love and appreciation for the tallgrass prairie, it is most likely that he would support the establishment of a tallgrass prairie national park.

5. **Analysis (4)** Increased soil erosion was an effect, not a cause, of the destruction of the tallgrass prairie.

Exercise 3, pages 126–127

1. **Evaluation (3)** Barbarians such as the Manchus were assimilated into Chinese culture and thus were not a catalyst for change. Because power became centralized during Communism, there was a change in power structure. Because Buddhism was an exception to outside influences, it had an effect on Chinese culture. The last paragraph states that although power is centralized, the provinces continue to be important. The only statement that cannot be concluded from the passage is that Chinese painting changed little until the mid-19th century.

2. **Application (2)** A Chinese sheng, or province, is most similar to a state of the United States. It forms the next level of government below the national government. The Chinese provinces are "centres of political and economic authority and …the focus of regional identification and loyalty." The same could be said of American states.

Exercise 4, pages 128–130

1. **Comprehension (2)** In the earliest year, 900, all the largest cities were located in Asia. While Egypt in Africa was the site of some of the world's earliest cities, that information is not given by these charts.

2. **Comprehension (2)** All of the five largest cities in 1900 were either in North America or Europe, the continents whose countries surround the North Atlantic. To become the largest in 1900, they must have been growing in the nineteenth century.

3. **Evaluation (3)** Since at different times, different cities in China were among the world's largest, the centers of power and commerce could not have remained constant.

4. **Application (4)** According to the information on the chart, the first major evidence of the impact of the Industrial Revolution appears during the 19th century, since at the end of that century, the largest cities had grown to unprecedented size.

5. **Evaluation (5)** Before the Industrial Revolution, travel was far more difficult. As a result, tourism would have had a minor impact on the growth of cities. All the other reasons given had a major impact on the growth of pre-industrial cities.

6. **Analysis (3)** The rate of industrialization can be measured by the slope of the graph lines. Where the line has the highest slope, or moves upward most rapidly, the growth is fastest. Japan was the country that had the most rapid period of industrialization, that period being during the middle of the twentieth century.

7. **Analysis (4)** While (1), (2), and (3) might have some positive impact on economic prosperity, which could lead to increased urbanization, the best answer is (4) since people need jobs in order to move from rural areas to the cities. Rasing tariffs (5) could invite retaliation and not result in much net gain for the society.

Exercise 5, pages 133–135

1. **Comprehension (4)** According to the passage, power plant emissions are the single greatest source of SO_2 and NO_x emissions. Choice (4) is the only strategy that would directly try to reduce the number of power plants.

2. **Analysis (2)** The fact that sunlight increases the rate of the acidic reactions is not an argument to reduce SO_2 and NO_x emissions. All the other choices give direct examples of the damage caused by acid rain.

3. **Analysis (4)** The other four statements all support the recommendations for protecting wetlands.

4. **Analysis (1)** Since the U.S. Environmental Protection Agency has done this analysis of wetlands and made the recommendations, it is reasonable to assume that the government is responsible for environmental protection, even though it is never directly stated in the passage.

Exercise 6, pages 136–139

1. **Comprehension (2)** The passage states that the purpose of the First Continental Congress was to demand the colonists' rights as British citizens.

2. **Comprehension (2)** The passage states that "by the time of the Second Continental Congress in May 1775, hostile encounters had already taken place between the English soldiers and the colonists."

3. **Application (2)** The struggle of India for its independence from Great Britain is the only event that can be compared to the American colonists' fight against Great Britain since both ultimately won freedom and established democracies. The other choices are not examples of anticolonial wars.

4. **Comprehension (3)** After the French and Indian War ended in 1763, Great Britain needed to pay its huge war debt. It passed the Stamp Act of 1765 and the Townshend Acts of 1767 to help pay for the war.

5. **Analysis (2)** The maps show more dots in the North than in the South. Moreover, the larger population centers are shown to be in the North. Since industry was related directly to population growth, you can infer that there was more industry in the northern states than in the southern states during the period 1870–1900.

6. **Comprehension (4)** From the maps it appears that industries and the cities that grew up around them were usually established near bodies of water such as the Atlantic Ocean, the Great Lakes, and the Mississippi River.

7. **Evaluation (1)** Even though the Continental Congress first tried to settle its differences with Great Britain nonviolently, the American Revolution created a change in government through a violent war. In contrast, there is no evidence in the passage or the maps of the Industrial Revolution creating change through violence.

Exercise 7, pages 142–144

1. **Analysis (4)** At the time the posters were printed, patriotic enthusiasm for World War II was high, as was the popularity of Norman Rockwell. Rockwell's art was able to capture the essence of Roosevelt's message by showing serious common people apparently engaged in prayer. It would be engaging in present-mindedness to think that the potential resale value of the posters was a major issue. Collectibles of all types have become much more popular and valuable in recent years.

2. **Evaluation (3)** With their persecution of the Jews, the Nazis clearly were a threat to the freedom of worship. While the Bill of Rights guaranteed the separation of church and state, it also guaranteed the right of all citizens to follow the religion of their choice. It was appropriate for the United States government to protect that right.

3. **Analysis (2)** While the role of women in preindustrial America was an important precursor to the Women's Rights movement, it was not as important as the pulling of women into important economic roles outside the home as a result of the Industrial Revolution. Choices (3) and (5) also played a role in the development of the Women's Rights movement, but they are not nearly as important as choice (2). Choice (4) was a negative development that tended to hamper women.

4. **Evaluation (5)** The assertion that women's clothing such as corsets and petticoats emphasized female separation from the world of activity is best supported by the example of the development of bloomers.

Exercise 8, pages 146–148

1. **Comprehension (1)** Since it is listed with Taxes, Duties, and Excises, the most likely meaning of impost is a tax.

2. **Evaluation (4)** While Letters of Marque are an anachronism, they do not pose a problem or a threat. Therefore, it is unreasonable to go through the long, difficult, and costly amendment process just to remove something that is out of date and never used.

3. **Analysis (3)** The Constitution was written in 1787. The first airplane flight was in 1903, more than 100 years later.

4. **Application (1)** Since the Internet deals with interstate and international commerce, paragraph 3 would apply even though the Internet did not exist in 1787.

5. **Application (4)** The human rights abuses of Serbia could have been considered Offenses against the Law of Nations.

Exercise 9, pages 149–152

1. **Application (2)** Catton said that "we move to make a living reality out of the great ideal of equality of all Americans. . . ." Based on that, you could assume that Bruce Catton would most likely support the actions of the civil rights workers of the sixties, who were working for equality for African Americans.

2. **Evaluation (2)** Bruce Catton repeatedly points out that the Civil War obligates Americans to promote freedom at home and abroad.

3. **Comprehension (2)** The main idea of the passage is that African Americans adapted their heritage to the constraints of slavery.

4. **Comprehension (2)** Africans who were captured as slaves were constrained by their new circumstances that included the racial structure of enslavement as well as the American class structure and the prevailing economic conditions. Their pre-existing roles did not constrain them.

5. **Analysis (2)** While all the other differences are true, the most striking and important difference is that the Irish immigrants in steerage are traveling to survive, while the passengers of the Flying Clipper are going on a pleasure-filled vacation.

6. **Analysis (4)** The following facts about the Clipper are true: travelers did have to cope with long flights, Clippers were the largest commercial planes at the time, and the Clipper was the largest flying boat ever built. However, the only thing one can assume from the poster an the information given is that the Clipper could carry passengers as well as mail to exotic places. One cannot assume from the poster that Hawaiians could not afford to travel.

Chapter Review, pages 153–156

1. **Analysis (1)** The map shows Virginia favoring secession, while West Virginia opposed it. Before this vote, Virginia had been one state, but it split in two over the issue of secession, with the western part loyal to the Union becoming the new state of West Virginia.
2. **Comprehension (2)** Texas seceded from the Union despite the fact that only its eastern part voted to do so.
3. **Analysis (3)** Of the states listed, only Missouri was a slave state that was not part of the Confederate states.
4. **Evaluation (1)** The facts in the passage all support the conclusion that Lieberman being Jewish had no negative impact on Al Gore's candidacy. This conclusion supports the findings in the poll.
5. **Analysis (1)** The best modification of the hypothesis would be that air conditioning made modern industrial and commercial life possible. This would still leave room for the existence of the preindustrial tropical cities of the ancient world, while maintaining the heart of the writer's argument.
6. **Application (1)** Applying the theory of the importance of air conditioning in the development of hot regions, a reasonable conjecture would be that the South and West, the hottest regions of the United States, might still be underdeveloped.
7. **Evaluation (5)** Looking for Taino artifacts or comparing their customs to the modern Caribbeans would not prove that they still exist today. The passage states that historical records from the 16th century show the Taino as extinct; therefore, they would not be helpful. Visiting villages in Puerto Rico and Cuba may not give any specific information either. Studying and comparing the characteristics and traditions of those claiming to be Taino would be most helpful in proving their existence.
8. **Application (2)** Given the surprising survival of the Taino claimed in this passage, it would be reasonable to search for the survivors of other ancient ethnic groups. If the descendants of the Taino survived, other ancient ethnic groups might have present-day survivors as well.

Chapter 6

Exercise 1, pages 160–161

1. **Application (2)** Sardes is located exactly in the center of Herodotus's world.
2. **Comprehension (4)** Herodotus mapped where he had been.
3. **Application (3)** A compass is an instrument used to help navigate by showing in which direction one is traveling.
4. **Comprehension (1)** The continent south of the Mediterranean Sea is called Africa today.

Exercise 2, pages 164–165

1. **Analysis (1)** The author makes a case for regional boundaries that consider characteristics other than traditional state lines.
2. **Application (4)** By looking at the map and reading the names of the regions, the only element that has no bearing on a region's identity is its connection to the federal government in Washington.
3. **Comprehension (5)** Because of the differences in climate, topography, industry and culture, one can assume that elements of life are different in every region.

Exercise 3, page 168

1. **Comprehension (3)** The main point of the passage is that humans contribute to the spread of deserts.
2. **Analysis (5)** This passage is clearly written from the point of view of someone who is concerned about environments.
3. **Analysis (1)** Everything but oil would be affected negatively by desertification.

Exercise 4, page 170

1. **Application (II)** The Inuit
2. **Application (II)** The Inuit
3. **Application (I)** The BaMbuti
4. **Application (III)** both the BaMbuti and the Inuit
5. **Application (IV)** Neither the BaMbuti nor the Inuit. The BaMbuti are hunters and gatherers. Even though they get enough food, there is no indication that they don't have to travel distances to get it.

Exercise 5, page 173

1. **Analysis (4)** Only the person walking doesn't offer much evidence of the history of the city.
2. **Evaluation (5)** The photograph reflects centuries of change within a single place.

Exercise 6, pages 175–176

1. **Comprehension (3)** The photographs are one form of tangible proof that Auschwitz-Birkenau was a horrific place.
2. **Analysis (1)** All that can be said for sure is that, fortunately, there were survivors and witnesses. Most unfortunate is that concentration camps were indeed replicated in the last half of the 20th century in such places as Cambodia and Bosnia.
3. **Evaluation (5)** The deportees were the victims of the camp. Everyone else bore some responsibility.

Chapter Review, pages 177–181

1. **Evaluation (2)** Since Europe was not one of the major areas in which food production originated, the map does not support the conclusion that civilization first developed in Northern Europe.
2. **Comprehension (5)** There is evidence in the graph to support only a description of population shifts amid a drought.
3. **Evaluation (4)** If there wasn't concern over the survival of the turtles, then a sign wouldn't be needed.
4. **Comprehension (5)** The tone of the paragraph clearly indicates that the author is in sympathy with poor communities and is outraged on their behalf. She is likely, then, to be an advocate for them. There is no evidence to support choices (1)–(3), and the tone is at odds with choice (4).
5. **Evaluation (2)** Low income people and the communities in which they live are often ignored or "dumped on" because it is assumed that they lack the skills and/or interest to be aware and speak up on their own behalf.
6. **Analysis (2)** The passage emphasizes the issue of starvation. There is not enough information in the passage to support the other statements.
7. **Analysis (4)** No evidence was provided that rents were increased during the famine.
8. **Comprehension (5)** The cartoon depicts a concern that there are not enough resources.

Chapter 7

Exercise 1 (all application), page 184

1. oligarchy
2. monarchy
3. dictatorship
4. democracy

Exercise 2, pages 187–188

1. **Comprehension (4)** As shown on the chart, the "Great Compromise" involved the creation of a two-house federal legislature to allow for fairness in representation.
2. **Comprehension (1)** Counting only three-fifths of the slave population penalized the southern states because it meant that they would have fewer representatives in the House of Representatives.
3. **Comprehension (3)** The Bill of Rights was an important addition to the Constitution because it guaranteed rights to the citizens.
4. **Comprehension(3)** Given the complexity of the issues involved and the diversity of views represented, it is clear that the convention called for a great deal of creative problem solving.

Exercise 3 (all application), page 190

1. (e)
2. (a)
3. (c)
4. (f)
5. (d)

Exercise 4, pages 191–192

1. **Comprehension (1)** The issue was one that concerned Fifth Amendment rights.
2. **Application (5)** Prison guards are the only ones not involved in the arrest and trial of a criminal suspect.
3. **Evaluation (2)** The Supreme Court hears cases that have broad implications. Miranda's innocence was not the issue. Other courts had heard the case, and it is the Supreme Court's responsibility to interpret the Constitution, not to cast judgement on it or change it.

Exercise 5 (all comprehension), page 193

2. legislative, executive
3. legislative, executive
4. legislative, executive
5. judicial, legislative
6. executive, legislative

Exercise 6, page 195

1. **Application (4)** The Fifth Amendment includes the "right to remain silent," one of the rights read to an accused. The Sixth Amendment gives the accused the right to call a lawyer.
2. **Application (3** The First Amendment guarantees the freedoms of speech and assembly.
3. **Application (1)** The terms "cruel and unusual punishment" can be interpreted in several ways.
4. **Application (4)** All criminal suspects are guaranteed the right to a fair trial with an impartial, or unopinionated, jury.

Exercise 7, page 198

1. **Analysis (1)** The cartoon makes it clear that there are still serious issues concerning civil rights, but they have more to do today with economic class and clout than skin color.
2. **Evaluation (3)** The cartoon is the only evidence we have about the artist. To assume anything else about him or her would require speculation beyond the evidence.

Exercise 8, pages 200–201

1. **Comprehension (2)** The graph reveals that for at least forty years low voter turnout has been a constant issue.

2. **Evaluation (1)** Voter outreach programs and bilingual ballots would be likely to encourage voter participation.

Exercise 9, pages 202–203

1. **Comprehension (2)** Speaker B's main point is that if people can only stay in office for a short period of time, there will be no experienced legislators to handle the complex work of the Congress.
2. **Evaluation (1)** The bottom line for both speakers is that strong, respectable people should serve in government.

3. **Application (4)** This example would emphasize Speaker A's point about the "rotten" aspect of career politicians.

Exercise 10, page 205

1. **Analysis (3)** Only an opportunity to hear the real concerns of voters would be valuable, given the ways in which television "packages" candidates and strays from the issues of greatest interest.

Exercise 11, pages 207–208

1. **Application (1)** The man is over 65 and earned less than $8,300.
2. **Comprehension (3)** The form states, "Do not include Social Security benefits unless you are married . . ."

Exercise 12 (all application), page 209

1. A & II
2. B & I
3. A & I
4. B & II

Chapter Review, pages 211–215

1. **Analysis (3)** Calling a document "powerful" is expressing an opinion. All of the other statements are facts.
2. **Evaluation (2)** From the excerpt, it is evident that Jefferson was concerned about people's rights.
3. **Comprehension (5)** The paragraph describes the rights and freedoms people should be entitled to.
4. **Application (5)** Because the speaker advocates a return to an earlier policy (arming oneself as in the Old West), the speaker may be considered reactionary.
5. **Application (2)** Because the speaker advocates social improvement through government action, the speaker may be considered a liberal.
6. **Application (4)** Because the speaker advocates maintaining the existing order (the law should remain the way it is), the speaker may be considered conservative.
7. **Application (3)** Because the speaker believes in avoiding extreme changes based on the belief that current laws on the books need only to be enforced, the speaker may be considered moderate.

8. **Application (1)** Because the speaker advocates stopping the manufacture of guns immediately, the speaker may be considered a radical.

9. **Application (2)** The Southern African example meets the criteria that Rehnquist mentions: a written constitution and independence from other authorities.

10. **Application (3)** Because justices are appointed for life, they are able to maintain political detachment.

11. **Comprehension (1)** The chart indicates that third parties don't generally receive a significant percentage of the vote.

12. **Analysis (4)** Based on her background and the historical period of which she was a part, Ms. Blackwell must have suffered the prejudice of others.

Chapter 8

Exercise 1, page 218

1. **Application (e)** Green Thumb is a producer because it makes a product.

2. **Application (c)** Trucks are one method of distribution.

3. **Application (a)** Consumers purchase goods and services.

4. **Application (b)** The plants are the product, or goods, that Green Thumb sells.

5. **Application (d)** The salespeople provide services, such as assistance with a purchase and instruction on how to grow and care for plants.

Exercise 2, pages 219–220

1. **Application (4)** The Egyptian pharaoh technically owned everything and controlled all economic activity. These are elements of a command economy.

2. **Application (1)** Great Britain is considered to have had the world's first capitalist economy. The means of production was privately owned, and the economy was based on free markets.

3. **Application (5)** The economy of the self-sufficient Mohegan villages was a part of village life, and could not be separated from it. It would be considered a primitive economy.

4. **Application (2)** Even though much of the economy is in private hands, the Swedish government exercises considerable control over property and the distribution of income. The Swedish economy is an example of socialism.

Exercise 3, pages 221–222

1. **Analysis (1)** While one of the keys to Europe's economic growth was its fragmented political authority, in the United States, the strong central government from the beginning protected individual rights and promoted economic development.

2. **Comprehension (4)** The top priority of the rulers of China was to maintain control. One of the by-products of this control was the stifling of innovation, which could be seen as threatening the established order.

3. **Application (3)** Since the passage claims that the foundation of the modern economy was the political fragmentation in Europe, it is a reasonable conclusion that without that fragmentation, the modern economy might never have developed in Europe at all.

Exercise 4, pages 223–224

1. **Comprehension (3)** The first glass is worth 2 dollars and the fourth glass is worth 0.5 dollars. Therefore the fourth glass is worth 1.5 dollars less.

2. **Comprehension (5)** Each glass is worth less than the previous one. The fourth glass is worth 0.5 dollars, and 0.3 dollars is the only one of the choices less than 0.5 dollar.

Exercise 5, pages 226–227

1. **Evaluation (4)** Answers **(1)** and **(2)** do not correspond with what the graph shows. **(3)** and **(5)** may be true statements, but this is not the information given in the graph. According to the graph, the number of men in the labor force has decreased while the number of women working has increased; however, in both cases, the percent has leveled off.

2. **Comprehension (1)** The graph clearly shows that the percent of women in the labor force has been steadily increasing for half a century. The graph does not give an explanation of why this might be happening or whether or not the trend will continue.

3. **Analysis (2)** After reaching a peak in 1980, average hourly earnings either held steady or declined for the next 15 years when corrected for inflation.

Exercise 6, pages 228–230

1. **Application (4)** Since the period of unemployment is during the cold weather of winter, it is seasonal unemployment.
2. **Application (2)** The introduction of the computer has caused a fundamental, permanent change in many businesses, causing structural unemployment.
3. **Application (1)** The unemployment rate for construction workers is related to the overall health of the economy, and therefore, can be considered cyclical unemployment.
4. **Comprehension (2)** The highest point on the graph is the year with the greatest growth rate. That high point was in 1882.
5. **Evaluation (3)** All three wars occurred during periods of economic growth. The data seems to indicate that the wars helped cause that growth.
6. **Analysis (3)** By plotting the unemployment rate and the GDP growth rate on one graph, the author was able to clearly show that they had a roughly inverse relationship.

Exercise 7, pages 231–234

1. **Evaluation (5)** Based on Plunkitt's definition of "honest graft" and "dishonest graft," you should have arrived at the judgment that political bosses appeared to have no sense of right and wrong.
2. **Comprehension (4)** According to the information in the passage, another name for "honest graft" as described by Plunkitt might be profiting from inside information on government purchases.
3. **Comprehension (4)** Plunkitt describes blackmailing gamblers, saloonkeepers, and disorderly people as practicing dishonest graft. Extorting money to ignore illegal activity is blackmail.
4. **Comprehension (4)** The rich businesses filling the back row were the true bosses of the Senate.
5. **Comprehension (2)** The Mail Trust is entering under the sign "Entrance for Monopolists." Therefore, it is reasonable to conclude that a trust is a monopoly.

6. **Application (5)** When people purchase products, they usually pay a sales tax. The other choices do not involve the retail sale of ordinary goods.
7. **Application (4)** The money paid out is based on the ownership of real estate, so the tax is a property tax. The other choices do not involve the continued ownership of real estate.
8. **Application (3)** Because Raul Rodriguez made a profit on the sale of real estate, the money paid out was a capital gains tax. The other choices do not involve the sale of real estate.
9. **Application (2)** Because Mr. Reed had been paying a Social Security tax on his earnings, he was entitled to payments from this fund after retirement. None of the other taxes result in benefit payments.

Exercise 8, pages 236–238

1. **Evaluation (1)** The IDA is supposed to give the most to the poorest countries, as long as they have a track record of success. Since 47% of new commitments went to Sub-Saharan Africa, 20% more than to any other region, there is sufficient evidence to conclude that Sub-Saharan Africa is the poorest region in the world.
2. **Evaluation (4)** It would be very unlikely for the web site to highlight the failures of the IDA, since an official web site usually would emphasize the positive.
3. **Comprehension (2)** The mission statement given in the second sentence gives the main idea of the entire passage, which is that the IDA supports programs to reduce poverty and improve the quality of life in its poorest member countries. The other choices are details that support this main idea.

Exercise 9, pages 240–241

1. **Evaluation (1)** The cartoon exaggerates and satirizes just how far some people might go to get a tax deduction.
2. **Comprehension (2)** The debit card can draw only on available funds, which suggests that the user cannot run up a debt with the card. There is no support for the other choices.
3. **Application (1)** The government would be able to spend only the money it actually had, thus limiting spending. Neither spending nor debt would be increased. A national "debit card" might keep the debt in check, but it wouldn't necessarily save enough to make the debt go away or reduce the government's responsibility.

Exercise 10, pages 242–244

1. **Evaluation (3)** These examples show such an extreme unequal distribution of wealth that it is reasonable to conclude that too much wealth is concentrated in the hands of too few people. There is no support in the passage for the other choices.

2. **Analysis (3)** Since the graph shows a substantial decline in the relative wealth of the bottom 40%, especially when compared to the top 5%, a tax cut that concentrates its benefits on households in the bottom 40% would appear to be one way of reducing the inequity. Since so much of the American economy is consumer based, increasing the purchasing power of the greatest number of people would be a reasonable policy recommendation.

3. **Analysis (1)** Giving more money to the rich in order to benefit the poor is also known as the trickle-down theory. The cartoonist is implying that wealth will trickle down right back to the rich.

Exercise 11, pages 246–247

1. **Comprehension (1)** The passage is completely about Great Britain, eliminating choice (2) as too broad. (3), (4), and (5) are all details supporting the main idea, that because it was the birthplace of the Industrial Revolution, Great Britain became the richest nation on earth.

2. **Analysis (2)** The greatest difference between the industrialization of America in the 20thcentury and that of Great Britain in the 19th is that petroleum and electricity replaced coal and steam as the primary energy sources, opening up many new possibilities.

3. **Evaluation (3)** According to the evidence given by the factory girl, factory work helped young women out of poverty. Her testimony seems to contradict choices (1), (2), and (5). It also seemed that rather than saving, she used more money to purchase additional things, eliminating choice (4).

4. **Analysis (2)** The whole point of the cartoon appears to be that these middlemen, although aware of their uselessness, have no intention of changing anything, since that would eliminate themselves.

Chapter Review, pages 248–251

1. **Evaluation (3)** The devastation of the two world wars is a much more plausible explanation of Europe's decline than any of the other choices.

2. **Comprehension (4)** Choice (4) summarizes choices (3) and (5), which are two examples of innovation. The ancient Roman economy was not revived in mainland Europe. The fertile land had been known about. It was the invention of new tools and techniques that allowed its exploitation.

3. **Analysis (4)** The cartoon is a humorous way of saying that apartments are getting much too expensive. It's an exaggeration that the only way to afford a place to live is to have an oil rig in your home, but it makes the point of how unaffordable housing is becoming.

4. **Evaluation (2)** Since the Gross Domestic Product per person of the United States is more than ten times greater than the per person GDP of Ukraine, it is reasonable to conclude that the United States could afford to pay its workers higher wages.

5. **Analysis (3)** The politicians who are robbing the New York City Treasury are being saluted by the police, while a poor person stealing bread for his family is being beaten.

6. **Comprehension (2)** President Eisenhower was concerned that the military and the arms industry would get so large that they would have too much influence on decision making, in particular, in making decisions that would keep them large.

7. **Application (1)** Even though the military threat to the United States had been greatly reduced, President George W. Bush pushed for a large increase in the military budget. Despite rhetoric of the need to protect ourselves, it is more likely that what is being protected is our huge military and the industries that support and supply it.

8. **Comprehension (2)** In 1920 the CPI was 20.0. In 1940, it was 14.0. This was the only 20-year period in which the CPI was lower at the end than it was at the beginning.

9. **Analysis (4)** Except for 1920 the highest inflation rates on the table were 9.1% in 1975 and 13.5% in 1980.

Chapter 9

Exercise 1, pages 254–255

1. **Analysis (1)** From the pictures we can reasonably infer (2)–(5). The only thing that cannot be inferred is that the older, more labor-intensive machine made a product of poorer quality.

2. **Application (2)** The factory worker would have lost his or her job when a computerized machine replaced the older, human-operated one.

Exercise 2, page 257

1. **Application (4)** Property plot maps and deeds of property and sale can be traced to surveyor charts and diagrams, the U.S. Constitution to the Code of Hammurabi, and calendars to the understanding of the movement of planets. While the paragraph mentions arithmetic and calculation there is no reference to a device to enable computing.

2. **Analysis (3)** The message of the numerous examples of a variety of innovations is that cities can offer an environment in which invention can thrive.

Exercise 3, pages 258–259

1. **Analysis (2)** Because of the overall poor working conditions, it would have been extremely surprising to find increases in wages. The system was not designed to support the average worker, but rather to exploit him or her.

2. **Application (3)** To be able to enroll in an American university in the 1800s meant that you were financially comfortable. Sons of the middle and upper classes attended college, but not someone who needed to work just to have enough to eat. All of the other choices are examples of people who worked in the mills because they had to.

3. **Analysis (3)** The labor organizing movement is the most logical choice of something to emerge from a time most strongly associated with issues of work and industry.

Exercise 4, page 260

1. **Analysis (3)** Based on the passage only (3) is a matter of fact and not opinion or overgeneralization.

2. **Analysis (4)** In the passage the author refers broadly to "The American" as if there was only one type, and describes that type as a businessperson living in the suburbs. The other choices are contradicted by the passage.

3. **Evaluation (4)** The expansiveness of the nation is no longer a powerful idea in the minds of most Americans.

Exercise 5, pages 263–264

1. **Comprehension (2)** The balance among job types is the most striking aspect of the graph of 1900 in contrast to that of 1998.

2. **Analysis (5)** While the airplane has caused some changes in employment, it has had the least impact of the choices given in the three sectors shown.

3. **Evaluation (2)** The computer industry is one of the few industries not to have slowed in this period. In fact it is because of the increased presence of computers in other industries that fewer workers were required in them.

Exercise 6, page 265

1. **Comprehension (1)** The only reasonable inference that can be made from the cartoon is that the practice of medicine was not very advanced by today's standards.

2. **Analysis (3)** The purpose of most cartoons is to satirize something. In this case it was the extreme concern that people had about a vaccine that came from a cow.

Exercise 7, pages 266–267

1. **Comprehension (4)** The first two sentences emphasize the Mayos' contribution in terms of the practice and refinement of essential medical procedures.

2. **Analysis (3)** The logical effect of the Mayos' work, as reported in this passage, was that it impacted the work of other doctors as well.

Exercise 8, pages 268–269

1. **Analysis (1)** The author's tone makes the point that she thinks the press has taken an overly alarmist position regarding cloning.

2. **Application (4)** Only chimpanzee language is not something that humans are or have been responsible for developing.

Exercise 9, pages 270–271

1. **Comprehension (3)** While those who cannot afford a computer and phone have more difficulty accessing the web, they can still do it through libraries and community centers.

2. **Comprehension (4)** The support for (4) lies in the second paragraph with its emphasis on profound change in the past, present, and future.

3. **Analysis (1)** The assumption made here, whether or not it is true, is that everyone (a generalization) has been impacted by technology. The other statements are not assumptions but observations.

Exercise 10, pages 274–275

1. **Comprehension (2)** The lowest bar on the entire graph is that identified with African Americans.

2. **Comprehension (1)** The graph and chart clearly show that income is a determining factor as to whether someone owns a computer.

3. **Application (3)** Since income is such an important factor in terms of access to technology and, therefore, information, it stands to reason that the person interested in obtaining support for low-income neighborhoods could use these statistics to help his or her cause.

Chapter Review, pages 277–282

1. **Application (4)** Bows and arrows were used for hunting and thus did not contribute to the shift to agriculture.

2. **Analysis (3)** The agricultural lifestyle, as opposed to the nomadic one, enabled people to stay in one place and survive more easily.

3. **Analysis (5)** Although many inventions do have an impact on society the inventors, like Edison with his phonograph, often did not start out with that intention.

4. **Application (5)** Cordless and cell phones are the only items mentioned that are inventions designed to make life easier for everyone.

5. **Application (1)** The need for a polio vaccine was true and urgent, thus inspiring its invention.

6. **Analysis (1)** If anything, business at the shopping mall has probably decreased due to the cuts in local consumers' incomes.

7. **Evaluation (1)** The author writes "since most of us are educated . . . we value the sonnet and think that a button is just a button." This is an assumption about the readers that may not be true.

8. **Evaluation (3)** By pointing out that many people appreciate the sonnet for certain reasons and that many other people appreciate the button for other, different reasons, the passage is saying that you can't evaluate one invention as better than another.

9. **Comprehension (5)** The speed with which technology changes is the point of this cartoon.

10. **Analysis (3)** This is an illustration of the tremendous impact that information, or lack thereof, can have on people's lives. In this case, it affected people's basic freedom.

Chapter 10

Exercise 1, pages 285–288

1. **Application (4)** The development of writing would most likely occur in a place that had a large concentration of people. Writing actually did develop first in the cities of Sumeria and Egypt.

2. **Application (4)** Modern cities still have financial districts.

3. **Analysis (5)** Such large numbers of people lived in cities that it became impossible to organize them strictly on kinship lines.

4. **Comprehension (3)** According to the passage the Greeks adopted the alphabet from Oriental civilizations.

5. **Application (1)** Over the past one hundred years, the United States has been the leading innovator and cultural leader in the world.

6. **Analysis (3)** Valid criteria of intelligence and creativity can be established.

Exercise 2, pages 289–292

1. **Comprehension (2)** It is reasonable to conclude that the Native Americans had domesticated the many plants, since the article states that the Europeans brought plants from America back to Europe.

2. **Analysis (1)** Though it is never directly stated, it is clear from the passage that the author assumes that the exchange of food benefited everyone, since he never gives a negative consequence of the food exchange, but gives very positive examples.

3. **Analysis (3)** Exporting slaves was most disruptive to Western Africa. No other thing traded was as destructive to the exporting area as Western Africa's loss of a significant part of its population.

4. **Analysis (2)** Just as the United States expanded west until it reached the Pacific Ocean, Russia expanded east until it reached the Pacific Ocean.

5. **Comprehension (5)** While missionaries converted native peoples (2), they shared their European culture and tastes (1) which, in turn, influenced the art of other cultures (3). They were also influenced by art from other cultures (4). The statement that does not describe missionaries is (5). Missionaries are sent to convert other peoples to their religion, and the passage does not mention the influence of native religions in Europe.

6. **Evaluation (3)** The level of imports and exports of the Russian Federation is so low compared to the United States, Germany, and Japan that it is reasonable to conclude that the power of the Soviet Union was not based on its economic strength and productivity.

7. **Evaluation (4)** Since Belgium and China are so vastly different in size and population, they provide strong evidence that the economic strength of a nation is not necessarily tied to its size or number of people.

Exercise 3, pages 294–295

1. **Comprehension (2)** The passage's main idea is that Britain's economic impact on the colonies was far greater than the colonies' impact on the British. The first paragraph emphasizes the colonies' lack of major economic impact on Britain, while the second paragraph describes the enormous economic impact Britain had on its colonies.

2. **Analysis (3)** In the 19th century, former European colonies were swept by independence movements based on a desire for self-determination and the affirmation of local culture. The passage makes clear that economics was not the primary motive. The prominence of the United States was not as well-established when these countries became independent as it is today.

3. **Evaluation (2)** Most likely the railroad would still have been built entirely within the territory of the United States. Therefore, the route would have been built farther north.

4. **Evaluation (1)** The evidence shows that the United States provoked the war and ended up taking by force what it originally had wanted and was willing to purchase.

5. **Evaluation (4)** The Spanish conquest of the Incas is the only one of the choices in which the conqueror plundered the conquered. The Spanish took a great amount of gold from the Incas.

6. **Analysis (1)** The examples given all support the notion that the productivity of the dominant culture determines the standard of living of an area. When a more advanced culture withdrew from an area and it reverted to control by a less advanced culture, the standard of living actually declined.

Exercise 4, pages 299–301

1. **Application (2)** Spain and Portugal did not invest in their own nations with the wealth they gained from the New World. As a result when the wealth ran out, they were left as poor countries. The same could happen to nations of the Middle East if they do not invest any of their wealth from oil sales into the economic development of their own countries.

2. **Analysis (2)** The passage argues that Spain's failure to invest in its own economic development led to its decline. Therefore, even if the Spanish Armada had been successful, eventually one of the economically developing nations of Northern Europe would have surpassed Spain.

3. **Evaluation (5)** The fact that Bruegel was famous for depicting common people has no bearing at all on whether or not the interpretation of *The Big Fish Eat the Little Fish* is correct.

4. **Analysis (2)** The big fish is stuffed to overflowing with little fish. It appears that it died of overeating.

5. **Comprehension (2)** According to the map, France and England became rivals in the establishment of some settlements in the New World. The map shows that they both claimed a large portion of Canada.

6. **Comprehension (1)** According to the map the greatest amount of territory was claimed by Spain.

Exercise 5, pages 304–308

1. **Analysis (1)** The other four choices all support the conclusion that modern monotheist religions adopted important beliefs, morality, and ethics from ancient Middle Eastern religions.

2. **Analysis (5)** Given the information in the passage, it appears most likely that despite many similarities between the old and new religions, leaders of the monotheist religions felt that the polytheistic religions were violent and sensuous, promoting barbarous and immoral practices.

3. **Analysis (1)** In the engraving the Bible has more weight, or is more important, than all the members of the Catholic clergy. The engraver was supporting the Protestant Reformation, believing that it was returning the Bible to its true importance.

4. **Analysis (5)** Napoleon's attempt to unite Europe by force created an upsurge of nationalism to oppose and finally defeat it, despite the very real advances that he introduced.

5. **Comprehension (3)** Ferdinand VII, from the Bourbon family, was king of Spain.

6. **Analysis (1)** While he considers the two-party system an ingenious method of social control, Zinn does not believe that it was the result of a deliberate plot. It evolved naturally, almost by accident, and once in place, has been remarkably stable.

Exercise 6, pages 310–312

1. **Comprehension (5)** The Helsinki Agreements state, "The participating states respect human rights and fundamental freedoms." Since the Soviet Union signed the Helsinki Agreements it agreed to abide by their provisions.

2. **Analysis (1)** Since only a small percent of the United States economy was linked to Asia, the Asian economic crisis did not have a great enough negative impact to stop the growth of the U.S. economy.

3. **Application (3)** Ontario, like Quebec, is a province of Canada. It also borders Quebec. According to the information in the passage, it is reasonable to predict that Quebec's trade with Ontario would be greater than its trade with any of the other choices.

4. **Analysis (4)** The point of the cartoon is that many of our decisions do not depend only on getting the lowest price. The cartoon shows an absurd consequence of price being the only consideration.

5. **Analysis (5)** The skills, education, and work ethic of American labor is what makes it so valuable and able to compete internationally. The main competition for the United States comes from the other high wage nations, not from the low-wage countries.

Exercise 7, pages 314–320

1. **Comprehension (5)** While all the other possibilities are facts stated in the passage, the author attributes the spread of the plague to Europe to the passengers of a boat that landed in Sicily.

2. **Analysis (4)** In general, the disease spread from south to north.

3. **Comprehension (3)** The graph shows that the most people with HIV/AIDS are from Sub-Saharan Africa. The passage also states that Sub-Saharan Africa has been hit the worst by the epidemic.

4. **Evaluation (2)** So many millions are already infected that low cost drug treatment would have the greatest positive impact. Public relations campaigns might have some impact, but most people involved with promiscuous sex or narcotic drugs are unlikely to respond to such campaigns. Free condoms and needles can slow down the spread of HIV, but since the disease is already so widespread, this solution would not have as large a positive impact as drug treatment.

5. **Analysis (3)** The civil war in the Congo is the only choice that did not benefit African people.

6. **Analysis (1)** When Truman said, "Those with competing philosophies have stressed—and are shamelessly distorting—our shortcomings," he was referring to the Communists.

7. **Analysis (4)** Rebuilding black institutions that reach out to young black people appears to be more important than more government programs.

8. **Analysis (3)** It was how black people responded to their oppression that helped them survive more than a knowledge of who their oppressor was.

9. **Comprehension (1)** *Miscegenation* means the "mixture of races." The practice has always been so common in Brazil that parents looking like members of one race would not be surprised if their child had different racial characteristics.

Chapter Review, pages 321–326

1. **Analysis (4)** When Gorbachev buried Soviet totalitarianism, long-suppressed nationalistic feelings throughout the former Soviet Union immediately began to reemerge after years of being hidden.

2. **Analysis (4)** The image of a ghost rising out of a graveyard is meant to symbolize apprehension.

3. **Evaluation (5)** Since the United States has the highest gun ownership and the highest rate of gun deaths, there seems to be a correlation between the two facts. Therefore, the graph would support a reduction of gun ownership in the United States as a means of reducing gun deaths.

4. **Comprehension (5)** Of all the countries on the chart, Japan has by far the lowest rate of gun deaths.

5. **Comprehension (1)** All the details in the paragraph support the main idea that the "prison-industrial complex" has been targeting young black men.

6. **Evaluation (3)** The writer makes clear throughout the passage that the massive increase in prisons and the prison population is a disaster, especially to the black community.

7. **Comprehension (2)** It was the economic structures that were in place in Europe that created the conditions that encouraged the Industrial Revolution.

8. **Comprehension (1)** The United States was one nation, while Europe was fragmented into many independent nations. All the other conditions for industrialization was shared by the United States and Europe.

9. **Application (2)** Articles 1 and 3 are most similar to the Declaration of Independence, which states, "We hold these truths to be self-evident. That all men are created equal. That they are endowed by their creator with certain unalienable rights. That among these are life, liberty, and the pursuit of happiness."

10. **Application (5)** Articles 18, 19, and 20 contain guarantees that are most similar to those contained in the Bill of Rights.

11. **Analysis (4)** While marriage is certainly protected in the United States, it is not explicitly addressed in the Constitution or its amendments. All the other choices are mentioned either in the Constitution or in its amendments.

Glossary

A

Amendment (Constitutional) Changes in, or additions to, a constitution. In the United States, an amendment must be proposed by a two-thirds vote of both houses of Congress or by a convention called by Congress at the request of two-thirds of the state legislatures. Ratified by approval of three-fourths of the states.

Articles of Confederation The first constitution of the United States (1781). Created a weak national government; replaced in 1789 by the Constitution of the United States.

Authority Power to influence or command thought, opinion, or behavior.

B

Balance of Trade The difference between the total amount of exports and imports for a country in one year.

Barter The direct exchange of one good or service for another without the use of money.

B.C.E. and C.E. Before the Common Era (formerly known as B.C.) and Common Era (formerly known as A.D.).

Bicameral A legislative body composed of two houses.

Bill of Rights The first ten amendments to the United States Constitution. Ratified in 1791, these amendments limit governmental power and protect basic rights and liberties of individuals.

Bureaucracy Administrative organizations that implement government policies.

Business Cycle The periods of recession and expansion that an economy goes through because production does not increase continuously over time.

C

Cabinet Secretaries, or chief administrators, of the major departments of the federal government. Cabinet secretaries are appointed by the president with the consent of the Senate.

Capital Manufactured resources such as tools, machinery, and buildings that are used in the production of other goods and services (e.g., school buildings, books, tables, and chairs are some examples of capital used to produce education). This is sometimes called real capital.

Case Study An in-depth examination of an issue.

Checks and Balances The Constitutional mechanisms that authorize each branch of government to share powers with the other branches and thereby check their activities. For example, the president may veto legislation passed by Congress; the Senate must confirm major executive appointments; and the courts may declare acts of Congress unconstitutional.

Citizen A member of a political society who owes allegiance to a government and is entitled to its protection.

Civil Rights The protections and privileges of personal liberty given to all U.S. citizens by the Constitution and Bill of Rights.

Civilization An advanced state of a society possessing historical and cultural unity.

Common or Public Good To the benefit, or in the interest, of a politically organized society as a whole.

Communism A political and economic system in which factors of production are collectively owned and directed by the state.

Competitive Behavior When a business or individual acts in a self-interested way intending to increase wealth or personal gain.

Social Studies

Concurrent Powers   Powers that may be exercised by both the federal and state governments (e.g., levying taxes, borrowing money and spending for the general welfare).

Confederate   Of, or pertaining to, a group of states more or less permanently united for common purposes. In the United States, the southern states that seceded from the Union before the Civil War are referred to as the "Confederate States."

Conservatism   A general preference for the existing order of society and an opposition to all efforts to bring about rapid or fundamental change in that order.

Consumer   A person or organization that purchases or uses a product or service.

Consumer Sovereignty   The power consumers have in directing market economies because goods and services are produced and exchanged mostly to satisfy consumer wants.

Criminal Justice   The branch of law that deals with disputes or actions involving criminal penalties. It regulates the conduct of individuals, defines crimes, and provides punishment for criminal acts.

Cultural Diffusion   The adoption of an aspect (or aspects) of another group's culture, such as the spread of the English language.

Cultural Landscape   The visual outcome of humans living in a place.

Culture   The learned behavior of people, such as belief systems and languages, social relations, institutions, organizations, and material goods such as food, clothing, buildings, technology.

D

Deflation   A general lowering of prices. The opposite of inflation.

Delegated Powers   Powers granted to the national government under the Constitution, as enumerated in Articles I, II and III.

Demand   How much a consumer is willing and able to buy at each possible price.

Democracy   The practice of the principle of equality of rights, opportunity, and treatment.

Demographics   The statistical data of a population (e.g., average age, income, education).

Developed Nation   A country with high levels of well-being, as measured by economic, social, and technological sophistication.

Developing Nation   A country with low levels of well-being, as measured by economic, social, and technological sophistication.

Dictatorship   A system of government in which one person has absolute authority, including complete domination of the citizens' lives. The most basic of citizens' rights are taken away in order to guarantee the leader's hold on power.

Distribution   The arrangement of items over an area.

Due Process of Law   The right of every citizen to be protected against arbitrary action by government.

E

Economic Growth   An increase in an economy's ability to produce goods and services, which brings about a rise in standards of living.

Ecosystem   The interaction of all living organisms with each other and with the physical environment.

Emigration   People leaving a country (or other political unit) to live in another country.

Entrepreneur   A person who organizes, operates, and assumes the risk for a business venture.

Environment   Everything near and on the Earth's surface. Natural or physical environment refers to climate, biosphere, hydrosphere, soil, and geology. Human or cultural environment refers to aspects of the environment produced by humans.

Equal Protection Clause   The Fourteenth Amendment provision that prohibits states from denying equal protection of the laws to all people; that is, discriminating against individuals in an arbitrary manner, such as on the basis of race.

Equal Protection of the Law   The idea that no individual or group may receive special privileges from, nor be unjustly discriminated by, the law.

Exchange Rate   The price of one currency in terms of another (e.g., pesos per dollar).

F

Federal Reserve System   A system of 12 district banks and a Board of Governors that regulates the activities of financial institutions and controls the money supply.

Federal Supremacy   Article VI of the Constitution providing that the Constitution and all federal laws and treaties shall be the "supreme Law of the Land." Therefore, all federal laws take precedence over state and local laws.

Federalism   A form of political organization in which governmental power is divided between a central government and territorial subdivisions—in the United States, among the national, state, and local governments.

Federalist Papers   A series of essays written by Alexander Hamilton, John Jay, and James Madison that were published to support the adoption of the proposed United States Constitution.

Federalists   Advocates of a strong federal government and supporters of the adoption of the U.S. Constitution.

Feudalism   Political and economic system in which a lord required services from a vassal, and in return granted the vassal certain privileges, such as control over a castle and the surrounding territory.

Fiscal Policy   How the government uses taxes and/or government expenditures to change the level of output, employment, or prices.

Foreign Policy   Policies of the federal government directed to matters beyond U.S. borders, especially relations with other countries.

Free Enterprise   The freedom of private businesses to operate competitively, for profit, and without government controls.

Freedom of Expression   The freedoms of speech, press, assembly, and petition that are protected by the First Amendment.

Freedom of the Press   Freedom to print or publish without governmental interference.

G

Genocide   The systematic destruction of an entire cultural or ethnic group.

Global Warming   The progressive gradual rise of the earth's surface temperature thought to be caused by the greenhouse effect and responsible for changes in global climate patterns.

Globalization   The integration and democratization of the world's culture, economy, and infrastructure through transnational investment, rapid proliferation of communication and information technologies, and the impacts of free-market forces on local, regional and national economies.

Government   A political organization constituting the individuals and institutions authorized to formulate public policies and conduct affairs of state.

Great Compromise   An agreement made at the Constitutional Convention of 1787 that balanced the interest of the small and large states, resulting in the United States Senate being made up of two Senators from each state and a House of Representatives based on population.

Gross Domestic Product   A measure of how much an economy produces within its borders each year, stated in the dollar value of final goods and services.

Gross National Product   A measure of the total amount of goods and services produced by an economy, both domestically and internationally.

H

Hemisphere   The northern or southern half of the earth divided by the equator or the eastern or western half divided by a meridian.

Human Capital   The knowledge and skills that enable workers to be productive.

Human Characteristics   The pattern that people make on the surface of the Earth, such as cities, roads, canals, farms, and other ways people change the Earth.

I

Immigration   People moving to a country (or other political unit).

Impeachment   The act of accusing a public official of misconduct in office by presenting formal charges against him or her by the lower house, with a trial to be held before the upper house.

Imperialism   The practice by which powerful nations or peoples seek to extend and maintain control or influence over weaker nations or peoples.

Inalienable Rights   Fundamental rights of the people that may not be taken away. A phrase used in the Declaration of Independence.

Incentive   A benefit offered to encourage people to act in certain ways.

Income Tax   A percentage of wages, profits, and other income paid to federal, state, and local governments.

Inflation   A general rise in the level of prices.

Initiative   A form of direct democracy in which the voters of a state can propose a law by gathering signatures and having the proposition placed on the ballot.

Innovation   The process of putting an invention to use and modifying it as the situation demands.

Interdependence   Reliance on people in other places for information, resources, goods, and services.

Invention   An adaptation of a discovery to practical use.

Isolationism   The belief that the United States should not be involved in world affairs and should avoid involvement in foreign wars.

J

Judicial Review   The doctrine that permits the federal courts to declare unconstitutional, and thus null and void, acts of the Congress, the executive, and the states. The precedent for judicial review was established in the 1803 case of *Marbury* v. *Madison*.

Justice   Fair distribution of benefits and burdens, fair correction of wrongs and injuries, or use of fair procedures in gathering information and making decisions.

L

Land Use   How people use the Earth's surface (e.g., urban, rural, agricultural, range, forest); often subdivided into specific uses (e.g., retail, low-density housing, industrial).

Landform   A description of the Earth's shape at a certain place (e.g., mountain range, plateau, flood plain).

Latitude   The distance north or south of the equator, measured in degrees along a line of longitude.

Legend   The map key that explains the meaning of symbols on a map.

Liberalism   A political viewpoint or ideology that advocates political change in the name of progress, especially social improvement through governmental action.

Liquidity   The ease and speed with which something can be turned into cash (e.g., one can more quickly sell a common stock than a house; therefore, the stock is a more liquid asset than a house).

Longitude   Distance east or west, almost always measured in relation to the prime meridian that runs north and south through Greenwich, England.

M

Macroeconomics   The branch of economics that considers the overall aspects and workings of a national economy such as national output, price levels, employment rates, and economic growth.

Magna Carta   Document signed by King John of England in 1215 A.D. that limited the king's power and guaranteed certain basic rights. Considered the beginning of constitutional government in England.

Market   Any setting in which exchange occurs between buyers and sellers.

Market Economic System   A system in which most resources are owned by individuals and the interaction between buyers and sellers determines what is made, how it is made, and how much of it is made.

Market Price   The price at which the quantity of goods and services demanded by consumers and the quantity supplied by producers are the same. This is sometimes called the equilibrium price.

Mayflower Compact   The document drawn up by the Pilgrims in 1620, while on the Mayflower, before landing at Plymouth Rock. The Compact provided a legal basis for self-government.

Mercantilism   An economic and political policy in which the government regulates the industries, trade, and commerce with the national aim of obtaining a favorable balance of trade.

Microeconomics   The branch of economics concerned with the decisions made by individuals, households, and firms and how these decisions interact to form the prices of goods and services and the factors of production.

Moderate   Generally, a "middle-of-the-road" set of beliefs, rather than an ideology. Moderates of all political parties usually share the traits of pragmatism, an aversion to ideology or ideological excesses, and willingness to compromise.

Monarchy   A type of government in which political power is exercised by a single ruler under the claim of divine or hereditary right.

Monetary Policy   Management of the money supply and interest rates to influence economic activity.

Money   Any medium of exchange that is widely accepted in payment for goods and services and in settlement of debts.

Mortgage   A legal document that pledges a house or other real estate as security for repayment of a loan. By providing a guarantee that the loan will be paid back, a mortgage enables a person to buy property without having the funds to pay for it outright.

N

National Security   Condition of a nation's safety from threats, especially threats from external sources.

Natural Disaster   A process taking place in the natural environment that destroys human life, property, or both (e.g., hurricane, flooding).

Natural Resource   Naturally occurring material such as plants, animals, mineral deposits, soils, clean water, clean air, and fossil fuels, which can be used by people.

P

Pluralism   The acceptance of many groups in society.

Poverty   The condition of having insufficient resources or income. In its most extreme form, poverty is a lack of basic human needs, such as adequate and nutritious food, clothing, housing, clean water, and health services.

Price Ceilings   Government policy that prevents the price of a good or service from exceeding a particular level (e.g., rent control or the price of gasoline during the 1970s).

Principle   A basic rule that guides or influences thought or action.

Producers   People who change resources into an output that tends to be more desirable than the resources were in their previous form (e.g., when people produce french fries, consumers are more inclined to buy them than the oil, salt, and potatoes individually).

Profit   The monetary difference between the cost of producing and marketing goods or services and the price subsequently received for those goods or services.

Progress   A series of improvements in human life marked by inventions and discoveries.

Progressive Tax   A tax structure where people who earn more are charged a higher percentage of their income (e.g., the federal income tax).

Property Rights   The rights of an individual to own property and keep the income earned from it.

Property Tax   Money paid by property owners in local communities to local government to offset expenses of services provided including street construction and maintenance and often public schools.

Proportional Tax   A tax structure where all people pay about the same percentage of their incomes in taxes (e.g., a flat-rate tax).

Protectionism The practice of protecting domestic industries from foreign competition by imposing import duties or quotas.

Public Service Service to local, state, or national communities through appointed or elected office.

Q

Quota A limit on how much of a good can be imported. The limit is set either by quantity or by the dollar value.

R

Radical A person who advocates sweeping changes in the laws and methods of government with the least delay.

Ratify To confirm by expressing consent, approval, or formal sanction.

Reactionary A political philosophy that advocates for the resisting of change and a return to an earlier social order or policy.

Referendum A form of direct democracy in which citizens of a state, through gathering signatures, can require that a legislative act come before the people as a whole for a vote. The process also allows the legislature to send any proposal for a law to the people for a vote.

Refugee A person who has fled or been expelled from his or her country of origin because of natural disaster, war or military occupation, or fear of religious, racial, or political persecution.

Region A larger-sized territory that includes many smaller places, all or most of which share similar attributes, such as climate, landforms, plants, soils, language, religion, economy, government or other natural or cultural attributes.

Regressive Tax A tax structure where people who earn more pay a smaller percentage of their income in taxes (e.g., sales taxes).

Representative Democracy A form of government in which power is held by the people and exercised indirectly through elected representatives who make decisions.

Republican Government A system of government in which power is held by the voters and is exercised by elected representatives responsible for promoting the common welfare (e.g., the United States government).

Resources Land, labor, capital, and entrepreneurship used in the production of goods and services.

Return How well you do by investing in one asset as opposed to another (e.g., if you buy a house in an up-and-coming neighborhood, you expect a better return when you sell it than if you buy a house next to where a new freeway is going to be built).

Revolution A complete or drastic change of government or society and the rules which are followed by that government or society.

Risk How much uncertainty accompanies your choice of investment (e.g., if you lend money to someone who has just escaped from prison, you are taking more of a risk than if you lend money to your mother).

Rule of Law The principle that every member of a society, even a ruler, must follow the law.

S

Scale The relationship between a distance on the ground and the distance on a map. For example, the scale 1:100,000 means that one unit of distance (e.g., an inch or millimeter) on the map equals 100,000 of these units on the Earth's surface.

Scarce A good or service that is insufficient in quantity to satisfy the demand or need for it.

Science A branch of systematic study concerned with the observation and classification of facts and the establishment of laws based on data.

Separation of Powers The division of governmental power among several institutions that must cooperate in decision-making.

Social Security The use of contributions made by workers and employers through a social security tax to provide income to people and their families during retirement or in the case of unemployment, disability, or death.

Socialism   An economic system in which property and the distribution of income are subject to social and governmental control rather than individual determination of market forces.

Sovereignty   The ultimate, supreme power in a state (e.g., in the United States, sovereignty rests with the people).

Spatial   Pertaining to distribution, distance, direction, areas and other aspects of space on the Earth's surface.

Specialization   When a business focuses on producing a limited number of goods and leaves the production of other goods to other businesses. Specialization also describes how each person working to produce a good might work on one part of the production instead of producing the whole good (e.g., in a shoe factory one person cuts the leather, another person sews it, another glues it to the sole).

Standard of Living   The overall quality of life that people experience.

Suffrage   The right to vote.

Supply   The quantity of a product or service a producer is willing and able to offer for sale at each possible price.

T

Tariff   A tax on an imported good.

Technology   The application of processes, methods, or knowledge to achieve a specific purpose.

Theocracy   Any government in which the leaders of the government are also the leaders of the religion and they rule as representatives of the deity.

Totalitarianism   A centralized government that does not tolerate parties of differing opinion and that exercises dictatorial control over many aspects of life.

Treaty   A formal agreement between sovereign nations to create or restrict rights and responsibilities. In the United States, all treaties must be approved by a two-thirds vote in the Senate.

U

Unitary Government   A government system in which all governmental authority is vested in a central government from which regional and local governments derive their powers (e.g., Great Britain and France, as well as the American states within their spheres of authority).

United Nations   An international organization composed of most of the nations of the world, formed in 1945, to promote global peace, security, and economic development.

Urbanization   The process of an increasing number of people moving to cities to work and live, and the development that results.

V

Veto   A privileged single vote that, according to some systems of rules for decision-making, has the effect of blocking or negating a majority decision. In the United States, the President may veto a bill passed by majorities in both houses of Congress, preventing it from becoming law unless each house then re-passes the bill by a two-thirds majority.

Voluntary Exchange   Trade between people when each one feels he or she is better off after the trade (e.g., if you sell your old exercise bike for cash, you gain because you would rather have the cash than the bike, but the other person gains because he or she would rather have the bike than the cash).

W

Wealth   An accumulation of goods having economic value.

Index

Useful Websites

The following web sites contain interesting and useful information about the subject areas covered on the GED Social Studies Test.

World History

http://www.hyperhistory.com/online_n2/History_n2/a.html

Background information and maps about many periods of world history, from prehistory to the present

http://www.cnn.com

Current events from around the world, including the United States

http://europeanhistory.about.com

European history from the Age of Exploration to the present

http://history1900s.about.com

History of the 20th century

American History

http://www.whitehouse.gov

Official web site of the White House—information about the current president and his staff and programs as well as historical information about the White House and former presidents

http://americanhistory.about.com

American history from the time of the first explorers to the present

http://memory.loc.gov

Library of Congress's historical site—information and documents about American history from original sources

http://www.historyplace.com

Information, documents, and photos about American history, from the time of the explorers to the present

Civics & Government

http://www.whitehouse.gov

Official web site of the White House—information about the Executive Branch of government and the current president

http://www.supremecourtus.gov

Information about the U.S. Supreme Court, including historical information, information about the justices, and Supreme Court decisions

http://www.senate.gov

Current Senate membership, issues being debated, and historical information

http://www.house.gov

Current House of Representatives membership, information about members, issues being debated, and historical information

Economics

http://economics.about.com

Explanations of economic terms and topics as well as information about current economic situations

http://www.nationalcouncil.org

Official site of the National Council on Economic Education—online lessons about economic concepts as well as information on personal finances

http://ecedweb.unomaha.edu/teach.htm

Resources for teachers and students of economics at all levels, including lesson plans and clear explanations of economic concepts

http://www.federalreserve.gov

Web site of the Federal Reserve board—information about the Federal Reserve system as well as information about current decisions and issues facing the Federal Reserve

Geography

http://geography.about.com

A wide range of geographic topics, including maps, atlases, and a geography glossary

http://www.census.gov

Official web site of the U.S. Census Bureau—the latest demographic information from the 2000 census

http://www.smithsonianmag.si.edu

Web site for the Smithsonian Institution's magazine—current information about geography and geographic issues

http://www.geographynetwork.com

Maps and information about U.S. and world geography as well as links to other geography sites